# BROKEN PEOPLE

## Caste Violence Against India's "Untouchables"

**Human Rights Watch**
New York • Washington • London • Brussels

ISBN 1-56432-228-9
Library of Congress Catalog Card Number 99-61749

Cover photos by Smita Narula. © Human Rights Watch 1998.
Top photo: Survivors of a massacre in Bihar.
Bottom photo: Children of manual scavengers in Gujarat.
Cover design by Rafael Jiménez

Addresses for Human Rights Watch
350 Fifth Avenue, 34th Floor, New York, NY 10118-3299
Tel: (212) 290-4700, Fax: (212) 736-1300, E-mail: hrwnyc@hrw.org

1522 K Street, N.W., #910, Washington, DC 20005-1202
Tel: (202) 371-6592, Fax: (202) 371-0124, E-mail: hrwdc@hrw.org

33 Islington High Street, N1 9LH London, UK
Tel: (171) 713-1995, Fax: (171) 713-1800, E-mail: hrwatchuk@gn.apc.org

15 Rue Van Campenhout, 1000 Brussels, Belgium
Tel: (2) 732-2009, Fax: (2) 732-0471, E-mail:hrwatcheu@skynet.be

Web Site Address: http://www.hrw.org

Listserv address: To subscribe to the list, send an e-mail message to
majordomo@igc.apc.org with "subscribe hrw-news" in the body of the message
(leave the subject line blank).

Human Rights Watch is dedicated to
protecting the human rights of people around the world.

We stand with victims and activists to prevent
discrimination, to uphold political freedom, to protect people from inhumane
conduct in wartime, and to bring offenders to justice.

We investigate and expose
human rights violations and hold abusers accountable.

We challenge governments and those who hold power to end abusive practices
and respect international human rights law.

We enlist the public and the international
community to support the cause of human rights for all.

# HUMAN RIGHTS WATCH

Human Rights Watch conducts regular, systematic investigations of human rights abuses in some seventy countries around the world. Our reputation for timely, reliable disclosures has made us an essential source of information for those concerned with human rights. We address the human rights practices of governments of all political stripes, of all geopolitical alignments, and of all ethnic and religious persuasions. Human Rights Watch defends freedom of thought and expression, due process and equal protection of the law, and a vigorous civil society; we document and denounce murders, disappearances, torture, arbitrary imprisonment, discrimination, and other abuses of internationally recognized human rights. Our goal is to hold governments accountable if they transgress the rights of their people.

Human Rights Watch began in 1978 with the founding of its Europe and Central Asia division (then known as Helsinki Watch). Today, it also includes divisions covering Africa, the Americas, Asia, and the Middle East. In addition, it includes three thematic divisions on arms, children's rights, and women's rights. It maintains offices in New York, Washington, Los Angeles, London, Brussels, Moscow, Dushanbe, Rio de Janeiro, and Hong Kong. Human Rights Watch is an independent, nongovernmental organization, supported by contributions from private individuals and foundations worldwide. It accepts no government funds, directly or indirectly.

The staff includes Kenneth Roth, executive director; Michele Alexander, development director; Reed Brody, advocacy director; Carroll Bogert, communications director; Cynthia Brown, program director; Barbara Guglielmo, finance and administration director; Jeri Laber special advisor; Lotte Leicht, Brussels office director; Patrick Minges, publications director; Susan Osnos, associate director; Jemera Rone, counsel; Wilder Tayler, general counsel; and Joanna Weschler, United Nations representative. Jonathan Fanton is the chair of the board. Robert L. Bernstein is the founding chair.

The regional directors of Human Rights Watch are Peter Takirambudde, Africa; José Miguel Vivanco, Americas; Sidney Jones, Asia; Holly Cartner, Europe and Central Asia; and Hanny Megally, Middle East and North Africa. The thematic division directors are Joost R. Hiltermann, arms; Lois Whitman, children's; and Regan Ralph, women's.

The members of the board of directors are Jonathan Fanton, chair; Lisa Anderson, Robert L. Bernstein, William Carmichael, Dorothy Cullman, Gina Despres, Irene Diamond, Adrian W. DeWind, Fiona Druckenmiller, Edith Everett, Michael E. Gellert, Vartan Gregorian, Alice H. Henkin, James F. Hoge, Stephen L. Kass, Marina Pinto Kaufman, Bruce Klatsky, Josh Mailman, Yolanda T. Moses, Samuel K. Murumba, Andrew Nathan, Jane Olson, Peter Osnos, Kathleen Peratis, Bruce Rabb, Sigrid Rausing, Orville Schell, Sid Sheinberg, Gary G. Sick, Malcolm Smith, Domna Stanton, and Maya Wiley. Robert L. Bernstein is the founding chair of Human Rights Watch.

# ACKNOWLEDGMENTS

This report was researched and written by Smita Narula, researcher for the Asia division of Human Rights Watch. It is based on research conducted from January to March and July to August 1998. More than 300 Dalit men and women were interviewed. Interviewees were chosen on the basis of their willingness and ability to speak freely with Human Rights Watch; no interviews were conducted under circumstances that presented the risk of retaliation. Human Rights Watch also spoke with more than one hundred government officials, social workers, Dalit activists, and attorneys.

The report was edited by Patricia Gossman, senior researcher for the Asia division of Human Rights Watch, Wilder Tayler, general counsel, and Cynthia Brown, program director. Production assistance was provided by Tom Kellogg, associate for the Asia division of Human Rights Watch, Alex Frangos, associate, Human Rights Watch, and Raj Barot, intern. Scott Campbell, consultant to Human Rights Watch, assisted with the research in Bihar.

Human Rights Watch would like to thank the following people and organizations for their generous assistance: Henri Tiphagne and members of People's Watch, Tamil Nadu; members of Bihar Dalit Vikas Samiti, Bihar; Sudha Varghese of Nari Gunjan, Bihar; Vivek Pandit and members of Samarthan, Maharashtra; Martin Macwan and members of Navsarjan, Gujarat; Paul Divakar of Sakshi, Andhra Pradesh; Ruth Manorama of the National Federation for Dalit Women; Henry Thiagaraj of the Dalit Liberation Education Trust, Tamil Nadu; and Kathy Sreedhar of the Holdeen India Fund, Washington, D.C.

We also thank the many people who prefer, for their own well-being and that of their organizations, that their names not be mentioned — an unfortunate indicator of the volatility surrounding the issue of caste conflict in India. We would like to express our gratitude to the many Dalit men, women, and children who spoke with us, recounting their personal experiences of hardship and violence. They made this report possible.

Finally, we acknowledge with appreciation the support of the Ford Foundation, which provided funding that has enabled Human Rights Watch to pursue caste and gender-related research and advocacy in India.

The recommendations for this report were drafted in consultation with over forty activists during two sets of meetings convened by Human Rights Watch in July and August 1998 in Bangalore and New Delhi, respectively. Activists and lawyers from eight states and New Delhi took part, representing prominent Dalit rights and women's rights organizations, and national civil liberties and human rights organizations. We wish to thank them for their participation and invaluable contributions.

Participants' names and organizations are listed by state.

*Tamil Nadu*: Henri Tiphagne, C. J. Rajan, and Vincent, People's Watch; Henri Thiagaraj and James Antony, Dalit Liberation Education Trust; V. P. Epsibai, Tamil Nadu Dalit Women's Integration Movement; S. A. Maniraj, Tamil Nadu Women's Forum; A. Vinoth, Athi Tamilar Viduthalaiiyyakkam; P. Chandrabose, Dalit Liberation Movement. *Karnataka*: Ruth Manorama, National Federation of Dalit Women and Women's Voice; Aloysius SJ, Lazar SJ, John SJ, Indian Social Institute; Jyothi Raj, H. M. Amitha, Rural Education for Development Society; Sam A. Chelladurai, HAKKU; Ashwini Madhyasta, Anekal Rehabilitation, Education and Development Centre. *Andhra Pradesh*: N. Paul Divakar, V. Nanda Gopal, SAKSHI; Bejawada Wilson, Safai Karmachari Andolan; L. Jaya, Vedika; G. Sathyavathi, Rural Awareness and Development Society; P. Chennaiah, Andhra Pradesh Vyavasaya Vruthi Darula Union; *Maharashtra*: John Samuel, National Centre for Advocacy Studies; P. A. Sebastian, Indian People's Human Rights Commission; *Orissa*: R. K. Nayak, Sashmi Nayak, NISWASS; *Rajasthan*: P. L. Mimroth, Promila, Society of Depressed People for Social Justice; Geeta Deepika Rawatt, Sasvika; *Bihar*: Sudha Varghese, Nari Gunjan; Radha Mohan Singh, Bihar Dalit Vikas Samiti. *Gujarat*: Martin Macwan, Navsarjan; Meera Velayudhan, Institute for Environmental and Social Concerns. *New Delhi*: Dr. Walter Fernandes, Programme for Tribal Studies, Indian Social Institute; Dr. P. D. Mathew, Programme for Legal Aid, Indian Social Institute; Dr. Ambrose Pinto, Executive Director, Department of Research, Indian Social Institute; Dr. Sanjeeb K. Behera, Programme for Scheduled Castes, Indian Social Institute; Bhagwan Das, Dalit Solidarity, Asian Centre for Human Rights; South Asian Human Rights Documentation Centre.

I am a twenty-six-year-old Dalit agricultural laborer. I earn Rs. 20 [US$0.50] a day for a full day's work. In December 1997, the police raided my village... The superintendent of police [SP] called me a pallachi, which is a caste name for prostitute. He then opened his pant zip... At 11:00 a.m. the sub-collector came. I told the collector that the SP had opened his zip and used a vulgar word. I also told him that they had broken my silver pot. The SP was angry I had pointed him out...

The next morning the police broke all the doors and arrested all the men in the village... The SP came looking for me. My husband hid under the cot. My mother was with me at the time. I was in my night clothes. The police started calling me a prostitute and started beating me. The SP dragged me naked on the road for one hundred feet. I was four months pregnant at the time... A sixty-year-old woman asked them to stop. They beat her too and fractured her hands... They brought me to the police station naked... Fifty-three men had been arrested. One of them took off his lungi [wrap-around cloth] and gave it to me to cover myself.

I begged the police officers at the jail to help me. I even told them I was pregnant. They mocked me for making such bold statements to the police the day before. I spent twenty-five days in jail. I miscarried my baby after ten days. Nothing has happened to the officers who did this to me....

— Guruswamy Guruammal, Madurai, Tamil Nadu

# TABLE OF CONTENTS

# GLOSSARY

**Atrocities Act:** The Scheduled Castes and Scheduled Tribes (Prevention of Atrocities) Act, 1989.

**Atrocities Rules:** The Scheduled Castes and Scheduled Tribes (Prevention of Atrocities) Rules, 1995.

**Backward castes:** those whose ritual rank and occupational status are above "untouchables" but who themselves remain socially and economically depressed. Also referred to as Other Backward Classes (OBCs) or Shudras (who constitute the fourth major caste category in the caste system).

**BDVS:** Bihar Dalit Vikas Samiti (Bihar Dalit Development Organization).

**Bhangis:** a Dalit community of manual scavengers in Gujarat.

**Bhumihar:** a powerful upper-caste community in Bihar.

**Bill hook:** an agricultural tool with a hooked blade.

**BJP:** Bharatiya Janata Party, head of India's current coalition government.

**Caste Hindus:** those falling within the caste system, or all non-Dalits.

**CRPF:** Central Reserve Police Force, the largest of the paramilitary forces in India.

**Dalits:** literally meaning "broken" people, a term employed by rights activists to refer to "untouchables."

**Devadasis:** literally meaning "servants of god," referring to those forced into temple prostitution.

**DGP:** Deputy General of Police.

**DPI:** Dalit Panthers of India.

**DSP:** Deputy Superintendent of Police.

**FIR:** The First Information Report, the first report, recorded by police, of a crime.

**Goonda:** A habitual criminal, usually associated with a criminal gang.

**Lathi:** A police baton, frequently carried by Indian police. It is approximately one meter in length, two to five centimeters in diameter, and usually made of wood.

**Lathi-charge:** the act of charging a crowd with a baton.

**Lower castes:** those relatively lower in the caste system, including Dalits.

**Manual scavengers:** see below under "safai karamcharis."

**Naxalites:** groups with a Marxist/Leninist/Maoist orientation engaged in a militant struggle to achieve higher wages and more equitable land distribution in Bihar and other states.

**NGO:** nongovernmental organization.

**NHRC:** The National Human Rights Commission of India.

**OBCs:** Other Backward Classes, see above under "backward castes."

**Pallars:** a Dalit community in Tamil Nadu.

**Pakhis:** a Dalit community of manual scavengers in Andhra Pradesh.

**Panchayat:** village council.

**PCR Act:** Protection of Civil Rights Act, 1955.

**PUCL:** People's Union for Civil Liberties, the country's largest civil liberties organization.

**Pucca:** solid, in reference to houses made of brick.

**PUDR:** People's Union for Democratic Rights, a well-respected national human rights organization.

**Ranvir Sena:** a private militia of upper-caste landlords in Bihar.

**Reservations:** quotas for various lower castes allowing for increased representation in education, government jobs, and political bodies (provided as compensation for past mistreatment).

**Safai karamcharis:** cleaning workers or manual scavengers engaged in, or employed for, manually carrying human excreta or any sanitation work.

**Scheduled castes:** a list of socially deprived ("untouchable") castes prepared by the British Government in 1935. The schedule of castes was intended to increase representation of scheduled-caste members in the legislature, in government employment, and in university placement. The term is also used in the constitution and various laws.

**Scheduled tribes:** a list of indigenous tribal populations who are entitled to much of the same compensatory treatment as scheduled castes.

**SHRC:** State Human Rights Commission.

**Sikkaliars:** a Dalit community of manual scavengers in Tamil Nadu.

**SP:** Superintendent of Police

**SRPF:** State Reserve Police Force, an armed branch of the police that is called in during times of emergency.

**TADA:** Terrorism and Anti-Disruptive Activities Act.

**Thevars:** a powerful "backward caste" in Tamil Nadu.

**"Untouchability":** the imposition of social disabilities on persons by reason of their birth in certain castes.

**"Untouchables":** those at the bottom of or falling outside the caste system. Administrative parlance now employs the term "scheduled castes" while rights activists and the population more generally employ the term "Dalits."

**Upper castes:** technically those occupying the first three major caste categories (thereby excluding the backward castes). Those interviewed for this report, however, often use the term to refer to all non-Dalit Hindus.

# I. SUMMARY

*When we are working, they ask us not to come near them. At tea canteens, they have separate tea tumblers and they make us clean them ourselves and make us put the dishes away ourselves. We cannot enter temples. We cannot use upper-caste water taps. We have to go one kilometer away to get water... When we ask for our rights from the government, the municipality officials threaten to fire us. So we don't say anything. This is what happens to people who demand their rights.*

— A Dalit manual scavenger, Ahmedabad district, Gujarat[1]

*Thevars [caste Hindus] treat Sikkaliars [Dalits] as slaves so they can utilize them as they wish. They exploit them sexually and make them dig graveyards for high-caste people's burials. They have to take the death message to Thevars. These are all unpaid services.*

— Manibharati, social activist, Madurai district, Tamil Nadu[2]

*In the past, twenty to thirty years ago, [Dalits] enjoyed the practice of "untouchability." In the past, women enjoyed being oppressed by men. They weren't educated. They didn't know the world... They enjoy Thevar community men having them as concubines... They cannot afford to react, they are dependent on us for jobs and protection... She wants it from him. He permits it. If he has power, then she has more affection for the landlord.*

— A prominent Thevar political leader, Tamil Nadu[3]

More than one-sixth of India's population, some 160 million people, live a precarious existence, shunned by much of society because of their rank as

---

[1]Human Rights Watch interview, Ahmedabad district, Gujarat, July 23, 1998. See explanation of manual scavenging below in this section and in Chapter VII.
[2]Human Rights Watch interview, Madurai district, Tamil Nadu, February 17, 1998.
[3]Human Rights Watch interview, Madurai city, Tamil Nadu, February 18, 1998.

1

"untouchables" or Dalits—literally meaning "broken" people[4]—at the bottom of India's caste system. Dalits are discriminated against, denied access to land, forced to work in degrading conditions, and routinely abused at the hands of the police and of higher-caste groups that enjoy the state's protection. In what has been called India's "hidden apartheid," entire villages in many Indian states remain completely segregated by caste. National legislation and constitutional protections serve only to mask the social realities of discrimination and violence faced by those living below the "pollution line."

Despite the fact that "untouchability" was abolished under India's constitution in 1950,[5] the practice of "untouchability"—the imposition of social disabilities on persons by reason of their birth in certain castes— remains very much a part of rural India. "Untouchables" may not cross the line dividing their part of the village from that occupied by higher castes. They may not use the same wells, visit the same temples, drink from the same cups in tea stalls, or lay claim to land that is legally theirs. Dalit children are frequently made to sit in the back of classrooms, and communities as a whole are made to perform degrading rituals in the name of caste.

Most Dalits continue to live in extreme poverty, without land or opportunities for better employment or education. With the exception of a minority who have benefited from India's policy of quotas in education and government jobs, Dalits are relegated to the most menial of tasks, as manual scavengers, removers of human waste and dead animals, leather workers, street sweepers, and cobblers. Dalit children make up the majority of those sold into bondage to pay off debts to upper-caste creditors. Dalit men, women, and children numbering in the tens of millions work as agricultural laborers for a few kilograms of rice or Rs. 15 to Rs. 35 (US$0.38 to $0.88) a day.[6] Their upper-caste employers frequently use caste as a cover for exploitative economic arrangements: social sanction of their status as lesser beings allows their impoverishment to continue.

Dalit women face the triple burden of caste, class, and gender. Dalit girls have been forced to become prostitutes for upper-caste patrons and village priests. Sexual abuse and other forms of violence against women are used by landlords and the police to inflict political "lessons" and crush dissent within the community.

---

[4]"Dalit" is a term first coined by Dr. B. R. Ambedkar, one of the architects of the Indian constitution of 1950 and revered leader of the Dalit movement. It was taken up in the 1970s by the Dalit Panther Movement, which organized to claim rights for "untouchables," and is now commonly used by rights activists.
[5]The abolishment of "untouchability" was made enforceable through the Protection of Civil Rights Act, 1955.
[6]The conversion rate used throughout this report is US$1 to Rs. 40.

According to a Tamil Nadu state government official, the raping of Dalit women exposes the hypocrisy of the caste system as "no one practices untouchability when it comes to sex."[7] Like other Indian women whose relatives are sought by the police, Dalit women have also been arrested and tortured in custody as a means of punishing their male relatives who are hiding from the authorities.

The plight of India's "untouchables" elicits only sporadic attention within the country. Public outrage over large-scale incidents of violence or particularly egregious examples of discrimination fades quickly, and the state is under little pressure to undertake more meaningful reforms. Laws granting Dalits special consideration for government jobs and education reach only a small percentage of those they are meant to benefit. Laws designed to ensure that Dalits enjoy equal rights and protection have seldom been enforced. Instead, police refuse to register complaints about violations of the law and rarely prosecute those responsible for abuses that range from murder and rape to exploitative labor practices and forced displacement from Dalit lands and homes.

Political mobilization that has resulted in the emergence of powerful interest groups and political parties among middle- and low-caste groups throughout India since the mid-1980s has largely bypassed Dalits. Dalits are courted by all political parties but generally forgotten once elections are over. The expanding power base of low-caste political parties, the election of low-caste chief ministers to state governments, and even the appointment of a Dalit as president of India in July 1997 all signal the increasing prominence of Dalits in the political landscape but cumulatively have yet to yield any significant benefit for the majority of Dalits. Laws on land reform and protection for Dalits remain unimplemented in most Indian states.

Lacking access to mainstream political organizations and increasingly frustrated with the pace of reforms, Dalits have begun to resist subjugation and discrimination in two ways: peaceful protest and armed struggle. Particularly since the early 1990s, Dalit organizations have sought to mobilize Dalits to protest peacefully against the human rights violations suffered by their community. These movements have quickly grown in membership and visibility and have provoked a backlash from the higher-caste groups most threatened—both economically and politically—by Dalit assertiveness. Police, many of whom belong to these higher-caste groups or who enjoy their patronage, have arrested Dalit activists, including social workers and lawyers, for activity that is legal and on charges that show the police's political motivation. Dalit activists are jailed under preventive detention

---

[7]Human Rights Watch interview, Madras, February 13, 1998.

statutes to prevent them from holding meetings and protest rallies, or charged as "terrorists" and "threats to national security." Court cases drag on for years, costing impoverished people precious money and time.

Dalits who dare to challenge the social order have been subject to abuses by their higher-caste neighbors. Dalit villages are collectively penalized for individual "transgressions" through social boycotts, including loss of employment and access to water, grazing lands, and ration shops. For most Dalits in rural India who earn less than a subsistence living as agricultural laborers, a social boycott may mean destitution and starvation.

In some states, notably Bihar, guerrilla organizations advocating the use of violence to achieve land redistribution have attracted Dalit support. Such groups, known as "Naxalites,"[8] have carried out attacks on higher-caste groups, killing landlords, village officials and their families and seizing property. Such attacks on civilians constitute gross violations of international humanitarian law. Naxalite groups have also engaged in direct combat with police forces.

In response, police have targeted Dalit villagers believed to be sympathetic to Naxalites and have conducted raids in search of the guerrillas and their weapons. While there is no question that the Naxalites pose a serious security threat and that the police are obliged to counter that threat, the behavior of the police indicates that the purpose of the raids is often to terrorize Dalits as a group, whether or not they are members of Naxalite organizations. During the raids, the police have routinely beaten villagers, sexually assaulted women, and wantonly destroyed property.

Higher-caste landlords in Bihar have organized private militias to counter the Naxalite threat. These militias, or *senas*, also target Dalit villagers believed to be sympathetic to Naxalites. Senas are believed responsible for the murders of many hundreds of Dalits in Bihar since 1969. One of the most prominent militias, the Ranvir Sena, has been responsible for the massacre of more than 400 Dalit villagers in Bihar between 1995 and 1999. In one of the largest of such massacres, on the night of December 1, 1997, the Ranvir Sena shot dead sixteen children, twenty-seven women, and eighteen men in the village of Laxmanpur-Bathe, Jehanabad

---

[8]The term "Naxalite" is derived from Naxalbari in the northern region of Western Bengal where, under the leadership of Kanhu Sanyal, the concept of "forcible protest against the social order relating to holding of property and sharing of social benefits" originated. National Human Rights Commission, *Annual Report 1996-1997* (New Delhi: Government of India, 1998), p. 106. The Naxalite movement, which organizes peasants to bring about land reform through radical means including violence, was virtually crushed in West Bengal in the early 1970s but has a strong following in parts of Bihar and the southern state of Andhra Pradesh.

district Bihar. Five teenage girls were raped and mutilated before being shot in the chest. The villagers were reportedly sympathetic to a Naxalite group that had been demanding more equitable land redistribution in the area. When Ramchela Paswan returned home from the fields, he found seven of his family members shot: "I started beating my chest and screaming that no one is left...."[9] When asked why the sena killed children and women, one sena member responded, "We kill children because they will grow up to become Naxalites. We kill women because they will give birth to Naxalites."[10]

The senas, which claim many politicians as members, operate with impunity. In some cases, police have accompanied them on raids and have stood by as they killed villagers and burned down their homes. On April 10, 1997, in the village of Ekwari, located in the Bhojpur district of Bihar, police stationed in the area to protect lower-caste villagers instead pried open the doors of their residences as members of the sena entered and killed eight residents. In other cases, police raids have followed attacks by the senas. Sena leaders are rarely prosecuted for such killings, and the villagers are rarely or inadequately compensated for their losses. Even in cases where police are not hostile to Dalits, they are generally not accessible to call upon: most police camps are located in the upper-caste section of the village and Dalits are simply unable to approach them for protection.

In the southern districts of Tamil Nadu, clashes between Pallars (a community of Dalits) and Thevars (a marginally higher-caste non-Dalit community) have plagued rural areas since 1995. New wealth among the Pallars, who have sent male family members to work in Gulf states and elsewhere abroad, has triggered a backlash from the Thevars as the Pallars have increasingly been able to buy and farm their own lands or look elsewhere for employment. At the same time, a growing Dalit political movement has provided the Pallars with a platform for resisting the still-prevalent norms of "untouchability." While some Dalits have joined militant groups in Tamil Nadu, such groups have generally engaged in public protests and other political activities rather than armed resistance. The Thevars have responded by assaulting, raping, and murdering Dalits to preserve the status quo.

Local police, drawn predominantly from the Thevar community, have conducted raids on Dalit villages, ostensibly to search for militant activists. During the raids they have assaulted residents, particularly women, and detained Dalits under preventive detention laws. With the tolerance or connivance of local

---

[9] Human Rights Watch interview, Jehanabad district, Bihar, February 25, 1998.
[10] Human Rights Watch interview, New Delhi, February 21, 1998.

officials, police have also forcibly displaced thousands of Dalit villagers. During one such raid, Guruswamy Guruammal, a pregnant, twenty-six-year-old Dalit agricultural laborer, was stripped, brutally beaten, and dragged through the streets naked before being thrown in jail. She told Human Rights Watch, "I begged the police officers at the jail to help me. I even told them I was pregnant. They mocked me for [having made] bold statements to the police the day before. I spent twenty-five days in jail. I miscarried my baby after ten days. Nothing has happened to the officers who did this to me."[11]

Excessive use of force by the police is not limited to rural areas. Police abuse against the urban poor, slum dwellers, Dalits, and other minorities has included arbitrary detention, torture, extrajudicial executions and forced evictions. Although the acute social discrimination characteristic of rural areas is less pronounced in cities, Dalits in urban areas, who make up the majority of bonded laborers and street cleaners, do not escape it altogether. Many live in segregated colonies which have been targets of police raids. This report documents a particularly egregious incident in a Dalit colony in Bombay in July 1997, when police opened fire without warning on a crowd of Dalits protesting the desecration of a statue of Dalit cultural and political hero Dr. B. R. Ambedkar.[12] The firing killed ten and injured twenty-six.

---

[11]Human Rights Watch interview, Madurai, February 18, 1998.

[12]Dr. B. R. Ambedkar was born in 1891 into the "untouchable" Mahar caste of Maharashtra and is widely regarded as one of the most ardent and outspoken advocates of the rights of Dalits in twentieth-century India. At a time when less than 1 percent of his caste was literate, he obtained a Ph.D. from Columbia University in New York and a D.Sc. from the University of London. His earliest efforts involved establishing a Dalit movement in Maharashtra by founding newspapers, holding conferences, forming political parties, and opening colleges and other educational institutions for the welfare of Dalits. During the 1930s, as a delegate at the London Roundtable Conferences, he stated the case for Dalits as a minority entitled to its own electorate. Ambedkar also led campaigns for religious rights for Dalits, including lifting prohibitions on allowing Dalits to enter temples. Eventually he advocated conversion to other religions, most notably Buddhism. He is perhaps best known for improving the status of Dalits through the drafting of relevant articles in the Indian constitution. He was named the minister for law in the first Nehru cabinet in independent India and served as chairman of the drafting committee for the constitution. Stephen Hay, *Sources of Indian Tradition. Volume Two: Modern India and Pakistan*. Second Edition. (New Delhi: Penguin Books India, 1988), pp. 324-333 and pp. 339-348. See also Dhananjay Keer, *Dr. Ambedkar: Life and Mission* (Bombay: Popular Prakashan Private Limited, 1990); Verinder Grover, ed., *Bhimrao Ramji Ambedkar: A Biography of his Vision and Ideas* (New Delhi: Deep and Deep Publications, 1998).

Dalits throughout the country also suffer in many instances from de facto disenfranchisement. During elections, those unpersuaded by typical electioneering are routinely threatened and beaten by political party strongmen in order to compel them to vote for certain candidates. Already under the thumb of local landlords and police officials, Dalit villagers who do not comply have been murdered, beaten, and harassed.

Police and upper-caste militias, operating at the behest of powerful political leaders in the state, have also punished Dalit voters. In February 1998, police raided a Dalit village in Tamil Nadu that had boycotted the national parliamentary elections. Women were kicked and beaten, their clothing was torn, and police forced sticks and iron pipes into their mouths. Kerosene was poured into stored food grains and grocery items and police reportedly urinated in cooking vessels. In Bihar, political candidates ensure their majority vote with the help of senas, whose members kill if necessary. The Ranvir Sena was responsible for killing more than fifty people during Bihar's 1995 state election campaign. The sena was again used to intimidate voters in Ara district, Bihar, during the February 1998 national parliamentary elections.

Dalits who have contested political office in village councils and municipalities through seats that have been constitutionally "reserved" for them have been threatened with physical abuse and even death in order to get them to withdraw from the campaign. In the village of Melavalavu, Madurai district Tamil Nadu, following the election of a Dalit to the village council presidency, members of a higher-caste group murdered six Dalits in June 1997, including the elected council president, whom they beheaded. As told to Human Rights Watch by an eyewitness, the leader of the attack "instructed the Thevars [caste Hindus] to kill all the Pariahs [Dalits]... They pulled all six out of the bus and stabbed them on the road... Five Thevars joined together, put Murugesan [the Dalit president] on the ground outside the bus, and chopped off his head, then threw it in a well half a kilometer away... Some grabbed his hands, others grabbed his head, and one cut his head... They deliberately took the head and poured the blood on other dead bodies."[13] As of February 1999, the accused—who had been voted out of their once-secure elected positions—had not been prosecuted. Those arrested were out on bail, while the person identified as the ringleader of the attack was still at large.

---

[13]Human Rights Watch interview, Madurai district, Tamil Nadu, February 15, 1998.

The Scheduled Castes and Scheduled Tribes[14] (Prevention of Atrocities) Act, enacted in 1989, provides a means to address many of the problems Dalits face in India. The act is designed to prevent abuses and punish those responsible, establish special courts for the trial of such offenses, and provide for victim relief and rehabilitation. A look at the offenses made punishable by the act provides a glimpse into the retaliatory or customarily degrading treatment Dalits may receive. The offenses include forcing members of a scheduled caste or scheduled tribe to drink or eat any inedible or obnoxious substance; dumping excreta, waste matter, carcasses or any other obnoxious substance in their premises or neighborhood; forcibly removing their clothes and parading them naked or with painted face or body; interfering with their rights to land; compelling a member of a scheduled caste or scheduled tribe into forms of forced or bonded labor; corrupting or fouling the water of any spring, reservoir or any other source ordinarily used by scheduled castes or scheduled tribes; denying right of passage to a place of public resort; and using a position of dominance to exploit a scheduled caste or scheduled tribe woman sexually.

The potential of the law to bring about social change has been hampered by police corruption and caste bias, with the result that many allegations are not entered in police books. Ignorance of procedures and a lack of knowledge of the act have also affected its implementation. Even when cases are registered, the absence of special courts to try them can delay prosecutions for up to three to four years. Some state governments dominated by higher castes have even attempted to repeal the legislation altogether.

Between 1994 and 1996, a total of 98,349 cases were registered with the police nationwide as crimes and atrocities against scheduled castes. Of these, 38,483 were registered under the Atrocities Act for the sorts of offenses enumerated above. A further 1,660 were for murder, 2,814 for rape, and 13,671

---

[14]The term "scheduled castes," by which Dalits are also called, refers to a list of socially deprived ("untouchable") castes prepared by the British Government in 1935. The schedule of castes was intended to increase representation of scheduled-caste members in the legislature, in government employment, and in university placement. The term is also used in the constitution and various laws.   Pauline Kolenda, *Caste in Contemporary India: Beyond Organic Solidarity* (Menlo Park: The Benjamin/Cumming Publishing Co., 1978), p. 128. The term "scheduled tribes" refers to a list of indigenous tribal populations who are entitled to much of the same compensatory treatment as scheduled castes.

for hurt.[15]  Given that Dalits are both reluctant and unable (for lack of police cooperation) to report crimes against themselves, the actual number of abuses is presumably much higher.  The National Commission for Scheduled Castes and Scheduled Tribes has reported that these cases typically fall into one of three categories: cases relating to the practice of "untouchability" and attempts to defy the social order; cases relating to land disputes and demands for minimum wages; and cases of atrocities by police and forest officials.

Although this report focuses primarily on abuse against Dalit communities that have begun to assert themselves economically or organize themselves politically, it also examines the weakest sectors of the population: those with no political representation, living in the poorest of conditions, and made to perform the most degrading of tasks with little or no remuneration.  To eke out a subsistence living, Dalits throughout the country, numbering in the tens of millions, are driven to bonded labor, manual scavenging, and forced prostitution under conditions that violate national law and their basic human rights.

An estimated forty million people in India, among them fifteen million children, are bonded laborers, working in slave-like conditions in order to pay off a debt.  A majority of them are Dalits.  According to government statistics, an estimated one million Dalits are manual scavengers who clear feces from public and private latrines and dispose of dead animals; unofficial estimates are much higher.  An activist working with scavengers in the state of Andhra Pradesh claimed, "In one toilet there can be as many as 400 seats which all have to be manually cleaned.  This is the lowest occupation in the world, and it is done by the community that occupies the lowest status in the caste system."[16]  In India's southern states, thousands of girls are forced into prostitution before reaching the age of puberty.  Devadasis, literally meaning "female servant of god," usually belong to the Dalit community.  Once dedicated, the girl is unable to marry, forced to become a prostitute for upper-caste community members, and eventually auctioned off to an urban brothel.

This report is about caste, but it is also about class, gender, poverty, labor, and land.  For those at the bottom of its hierarchy, caste is a determinative factor for the attainment of social, political, civil, and economic rights.  Most of the conflicts documented in this report take place within very narrow segments of the caste

---

[15]National Commission for Scheduled Castes and Scheduled Tribes, *National Crime Records Bureau (M.H.A.), Statement Showing Cases Registered with the Police Under Different Nature of Crimes and Atrocities on Scheduled Castes and Scheduled Tribes from 1994 to 1996* (New Delhi: Government of India, 1997).
[16]Human Rights Watch interview, Bangalore, July 26, 1998.

hierarchy, between the poor and the not-so-poor, the landless laborer and the small landowner. The differences lie in the considerable amount of leverage that the higher-caste Hindus or non-Dalits are able to wield over local police, district administrations, and even the state government.

Investigations by India's National Commission for Scheduled Castes and Scheduled Tribes, the National Human Rights Commission, the National Police Commission, and numerous local nongovernmental organizations all concur that impunity is rampant. In cases investigated for this report, with the exception of a few transfers and suspensions, no action has been taken against police officers involved in violent raids or summary executions, or against those accused of colluding with private actors to carry out attacks on Dalit communities. Moreover, in many instances, repeated calls for protection by threatened Dalit communities have been ignored by police and district officials.

The "National Agenda for Governance," the election manifesto for the Bharatiya Janata Party (BJP), which came to power in the February 1998 elections, outlines a program of action for the "upliftment" of scheduled castes and scheduled tribes. It promises to take steps to establish "a civilised, humane and just civil order... which does not discriminate on the grounds of caste, religion, class, colour, race or sex"; ensures the "economic and educational development of the minorities"; safeguards the interests of scheduled castes, scheduled tribes and backward classes by "appropriate legal, executive and societal efforts and by large scale education and empowerment"; provides "legal protection to existing percentages of reservation in educational institutions at the State level"; and removes "the last vestiges of untouchability." However, to date, the Indian government has done little to fulfill its promises to Dalits.

A national campaign to highlight abuses against Dalits spearheaded by human rights groups in eight states began to focus national and international attention to the issue in 1998. The recommendations for this report were drafted in consultation with more than forty activists who have been working closely on the campaign. In publishing this report now, Human Rights Watch adds its voice to theirs in calling upon the Indian government to implement the recommendations outlined in this report, to fulfill the commitments made regarding scheduled castes in the National Agenda for Governance, and to take immediate steps to prevent and eliminate caste-based violence and discrimination. We further urge the international community to press the Indian government to bring its practices into compliance with national and international law.

# II. RECOMMENDATIONS

In upholding constitutional guarantees of equality, freedom, justice and human dignity, the government of India should demonstrate its commitment to the eradication of caste violence and caste-based discrimination by implementing the following recommendations at the earliest possible date.

In particular, the government should implement measures designed to ensure that states abolish the practice of "untouchability," in compliance with Article 17 of the constitution; commit to taking steps to prevent further violence and prosecute both state and private actors responsible for caste-motivated attacks on Dalit communities; enforce the Scheduled Castes and Scheduled Tribes (Prevention of Atrocities) Act, 1989 and other relevant legislation; and educate state agents and the Indian population on the rights and constitutional freedoms of all citizens.

Immediately and without fail, the government should disband the Ranvir Sena, prosecute and punish state and private actors responsible for abuses documented in this report, and place a high priority on the protection of Dalit women. Naxalite groups have also committed egregious abuses, including murders of landlords and their family members. Human Rights Watch condemns all such attacks on civilians.

Many of the recommendations that follow complement the major areas of action outlined above. In addition, Human Rights Watch recognizes that the problem of caste violence and caste-based discrimination cannot be resolved without a meaningful commitment to land and wage reform.

## Recommendations to the Government of India
*The Indian government should fully implement the provisions of the Scheduled Castes and Scheduled Tribes (Prevention of Atrocities) Act, 1989 and the Scheduled Castes and Scheduled Tribes (Prevention of Atrocities) Rules, 1995. In particular it should:*

- Ensure that states constitute and oversee state- and district-level vigilance and monitoring committees, as required by Rules 16 and 17 of the Scheduled Castes and Scheduled Tribes (Prevention of Atrocities) Rules, 1995, for the purpose of properly implementing the Scheduled Castes and Scheduled Tribes (Prevention of Atrocities) Act, 1989 [hereinafter the Atrocities Rules and the Atrocities Act]. This effort should ensure that a sufficient number of investigators (including appropriate representation of Dalit men and women) are included in the committees to guarantee full implementation of the act. Given the number of potential cases, the government should enlist lawyers,

11

social workers, medical personnel, teachers, civil servants, and others involved in Dalit issues as investigators. Nongovernmental organization (NGO) representatives should also be consulted in the recruitment of investigators. Committees should submit their reports to district collectors to pursue prosecution. In turn, collectors should report on actions taken during committee meetings. Reports published by the committee should be made public, and in-depth training should be provided to district officials charged with enforcing the act.

- Ensure that states establish special courts in every revenue district and appoint special public prosecutors to try cases arising under the Atrocities Act.

- Ensure strict implementation of the Atrocities Act, as regards victims of violent abuse and other "atrocities." Each police station should have a scheduled caste/scheduled tribe atrocities cell to handle investigations of abuses and alleged violations of the Atrocities Act. Each revenue district should also have a special deputy superintendent of police charged with investigating atrocities under the act. In keeping with the Atrocities Rules, police who refuse to register cases under the act should be punished accordingly. For full implementation of the act, these cells should be statutorily empowered to receive and address complaints of violations under the act and complaints of official misconduct. They should also be able to file "first information reports" (FIRs), the first step in prosecution of a criminal charge, when abuses are committed against Dalits. The cells should work closely with the vigilance and monitoring committees established under the Atrocities Rules to ensure full enforcement.

- Ensure immediate and full compensation by the district administration to victims of atrocities as per the Atrocities Rules. The value of property destroyed and crops damaged should be included in the compensation schedule. The committees appointed by the government under the rules to estimate loss should include NGOs in addition to government officials. In accordance with Rule 11, the district administration should also ensure that victims' trial expenses are paid.

- Provide training to district officials charged with enforcing the Atrocities Act and ensure that a copy of the act (translated into the local language) and accompanying rules are easily available and prominently posted in all local level police stations and available in all courts trying cases under the act.

- Statutorily empower the National Commission for Scheduled Castes and Scheduled Tribes to oversee implementation of the Atrocities Act in all states. Strengthen the capacity of the National Commission for Scheduled Castes and Scheduled Tribes to operate legal cells and open branch offices in all states with enough financial resources and powers to initiate prosecution of cases. As recommended by the commission, amend Article 338 of the constitution to empower the commission to issue directions for corrective action and implement its findings.

- Strengthen the capacity of the National Human Rights Commission and the National Commission for Women to operate branch offices in all states with enough financial resources and powers to initiate prosecution of cases. Amend the Protection of Human Rights Act, 1993 so that national and state human rights commissions are not automatically exempted from inquiring into matters already pending before a state commission or any other commission duly constituted under any law.

- Establish a civilian review board or civilian ombudsman committee comprising judges and lawyers to monitor police stations and ensure that Supreme Court guidelines on treatment of persons in custody, as established in *D. K. Basu v. State of West Bengal*, are strictly enforced. NGO input should also be solicited. Ensure that complaints against law enforcement personnel are promptly and thoroughly investigated by adequately trained investigatory staff. The agency should have the power to subpoena documents, summon witnesses, and enter the premises of police stations, lock-ups, and detention centers to conduct thorough investigations.

- Implement the recommendations made by the National Police Commission in 1980, specifically those that call for a mandatory judicial inquiry in cases of alleged rape, death, or grievous injury of people in police custody and the establishment of investigative bodies whose members should include civilians as well as police and judicial authorities.

- Ensure that each police station has adequate female police personnel, consistent with recommendations made by the National Commission for Scheduled Castes and Scheduled Tribes. Female police should record complaints submitted by women. Each police station should also have adequate scheduled caste and scheduled tribe personnel and enough financial resources to carry out investigations.

- Ensure strict implementation of the bonded labor-related provisions of the Atrocities Act. As Dalits constitute the majority of bonded laborers, the government should ensure that states and districts establish and oversee bonded labor vigilance committees, as required by the Bonded Labour (System) Abolition Act, 1976. The government should ensure that a sufficient number of investigators can be included in the committee to guarantee implementation of the act. Lawyers, social workers, teachers, civil servants, and others with ties to bonded laborers and their families should be enlisted as investigators. Nongovernmental organization representatives should be consulted in the recruitment of investigators. The government should provide in-depth training to district officials charged with enforcing the Bonded Labour (System) Abolition Act, 1976, as directed by the Supreme Court in *Neeraja Chaudhary v. State of Madhya Pradesh*, 1984.

- Ensure appropriate implementation of the Employment of Manual Scavengers and Construction of Dry Latrines (Prohibition) Act, 1993, including prosecution of officials responsible for the perpetuation of the practice and non-rehabilitation of affected scavenger communities, the majority of which are Dalits. The government should ensure that states and districts constitute and oversee vigilance and monitoring committees with adequate representation of NGOs, women, and members of the scavenger communities. State governments should also train district officials charged with enforcing the act.

- Implement measures designed to ensure that states are in compliance with Article 45 of the constitution, which mandates free and compulsory education for all children up to the age of fourteen. Primary education is the first step in breaking the cycle of discrimination and caste-based employment.

- Incorporate education on relevant legislation for Dalits and women into school curricula (including education on the Atrocities Act and the Protection of Human Rights Act, 1993).

- Launch a nationwide public awareness campaign regarding the legal prohibition of "untouchability," "atrocities" and other forms of discrimination and violence against Dalits. This campaign should explain in simple terms what actions are legally prohibited, what recourse is available to Dalits and their families, and what the procedures are for filing an FIR. It should also include a program of public service announcements in all states aimed at sensitizing the population on Dalit issues and creating awareness of Dalit rights.

- Make available to the public government studies on issues affecting Dalits. Specifically, the government should release the white paper on reservations and the white paper on land reform. The first outlines the extent to which constitutional reservations have been implemented at the state and central level since independence. In particular, attention should be given to implementation of reservations in all ministries, in the secretariats of the prime minister and president, and in the police and judiciary. The second outlines the extent to which tenancy acts and acts that establish ceilings on single landowners' holdings have been implemented in all states.

- Ensure that adequate financial resources are allocated to the proper functioning of the newly constituted government bodies under the seventy-third and seventy-fourth amendments to the Indian constitution. These amendments provide that in every *panchayat* (village council) and every municipality, seats shall be reserved for scheduled-caste and scheduled-tribe members in proportion to their representation in the population. Among the seats reserved for the scheduled castes and scheduled tribes, not less than one-third shall be reserved for women belonging to those castes or tribes. The government should work with intergovernmental and nongovernmental organizations to provide appropriate training to elected members of rural and urban bodies, including gender and caste sensitivity training. Women should take part in legal literacy workshops, and all those appointed to reserved panchayat positions should be provided legal protection to ensure that they are able to perform their duties.

*The Indian government should provide full cooperation to relevant United Nations bodies in the implementation of the following recommendations:*

- Invite the Working Group on Arbitrary Detention, and the Special Rapporteurs on Torture, on Extrajudicial, Summary and Arbitrary Executions, and on Violence against Women to visit India. The government should encourage them to include in their investigations allegations of illegal detention, abuse, and deaths of Dalits in police custody, of fake encounter killings, and of violence against Dalit women, including abuse by the police and by private upper-caste militias.

- Implement the recommendations of the 49th session of the Committee on the Elimination of Racial Discrimination (CERD). In particular, the government should implement the recommendation that "special measures be taken by the authorities to prevent acts of discrimination towards persons belonging to the scheduled castes and tribes, and in the case where such acts have been committed, to conduct thorough investigations, to punish those found responsible and provide just and adequate reparation to the victims." As per committee recommendations, the committee's findings should be available to the public in local languages.

- Promptly submit the Indian government's next periodic report on compliance with the International Convention on the Elimination of All Forms of Discrimination to CERD, as this has been overdue since January 4, 1998. As requested by CERD, the report should include "detailed information on the legislative aspects and the concrete implementation of the Directive Principles of the State Policy of the Constitution," as well as information on the powers and functions of the National Commission for Scheduled Castes and Scheduled Tribes.

- Promptly submit the Indian government's initial report on compliance with the Convention on the Elimination of All Forms of Discrimination against Women to the Committee on the Elimination of Discrimination against Women, as this has been overdue since August 8, 1994.

- Ratify the United Nations Convention against Torture and Other Forms of Cruel, Inhuman, or Degrading Treatment or Punishment, 1984.

## Recommendations to All State Governments

*In addition to recommendations outlined for the government of India, state governments should implement the following recommendations at the earliest possible date:*

- Ensure full implementation of the Scheduled Castes and Scheduled Tribes (Prevention of Atrocities) Act, 1989, including the appointment of special courts, special prosecutors, and vigilance and monitoring committees. Provide training in proper procedures under the act to judges and prosecutors charged with trying atrocities cases. (See related recommendations under Recommendations to the Government of India.)

- Ensure ratification and implementation of the Bonded Labour (System) Abolition Act, 1976 and ratify and implement the Employment of Manual Scavengers and Construction of Dry Latrines (Prohibition) Act, 1993. (See related recommendations under Recommendations to the Government of India.)

- Implement measures designed to ensure that states are in compliance with Article 46 of the constitution, which directs states to promote with special care the educational and economic interests of the scheduled castes and scheduled tribes and to protect them from social injustice and all forms of economic exploitation.

- Study and publicize the extent to which land and wage reforms have been implemented in the state. In particular, state governments should determine industry compliance with minimum and living wage standards, particularly those industries that employ a majority of Dalits, as well as the status of land reforms, land ceiling laws, and distribution of surplus land. The study should also review proof of ownership in land records, the extent of encroachment on scheduled caste/scheduled tribe lands. NGO participation should be ensured in the investigations.

- Take immediate steps to prevent further violence, social boycotts, and other forms of discrimination against Dalits and to investigate and punish those responsible for attacks and acts of discrimination in affected districts. Any officials or members of the police who fail to respond to repeated calls for protection from villagers, or fail to prosecute acts of violence or discrimination should also be prosecuted.

- Take decisive steps to ensure police agents use deadly force only as a last resort to protect life. Police agents should act in accordance with guidelines established in relevant state police manuals that meet international standards on use of force. The United Nations Basic Principles on the Use of Force or Firearms by Law Enforcement Officials emphasize that the use of force and firearms should be in consonance with respect for human rights and that deadly force should not be used against persons unless "strictly unavoidable in order to protect life."

- Take decisive steps to ensure that police do not conduct raids on villages or engage in arbitrary and unlawful destruction and seizure of property in response to caste clashes. Police involved in such activities should be promptly investigated by an independent judicial body and prosecuted accordingly.

- Ensure that investigations of complaints of violence against women include women investigators. Amend the Criminal Procedure Code so that rape victims are not restricted to approaching government hospitals for medical examinations and can instead be examined by any registered practitioner for the purposes of gathering evidence.

- Establish independent monitoring agencies to review cases of Dalits and Dalit activists detained under detention laws. All cases found to be without merit, or in violation of proper detention procedures, should be withdrawn.

- Compile and release state-level statistics on the number of atrocities committed against Dalits, the number of cases registered under the Atrocities Act, and the extent to which reservations have been implemented in the state. States should ensure that all NGOs and citizens have access to this information.

- Investigate the process of recruitment of police officers in the state to ensure that requirements of reservations for scheduled castes and scheduled tribes are met and that monetary bribes are not part of the police and judicial recruitment process. Prosecute and punish those found to have engaged in bribes or extortion while registering cases or conducting raids.

- Ensure speedy review and publication of findings by commissions of inquiry appointed by the state to investigate abuses against Dalits.

**Recommendations Specific to Abuses Documented in this Report**
*Naxalites and other armed opposition groups are at all times obliged to respect minimum standards of humane behavior. These standards require that civilians and other protected persons be treated humanely, with specific prohibitions on murder, torture, or cruel, humiliating or degrading treatment. Groups engaging in armed struggle should look to the provisions of Common Article 3 of the Geneva*

*Conventions for additional guidance on the legal foundations of these basic principles. Additionally, the state government of Bihar should:*

- Appoint an independent judicial body to investigate and punish those responsible for attacks in affected districts, including any officials or members of the police who failed to respond to repeated calls for protection for villagers or to prosecute previous acts of violence.

- Make special efforts to investigate and prosecute those responsible for attacks on women during the Laxmanpur-Bathe massacre of December 1997, and other massacres.

- Investigate the role of the police in conducting raids on villages in the aftermath of massacres and in illegally destroying or seizing property. Police responsible for such abuses should be prosecuted and punished accordingly. Dalits who have lost property during such raids should be compensated.

- Disband the Ranvir Sena, an upper-caste private militia which has been implicated in the massacre of hundreds of Dalits since 1994.

- Provide full security to villagers against further private militia attacks. Relocate village-based police pickets away from upper-caste areas to areas more accessible and secure for lower-caste communities.

- Ensure that in all districts affected by caste clashes (particularly in Jehanabad, Patna, and Bhojpur) at least one senior officer is a member of the Dalit community.

*The state government of Maharashtra should:*

- Prosecute officers found guilty of killing and injuring hundreds of Dalits in Bombay's Ramabai colony on July 11, 1997 when members of the Special Reserve Forces fired indiscriminately into a crowd of Dalits protesting the desecration of a statue of Dr. B. R. Ambedkar.

- Prosecute and punish those officials held responsible by the Gundewar commission for the Ramabai killings.

*The state government of Tamil Nadu should:*

• Use an independent judicial body to promptly investigate and prosecute police involved in raids on villages during the southern district clashes from July 1995 to December 1998. Dalits who lost property during such raids should be compensated.

• Ensure that in all southern districts affected by caste clashes (particularly Tuticorin, Tirunelveli, Virudhunagar, Ramanathapuram, Sivagangai, Madurai, and Theni) at least one senior officer is a member of the Dalit community.

**Recommendations to the United Nations**

• The Secretary-General of the United Nations and the United Nations High Commissioner for Human Rights should ensure that all United Nations agencies working in India pay particular attention to the issue of caste violence and caste discrimination and develop programs and strategies designed to curb abuse and encourage accountability.

• Agencies should establish consultative mechanisms to seek Dalit NGO input in project design and evaluation.

• The World Health Organization should investigate and publicize the adverse health consequences arising from the practice of manual scavenging and promote measures to eliminate exposure of Dalits to hazardous work conditions.

• U.N. agencies that have programs for women in India, including WHO, UNDP, UNICEF, and UNIFEM, should use these programs to focus attention on the human rights implications of violence against Dalit women, including the role of official forces in perpetuating that violence.

• UNIFEM, in conjunction with the Indian government and NGOs, should expand its efforts in providing legal training to rural women elected as panchayat members.

**Recommendations to the World Bank and Other International Lending Institutions**
*The World Bank and other international lending institutions operational in India should:*

• Ensure that anti-discrimination measures are built into World Bank and Asian Development Bank-funded projects in areas where the problems of caste violence and caste discrimination are severe. As part of its commitment to good governance, the World Bank, as well as other international lending institutions, should establish ongoing dialogue with Dalit NGOs at all stages of the decision-making process—before a loan is released, while the project is being implemented, and in the course of any post-project evaluation.

• Prior to approval of projects, and in consultation with NGOs, investigate the effect of proposed policies and programs on caste violence, caste discrimination, and discrimination against Dalit women, and explore ways in which programs could help alleviate violence and discrimination.

**Recommendations to India's Donors and Trading Partners**
*India's donors and trading partners should:*

• Encourage India to adopt the recommendations outlined above and use every opportunity to raise the problem of caste violence both publicly—at international meetings, congressional or parliamentary hearings, and in press conferences—and privately, at Consultative Group meetings and in meetings with relevant officials.

• Work to develop programs and strategies for bilateral and multilateral aid programs to India that would make funds available to promote legal literacy programs aimed at educating Dalits and in particular Dalit women on the laws that are designed to protect them; train rural women who are elected to panchayats; launch a series of sensitization campaigns aimed at educating the population on the rights of Dalits and human rights in general; set up the various independent monitoring agencies described above; strengthen the capacity of the National Commission for Scheduled Castes and Scheduled Tribes, the National Human Rights Commission, and the National Commission for Women to operate legal cells and open branch offices in all states; and train judicial and law enforcement personnel—particularly investigators of caste violence—on crimes against Dalits and gender-based crimes against Dalit women. Programs should also be devised that would enhance the recruitment of women investigators.

- Encourage India to implement the recommendations of the National Police Commission and to invite the United Nations Special Rapporteurs on Torture, Extrajudicial Executions, and Violence against Women.

## III. THE CONTEXT OF CASTE VIOLENCE

The constitution has merely prescribed, but has not given any description of the ground reality. We can make a dent only if we recognise the fact that the caste system is a major source, indeed an obnoxious one, of human rights violations.

— R. M. Pal, "The Caste System and Human Rights Violations"[17]

With little land of their own to cultivate, Dalit men, women, and children numbering in the tens of millions work as agricultural laborers for a few kilograms of rice or Rs. 15 to Rs. 35 (US$0.38 to $0.88) a day. Most live on the brink of destitution, barely able to feed their families and unable to send their children to school or break away from cycles of debt bondage that are passed on from generation to generation. At the end of day they return to a hut in their Dalit colony with no electricity, kilometers away from the nearest water source, and segregated from all non-Dalits, known as caste Hindus. They are forbidden by caste Hindus to enter places of worship, to draw water from public wells, or to wear shoes in caste Hindu presence. They are made to dig the village graves, dispose of dead animals, clean human waste with their bare hands, and to wash and use separate tea tumblers at neighborhood tea stalls, all because—due to their caste status—they are deemed polluting and therefore "untouchable." Any attempt to defy the social order is met with violence or economic retaliation.

As documented throughout this report, the perpetuation of human rights abuses against India's Dalit population is intimately connected to police abuse. Local police officials routinely refuse to register cases against caste Hindus or enforce relevant legislation that protects Dalits. Prejudiced by their own caste and gender biases, or under the thumb of influential landlords and upper-caste politicians, police not only allow caste Hindus to act with impunity but in many cases operate as agents of powerful upper-caste groups to detain Dalits who organize in protest against discrimination and violence, and to punish Dalit villagers because of their suspected support for militant groups.

Under constitutional provisions and various laws, the state grants Dalits a certain number of privileges, including reservations (quotas) in education, government jobs, and government bodies. The Scheduled Castes and Scheduled

---

[17]Dr. R. M. Pal, "The Caste System and Human Rights Violations," in *Human Rights from the Dalit Perspective* [no date] (Madras: Dalit Liberation Education Trust), p. 23.

Tribes (Prevention of Atrocities) Act, 1989 was designed to prevent abuses against members of scheduled castes and scheduled tribes and punish those responsible. Its enactment represented an acknowledgment on the part of the government that abuses, in their most degrading and violent forms, were still perpetrated against Dalits decades after independence. The laws, however, have benefited very few and, due to a lack of political will, development programs and welfare projects designed to improve economic conditions for Dalits have generally had little effect. Dalits rarely break free from bondage or economic exploitation by upper-caste landowners.

Political parties have frequently fashioned their manifestos and campaign slogans around the need for "upliftment" of these marginalized sectors, while political leaders, mostly drawn from higher castes, offer the promise of equal status and equal rights.[18] It would be difficult to convince the Dalits of Dholapur district, Rajasthan, that, fifty years after independence, the government had done anything to end the violence and discrimination that have ruled their lives. In April 1998, a Dalit of the area was assaulted by an upper-caste family who forcibly pierced his nostril, drew a string through his nose, paraded him around the village, and tied him to a cattle post—all because he refused to sell *bidis* (hand-rolled cigarettes) on credit to the nephew of the upper-caste village chief.[19] The message sent from the judiciary on caste discrimination is equally grim: in July 1998 in the state of Uttar Pradesh, an Allahabad High Court judge had his chambers "purified with Ganga *jal*" (water from the River Ganges), because it had earlier been occupied by a Dalit judge.[20]

The remainder of this chapter describes the basic tenets of the caste system, the context for the abuses described in this report, the political movements they have helped fuel, and the legal framework of the government's response.

## The Caste System

India's caste system is perhaps the world's longest surviving social hierarchy. A defining feature of Hinduism, caste encompasses a complex ordering of social groups on the basis of ritual purity. A person is considered a member of the caste into which he or she is born and remains within that caste until death, although the particular ranking of that caste may vary among regions and over time. Differences

---

[18]Kothapalli Wilson, "Human Rights in a Caste Society, An Indian Perception" (Madras: Dalit Liberation and Education Trust), [no date], pp. 3-4.
[19]*Indian Express* (Bombay), April 28, 1998.
[20]"LS Concerned at 'purifying' act by HC judge," *Times of India* (Bombay), July 23, 1998.

in status are traditionally justified by the religious doctrine of *karma*, a belief that one's place in life is determined by one's deeds in previous lifetimes. Traditional scholarship has described this more than 2,000-year-old system within the context of the four principal *varnas*, or large caste categories. In order of precedence these are the Brahmins (priests and teachers), the Ksyatriyas (rulers and soldiers), the Vaisyas (merchants and traders), and the Shudras (laborers and artisans). A fifth category falls outside the varna system and consists of those known as "untouchables" or Dalits; they are often assigned tasks too ritually polluting to merit inclusion within the traditional varna system.[21]

Within the four principal castes, there are thousands of sub-castes, also called *jatis,* endogamous groups that are further divided along occupational, sectarian, regional and linguistic lines. Collectively all of these are sometimes referred to as "caste Hindus" or those falling within the caste system. The Dalits are described as *varna-sankara*: they are "outside the system"—so inferior to other castes that they are deemed polluting and therefore "untouchable." Even as outcasts, they themselves are divided into further sub-castes. Although "untouchability" was abolished under Article 17 of the Indian constitution, the practice continues to determine the socio-economic and religious standing of those at the bottom of the caste hierarchy. Whereas the first four varnas are free to choose and change their occupation, Dalits have generally been confined to the occupational structures into which they are born.

### "Untouchability" and Segregation

A 1997 report issued by the National Commission for Scheduled Castes and Scheduled Tribes underscored that "untouchability"—the imposition of social disabilities on persons by reason of their birth in certain castes—was still practiced in many forms throughout the country. The report described a number of social manifestations of caste-based discrimination in the 1990s: scheduled-caste bridegrooms were not permitted to ride a mare in villages, a marriage tradition; scheduled castes could not sit on their *charpoys* (rope beds) when persons of other castes passed by; scheduled castes were not permitted to draw water from common

---

[21]See generally, Ainslie Embree, ed., *Sources of Indian Tradition: From the Beginnings to 1800* (New York: Columbia Univ. Press, 1988); Pauline Kolenda, *Caste in Contemporary India: Beyond Organic Solidarity* (Menlo Park: Benjamin/Cumming Publishing Co., 1978); M. N. Srinivas, ed., *Caste: Its Twentieth Century Avatar* (New Delhi: Viking, 1996).

wells and hand-pumps; and in many tea-shops and *dhabas* (food stalls), separate crockery and cutlery were used for serving the scheduled castes.[22]

The prevalence of "untouchability" practices was also noted by the United Nations Committee on the Elimination of Racial Discrimination in 1996, while reviewing India's tenth to fourteenth periodic reports under the Convention on the Elimination of All Forms of Racial Discrimination:[23]

> Although constitutional provisions and legal texts exist to abolish untouchability and to protect the members of the scheduled castes and tribes, and social and educational policies have been adopted to improve the situation of members of the scheduled castes and tribes and to protect them from abuses, widespread discrimination against those people, and the relative impunity of those who abuse them, points to the limited effect of these measures. The Committee is particularly concerned at reports that people belonging to the scheduled castes and tribes are often prevented from using public wells or from entering cafes or restaurants and that their children are sometimes separated from other children in schools, in violation of article 5 (f) of the Convention.[24]

Most Dalits in rural areas live in segregated colonies, away from the caste Hindus. According to an activist working with Dalit communities in 120 villages in Villapuram district, Tamil Nadu, all 120 villages have segregated Dalit colonies. Basic supplies such as water are also segregated, and medical facilities and the better, thatched-roof houses exist exclusively in the caste Hindu colony. "Untouchability" is further reinforced by state allocation of facilities; separate

---

[22]National Commission for Scheduled Castes and Scheduled Tribes, *Highlights of the Report for the Years 1994-95 & 1995-96* (New Delhi: Government of India, 1997), p. 2. The National Commission for Scheduled Castes and Scheduled Tribes is a constitutional body set up pursuant to Article 338 of the Indian constitution. It has been entrusted with the responsibility of ensuring that the safeguards and protections which have been given to scheduled castes and tribes are implemented by the various implementing agencies.

[23]In its review the committee noted that the situation of scheduled castes fell within the scope of the convention. See also Chapter X for more on the convention and its applicability to Dalits.

[24]Consideration of Report by India to the Committee on the Elimination of Racial Discrimination, CERD/C/304/Add.13, September 17, 1996.

facilities are provided for separate colonies. Dalits often receive the poorer of the two, if they receive any at all.[25]

As part of village custom, Dalits are made to render free services in times of death, marriage, or any village function. During the Marama village festival in Karnataka state, caste Hindus force Dalits to sacrifice buffalos and drink their blood. They then have to mix the blood with cooked rice and run into the village fields without their *chappals* (slippers). The cleaning of the whole village, the digging of graves, the carrying of firewood, and the disposal of dead animals are all tasks that Dalits are made to perform.[26]

In villages where Dalits are a minority, the practice of "untouchability" is even more severely enforced. Individual attempts to defy the social order are frequently punished through social boycotts and acts of retaliatory violence further described below. Activists in Tamil Nadu explained that large-scale clashes between caste communities in the state's southern districts have often been triggered by Dalits' efforts to draw water from a "forbidden" well or by their refusal to perform a delegated task. Dalits have responded to ill-treatment by converting, en masse, to Buddhism, Christianity, and sometimes Islam. Once converted, however, many lose access to their scheduled-caste status and the few government privileges assigned to it. Many also find that they are ultimately unable to escape treatment as "untouchables."

## The Relevance of Land

The caste system is an economic order. It prevents someone from owning land or receiving an education. It is a vicious cycle and an exploitative economic arrangement. Landowning patterns and being a high-caste member are co-terminous. Also there is a nexus between [being] lower-caste and landlessness... Caste is a tool to perpetuate exploitative economic arrangements.

— R. Balakrishnan, chairman, Tamil Nadu Commission for Scheduled Castes and Scheduled Tribes[27]

---

[25]Human Rights Watch interview with Nicholas, director of Integrated Rural Development Society, Madras, February 14, 1998. In Tamil Nadu, the father's given name, which comes before one's given name (often in the form of an initial), often serves as the family name for his children. Throughout the country, Dalits and lower castes also use their caste name as their last name. Many of the people interviewed in this report, therefore, identified themselves only by their given name, and not their caste name or their father's name.

[26]Human Rights Watch interview with activists in Karnataka, Bangalore, July 26, 1998.

[27]Human Rights Watch interview with R. Balakrishnan, chairman of the Tamil Nadu Commission for Scheduled Castes and Scheduled Tribes, Madras, February 13, 1998.

Most Dalit victims of abuse are landless agricultural laborers.[28] According to the 1991 census, 77 percent of the Dalit workforce is in the primary (agricultural) sector of the economy. Those who own land often fall into the category of marginal landowners.[29] Land is the prime asset in rural areas that determines an individual's standard of living and social status.[30] Lack of access to land makes Dalits economically vulnerable; their dependency is exploited by upper- and middle-caste landlords and allows for many abuses to go unpunished.

India's policy of economic liberalization is also having an effect on Dalits and their livelihood. As the public sector shrinks due to privatization, the reservations model is affecting—and able to assist—fewer people, inasmuch as government-related jobs are being drastically reduced. Globalization has also led to coastal lands increasingly being acquired by multinationals (via the central government) for aquaculture projects. Dalits are the main laborers and tenants of coastal land areas and are increasingly being forced to leave these areas—to live as displaced people, for the most part—as foreign investment rises.[31]

Land reform and increased wages for rural laborers are the central demands of most leftist guerrilla organizations active in West Bengal, Bihar, and Andhra Pradesh. Private landlord militias and state security forces have targeted civilians thought to be guerrilla sympathizers. The failure of most state governments to implement land reform legislation has only added to the sense of economic vulnerability that fuels militant movements. In Bihar in particular, guerrillas enjoy Dalit support, as most of the Dalit community lives on the edge of starvation. Laws and regulations that prohibit alienation of Dalit lands, set ceilings on a single landowner's holdings, or allocate surplus government lands to scheduled castes and scheduled tribes have been largely ignored, or worse, manipulated by upper castes with the help of district administrations.

In 1996 a nongovernmental organization undertook a door-to-door survey of 250 villages in the state of Gujarat and found that, in almost all villages, those who had title to land had no possession, and those who had possession had not had their land measured or faced illegal encroachments from upper castes. Many had no

---

[28]Studies conducted by the National Commission for Scheduled Castes and Scheduled Tribes.

[29]"Social Conflict," *The Pioneer* (Delhi), December 30, 1997.

[30]National Commission for Scheduled Castes and Scheduled Tribes, *Highlights of Fourth Report* (New Delhi: Government of India, 1998), pp. 4-5.

[31]See also, Anand Teltumbde, "Impact of Economic Reforms on Dalits in India," (A Paper Presented in the Seminar on 'Economic Reforms and Dalits in India' Organized by the University of Oxford, Oxford, UK, on November 8, 1996), www.foil.org/inspiration/ambedkar/ecoreforms.html.

record of their holdings at all. Even those who had been offered land under agrarian reform legislation refused to accept it for fear of an upper-caste backlash.

In the late 1980s in Chenaganambatti village in Madurai district, Tamil Nadu, 9.5 acres of idle land belonging to a temple under the Hindu Religious Endowment Act were auctioned and sold to villagers for cultivation. At the time, some 500,000 acres of such idle land existed in Tamil Nadu. Caste Hindus did not allow Dalits to take part in the auction. In 1989 Dalits began demanding participation and, in 1992, finally succeeded in entering the auction. Caste Hindus protested and appealed to the commissioner of the Hindu Religious Endowment Act, a central government official. The commissioner decreed that the lands, once bought at auction, legally belonged to the Dalits. One month later, and in broad daylight, one hundred members of the Kallar community, an upper-caste group, invaded and destroyed nine acres of paddy (rice) fields belonging to Dalits. In subsequent attacks, the Kallars murdered two Dalit men and assaulted three Dalit women, who sustained head injuries. As the leader of the Dalit Panthers movement in Tamil Nadu (see below) recalled:

> They just cut their throat on the road. Even though the land belongs to Dalits, they [the Dalit owners] cannot plow it, even today. The accused were never punished. No trial took place.[32]

## Social Boycotts and Retaliatory Violence

> Whenever Dalits have tried to organise themselves or assert their rights, there has been a backlash from the feudal lords resulting in mass killings of Dalits, gang rapes, looting and arsoning, etc. of Harijan [Dalit] basties [villages].
>
> — National Commission for Scheduled Castes and Scheduled Tribes[33]

Whether caste clashes are social, economic, or political in nature, they are premised on the same basic principle: any attempt to alter village customs or to demand land, increased wages, or political rights leads to violence and economic retaliation on the part of those most threatened by changes in the status quo. Dalit

---

[32]Human Rights Watch interview with Tirumavalavan of the Dalit Panthers of India, Madras, February 13, 1998.

[33]National Commission for Scheduled Castes and Scheduled Tribes, *Highlights of the Report of the National Commission for Scheduled Castes and Scheduled Tribes for the Years 1994-95 & 1995-96* (New Delhi: Government of India, 1997), p. 2.

communities as a whole are summarily punished for individual transgressions; Dalits are cut off from their land and employment during social boycotts, women bear the brunt of physical attacks, and the Atrocities Act is rarely enforced.

Describing one such boycott, a village resident and social worker in the Marathwada region of eastern Maharashtra recalled:

> The upper caste got together and said that we touched their god so we shouldn't live here. They put a social boycott on all the Dalits. We could not enter their land, we could not work for them, we could not get wood, we could not buy goods from their stores, and we could not grind grain in the flour mill. We were not even allowed to go near the wells in upper-caste territory to fetch water. We could use our government pumps, but that wasn't enough.[34]

The social boycott is reinforced when the village council levies fines against caste Hindus who refuse to participate in it. In villages in Karnataka state, upper castes are generally fined Rs. 501 (US$12.53) for giving employment to Dalits during a social boycott.[35]

## Violence Against Dalit Women

As Human Rights Watch was told by a government investigator in Tamil Nadu, "[n]o one practices untouchability when it comes to sex."[36] Rape is a common phenomenon in rural areas. Women are raped as part of caste custom or village tradition. According to Dalit activists, Dalit girls have been forced to have sex with the village landlord.[37] In rural areas, "women are induced into prostitution (Devadasi system)..., which [is] forced on them in the name of religion."[38] The

---

[34]Human Rights Watch interview, Usgaon, Maharashtra, January 29, 1998. The boycott took place in 1992, arising from Dalits attempting to enter the village temple.

[35]Human Rights Watch interview with Karnataka activists, Bangalore, July 26, 1998.

[36]Human Rights Watch interview with R. Balakrishnan, director of Tamil Nadu chapter of National Commission for Scheduled Castes and Scheduled Tribes, Madras, February 13, 1998.

[37]Dr. R. M. Pal, "The Caste System...," p. 19.

[38]"Statement made by the Dalit Liberation Education Trust on the Situation of Untouchable People (Dalits) in South Asia region, at the World Conference on Human Rights of the United Nations on 24th June 93 at Astoria Centre, Vienna during the 11th meeting of the Main Committee," Annexure I in *Human Rights from the Dalit Perspective* (Madras: Dalit Liberation Education Trust), p. iii.

prevalence of rape in villages contributes to the greater incidence of child marriage in those areas. Early marriage between the ages of ten years and sixteen years persists in large part because of Dalit girls' vulnerability to sexual assault by upper-caste men; once a girl is raped, she becomes unmarriageable. An early marriage also gives parents greater control over the caste into which their children are married.

Dalit women are also raped as a form of retaliation. Women of scheduled castes and scheduled tribes are raped as part of an effort by upper-caste leaders to suppress movements to demand payment of minimum wages, to settle sharecropping disputes, or to reclaim lost land. They are raped by members of the upper caste, by landlords, and by the police in pursuit of their male relatives.

Despite overwhelming evidence to the contrary, upper-caste leaders deny the prevalence of sexual abuse against Dalit women. A prominent leader of the Thevar community in Tamil Nadu, who wished to remain anonymous, vehemently denounced the assertion that sexual relations between Dalit laborers and their landowning employers were nonconsensual.[39]  The very practice of "untouchability," he explained, was until recently looked upon favorably by Dalits. He added that in the present day, the practice has almost completely disappeared. In an interview with Human Rights Watch, he claimed:

> In the past, twenty to thirty years ago, *harijans* [Dalits] enjoyed the practice of "untouchability." In the past, women enjoyed being oppressed by men. They weren't educated. They didn't know the world. Ladies would boast to others that my husband has more wives. Most of Dalit women enjoy relations with Thevar men. They enjoy Thevar community men having them as concubines. It is not done by force. Anything with Dalits is not done by force. That's why they don't react. They cannot afford to react, they are dependent on us for jobs and protection. Harijans formerly enjoyed their masters. "Untouchability" was there in various forms, but because of education, economic improvement, now in 95 percent of places, "untouchability" is not practiced. Thevars never say anything against them. Without Dalits we cannot live. We want workers in the fields. We are landholders. Without them we cannot cultivate or take care of our cattle. But Dalit women's relations with Thevar men are not out of economic

---

[39]Thevars are a powerful "backward caste" in Tamil Nadu. For more on backward castes, see below.

dependency. She wants it from him. He permits it. If he has power, then she has more affection for the landlord.[40]

Attacks on Dalit women during massacres, police raids, and caste clashes are discussed throughout this report. Dalit women are easy targets for any perpetrator because upper castes consider them to be "sexually available" and because they are largely unprotected by the state machinery. The Bathani Tola massacre in Bihar in 1996[41] epitomizes this phenomenon.

The "landlords" wanted to reassert their feudal tyranny over the poor who have started becoming more vocal and by attacking the most vulnerable, women and children, they sent a clear message that they would not allow anyone to disturb the social structure... Women were raped and hacked. The huts and small houses in which the victims took shelter were burnt down. The shrill cries failed to draw the attention of the police posted a kilometre and a half away because their food came from the landlords' houses.[42]

**The Role of the Police**

In 1979 the government of India constituted the National Police Commission to analyze the factors behind the dismal performance of the police throughout the country. The commission's eight-volume report, which includes recommendations to address the problem, is still considered by government officials and civil rights activists to be the most comprehensive and definitive document on the issue. Moreover, the problems of corruption, police brutality, and impunity documented in the report persist to this day. A *Times of India* editorial by a New Delhi-based human rights activist summarized the findings of the report as follows:

---

[40]Human Rights Watch interview, Madurai, Tamil Nadu, February 18, 1998.

[41]See details in Chapter IV. Nineteen Dalits and Muslims, mostly women and children, were killed by members of the Ranvir Sena, a private militia of upper-caste landlords, in Bathani Tola (a Dalit hamlet of Barki Kharaon village) in July 1996. The attack was reportedly an effort to weaken the resolve of CPI(M-L), a leftist guerrilla organization, and to prevent a labor boycott on hundreds of acres of land.

[42]Neena Bhandari, "Sexual Assaults on Women: Women are being sexually violated in India for various reasons including land disputes and caste conflicts," [no date] Inter Press Service.

The sum of the report, in fact, detail and verify what common sense tells us. Subversion begins at recruitment which is rife with patronage. Promotions follow suit depending on the "reach" of lucky people. Transfers substitute for punishment as a bad egg is foisted on one community after another. At the police station, a normal young recruit enters such a strong atmosphere of routine violence that in a few years he has been molded into something quite unrecognisable. Low pay, bad housing, little insurance against the hazards of police work, absurdly long hours, practically no forensic support to assist in crime detection, and punishing demands for results, all confirm the ordinary policeman's need for a "Godfather" to guide him through the thickets of survival. Favour for favour then ensures that the only agency legally allowed to use force against citizens gets transformed into a powerfully armed untamed assemblage that masquerades as the Law.[43]

The National Police Commission's recommendations include a section on "police and the weaker sections," which detailed police abuses specific to scheduled castes. The section noted that "complaints against the police in their handling of cases arising from atrocities against Scheduled Castes often relate to refusal to register complaints, delayed arrival on the scene, half-hearted action while investigating specific cases, extreme brutality in dealing with accused persons belonging to weaker sections, soft treatment of accused persons belonging to influential sections, making arrests or failing to make them on malafide considerations, etc."[44]

Two decades later, none of the commission's recommendations have been adopted, and police continue to detain, torture and extort money from Dalits without much fear of punishment. Frustration with the police has also helped to fuel armed and unarmed Dalit movements.

## Dalit Political Movements

In addition to a growing number of lower-caste-based political parties and human rights movements, Dalits have taken part in struggles against the state and

---

[43]Maja Daruwala, "Cop Out on Police Reform," *Times of India*, August 13, 1998. Maja Daruwala is the director of the Commonwealth Human Rights Initiative, a New Delhi-based NGO.

[44]National Police Commission, "Police and the Weaker Sections of Society," Chapter XIX, *Third Report of the National Police Commission* (New Delhi: Government of India, 1980), p. 4.

their upper-caste counterparts since the 1960s to claim their rights; several of these movements have used arms and have advocated violence. While some Dalit leaders have argued that the fundamental rights of Dalits should be addressed within a constitutional framework, many non-urbanized Dalits have taken the position that their problems cannot be resolved without a militant struggle against those in power.

Mainstream political parties in India have generally adopted a top-down interventionist approach to Dalit problems, offering promises of loans, housing, and proper implementation of reservations (quotas allowing for increased representation in government jobs, education, and political bodies) as compensation for past mistreatment. Issues of "untouchability," temple entry,[45] violence, and economic exploitation were largely left unaddressed by the state and political parties. As the traditional political parties abandoned or avoided efforts to mobilize support among Dalits at the grassroots level, they paved the way for an autonomous Dalit leadership to emerge in the early 1990s. This new leadership has been threatening for backward and upper castes.

---

[45]Until 1917 the National Congress refused to take up social reform for fear of creating divisions within the growing nationalist movement. However, leaders such as Mohandas K. (Mahatma) Gandhi made the removal of "untouchability" a priority and declared that it was no less important than the political struggle for independence. In 1923, Congress began taking active steps toward the eradication of "untouchability" by educating and mobilizing support among caste Hindus. The campaign against "untouchability" was perhaps most vibrant in the state of Kerala, where the problem was particularly acute and where social reform movements had been active since the end of the nineteenth century. The Vaikam *satyagraha* (passive resistance) from 1924 to 1925 offered Gandhi his first opportunity to act on behalf of Dalits who were denied entry into temples and the use of roads outside the Vaikam temple in Kerala state. Gandhi negotiated with the Nambudri Brahmin trustees of the Vaikam temple and managed to convince the temple authorities to open the temple roads to all. Dalit leader B. R. Ambedkar had stated that for Dalits "the most important event in the country today is the satyagraha at Vaikam" but also pointed out that, after a year of protest, there had been few results. Dalits remained unable to enter the temple until 1936. The main weakness of the temple entry movement was that even while arousing people against "untouchability," it lacked a strategy for ending the caste system itself. Bipan Chandra, ed., *India's Struggle for Independence: 1857-1947* (New Delhi: Viking, 1988), pp. 230-234; Eleanor Zelliot, "Gandhi and Ambedkar: A Study in Leadership," in E. Zelliot, *From Untouchable to Dalit: Essays on the Ambedkar Movement* (New Delhi: Manohar Publications, 1992), pp. 160-165.

**Dalit Panthers of India**

During the 1960s and 1970s, the Dalit Panthers, and several groups with a Marxist/Leninist or Maoist orientation, emerged outside the framework of recognized political parties and parliamentary politics to confront the established powers. The Dalit Panthers were formed in the state of Maharashtra in the 1970s, ideologically aligning themselves to the Black Panther movement in the United States. During the same period, Dalit literature, painting, and theater challenged the very premise and nature of established art forms and their depiction of society and religion. Many of these new Dalit artists formed the first generation of the Dalit Panther movement that sought to wage an organized struggle against the varna system. Dalit Panthers visited "atrocity" sites, organized marches and rallies in villages, and raised slogans of direct militant action against their upper-caste aggressors.[46]

The determined stance of the Dalit Panthers served to arouse and unite many Dalits, particularly Dalit youths and students. The defeat of ruling party candidates and the boycott of elections in some areas forced the government to take notice of the movement: Panther leaders were often harassed and removed from districts for speaking out against the government and Hindu religion. They also became frequent targets of police brutality and arbitrary detentions. Disagreements over the future of the movement and the inclusion of other caste groups ultimately led to a dispersal of Dalit Panther leadership. The former aggressiveness and militancy of the Dalit Panthers have for the most part dissipated, though small splinter groups or groups that have adopted the name still survive.[47] In Tamil Nadu, for example, the Dalit Panthers of India have thrived since the 1980s as a nonviolent awareness-raising and organizing movement concentrating primarily on women's rights and land issues and claims. They are currently led by a man named Tirumavalavan. As documented in chapters V and VIII, their members are continually harassed and detained by the police.

---

[46]Sandeep Pendse, ed., *At Crossroads: Dalit Movement Today* (Bombay: Vikas Adhyayan Kendra, 1994), pp. 69-82.
[47]Ibid.

**Naxalites**

The origins of the Naxalite movement can be traced to a breakaway Maoist group in West Bengal, which in March 1967 split from the Communist Party of India (Marxist) (CPI(M)) over differences in ideology: while CPI(M) chose the parliamentary path to change, the Maoist group chose to engage in armed struggle. The group initiated a series of peasant uprisings beginning in a village in the state of West Bengal called Naxalbari, from which rebel leaders took the name "Naxalite." The peasant communities seized land, burned property records, and assassinated exploitative landlords and others identified as "class enemies." Although the uprising was brutally crushed within a few months, similar revolts broke out elsewhere in West Bengal and in other parts of India.[48]

By 1970, Naxalite groups had expanded their efforts to large areas of the countryside stretching from West Bengal to the southern state of Kerala. They engaged in a campaign of land seizure and violence against the police and security forces, as well as against political figures, civil servants, landlords, and other civilians. In many instances, land seizures and other demonstrations of peasant resistance forced landlords to flee their lands. The Naxalites' abuses included targeted assassinations and kidnappings of political figures and police officials. Naxalite groups also carried out bombings and arson in areas where they were likely to cause civilian casualties and summarily executed, and in some cases tortured to death, suspected police informers. All such practices constitute gross violations of international law. Although the Naxalite insurgency was brought to an end in most parts of the country by a brutal police crackdown designed to eliminate the militants and their supporters, the movement continues to survive, albeit with some splits and regroupings, in the rural areas of West Bengal, Orissa, Andhra Pradesh, and Bihar.

From the outset of the Naxalbari uprising, the government has resorted to extra-legal measures to deal with the Naxalite threat, including extrajudicial

---

[48]One such revolt began in 1967 in a tribal district in the forest regions of northeastern Andhra Pradesh known as Srikakulam. As a result of confrontations between landlords and tribal activists demanding better wages and land rights, armed tribal committees began seizing land and crops from local landlords. The police responded by imposing restrictions on public gatherings, raiding tribal villages, and arresting and killing several hundred villagers. In reprisal, Naxalite groups accelerated campaigns to eliminate "class enemies," which included landlords, money-lenders, and the police. By 1972 the insurgency was brought to an end, but Naxalite groups continue to operate in the state. Asia Watch (now the Asia division of Human Rights Watch), "Police Killings and Rural Violence in Andhra Pradesh," *A Human Rights Watch Report*, September 1992, pp. 8-9.

executions, torture, and forced disappearances. Most of the victims of police abuse are peasants and laborers.    Members and organizers of peasant unions are automatically labeled as Naxalites.  Tribal and Dalit villagers are often singled out as Naxalite sympathizers, while attacks on rural activists and striking laborers are sanctioned as part of a campaign to fight "Naxalite terrorism."  Senior police officers with a record of "killing Naxalites" even receive promotions, cash rewards, and favored postings.[49]

The significance of the Naxalite movement in Bihar's caste clashes is further discussed in Chapter IV.

### The Rise of the "Backward Castes"

For those within the four principal varnas, caste has not proved to be a completely rigid system.  Just as the higher ritual status of Brahmins does not necessarily translate into economic or political supremacy, those lower in the ranks are able to move up in the local hierarchy through the capture of political power, the acquisition of land, and migration to other regions.  A combination of these strategies and India's policy of quotas or reservations have particularly benefited the so-called backward castes, or Shudras.  Referred to as "other backward classes" (OBCs) in administrative parlance, backward castes are defined as those whose ritual rank and occupational status are above "untouchables" but who themselves remain socially and economically depressed.

Contrary to the general presumption that the OBCs belong to the deprived sections of Hindu society, few groups in independent India have made progress on a scale comparable to the OBCs.  However, it must be noted that the term OBCs is a problematic categorization.  One author writes that OBCs

> span such a wide cultural and structural arch as to be almost meaningless. There are at one extreme the dominant, landowning, peasant castes which wield power and authority over local Vaishyas and Brahmins, whereas at the other extreme are the poor, near-Untouchable groups living just above the pollution line. The category also includes many artisan and servicing castes.[50]

---

[49]Ibid., pp. 1-10.
[50]Meenakshi Jain, "Backward Castes and Social Change in U.P. and Bihar," in *Caste: Its Twentieth Century Avatar* (New Delhi: Viking, 1996), p. 136.

Some academics have divided Shudras into two clearly identifiable subcategories: upper Shudras and lower Shudras. In north India the upper Shudras comprise such economically powerful and politically aggressive groups as the Jats and Yadavs. The Jats, though not officially included in the OBC list, still regard themselves as the leaders of the backward castes.

The inclusion of so many heterogeneous groups within the OBC category has both made for its enormous size and has enabled its leaders to advocate their claim for special status and land in post-independence India. The first wave of land reform in the 1950s aimed at conferring ownership rights on existing tenants of land. Land reform legislation was responsible for displacing the large class of *zamindars* (large landowners) and creating a substantial class of medium-sized owner-cultivators, many of whom were OBCs. After cornering the benefits of this first wave of legislation, these groups attempted to block all subsequent land reform measures designed to benefit marginal farmers and the landless, who usually belonged to castes and groups lower on the social hierarchy, most notably Dalits.[51] Economic prosperity soon translated into political gains for OBCs, while the reservation system of quotas—successfully implemented—ensured them a presence in the state machinery.[52]

---

[51]Ibid., pp. 136-151.

[52]The Mandal Commission was appointed in December 1978 by then-Prime Minister Morarjibhai Desai. In 1980 the commission's report recommended that 27 percent of federal government jobs be reserved for OBCs and classified 3,743 sub-castes throughout the country as backward and deserving of special treatment through reservations in government employment and education. Most government officials ignored the report's recommendations until 1990, when then-Prime Minister V. P. Singh announced that his administration would implement the reservation scheme. The decision led to a violent public outcry, especially from students from lower-middle economic classes belonging to caste backgrounds that did not qualify under the reservation scheme. Thousands of students protested, boycotted classes, blocked traffic, destroyed public property, and engaged in violent confrontations with the police. Some students even set themselves on fire in protest. Widespread civil unrest and rioting, spurred on by the Bharatiya Janata Party, eventually led to the removal of Prime Minister V.P. Singh from office in November 1990 through a no confidence vote in Parliament. In September 1991 the newly installed government of Prime Minister P. V. Narasimha Rao announced that it would retain the reservation scheme recommended by the Mandal Commission Report and reserve an additional 10 percent for poorer members of the upper castes and non-Hindu minorities. In September 1993, in *Indra Sawhney v. Union of India*, the Supreme Court ruled the Mandal scheme constitutional. "Constitutional Fairness or Fraud on the Constitution? Compensatory Discrimination in India," *Case Western Reserve Journal of International Law*, Winter 1996 (28 Case W. Res.

In 1980 the National Police Commission noted a disturbing trend in caste conflicts between backward castes and scheduled castes:

> In the recent years we have also seen a new factor emerging in the social struggle in rural areas in which the "backward classes" have been surging forward to take up positions of power and control in society, knocking down the upper castes who had held sway in such positions all along in the past. In this process of marching forward, the backward classes tend to push back the Scheduled Castes and others who occupy the lower rung in the social hierarchical ladder. There is greater tension between structural neighbours in this hierarchy than between the top level and the bottom level.[53]

The pattern has since solidified such that caste clashes are far more prevalent between scheduled castes and backward castes than they are between these groups and upper castes. The Home Ministry's Annual Report for 1995 reported that caste-related incidents in Tamil Nadu, Bihar, and Maharashtra increased by 25 to 30 percent from previous years. A majority of these incidents were taking place between scheduled castes and OBCs.[54] The trend has continued, particularly in the state of Tamil Nadu, as documented in Chapter V.

**Legal Context**

The Constitution of India came into effect in 1950, the year that India became a republic and three years after India's independence from British rule. It embodies the principles of equality, freedom, justice, and human dignity and requires both state and central governments to provide special protection to scheduled-caste members, to raise their standard of living, and to ensure their equality with other citizens. To women, the constitution guarantees equal rights, liberty, justice and the right to live with dignity. Discrimination on the basis of religion and gender is prohibited, and compensation for past discrimination is promoted.[55]

---

J. Int'l L. 63).

[53] National Police Commission, "Police and the Weaker Sections of Society," Chapter XIX, *Third Report of the National Police Commission* (New Delhi: Government of India, 1980), p. 3.

[54] "Caste Tensions on the rise in Tamil Nadu, Maharashtra, Bihar: govt. report," *Times of India*, August 2, 1996.

[55] Women are given equal status with men in most respects, with the exception of personal laws—laws relating to marriage, divorce, adoption, and succession.

Building on constitutional provisions, the government of India has pursued a two-pronged approach to narrowing the gap between the socio-economic status of the scheduled-caste population and the national average. The first approach involves regulatory measures designed to ensure that relevant legal provisions are adequately implemented, enforced and monitored; the second focuses on increasing the self-sufficiency of the scheduled-caste population through financial assistance for self-employment activities and through development programs to increase education and skills.[56]

The protective component of this two-pronged strategy includes the implementation of legal provisions contained in the Protection of Civil Rights Act, 1955 and the Scheduled Castes and Scheduled Tribes (Prevention of Atrocities) Act, 1989; other state and central government laws; and reservations or quotas in the arenas of government employment and higher education.[57] India's policy of reservations is an attempt by the central government to remedy past injustices related to low-caste status. To allow for proportional representation in certain state and federal institutions, the constitution reserves 22.5 percent of seats in federal government jobs, state legislatures, the lower house of parliament, and educational institutions for scheduled castes and scheduled tribes. These protective measures are monitored by the National Commission for Scheduled Castes and Scheduled Tribes. The development measures for the educational, social, and economic upliftment of scheduled castes are administered by the Ministry of Welfare through the state governments.[58]

Like many of the protective measures described in this report, the reservation policy has not been successfully implemented for Dalits. In the highlights of its fourth report for the years 1996-97 and 1997-98, the National Commission for Scheduled Castes and Scheduled Tribes noted that reservations had only been provided in government services and stressed that reservations in defense forces and the judiciary should be enforced. It added that the private sector, which continues to enjoy government patronage in terms of concessional land, financing, and excise and sales tax relief, should also be brought under the purview of the

---

[56]Ministry of Welfare, *Annual Report 1995-1996* (New Delhi: Government of India, 1996), p. 8.

[57]For more detailed accounts of legal protections, see Chapter X.

[58]The provision of finances to members of scheduled castes and scheduled tribes for self-employment activities is administered through the National Scheduled Castes and Scheduled Tribes Finance and Development Corporation.

reservation policy.[59] Despite a large body of legislation and administrative agency mandates assigned exclusively to deal with the plight of scheduled castes, the persistence of caste-based prejudices and the denial of access to land, education, and political power have all contributed to an atmosphere of increasing intolerance. Violence against Dalits in their communities, which has steadily climbed since 1994, is only the most extreme form of that intolerance.

Between 1994 and 1996, a total of 98,349 cases were registered with the police nationwide as crimes and atrocities against scheduled castes. Of these, 38,483 were registered under the Atrocities Act. A further 1,660 were for murder, 2,814 for rape, and 13,671 for hurt.[60] Given that Dalits are both reluctant and unable (for lack of police cooperation) to report crimes against themselves, the actual number of abuses is presumably much higher. While there are not yet official figures available on killings and attacks in 1997 and 1998, the latest wave of attacks described in this and other reports confirms that the violence has continued.

---

[59]National Commission for Scheduled Castes and Scheduled Tribes, Highlights of Fourth Report (New Delhi, Government of India, 1998), p. 4.

[60]National Commission for Scheduled Castes and Scheduled Tribes, *National Crime Records Bureau (M.H.A.), Statement Showing Cases Registered with the Police Under Different Nature of Crimes and Atrocities on Scheduled Castes and Scheduled Tribes from 1994 to 1996* (New Delhi: Government of India, 1997).

## IV. THE PATTERN OF ABUSE: RURAL VIOLENCE IN BIHAR AND THE STATE'S RESPONSE

The organized killing of poor peasants and landless labourers by middle and upper caste landed armies and [the ensuing] retaliation by Marxist-Leninist organizations [Naxalites] have been flashpoints in the agrarian scene in Bihar over the last fifteen years. This is not a new phenomenon. What is relatively new however is the entry on the rural scene... of a new upper caste landed organization called the Ranbir Sena. It has, over the last three years, been responsible for a series of massacres of the rural poor, such that the names of obscure villages have become known to a wider public through the national press...

In a region where tragic massacres repeat themselves with monotonous regularity, the state's response is predictable and misdirected—setting up more police camps and increasing the financial allocation for anti-Naxalite operations... The issues remain the same; the landlord army is different each time. We are condemned to reiterate the same demands each time and like some ritual drama whose script is familiar to all, the same events are re-enacted each time, drawing the same reactions from the state... One has to remember that the dreadful reality of bloody massacres are the outcome of [the state's] refusal to address basic questions of agrarian struggle.

— People's Union for Democratic Rights, *Agrarian Conflict in Bihar and the Ranbir Sena*, October 1997[61]

The eastern state of Bihar, with a population of eighty-six million people, is notorious for its poverty and lawlessness and for an ongoing conflict between Naxalites and private upper-caste militias set against the backdrop of acute social disparities. Since independence, Bihar has consistently ranked among the worst of India's larger states in urbanization, production, and income; it has the highest number of very large landholders and one of the largest landless populations

---

[61]The People's Union for Democratic Rights is one of India's most respected national human rights organizations. Ranbir Sena is one of several spelling variations of the private militia's name. Others include Ranbeer and Ranveer Sena. Throughout this report, the organization is referred to as the Ranvir Sena.

among all Indian states.[62] Agrarian issues have long dominated the state's political life as the feudal nature of landholding has remained largely unchanged despite legislation establishing ceilings on the maximum amount of land one individual can own. Political leaders who depend on landed elites for support have had little interest in pursuing reforms. Wages for agricultural laborers are also among the lowest in the country. In many districts workers are not paid in money but instead often work a full day for as little as two kilograms of rice.

Since the 1960s, social activists advocating on behalf of low-caste groups have attempted, through various forms of peaceful protest, to pressure the government to institute land reforms; at the same time, Naxalite groups have advocated armed resistance and have carried out targeted assassinations of landlords. In turn, higher-caste landholders have retaliated by forming private militias, known as *senas* (armies), to fight the Naxalites and terrorize and kill low-caste villagers whom they believe to have provided support to the Naxalites, or who have organized to demand better wages and other reforms. Hundreds of Dalits have been killed in sena attacks since the early 1990s. The attacks frequently take place at night; in many cases, the victims, including women and children, have been shot in their beds while they were sleeping. Members of the senas have also raped women and girls during the attacks. They have often claimed responsibility for the attacks and have even announced beforehand which villages they planned to target. However, because the senas enjoy the patronage of powerful elites, they operate with impunity.

Rather than addressing the security needs of landless laborers most affected by the violence or provide protection to villagers at risk, a series of inefficient and corrupt state governments since the early 1970s has only exacerbated the problem. In many instances, government officials—many of whom are alleged to have caste ties or other affiliations with the senas—have acted as agents of the private armies and have turned a blind eye to the killings. State security forces have helped train the senas, and in some cases, police have accompanied the militias during their attacks on Dalit villages. Police have also conducted their own raids on Dalit villages in the aftermath of massacres carried out by upper-caste militias. The ostensible reason for police raids has been to capture suspected Naxalites, but the raids are frequently used to punish villagers suspected of sympathizing with the militant groups. Like the attacks by private militias, police raids have been characterized by violence, looting, and assaults on women. The state's response

---

[62]Lloyd I. and Susanne Hoeber Rudolph, *In Pursuit of Lakshmi: The Political Economy of the Indian State* (Chicago: University of Chicago Press, 1987), pp. 356, 375.

to militant activity by Naxalite groups and by the senas is conspicuously uneven. Sena members have rarely been prosecuted for acts of violence. Police routinely detain and charge suspected Naxalite militants, however, and many are killed in so-called encounters with the police.[63]

This chapter traces the conflict in Bihar since the birth of the Ranvir Sena, an upper-caste militia formed in 1994. Human Rights Watch investigated three massacres carried out by the Ranvir Sena and two raids conducted by the police in 1997 and 1998; documentation of those incidents, and additional information on other incidents, is provided below. The chapter also describes a pattern of state collusion and police complicity in sena attacks.

### The Context of the Conflict

Scheduled castes constitute close to 14 percent of the population in Bihar; most of the agricultural laborers belong to these castes. The four main upper castes in the region are the Brahmins, the Bhumihars, the Rajputs, and the Kayasthas. There are more than one hundred backward castes, the dominant of which are the Yadavs and the Kurmis. In 1996 and 1997 the state government was led by Laloo Prasad Yadav, president of the Rashtriya Janata Dal party and member of the Yadav backward caste; although his administration was dominated by upper castes. Laloo Prasad Yadav resigned in 1998; he was replaced as chief minister by his wife Rabri Devi.

The implementation of reservations in favor of the backward castes has improved their status throughout the state; the same has not held true of scheduled castes whose status continues to deteriorate. Central Bihar in particular has seen a consistent rise in abuses against scheduled castes since the early 1990s at the hands of upper castes and backward castes who employ them as laborers on their lands. Rapes and murders of Dalit women in particular have reportedly increased during this period.[64] As one long-time observer of violence in the state has noted,

---

[63]An "encounter" is an incident in which police claim to have fired on an armed assailant in self-defense. Both the prevalence and suspicious nature of so-called encounter killings throughout the country have transformed the term's definition, such that it now automatically connotes an extrajudicial execution by the police. For more on "encounters," see below.

[64]Sudhir Hindwan, "Factors behind caste conflict in Bihar," *Indian Express*, October 6, 1995. Given the reluctance of rape victims to come forward, exact data on the number of rapes are difficult to obtain. The killing of Dalit women during massacres, however, is well-documented in local human rights organization reports, press reports, and in this chapter. See also People's Union for Democratic Rights, *Agrarian Conflict in Bihar and the Ranbir*

"Disparities in socioeconomic hierarchy run alongside the caste hierarchy throughout Bihar although the degree of relationship may differ in some districts... Scheduled Castes invariably fall in the lowest category both socially and economically."[65] A 1995 analysis of available statistics by *The Pioneer,* a Delhi-based daily, concluded:

> [T]he distribution pattern of land and other resources is based on caste hierarchy. One-third of the upper castes have land worth more than Rs. 55,000 [US$1,375] whereas two-thirds of the scheduled caste households are landless and approximately one-fifth hold land with a total value of less than Rs. 5,000 [US$125].[66]

There is little organized official effort to bridge the class gap. Administrations that have governed the state since independence have not even succeeded in completing any land surveys.[67]  In the districts of central Bihar, money-lending, bonded labor, sexual assaults on rural women, and abuse of the landless class by landowners have all contributed to violent clashes between various castes.[68]  Successive Bihari governments have failed to implement land reforms and guaranties of minimum wages for agricultural laborers; as a result, disparities in wealth between landless Dalit laborers and their landed upper-caste and middle-caste counterparts have increased.[69]  The disparity and increasing economic exploitation have given rise to numerous militant leftist groups who have increased their membership, their political clout, and their weaponry since the 1970s. The central Bhojpur district of Bihar has long been a stronghold of these so-called Naxalite groups that operate under various political banners.  The increase in Naxalite activities has also ushered in a rise in the number of private upper-caste militias, including the Ranvir Sena, that have been responsible for killing hundreds of Dalit laborers between 1995 and 1998. In these areas of Bihar, a class struggle has escalated into an armed caste conflict.

---

*Sena* (New Delhi: October 1997).

[65]Sudhir Hindwan, "Caste iron jacket," *The Pioneer,* September 9, 1996.

[66]Sudhir Hindwan, "A question of economics, caste violence in Bihar has been prcmpted by class distinctions," *The Pioneer,* December 8, 1995.

[67]Venkitesh Ramakrishnan, "Massacre in Bihar: Landlord attack on Dalits and Muslims," *Frontline* (Madras), August 9, 1996, quoting sociologist K. K. Verma.

[68]Hindwan, "A question of economics...," *The Pioneer.*

[69]Ramakrishnan, "Massacre in Bihar...," *Frontline.*

## The "Naxalites"

Following the Naxalbari uprising in West Bengal in 1968 (see Chapter III), various Marxist-Leninist factions began calling for a militant peasant struggle against upper-caste domination in Bihar. An armed struggle in the countryside against semi-feudal interests, combined with area-wide seizures of land, were the groups' primary tactics. Throughout their history, Naxalite groups have engaged in attacks on civilians and abuses that directly violate international humanitarian law. Critical of the parliamentary tendencies of the Indian Communist movement, especially the Communist Party of India and Communist Party of India (Marxist), the Naxalites actively recruited Dalit and lower-caste peasants into their militant struggle. By 1998, Naxalite groups were operational in thirty-six out of fifty-four districts in Bihar.

The Naxalite groups are dominated by the Maoist Communist Centre (MCC), the Communist Party of India (Marxist-Leninist) Party Unity, and the Communist Party of India (Marxist-Leninist) (CPI(M-L)) Liberation.[70] In 1977 CPI (M-L) Liberation moved away from an emphasis on "annihilation of individual class enemies" to an attempt at organizing mass peasant movements through *Kisan Sabha* (peasants' organizations). In 1982 the group decided to enter parliamentary politics under the banner of the Indian People's Front (IPF). Though IPF won one parliamentary seat in 1989, and sent seven members in 1989 and six members in 1995 to the Bihar state assembly, its overall electoral success has since declined.[71]

While CPI(M-L) Liberation has pursued a parliamentary path, Party Unity and the Maoist Communist Centre have spearheaded a militant grassroots movement, that, in turn, has been targeted by Ranvir Sena attacks. Both the MCC and Party Unity are banned underground movements.[72] The MCC was responsible for the killing of at least fifty-four upper-caste Rajput community members in Dalelchak Baghaura in May 1987. The incident was the worst massacre in the state until the Ranvir Sena killing of sixty-one Dalits in Laxmanpur-Bathe on December 1, 1997.[73] MCC was also responsible for slitting the throats of forty-four upper-caste farmers in Bara village on February 12, 1992. Thirty-six died on the spot,

---

[70]Villagers interviewed for this report often used the term CPI(M-L) to collectively refer to Naxalites.

[71]Shishir K. Jha, *Prospects of Radical Change in Bihar: Recuperating the Diseased Heart of India,* www.foil.org/politics/shishir.html.

[72]Chandrakant Naidu, "Rise and rise of private armies," *Hindustan Times* (Delhi), December 14, 1997.

[73]Nalin Verma, "The Lull, After and Before the Storm" [Indian newspaper, publication illegible], December 1997.

and one died in the hospital. The killings were reportedly in retaliation for the murders of ten MCC supporters by the Savarna Liberation Front, an upper-caste Bhumihar militia, two months earlier.[74] MCC has also targeted police officers, who find themselves ill-equipped to respond.[75] According to press reports, 295 people were killed in Naxalite violence in 1995, 436 in 1996, and 424 in 1997. Not all clashes involve police: many of these deaths were attributed to interfactional fighting between Party Unity and MCC.[76]

On August 11, 1998, CPI(M-L) Party Unity merged with CPI (M-L) People's War, popularly known as the People's War Group (PWG). The merger was the culmination of five years of negotiations between the two underground movements. The unified party retained the name CPI(M-L) People's War. Ever since its founding in 1980, PWG has attempted to unify all Marxist-Leninist groups under its umbrella. Strongest in the southern and central states, its merger with Party Unity gave it a foothold in the north. Like MCC and Party Unity, PWG has advocated the use of violence against the upper castes in organizing Dalits to achieve land reform.[77] Firearms used by Naxalites are often looted or bought from

---

[74]Rajiv Ranjan Lal, "The Exploding Caste Volcano in Bihar," *The Illustrated Weekly of India* (Delhi), February 29 - March 6, 1992.

[75]Naidu, "Rise and rise...," *Hindustan Times.*

[76]"PWG-Party Unity merger may spark more violence in Bihar," *Rediff on the Net*, October 7, 1998, www.redifindia.com/news/1998/oct/07nxl.htm.

[77]"PWG hopes merger with Party Unity will boost cadre morale," *Rediff on the Net*, October 5, 1998, www.redifindia.com/news/1998/oct/05nxl.htm. On July 16, 1998, in Kurnool district in the state of Andhra Pradesh, at least eight and as many as thirty lower-caste villagers were hacked to death; their bodies were then thrown into one of a hundred houses that had been set on fire. The killings were reportedly carried out in retaliation for the murder of a high-caste community member by members of the People's War Group. Most of those killed in the massacre belonged to Dalit communities. Local police did not appear on the scene for more than ten hours. When they arrived, they cordoned off the affected area and did not allow any fact-finding teams to enter. Dalit villagers interviewed by a local human rights team several days later stated that many of their attackers were still present in the village and appeared to have police protection. Sakshi, "Interim Report of the Dalit Atrocity in the Vempenta Village of Kurnool District, Andhra Pradesh," July 21, 1998. Human rights NGOs asserted that the state had "completely colluded with the attackers in the name of countering the Naxalite problem" and that "the government has openly said that it will give outright support to whoever counters Naxalism." Human Rights Watch interview with members of Sakshi, an Andhra Pradesh-based human rights organization, Bangalore, July 25, 1998.

corrupt police.[78] As is typical of guerrilla organizations, Naxalites recruit members from villages where they operate and draw on the support of the local population. It does not follow, however, that all villagers in a Naxalite stronghold are members of the organization, though they may have relatives or neighbors who do belong.

### Caste Militias

Starting in the late 1960s, various upper-caste senas began to emerge in Bihar with the reported aim of containing Naxalite groups and protecting land belonging to upper castes. A look at their history reveals their political patronage. In 1969 the upper-caste Rajputs formed a militia named the Kuer Sena.[79] In 1979 the Kunwar Sena of Rajputs was formed; it disintegrated in 1986. The Sunlight Sena, also dominated by Rajputs, came into being in 1988. One of its founders was a former governor of the state of Tamil Nadu. The Brahmarshi Sena, which represented Bhumihars before the creation of the Ranvir Sena, was launched at a conference in Patna, Bihar's capital, in 1981. The Samajwadi Krantikari Sena, formed of Rajputs, was founded by a member of the state legislative assembly. The Bhumihar-dominated Savarna Liberation Front came into existence in 1990. Also known as the Diamond Sena, the militia was responsible for many massacres. On September 27, 1991, the sena beheaded seven Dalit and tribal laborers in Sawanbigha village in Jehanabad district. Soon thereafter, strongmen hired by landlords of Teendiha village in Gaya district beheaded nine laborers for their refusal to work as farm-hands for paltry wages.[80]

Like the upper castes, backward-caste landlords have cultivated private militias for protection. The Bhoomi Sena was formed by backward-caste Kurmis. Its founder was a former state minister and Janata Dal (People's Party) leader. The Lorik Sena was formed by the Yadav landlords of Jehanabad district,[81] while the Kisan Sangh is a militia of middle-caste landlords.[82]

---

[78]Human Rights Watch interview with People's Union for Democratic Rights, New Delhi, February 21, 1998.

[79]Arun Srivastava, "Caught in a caste spiral," *Indian Express*, April 5, 1997.

[80]"Mindless massacre: Bhumihar 'private army' strikes terror," *The Week* (Delhi), October 27, 1991.

[81]"Brutalisation of Bihar," *Sunday* (Calcutta), March 1 – 7, 1992.

[82]"Only living witness to Bihar massacre shot," *The Telegraph* (Calcutta), February 24, 1995.

Dalit victims and survivors of a Ranvir Sena massacre on December 1, 1997 in the village of Laxmanpur-Bathe, Jehanabad district, Bihar. (See page 60). The Ranvir Sena is a militia of upper-caste landlords. Sena members shot dead sixty-one Dalits: sixteen children, twenty-seven women, and eighteen men. Five teenage girls were raped and mutilated before being shot in the chest. The villagers were reportedly sympathetic to a Marxist-Leninist (Naxalite) group that had been demanding more equitable land redistribution in the area. The photos were taken on December 2, 1997. © Avdesh Kumar.

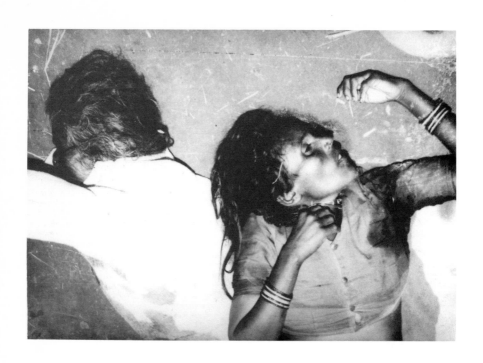

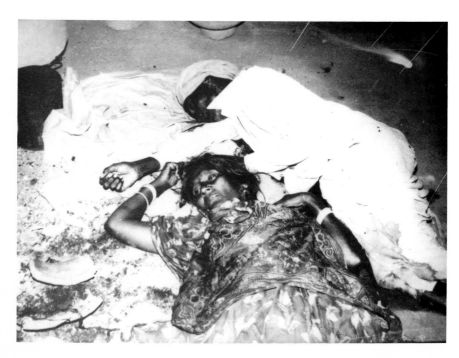

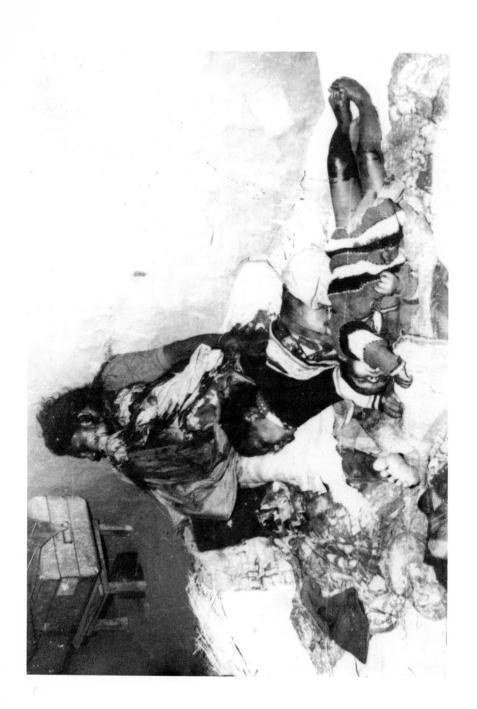

### Ranvir Sena

The Ranvir Sena was founded by upper-caste Bhumihars in Belaur village, Bhojpur district, in 1994.[83] It first made international headlines in July 1996 with its attack on Bathani Tola in Bhojpur district, Bihar, which left nineteen Dalits and Muslims, mostly women and children, dead. Sixty members of the sena reportedly descended on the village and set twelve houses on fire. Using *lathis*,[84] swords, and firearms, the attackers continued the onslaught for two and a half hours. The attack was reportedly in retaliation for the earlier killing of nine Bhumihars in Nadhi village, also in Bhojpur district, by the CPI(M-L).[85] The conflict began when CPI(M-L) began organizing the agricultural laborers to demand the statutory daily minimum wage of Rs. 30.75 (US$0.77). Landowners were only willing to pay Rs. 20 (US$0.50). CPI(M-L) members convinced laborers to refuse employment at that wage and called for an economic blockade against landowners. The attack on Bathani Tola, press reports claim, was an effort to weaken the resolve of CPI(M-L) cadres organizing in the village and to prevent a labor boycott on hundreds of acres of land.[86] None of the Ranvir Sena leaders were ever arrested for the Bathani Tola massacre.[87]

Since its inception, the Ranvir Sena has been implicated in killings, rapes and lootings in the villages of Belaur, Ekwari, Chandi, Nanaur, Narhi, Sarathau, Haibaspur, Laxmanpur-Bathe, Shankarbigha, and Narayanpur. On April 22, 1996, the sena gunned down five members of a marriage party in Nanaur village. The victims were believed to be CPI(M-L) supporters.[88] In 1997 the sena killed three Dalits in Jehanabad district for raising their voice against the rape of a Dalit girl by upper-caste youths.[89]

Human Rights Watch spoke to members of the Ranvir Sena about the organization's structure and ideology. Landowner Madan Singh of Ekwari village

---

[83]Srivastava, "Caught in a caste spiral," *Indian Express*. According to an article in *Times of India*, the Ranvir Sena was initially launched in the 1950s by a Bhumihar landlord named Ranvir Singh. In 1994 the army resurfaced under the leadership of landlord Dharikshan Chaudhary of Belaur village. Pravana K. Chaudhary, "Pvt. armies unleash terror in Bihar," *Times of India*, July 28, 1995.

[84]A heavy wooden cane or baton, often used by the police.

[85]"Laloo's land or lawless land?" *The Hindu* (Madras), July 21, 1996.

[86]Navin Upadhay, "Why does the Ranvir Sena kill?" *The Pioneer*, July 21, 1996.

[87]Human Rights Watch was unable to confirm whether CPI(M-L) members responsible for the murders in Nadhi village were prosecuted.

[88]Navin Upadhay, "Brothers in arms," *The Pioneer*, December 7, 1997.

[89]"Bloodshed in Bihar," *The Hindu*, April 13, 1997.

in Bhojpur district explained that sena membership was divided by districts and that all districts had a commander and at least 500 landowners "ready to take up arms." He confirmed that although Patna was the center, the sena was also present in Jehanabad, Aurangabad, Bhojpur, Rotas, Gaya, Bahuwan, and Baxar districts. As of 1998 sena members had also established a presence in Bhagalpur and Muzafarrpur.[90] Bhojpur, Patna and Jehanabad, also Naxalite-affected areas, have been centers of violence in the last several years.[91] According to Singh:

> Since 1970 there have been problems. It has been difficult for farmers. We cannot even get out of our house. They steal our crops and call strikes. We are farmers. That's how we earn. They destroy that. It's like kicking us in the stomach. We have to save ourselves and our crops. We need protection from Marxist/Leninists. After we got together, we began to give them an appropriate response, a jaw-breaking response. For all of Bhojpur district, we chose our men and from that year on, we have been battling with CPI(M-L). Those who have land are with us, and those who do not are with them.[92]

Upper- and lower-caste villagers in Ekwari claimed that Singh was on the CPI(M-L) hit-list. Another member of the sena, Arvind Singh, claimed that the CPI(M-L) had resolved to kill one rich landlord in each village: "They kill us and take our crops. To protect ourselves we started the Ranvir Sena."[93] According to members of Bihar Dalit Vikas Samiti (Bihar Dalit Development Organization, BDVS), a grassroots group active in the region for over ten years, the Ranvir Sena even has a program of life insurance: "Their families get paid Rs. 100,000 (US$2,500) if they get killed in a massacre, in the line of duty."[94] Reportedly, the

---

[90]Human Rights Watch interview with Madhan Singh, Ranvir Sena member, Bhojpur district, Bihar, February 27, 1998.

[91]Newspaper reports indicate that the sena is operational in sixteen districts with SOS calls being answered by many more districts. Faizan Ahmad, "Pregnant woman raped by high caste marauders in Bihar: Police aided Ranbir Sena cadres," *The Telegraph*, April 12, 1997.

[92]Human Rights Watch interview with Madhan Singh, Bhojpur district, Bihar, February 27, 1998.

[93]Human Rights Watch interview with Arvind Singh, Ranvir Sena member, Bhojpur district, Bihar, February 27, 1998.

[94]Human Rights Watch interview, Jehanabad district, Bihar, February 26, 1998.

Ranvir Sena has sophisticated arms, including semi-automatics bought with money raised through donation drives.[95]

### Confrontations over Land

Dissatisfied with the pace of reforms, or the lack thereof, the underground armed movement of CPI(M-L) first launched a "land grab" movement in the early 1970s. Under the protection of CPI(M-L), sharecroppers began harvesting crops on upper-caste land in Bihar's central districts as Naxalite cadres burned grain storages and imposed economic blockades on hundreds of acres of land that landlords were forcibly kept from cultivating. Blockades were often accompanied by labor strikes. The Ranvir Sena, and other senas before it, emerged to curb the movement and to quash its economic blockade.[96]

Wages in these areas have ranged from two kilograms of rice to Rs. 25 a day (US$0.63). Women have consistently been paid less. The Minimum Wages Act, legislated as early as 1948, and revised many times thereafter, now prescribes a daily wage of Rs. 32 (US$0.80), but Dalit demands for minimum wages have resulted in a violent backlash from landlords and their caste-based armies. According to government figures for 1995 and 1996, 84.9 percent of landowners in the state are marginal farmers owning less than five hectares each.[97] With landholding ranging between five and twenty *bighas* (3.1 to 12.4 acres),[98] even the slightest increase in wages paid to laborers would eat into the farmers' minimal profits.[99]

A representative from the People's Union for Democratic Rights (PUDR), a well-respected national human rights organization that has previously documented abuses by security forces, was a member of a fact-finding team that visited Bihar to investigate police raids on Dalit villages in the aftermath of massacres in 1997. He explained the relevance of land to the conflict:

> There are many fallow lands in these districts: at least thirty to forty acres in each village. With the Ranvir Sena in place, the land comes under the cultivation of landowners. Other villages have [Dalit]

---

[95]Human Rights Watch interview with People's Union for Democratic Rights, New Delhi, February 21, 1998; Kanhaiah Bhelari, "Waking up to death," *The Week*, December 14, 1997.
[96]"Danse macabre," *Sunday*, July 21 – 27, 1996.
[97]Raj Kamal Jha, "Belaur's road to nowhere: Landowners, dalits caught in a spiral of violence," *Indian Express*, July 21, 1996.
[98]In this region, one bigha equals 0.62 acres.
[99]Upadhay, "Why does the Ranvir...," *The Pioneer*.

cooperatives, villages where the CPI(M-L) is stronger. The money from the cooperatives goes to lawyers who are fighting cases filed by the police against them [Dalits]. Their major aim is revolution... Even marginal upper-caste farmers employ Dalits to push the wages down. The agricultural laborers are largely Dalits, so the upper castes are united in this way... Dalits don't live in the same settlements. The Mushahars, who are the lowest of the Dalits in these areas, are always segregated. They are also the poorest and the strength of these movements. They are the ones targeted in police raids and massacres when they are unorganized and unprotected by CPI(M-L). Their belongings are small, so it is easy to destroy their livelihood and take them to a stage of destitution.[100]

Between April 1995 and July 11, 1996, the date of the Bathani Tola massacre, forty-six people were killed on both sides in battles between the Ranvir Sena and CPI(M-L) in Bhojpur district.[101] According to press reports, over 400 people, many of them civilians, were killed in conflict between the two organizations in 1997.[102] Although the number of fatalities on both sides is high, the state's treatment of the two camps differs significantly, as described below.

The raping of women is a common tactic employed by members of the Ranvir Sena and other caste militias to spread terror in lower-caste communities.[103] In 1992 over one hundred Dalit women in the Gaya district of Bihar were reportedly raped by the Savarna Liberation Front.[104] Pregnant women and children have also been killed. When members of the People's Union for Democratic Rights asked the Ranvir Sena why they were killing children, they replied, "Because they will grow up to become Naxalites. We kill women because they will give birth to

---

[100]Human Rights Watch interview, New Delhi, February 21, 1998.
[101]Sujan Dutta, "Bhojpur revisited," [Indian newspaper, publication illegible], July 21, 1995.
[102]"Banned CPI-ML plans to avenge Monday's massacre," *Rediff on the Net*, December 3, 1997, www.redifindia.com/news/dec/03kill1.htm. The article adds that 436 people were killed in 1996, while 295 were killed in 1995. The figures also included police personnel.
[103]As a response to increased incidents of rape, the Dalit Sena Women's Wing, a militant vigilante group, was formed to train Dalit women in the use of guns. Members of the group are stationed in villages throughout Bihar with the reported aim of protecting Dalit communities against upper-caste violence. John Zubrzycki, "Lower Castes Still Stuck on India's Bottom Rung," *The Christian Science Monitor* (International), August 29, 1997.
[104]Ramakrishnan, "Massacre in Bihar...," *Frontline*.

Naxalites."[105] The sena has also been known to loot many of the houses they raid.

### Ranvir Sena Massacres and State Complicity

> The extent of political patronage extended to the Ranvir Sena can be gauged by the fact that while a large number of Naxalites are killed in "encounters" [with police] not a single Ranvir Sena man has been subjected to this fate. The administration awakes a little later when it comes to tackl[ing] these armies. The outfit [Ranvir Sena] had declared a few days before the Jehanabad [Bathe] carnage that it would soon make a national and international headline.
>
> — *The Pioneer*, December 12, 1997.[106]

In the districts of central Bihar, over 300 people were killed between 1995 and October 1997 in large-scale massacres committed by the Ranvir Sena.[107] Three massacres since October 1997 have increased number of deaths to over 400. Human rights activists add that many have also been killed in smaller confrontations. Extrajudicial executions of Naxalites, coupled with evidence of police collusion with the Ranvir Sena, as documented below, have led to charges that the sena is being backed by the state administration and non-left political parties to check the growing Naxalite movement.[108] Soon after a January 1999 sena massacre in Shankarbigha village, Jehanabad district, a senior police official was quoted as saying, "The administration would be happy if they kill the real extremists among the Naxalites, but they are killing soft targets like women and children and attacking villages of Dalits and weaker sections, which are unprotected."[109]

Like other senas before it, the Ranvir Sena enjoys considerable political patronage. The sena is said to be dominated by politicians from various parties, including Congress, the Janata Dal, and the Bharatiya Janata Party (BJP), which in

---

[105]Human Rights Watch interview with People's Union for Democratic Rights, New Delhi, February 21, 1998.

[106]Dhirendra K. Jha, "The running feud," *The Pioneer*, December 12, 1997.

[107]Faizan Ahmad, "Blood for blood, cries Ranbir Sena," *The Telegraph*, October 9, 1997.

[108]Upadhay, "Brothers in arms," *The Pioneer*, quoting Vinod Mishra, general secretary, CPI(M-L) Liberation; "Ranvir Sena is the only private army still active," *Times of India*, January 28, 1999.

[109]"Ranvir Sena is the only...," *Times of India*.

1998 led India's coalition central government.[110]   In turn, the BJP has enjoyed Bhumihar support in local elections, as described below.[111] Notorious Ranvir Sena leader Bharmeshwar Singh is also a known BJP activist.[112]  While Bihar's former Chief Minister Laloo Prasad Yadav, a member of a powerful backward caste, has accused the BJP of backing the sena, he himself has been blamed for only going after Naxalites, despite vows to disarm caste armies.[113]  Moreover, state agents at the village and district level are dominated by upper-caste members who often operate as "functionaries of mainstream political parties [and] are either active with or sympathize with the Ranbir Sena."[114]

According to press reports, in districts across central Bihar, and particularly in Bhojpur district,

> the police force has traditionally been dominated by Bhumihars and Rajputs.  Since the implementation of the Mandal reservations,[115] the OBCs too have been represented, but these are primarily Yadavs and Kurmis who also happen to be the new landowners in the districts. Caste as a factor in the police and administration is relevant in Bhojpur more than anywhere else in Bihar.[116]

The reported nexus between sena members and official paramilitary forces has also come under scrutiny:

---

[110]Inder Swahney, "Plans to smash Ranvir Sena network on anvil," *Times of India*, February 16, 1999; Bhelari, "Waking up...," *The Week.*

[111]An article in *Indian Express* reported that the landed gentry of Belaur (the village where the Ranvir Sena was founded in 1994) had decided to vote en bloc for the Bharatiya Janata Party during the February 1998 national parliamentary elections.  In an adjoining hamlet, a stronghold of the CPI(M-L), the residents were decidedly anti-BJP.  "Birthplace of CPIML, Ranvir Sena standby their 'saviours'," *Indian Express*, February 17, 1998.

[112]People's Union for Democratic Rights, *Agrarian Conflict in Bihar...*, p. 27.

[113]Ranjit Bhushan, "Caste bullets ricochet, rural violence spirals as caste 'armies' run amok," *Outlook*, April 9, 1997, quoting Laloo Prasad Yadav in an interview.

[114]People's Union for Democratic Rights, *Agrarian Conflict in Bihar...*, p. 33.

[115]See Chapter III, footnote 52.

[116]Raj Kamal Jha, "Officials ignored pleas for protection against Ranabir Sena," *Indian Express*, July 22, 1996.

According to the officials, the Sena goons received arms training from some former CRPF (Central Reserve Police Force) personnel.[117] Bhojpur [district]... has a tradition of sending its young to the Army and paramilitary forces. While on leave, the paramilitary personnel equip the Sena goons with the latest tactics, keeping them constantly ahead of the Naxalites.[118]

The licensing of guns for sena members came under attack in a report by the People's Union for Democratic Rights:

According to Home Ministry reports, the Ranbir Sena possesses 4,000 guns, both with and without licences. Until they actually fire their weapons, a group of Ranbir Sena members could be merely a group of landlords carrying legal arms. On the other hand, guns carried by labourers and poor peasants are likely to be unlicenced... The SSP [senior superintendent of police] gave an interesting explanation for not trying to withdraw licences from weapon-wielding members of the Ranbir Sena—that in the present state of agrarian conflict, the state could not protect all the bhumihars. Hence they had to be allowed to have guns for their own security and to safeguard their properties. When asked whether likewise the state was in a position to defend all dalits who did not possess weapons, he maintained a telling silence.[119]

Bihar is also notorious for instances of "booth-capturing" at election time; the practice of forcibly entering voting booths and stealing or rigging ballots.[120]

---

[117]Created in 1939, the Central Reserve Police Force is the largest of the paramilitary forces in India.

[118]Srivastava, "Caught in a caste spiral," *Indian Express*.

[119]People's Union for Democratic Rights, *Agrarian Conflict in Bihar...*, p. 31.

[120]The problem of booth-capturing in Indian elections is decades old. Following allegations of booth capturing, booth rigging, and intimidation of voters during the first phase of February 1998 national parliamentary elections in Bihar, the Election Commission ordered repolling in over 700 polling stations. "Repoll in 700 booths in Bihar ordered," *Indian Express*, February 19, 1998. According to the state home secretary, more than 1,100 people were arrested for booth-capturing and the tearing up of ballot papers. Moreover, fifteen people were killed, and dozens were injured in the thirty-four constituencies that went to the polls during the first phase. Police and paramilitary forces were also deployed in several pockets of Patna city. "EC cracks whip, scraps Patna polls," *INDOlink New from India*, February 21, 1998. www.indolink.com/INDNews/DNUmain/mn022198.html. During the

Political candidates ensure their majority vote with the help of senas, whose members kill if necessary. This phenomenon has been covered widely by the press and by human rights groups.[121] The Ranvir Sena was responsible for killing more than fifty people during Bihar's 1995 state election campaign.[122] A 1998 article noted the use of senas in Ara district, Bihar, during the February 1998 national parliamentary elections: "It is a measure of the chicanery and double-standards of most Ara politicians that when the opportunity arises, they do not hesitate in using the sena, though their public posture against the private army is holier than thou."[123]

The impunity with which Ranvir Sena leaders carry out their attacks—at election time and other times—provides further evidence of government support. The police record speaks for itself. None of the Ranvir Sena leaders have been prosecuted for the murder of nineteen Dalits and Muslims in Bathani Tola in 1996 and the murder of eleven in Haibaspur in 1997. In Ekwari village in April 1997, police pried open the doors of lower-caste homes and watched as sena members killed eight residents. No sena member was prosecuted. The officers were subsequently suspended, then transferred, but they, too, escaped prosecution. A December 1997 massacre in Laxmanpur-Bathe left at least sixty-one Dalits dead. According to survivors in the village, the attackers identified by eyewitnesses were never arrested. Villagers also received threats of a future attack and felt unprotected despite the presence of a police camp in the village. In January and February 1999, the Ranvir Sena killed over thirty people within seventeen days in

---

second phase of elections, seven deaths were reported, including that of a CPI(M-L) leader. Exchange of fire, snatching of ballots and ballot boxes, and intimidation of voters was also reported in several constituencies. "Second phase: 55% voting, nine deaths," *Indian Express*, February 23, 1998. Later in the year, during the state legislative assembly elections, police were given shoot-at-sight orders for those tampering with ballot boxes. "Maharashtra by-polls peaceful; firing, rigging in Bihar," *Indian Express*, June 4, 1998.
[121]*See*, for example, Jha, "The running feud," *The Pioneer*. According to a 1996 Associated Press report:

> Armies formed by local politicians have intimidated villages during every election in the underdeveloped farmland of northern India... On election day, hired thugs prevent many voters from reaching polling stations. Other voters arrive to find their ballots have already been cast. Sometimes, gunmen literally walk off with the ballot box, a tactic called booth capturing. Police, either overwhelmed or paid off, do little to interfere.

Arthur Max, "Private Armies," Associated Press, April 22, 1996.
[122]Ibid. See also People's Union for Democratic Rights, *Agrarian Conflict in Bihar...*, p. 23.
[123]Tara Shankar Sahay, "Only we are fighting the Ranvir Sena as it should be fought," *Rediff on the Net*, February 13, 1998, www.redifindia.com/news/1998/feb/13bihar1.htm.

Shankarbigha and Narayanpur villages. Sena members had announced the attack in local papers two weeks ahead of time. The state did nothing to stop them. According to an article in *The Statesman*, a Delhi-based daily, sena members were aided by the police in entering Narayanpur village.[124]

State intervention often comes to a halt after the distribution of paltry compensation packages and the posting of police camps in massacre-affected villages. Human Rights Watch investigations, and the investigations of a national ten-member civil rights team, found that in most villages police camps were located in the upper-caste areas, effectively inaccessible to Dalits and other lower-caste villagers.

Sena members who have been arrested have quickly been released on bail; none have been convicted.[125] By contrast, some Naxalites who have been prosecuted have been awarded death sentences.[126] Not only does the state treat the crimes of the two groups differently, but police and local officials openly tolerate the senas. On August 8, 1995, a little over two weeks after the killing of six Dalits in Sarathua village, the state government announced its decision to ban the Ranvir Sena.[127] Sena members continued to hold meetings and conventions to openly outline their strategy and response to Naxalite attacks. Several leaders wanted by the police were present during one such meeting held on October 8, 1997, in Belaur village, Bhojpur district. The local administration was reportedly fully aware of the meeting and its participants but did nothing to disarm the group or arrest the

---

[124]"11 mowed down by Ranvir gunmen," *The Statesman* (Delhi), February 11, 1999.

[125]According to a People's Union for Democratic Rights report, when sena members are arrested they are "given the option of presenting themselves in court at a later date rather than being arrested in the village. In jail, they receive much better treatment and food from their houses. One the other hand, when the poor are arrested, no such option is given to them. They are severely beaten, and often illegally detained in police custody." People's Union for Democratic Rights, *Agrarian Conflict in Bihar...*, p. 30.

[126]Eight suspected Naxalites were sentenced to death, and sixty-six Naxalites were sentenced to life imprisonment, for the Dalelchak Baghaura massacre of May 1987 which left at least fifty-four upper-caste Rajputs dead. "Death sentences awarded to eight accused," *Times of India*, December 10, 1995.

[127]"Ranbir Sena yet to be outlawed," *The Telegraph*, August 21, 1995. The six villagers killed were all said to be CPI(M-L) supporters. Raj Kumar, "Landlords gun down six Harijans in Bihar village," *Times of India*, July 27, 1995. The victims' family members received a relief and rehabilitation package amounting to Rs. 2,500,000 (US$62,500). "Relief for Bhojpur victims announced," *Times of India*, August 1, 1995.

wanted men.[128] Six massacres, and police complicity in the attacks, are described in detail below.

### Shankarbigha and Narayanpur

On the evening of January 25, 1999, at least twenty-two Dalit men, women and children were killed in the village of Shankarbigha, Jehanabad district, by members of the Ranvir Sena. The massacre was the fifth of its kind since July 1996 in which Dalit and lower-caste men, women and children were killed by the sena for their suspected allegiance to CPI(M-L) or MCC. According to press reports, members of the Ranvir Sena entered eight thatched huts in the village during the night and fired indiscriminately on the occupants. Many of the victims, including several children, were shot in the head and stomach at point-blank range. Police suspected that the attacks were in retaliation for the killing of two sena activists the week before by MCC members. According to Jehanabad District Magistrate P. Amrit, the killers shouted Ranvir Sena slogans throughout the attacks. The village is only ten kilometers away from Laxmanpur-Bathe, the site of the December 1997 sena massacre.[129] Ranvir Sena supporters told *Times of India* that the sena had planned to kill almost all the Dalits in the village, close to seventy people, but were unable to complete their task.

The police ignored early warnings that a massacre was likely. On January 8, 1999, a little over two weeks before the attack, Ranvir Sena leader Bharmeshwar Singh admitted in an interview to a local daily that the sena was planning an attack in Jehanabad district, "with renewed vigour [and] in a very calculat[ed] manner."[130] Singh also admitted that the sena had already chosen its target and was simply waiting for the "right time" to strike.[131] According the CPI(M-L) General Secretary Dipankar Bhattacharya, his group made a written submission to the local administration providing a list of villages deemed vulnerable to sena attacks. A list of "already-accused sena members" was also included.[132]

The National Human Rights Commission, a statutory body set up pursuant to the Protection of Human Rights Act, 1993, has asked the state government to investigate the massacre and prevent a recurrence of such incidents.[133] Twenty-four

---

[128]Ahmad, "Blood for blood...," *The Telegraph*.

[129]John Chalmers, "Massacre, religious woes mar India Republic Day," Reuters, January 26, 1999.

[130]P. Chaudary, "Fear stalks Jehanabad village," *Times of India*, January 28, 1999.

[131] "Clamour for Rabri's sack after Dalits massacre," *Indian Express*, January 28, 1999.

[132]"A Tale of Two Senas," *Times of India*, February 15, 1999.

[133]"NHRC asks Bihar Govt to probe massacre," *Deccan Herald* (Delhi), January 28, 1999.

people were arrested in late January 1999 in connection to the massacre, all of whom belong to the Bhumihar caste.[134] Activists are pessimistic, however, that any will be prosecuted.[135]

A little over two weeks after the Shankarbigha massacre, on the night of February 10, 1999, the sena attacked neighboring Narayanpur village. Sena members killed twelve and injured seven. According to press reports, over one hundred heavily armed sena members descended on the village during the night and forced their way into homes, shooting at will. The attack, which began at 9:00 p.m., lasted for one hour. The police did not arrive until 8:00 a.m. the following morning.[136] Bihar Governor Sunder Singh Bhandari stated that a "lack of vigil and alertness [had] led to a repeat of yet another strike by the Ranvir Sena."[137]

In a press release issued soon after the incident, the Ranvir Sena claimed responsibility for both massacres. Shamsher Bahadur Singh, leader and spokesman for the sena, stated that sena members were forced to "take up arms to save the honour, dignity, and life and property of the innocent farmers." The killings were meant as retaliation for the deaths of farmers at the hands of Naxalites over the past thirty years. The press release added:

> Our fight will continue till the extremists as well as the government lift the illegal economic blockade and release confiscated land, other properties, arms and ammunition, etc. of innocent farmers... Our main targets of future attacks will be Khakaria village in Jehanabad district, Akbarpur village under the Paliganj police station in Patna district and those villages where Naxal activists have let loose a reign of terror and become centres of extremists.[138]

On February 12, 1999, the Indian president dismissed the state government and imposed federal rule in Bihar, citing as the reason a breakdown of law and order and constitutional machinery. The following day, paramilitary forces numbering in the thousands were dispatched to the state. Two days later, on February 14, CPI(M-L) Liberation members reportedly gunned down seven people,

---

[134]P. K. Chaudary, S. Kumar, "Bihar to set up special court for Jehanabad trial," *Times of India*, January 28, 1999.
[135]Human Rights Watch telephone interviews with Bihar Dalit Vikas Samiti members in New Delhi and Patna, February 1999.
[136]Dipak Mishra and Satyendra Kumar, [no title], *Times of India*, February 12, 1999.
[137]"Ranvir Sena kills 12 Dalits," *The Tribune* (Delhi), February 12, 1999.
[138]"Ranvir Sena to carry on killings," *Times of India*, February [no date], 1999.

including four upper-caste Bhumihars who were said to be Ranvir Sena supporters, at Usri Bazaar, Jehanabad district. The police alleged that the attack was in retaliation for the killings in Shankarbigha and Narayanpur.[139] In early March 1999, the central government reversed its decision to impose president's rule. As of this writing, Bihar's state government, with Rabri Devi as the chief minister, had been reinstated. Sena leaders Bharmeshwar Singh and Shamsher Bahadur Singh had yet to be arrested.

### Laxmanpur-Bathe

On the evening of December 1, 1997, armed sena activists crossed the Sone river into the village of Laxmanpur-Bathe where 180 families lived. They raided fourteen Dalit homes and killed a total of sixty-one people: sixteen children, twenty-seven women, and eighteen men. In some families, three generations were killed. Twenty people were also seriously injured. As most of the men fled the village when the attack began, women and children numbered high among the fatalities. During the attack, at least five girls around fifteen years of age were raped and mutilated before being shot in the chest by members of the Ranvir Sena. Most of the victims allegedly belonged to families of Party Unity supporters; the group had been demanding more equitable land distribution in the area.

The village of Laxmanpur-Bathe has no electricity and is virtually inaccessible by road. In crossing the Sone river to reach the village, sena members reportedly also killed five members of the Mallah (fisherman) community and murdered the three Mallah boatmen who had ferried them across the river on their way back.[140] According to newspaper reports, the main reason for the attack was that the Bhumihars wanted to seize fifty acres of land that had been earmarked for distribution among the landless laborers of the village. A group of peasants, reportedly affiliated with Naxalite activity, was ready to take up arms against them.[141] Authorities apparently knew of the tensions but "had not cared to intervene in the land dispute and nip the trouble in the bud and instead allowed things to come to a head."[142] Following widespread publicity about the massacre,

---

[139]"7 killed in fresh Jehanabad violence," *Times of India*, February 14, 1999; "Cong begins to react, blasts Centre for Bihar killings," *Economic Times* (Delhi), February 16, 1999.
[140]Kalyan Chaudari, "The Jehanabad carnage," *Frontline*, December 26, 1997.
[141]Surendra Kishore, "61 massacred in Bihar as Ranvir Sena goes on killing spree," *Indian Express*, December 3, 1997; Chaudari, "The Jehanabad carnage," *Frontline*.
[142]"Murder and Mayhem," *The Hindu*, December 14, 1997.

Bihar Chief Minister Rabri Devi suspended the Jehanabad district superintendent of police and replaced several senior officers.[143]

Human Rights Watch visited the village on February 25, 1998. According to villagers who survived the attack, close to one hundred members of the Ranvir Sena arrived en masse and entered the front houses of the village: "Their strategy was to do everything simultaneously so that no one could be forewarned."[144] Human Rights Watch visited a house in which seven family members were killed. Only the father and one son survived. Vinod Paswan, the son, described the attack:

> Fifteen men surrounded the house, and five came in. My sister hid me behind the grain storage. They broke the door down. My sisters, brothers, and mother were killed... The men didn't say anything. They just started shooting. They yelled, "Long live Ranvir Sena," as they were leaving.[145]

At the time of the attack, the father, Ramchela Paswan, was away in the fields. When he returned, he found seven of his family members shot in his house: "I started beating my chest and screaming that no one is left. No one has been saved from my family. Then my son came out saying he that he had not been killed."[146] Human Rights Watch also interviewed seven female residents of the village, many of whom witnessed the rape, mutilation and murder of five girls. Thirty-two-year-old Surajmani Devi recounted what she saw:

> Everyone was shot in the chest. I also saw that the panties were torn. One girl was Prabha. She was fifteen years old. She was supposed to go to her husband's house two to three days later. They also cut her breast and shot her in the chest. Another was Manmatiya, also fifteen. They raped her and cut off her breast. The girls were all naked, and their panties were ripped. They also shot them in the vagina. There

---

[143]"Home Secy removed, SP suspended," *Hindustan Times*, December 3, 1997.

[144]Human Rights Watch interview with Bathe resident, Jehanabad district, Bihar, February 25, 1998.

[145]Human Rights Watch interview with Vinod Paswan, Jehanabad district, Bihar, February 25, 1998.

[146]Human Rights Watch interview with Ramchela Paswan, Jehanabad district, Bihar, February 25, 1998.

were five girls in all. All five were raped. All were fifteen or younger. All their breasts were cut off.[147]

Twenty-five-year-old Mahurti Devi was shot in the stomach but survived her injuries after extensive surgery. She had returned home after a dispute with her husband and was living in her mother's house. She recalled:

> They broke in and tried to open our box of valuables. They couldn't so they took my chain and earrings off my body. There were ten to twelve of them in the house. They didn't wear any masks. I said I had nothing. They said open everything. My mother was shot, and she fell down. They flashed a torch on my face. Then they shot me, and I fell down. The police took me to the hospital. After a three-day operation I came to, and the police took a report from me. Some people have been arrested, others are still free. They looted all the houses.[148]

At the time of the massacre, Jasudevi was at her husband's home in another village. She arrived in Bathe the morning after the attack to find her two sisters-in-law and her fifteen-year-old niece shot to death. "My niece was supposed to go to her husband's house the same day. She was expecting a child. When I found her it looked like she was trying to run away when she was shot."[149] Seven-year-old Mahesh Kumar was being held by his mother when she was shot. She fell forward and protected his body with her own. She then died.[150]

Local police had been aware of the possibility of violence long before the Bathe massacre. On November 25, 1997, sena leaders openly held a strategy meeting seven kilometers away from Bathe. Sena leader Shamsher Bahadur Singh had also been touring the area in the months before the massacre openly seeking donations from supporters. Police officers claimed to be aware of these meetings but dismissed them as routine—missing yet another opportunity to intervene and preempt a sena attack. One officer was quoted as saying, "It's like crying wolf.

---

[147]Human Rights Watch interview with Surajmani Devi, Jehanabad district, Bihar, February 25, 1998.

[148]Human Rights Watch interview with Mahurti Devi, Jehanabad district, Bihar, February 25, 1998.

[149]Human Rights Watch interview with Jasudevi, Jehanabad district, Bihar, February 25, 1998.

[150]Human Rights Watch interview with Bathe resident, Jehanabad district, Bihar, February 25, 1998.

The Communist Party of India (M-L) keeps sending us complaint letters every week, we can't take action every time."[151]

According to members of Bihar Dalit Vikas Samiti, a grassroots organization, the events that unfolded in Bathe were more complex than a random attack on a Dalit hamlet:

> CPI was organizing in Bathe because the residents were so poor and exploited, they couldn't even feed themselves after a full day's work. When they asked for more wages, they were beaten down even more. Some CPI(M-L) and Party Unity people had a split.[152] A few people left them and gave information about party activities to landlords. The landlords contacted Ranvir Sena in Bhojpur, saying that they needed help controlling them. The Ranvir Sena came out at 4:00 p.m. They ate and drank liquor with the landlords and attacked at 9:00 p.m. They had a list of whom to attack but got drunk and killed anyone and everyone.[153]

The activists also claimed that the purpose of Bathe was "to teach others not to rebel or raise a voice. In so doing women became vulnerable and were sexually assaulted... They raped women and cut off their breasts. A woman whose pregnancy was nearly complete was shot in the stomach. They said that otherwise the child will grow up to be a rebel."[154]

Life for most in the village has been disrupted. At the time of the Human Rights Watch visit, children were unable to go to school because a makeshift police camp had been located on school grounds. None of the adults were working.

---

[151]Yogesh Vajpayee, "Police was aware of Ranvir Sena attack," *Indian Express*, December 5, 1997.

[152]According to a press report, a year before the massacre the village was aligned with Party Unity but had since shifted to CPI(M-L) after the murder of Party Unity leader Chapit Ram. Party Unity members alleged that CPI(M-L) was behind the murder. "Bloodbath at night," *Rediff on the Net*, December 3, 1997, www.redifindia.com/news/dec/03kill2.htm. The same article also reported that villagers claimed that the killers shouted pro-sena slogans during the Bathe attack.

[153]Human Rights Watch interview with BDVS members, Jehanabad district, Bihar, February 26, 1998.

[154]Human Rights Watch interview with BDVS member, New Delhi, February 21, 1998.

Villagers complained, "There is no work, all has stopped. Since they [Bhumihars] are the landed families, our people don't get to work in their fields."[155]

Since the massacre, police protection in Bathe has remained grossly inadequate. The Bihar government announced soon after the Bathe killings that police would be deployed in the area to set up camp and maintain law and order. However, when parliamentary elections were later announced, the police force was directed to control election-related violence. Despite their dual assignment of controlling the Ranvir Sena and watching the polls, the police seemed more intent on conducting raids on Dalit villages in the name of controlling "extremism" and seeking out Naxalite cadres than on protecting Dalit villagers. According to a member of BDVS, "Bathe protection is near the poor but it only benefits the rich. Police always go to the landlords' houses... All their needs are taken care of by upper castes. If someone calls a meeting they won't come. They say we don't have time. They just do flag marches."[156]

At the time Human Rights Watch visited the village, the Dalit residents of Bathe feared another attack:

> Fifteen to twenty days ago we received a message that they will sprinkle petrol on the houses of villages and set them on fire—the houses of those that didn't get killed the first time around. We told the police. They said we are here so nothing will happen, but the police are protecting them. They are stationed in the Ranvir Sena *tola* [hamlet]. Police are helping the Ranvir Sena. The accused are moving around freely. So we feel that the culprits are being protected.[157]

Human Rights Watch also spoke to police officers stationed in the village school. Officer In-Charge Amay Kumar Singh informed us that a total of twenty-six police officers were present in the village. He claimed that the police arrived soon after the massacre. According to Singh, twenty-five of the twenty-six perpetrators identified by villagers had been arrested but at the time of the interview (two months after the events) had not been formally charged. He claimed

---

[155]Human Rights Watch interview with Bathe resident, Jehanabad district, Bihar, February 25, 1998.

[156]Human Rights Watch interview with BDVS member, Jehanabad district, Bihar, February 26, 1998.

[157]Human Rights Watch interview with Bathe resident, Jehanabad district, Bihar, February 25, 1998.

that the police were providing security for all villagers and that new threats had not been reported to them.

Like many officers, Singh claimed that police response to attacks is hindered by insufficient funding, infrastructure, and equipment for village-based police camps. These arguments fail, however, when one notes the frequency of police search and raid operations on remote Dalit villages. Though Singh believed that his officers had enough guns to provide security, and were able to communicate quickly with the area police station, he claimed that more men and more facilities were needed and that the roads to the village were in very poor condition. Road construction had begun soon after the massacre but came to a halt when "VIPs" stopped visiting the area. "We have no car. Look at our conditions. We are sleeping on the ground," Singh complained.[158] Deputy General of Police Saxena also reported that the local police station was poorly equipped and there was not enough personnel. "That's why we couldn't prevent this," he said.[159]

On January 9, 1998, nine people suspected to be supporters of the Ranvir Sena were killed by CPI(M-L) activists in Chouram village, forty-five kilometers from Jehanabad. The killings were reportedly in retaliation for the Bathe massacre. The attackers opened fire indiscriminately on the victims as they were returning home from a funeral.[160] Several Dalits in the Bathe area were subsequently taken into custody by the police. Bathe villagers claim that the sena members were actually killed by Marxist-Leninist party members who were not from their village: "Police have been harassing Dalits for fifteen kilometers around this village. No one cares about the sixty-one people who died here. Everyone cares about those nine. The Ranvir Sena says that they will take ninety for those nine killed."[161]

Despite the arrests immediately after the massacre, as of February 1999 none of the sena members responsible for the Bathe attack had been prosecuted.

### Ekwari

On the morning of April 10, 1997, members of the Ranvir Sena gunned down eight residents of Ekwari village in Bhojpur district in an operation that lasted two hours. Police officers stationed nearby forced open the villagers' houses and then

---

[158]Human Rights Watch interview with Amay Kumar Singh, Jehanabad district, Bihar, February 25, 1998.
[159]Kishore, "61 massacred in Bihar...," *Indian Express.*
[160]"CPI-ML kills nine Ranvir Sena activists," *Rediff on the Net,* January 10, 1998. www.redifindia.com/news/1998/jan/10kill.htm
[161]Human Rights Watch interview with Bathe resident, Jehanabad district, Bihar, February 25, 1998.

stood by and watched as the massacre took place. Seven of the eight killed belonged to the lower-caste Lohars, Chamars, Dhobis and Kahars. The village is known to many as the birthplace of CPI(M-L) in the 1970s. The head of the lower-caste hamlet in the village described the incident to Human Rights Watch:

> They were killed by the Ranvir Sena. We recognize them. The police were with them. They weren't shooting. They searched the houses. Then they left and Ranvir Sena came in and shot everyone. The police were still there. They were from the new police camp, not from outside. They sent more after the massacre. The sena killed to get more notoriety.[162]

An article in *The Telegraph*, a Calcutta-based daily, reported that the attackers raped two women before killing them: a fifteen-year-old girl and a woman who was eight months pregnant. A ten-year-old boy was shot in the head.

> The partisan role of the police could not have been clearer. While policemen pried open doors of houses, the Ranbir Sena activists followed them in and mowed the people down. Sunaina Devi, an eyewitness to the murder of her father-in-law and sister-in-law, said that when they refused to open their doors, the policemen broke them open and let the killers in... Sagar Mahato said he saw the police running away and watching from a distance.[163]

The article also reported that the CPI(M-L) Politburo member and member of legislative assembly, Ram Naresh Ram, claimed that the murders were premeditated and that police were bribed by the landlords. A probable cause of the conflict, a villager added, was that many acres of land were lying fallow in the village due to a blockade imposed by the CPI(M-L).[164]

The Bombay-based *Times of India* reported that the fifteen-year-old was raped in the presence of her father. The pregnant woman was said to be the relative of Jai Kahar, a veteran CPI(M-L) activist and a suspect in the murder of a landlord in the area the previous year. An eyewitness recounted, "Fifty people belonging

---

[162]Human Rights Watch interview with head of lower-caste hamlet, Bhojpur district, Bihar, February 27, 1998.
[163]Ahmad, "Pregnant woman raped...," *The Telegraph*.
[164]Ibid.

to upper caste cordoned off the entire small tola and started searching for firearms. I know them by their names. They are the landlords of this region. Indrajeet Singh, Binod Singh, Pankaj Singh, Ajay Singh are the main culprits who killed eight people in this tola."[165]

Human Rights Watch visited the village of Ekwari in February 1998. A police camp had been established in upper-caste territory, an area inaccessible to Dalits who were afraid to cross the road dividing the two parts of the village. When Human Rights Watch asked the villagers to take us to the police camp they responded, "We can't take you there. They are on Bhumihar land. No one is protecting us."[166]

An Ekwari village sub-inspector told Human Rights Watch that in his camp there were two sub-inspectors, one sub-inspector BMP (Bihar Military Police), and seventeen constables, making a total of twenty officers. A second camp located near the village fields had nineteen officers. The sub-inspector claimed that the police presence was sufficient to maintain law and order in the village. At the time of the massacre, he was on assignment at the police station eight kilometers away.

> There was a fight between CPI(M-L) and the Ranvir Sena. One Ranvir Sena member was killed. Eight CPI(M-L) were killed some days later. They were not members of CPI(M-L) but were killed based on caste. They have been fighting for years. People are killed on both sides. All have been arrested and charged. Thirty-six were named; approximately thirty were from the Ranvir Sena. All are in jail. There is only one absconder. He escaped from jail. When a CPI(M-L) dies, it's always the Ranvir Sena; when a Ranvir Sena dies it is always a CPI(M-L) who kills. We also caught the CPI(M-L) who killed the Ranvir Sena. We are here for now and most likely will stay for a while.[167]

In the aftermath of the killings, seven police officers were suspended. Another police camp officer claimed that the suspensions were a political move. "Both sides are political, so whenever there are problems there is a lot of pressure on the state, the superintendent of police, the district magistrate. So in order to

---

[165]Pranava K. Chaudary, "Ekwari carnage was backed by police," *Times of India*, April 13, 1997.
[166]Human Rights Watch interview with Ekwari village residents, Bhojpur district, Bihar, February 27, 1998.
[167]Human Rights Watch interview with Ekwari village sub-inspector, Bhojpur district, Bihar, February 27, 1998.

remove the pressure they suspend officers. The same officers come back on duty in a different police station."[168] When asked to describe the current situation, the sub-inspector responded that it was "peaceful and normal. There's been so much violence here that even one murder every few months is considered peaceful. Labor is an ongoing problem. It's a very old problem. Whenever killings take place, there is a strike. But now work is ongoing."[169]

Residents of the Dalit and backward-caste hamlet agreed. They explained that work had started again, but "there was a lot of fear" and little protection. Although CPI(M-L) is active in the village, the lower-caste villagers claim that the "Ranvir Sena is more powerful. They have rifles, semi-automatics, and guns. We only have sticks."[170] The head of the lower-caste section of the village was also apprehensive about the police and had little faith in the protection they provided.

> Police are here for law and order. They see what's going on, but they are allied with the Ranvir Sena. They get money and food from the forward castes so they favor the forward castes. The police don't care about the poor. We don't go to the police, nor any other state agencies. We asked for help from the Bhumihars to keep the killings low. They said they cannot control them even though the Bhumihar population belongs to the Ranvir Sena. We have no protection.[171]

According to the former deputy superintendent of police (DSP) for Bhojpur district, Bihar, the April 1997 attack was due to "police negligence":

> The police completely failed in giving protection. They went in one house, and the Ranvir Sena went into another. The guards did nothing to protect them. The Ranvir Sena killed everyone in the police's

---

[168]Human Rights Watch interview with Ekwari village police officer, Bhojpur district, Bihar, February 27, 1998.
[169]Human Rights Watch interview with Ekwari village sub-inspector, Bhojpur district, Bihar, February 27, 1998.
[170]Human Rights Watch interview with Ekwari village resident, Bhojpur district, Bihar, February 27, 1998.
[171]Human Rights Watch interview with head of lower-caste hamlet, Bhojpur district, Bihar, February 27, 1998.

presence. By the time the station police came, the Ranvir Sena had run away.[172]

The former DSP went on to describe the situation of women and children.

> There are 106 widows in Ekwari. At least fifty women have also been killed in the past several years. The Dalit men go to jail and get sentenced, while the Ranvir Sena has enough money to fight the case all the way to the Supreme Court. Dalit women are made homeless, and the children cannot go to school because the family needs the money to fight the cases against the men. The Ranvir Sena cares only about high numbers. They also rape the women. The police send innocent people to jail. No one can surrender for fear of so-called police encounters. They do not get justice from the police. That is the main factor.[173]

Even the landlords of the village (members of the Ranvir Sena) complained that the police, under pressure to maintain "law and order" in their jurisdiction, have arrested indiscriminately on both sides.

> First the police were with us, now they have left us. Since 1995 the police have really bothered us. In April, people were killed here. They killed one farmer and destroyed all crops. Seven CPI(M-L) were killed by Ranvir Sena for retaliation. The police just take care of the dead bodies. They don't really help. In response to the April massacre, the police destroyed a landowner's house after arresting him. They also arrested thirty-nine people. All landowners were innocent. They were not part of the Ranvir Sena. The police were also involved in the Ranvir Sena massacre. Seven people were suspended. The police are not with anybody they are trying to scare people. They always capture the innocent, even when CPI(M-L) strike.[174]

As of February 1999, none of the sena members or police officers responsible for the killings in Ekwari had been prosecuted.

---

[172]Human Rights Watch interview with former DSP Ramchandar Ram, Patna, March 1, 1998.

[173]Ibid.

[174]Human Rights Watch interview with Arvind Singh, Ranvir Sena member, Bhojpur district, Bihar, February 27, 1998.

**Haibaspur**

On March 23, 1997, ten landless laborers were killed in Haibaspur village in Patna district, Bihar, apparently for aligning themselves with the CPI(M-L) Party Unity. Before leaving the village, the Ranvir Sena inscribed its organization's name in blood on the rim of a dry well.[175] Party Unity forces retaliated within a month by killing six Ranvir Sena supporters on April 21, 1997.[176] According to BDVS activists, alcohol and the rape of Dalit women by the Bhumihar men played a role in the attack on the village:

> The Dalits made alcohol, and Bhumihars drank it. When Bhumihars fought among themselves, they went to the Mushahars [Dalits], gave them drinks, and got them to take revenge on their enemies by taking their field crops and so on. But the Dalits were working for both sides so the Bhumihars killed them. They were double-crossing them. They only gave them liquor to get them to do the work. Bhumihars give them money to make the liquor, then give some liquor to the Dalits to get them to do the work. Whoever makes alcohol also pays a commission to the police. When the Bhumihars came and drank, they also raped the Mushahar women. Mushahar men did not like it so they protested and were killed. The people killed were mostly innocent, but these are the two reasons it happened.[177]

According to an article in *The Hindu*, a Madras-based daily, although the police were informed immediately of the Haibaspur killings, they did not arrive on the scene until the following morning, after hearing that the chief minister was due to visit the site.[178] When Human Rights Watch spoke to villagers in February 1998, they said they were still afraid of another massacre and had received threats from neighboring upper-caste landholders.[179] Apart from the promise of small compensation packages, the state had done little to protect them.

---

[175]Ranjit Bhushan, "Caste bullets ricochet, rural violence spirals as caste 'armies' run amok," *Outlook*, April 9, 1997.

[176]Verma, "The Lull, After...".

[177]Human Rights Watch interview with BDVS members, Jehanabad district, Bihar, February 26, 1998.

[178]"Police arrived late at carnage scene," *The Hindu*, March 26, 1997.

[179]Human Rights Watch interview, Jehanabad district, Bihar, February 26, 1998.

### Bathani Tola

In response to the Ranvir Sena attack on the Dalit hamlet of Bathani Tola in July 1996 (see above), then-Home Minister Indrajit Gupta expressed dissatisfaction with police protection in the affected region. Even though four police camps had been posted in the area, Gupta charged that they were, "paralysed, impotent and did nothing."[180] Residents of the village claimed that most of the main perpetrators were still roaming freely in their village, though the police claimed to have arrested all sixty men involved.[181] A new police camp was soon set up near the site but was considered largely ineffective in checking threats from upper-caste landlords. "They are at the beck and call of the landlords. Their food comes from the landlords' houses. How can they render us justice?" one villager asked.[182]

Despite signs of rising tensions in the area, police neglected to shift their picket (booth) to Bathani Tola.[183] On July 26, 1996, the Bombay-based daily *Indian Express* reported that officials had received written notification of the possibility of an attack. In a letter dated July 4, 1996, to the district magistrate, the Bhojpur district committee of CPI(M-L) complained that the Ranvir Sena had "renewed its campaign of terror in the villages" and charged that the night before, "a gang of the Ranbir Sena [had] been engaged in indiscriminate firing."[184] The committee added that there was much tension and fear and urged the district magistrate to "take strong action immediately."[185] CPI(M-L) had also sent requests for protection on June 26, June 29, and July 2. According to press reports, Superintendent of Police S. N. Pradhan dismissed the letters as "routine."[186]

The killings took place on July 11. During the attack itself, the police reportedly made no attempts to intervene despite being on duty a "stone's throw" away from the scene.[187] Soon after the incident the chief minister suspended police officers stationed in camps near the tola,[188] but failed to prosecute them.

---

[180]Sabrina Inderjit, "Bihar carnage is a socio-political problem," *Times of India*, July 17, 1996.
[181]Ramakrishnan, "Massacre in Bihar...," *Frontline*.
[182]Ibid.
[183]Jha, "Officials ignored pleas...," *Indian Express*.
[184]Ibid.
[185]Ibid.
[186]Ibid.
[187]"Laloo's land or lawless land?" *The Hindu*.
[188]"Danse macabre," *Sunday*, July 21 – 27, 1996.

**Government Compensation Packages**

Instead of prosecuting accused sena members or taking action against colluding police officials, official action in cases of caste-based killings in Bihar has generally come to a halt after a few officers have been temporarily suspended and surviving family members have received the preliminary disbursements of their compensation money. The promised relief package has often included food rations, temporary manual labor jobs, and when the victims were Dalit and poor, an offer to build *pucca* (solid) houses. Solid houses are essential for instilling a sense of security for villagers whose flimsy mud huts are easier targets for police and sena raids. The government, however, has seldom followed through with promised relief packages.

In Shankarbigha, the government promised monetary compensation, a government job, and pucca housing to the victims' dependents.[189] Two and a half weeks later, in Narayanpur, the government promised Rs. 140,000 (US$3,500) to each of the victims' dependents.[190] In Bathe, the Paswan family lost seven of its members. It received Rs. 100,000 for every family member killed from the Bihar and central government, for a total of Rs. 1,400,000 (US$35,000). The family used the interest from the money to construct a new house. Even though the entire village remained vulnerable to future attacks, pucca houses were only provided to the families of those that were killed.[191] According to BDVS Director Dr. Jose Kananaikal, "Over 2,000 people have visited in the two months following Bathe. But now nobody cares. The chief minister also said they would get land, but that never happened. They also promised a school and a road, but that didn't happen either."[192]

When the chief minister arrived at the Haibaspur massacre site, he promised a compensation package to the families of the victims but failed to disarm the sena members responsible for the killings.[193] The government announced Rs. 120,000 (US$3,000) as compensation for each victim. It also assured work and food rations for three months and promised pucca houses for the entire Dalit hamlet. In February 1998, almost a year after the massacre, a civil rights fact-finding team reported that only Rs. 20,000 (US$500) had been paid, that no work or food rations

---

[189]Chaudary, "Bihar to set up...," *Times of India.*
[190]"Ranvir Sena kills...," *The Tribune.*
[191]Human Rights Watch interview, Jehanabad district, Bihar, February 25, 1998; All-India Civil Rights Team, "After Bathe Massacre, Findings of an All-Indian Civil Rights Team," *A Press Release by the All-India Civil Rights Team*, February 1998.
[192]Human Rights Watch interview, New Delhi, February 21, 1998.
[193]"A barbaric act," *The Hindu*, March 26, 1997.

had been provided, and that the houses had only been partially constructed. Moreover, police raids since the beginning of 1998 had destroyed the little construction that had taken place. Dalit residents were also unwilling to work in adjoining villages where they were earlier employed for fear of another orchestrated attack by their employers.[194]

### The State's Targeting of Naxalites

As noted above, although both the Naxalites and the private militias share the responsibility for increased violence and deaths in the state, the state's response to the Naxalites has been markedly different. Police have frequently operated as agents of the landed upper castes, conducting raids on Dalit villages and disguising killings as "encounters." According to a People's Union for Democratic Rights report, "The administration bans both the Ranveer Sena and the CPI(M-L) Party Unity but in effect treats them differently. [T]he judiciary is [also] influenced by the social and political background of the people concerned."[195] PUDR members also believe that the government is under pressure to show that the killings will be stopped, but its actions have focused primarily on Naxalite activities.

> Many are arrested under Criminal Procedure Code Section 107 for preventive detention. The Supreme Court has stated that the detention cannot be more than twenty-four hours, but in many cases it takes fifteen to thirty days to get a lawyer; sympathetic lawyers are already overburdened. The charges are bailable but they have no property, no surety. So they remain in jail for long periods of time... They won't settle land disputes because land is in the hands of landlords. So they treat it as a law and order issue and arrest and raid instead.[196]

### "Encounter" killings

The pattern of extrajudicial executions by security forces in disturbed areas and by police forces in Naxalite-affected areas has been documented by international human rights organizations and Indian civil liberties groups.[197] The

---

[194]All-India Civil Rights Team, "After Bathe Massacre...".

[195]Hemendra Narayan, "Caste, creed and carnage," *The Statesman*, December 12, 1997.

[196]Human Rights Watch interview with People's Union for Democratic Rights, New Delhi, February 21, 1998.

[197]*See*, for example, People's Union for Democratic Rights, *Encounters: A Report on Land Struggle in Bihar*, (New Delhi: April 1996). Extrajudicial killings have also been documented in previous Human Rights Watch reports. *See*, for example, Asia Watch (now

police routinely claim that the killings occur in so-called encounters. The People's Union for Civil Liberties, the largest civil rights organization in the country, has described the use of the term "encounter killing" as

> a unique contribution of the police in India to the vocabulary of human rights... it represents in most cases the taking into custody of an individual or a group, torture and subsequent murder. The death generally occurs as a result of the brutal torture or stage-managed extermination in an appropriate area. An official press release then elaborately outlines a confrontation, an encounter where the police claim to have fired in "self-defence."[198]

Such tactics have long been used against suspected Naxalites. In the southern state of Andhra Pradesh, the Naxalite threat has been used to justify state violence against all forms of peasant resistance and against other critics of state policy. Human Rights Watch has documented a pattern of systematic human rights violations that has formed part of the state government's counterinsurgency efforts. Since 1968, security forces have murdered hundreds of villagers, guerrilla group sympathizers, and suspected militants in the state. Human Rights Watch has also documented the degree to which security forces have colluded with powerful landlords to crush organized efforts by peasant movements to secure their rights to land and fair labor practices.[199]

These tactics have also been used in Bihar. On April 15, 1994, police reportedly killed eleven MCC members in an "encounter" in Gaya district, Bihar. According to a report by People's Union for Democratic Rights, since then, "there has been a significant rise in the number of people killed in this manner."[200] On

---

the Asia division of Human Rights Watch), *Kashmir Under Siege: Human Rights in India* (New York: Human Rights Watch, 1991), pp. 25 - 62; Asia Watch, *Punjab in Crisis: Human Rights in India* (New York: Human Rights Watch, 1991), pp. 37 - 89; Human Rights Watch/Asia, Physicians for Human Rights, *Dead Silence: The Legacy of Abuses in Punjab* (New York, Human Rights Watch, 1994), pp. 16 - 41.

[198]People's Union for Civil Liberties, "Murder by Encounter," [no date], in A.R. Desai, ed., *Violation of Democratic Rights in India* (Bombay: Popular Prakashan, 1986), p. 457. The phenomenon of disguising extrajudicial executions as killings committed in self-defense in the course of an armed engagement is, of course, not unique to India.

[199]Asia Watch (now the Asia division of Human Rights Watch), "Police Killings and Rural Violence in Andhra Pradesh," *A Human Rights Watch Report*, September 1992.

[200]People's Union for Democratic Rights, *Encounters: A Report...*, p. 2.

December 27, 1997, an "encounter" took place in Kodihara village, Patna district.

> At 5:30 a.m. that day, the police entered the village and caught hold of and beat people who were going out to work. There was a Naxalite squad in the village which noticed the arrival of the police and slipped away. The police fired at them but they escaped. Two of them hid in the fields nearby, but the police soon found them. The two of them handed over their weapons to the police and offered [to] surrender. But the police shot them dead in cold blood. This murder was seen by all the villagers assembled there.[201]

Villagers reported that after searching Kodihara, police moved on to Jhunauti. The raid on Jhunauti is described below.

Police have also repeatedly engaged in excessive use of force when dealing with Naxalites. On July 3, 1995, four Party Unity members were killed and eight arrested. The following month, the police fired into a crowd of 500 people gathered at a CPI(M-L) Liberation office in Begusurai town soon after they lathi-charged[202] a peaceful protest on land reforms. Five people were killed, and one was seriously injured. Sixty-five people, including twenty-nine women, were arrested on charges of rioting and illegal assembly. Three people were additionally charged with murder and attempted murder. All those arrested were severely beaten in police custody. In this incident, as in the two described above, the police claimed to have fired in self-defense, while villagers and other eyewitnesses claimed that the firing was one-sided. Post mortems were conducted immediately, and the bodies were quickly disposed of, eliminating any possibility of independent autopsies for verification of the manner of death.[203]

### Police raids

Under the pretext of seeking out Naxalite militants police have conducted raids on Dalit villages and falsely arrested those accused of harboring Naxalites. In some cases, federal paramilitary forces have been deployed. Like the private militias, police have sexually assaulted women and attacked children who remained behind after the men fled the villages. Women have also been arrested and taken into custody in order to punish their families and force their male relatives to

---

[201] All-India Civil Rights Team, "After Bathe Massacre...".
[202] The act of a charging a crowd using police canes or wooden batons.
[203] People's Union for Democratic Rights, *Encounters: A Report...*, pp. 12-13.

surrender. After the Ekwari village massacre of April 1997, police conducted search operations in neighboring lower-caste hamlets. Women were molested and beaten, and local residents alleged that police took Rs. 5,000 (US$125) from them.[204] As noted in a PUDR report:

> The loot of property and molestation of women by policemen in the course of [the post-Ekwari] search is a fairly common feature of routine police searches in poor settlements. So searches end up as punitive measures inflicted upon a section of the populace already targeted by the Ranbir Sena. Search operations in upper caste localities are not only rare but also very cursory.[205]

A ten-member team comprising members of seven civil liberties organizations visited sixteen villages in Patna and Jehanabad district, Bihar, in February 1998. Their mandate was to investigate reports of abuses committed by Bihar police deployed to protect Dalits in the aftermath of the 1997 massacres. The team's report described the raids:

> In the course of the raids, the police routinely abuse women in the most vulgar and offensive language... [T]here are no women police at all in the raid. It is the male police [who] enter the houses without consideration for the woman's privacy. They abuse the women whose sons/husbands they are looking for. One frequent [accusation] is that the woman has sent her husband away "so that she may sleep with the extremists." Women who are going to the fields in the early morning cold are forced to remove the *chaddar* [blanket] so that the police may see whether they are hiding any arms or ammunition underneath. These "suspicions" are only meant to insult and humiliate women.[206]

The report added:

> The raids are frequent and create fear and terror among the poorer classes who are suspected of harbouring Naxalites. These raids are

---

[204]People's Union for Democratic Rights, *Agrarian Conflict in Bihar...*, p. 6.
[205]Ibid., p. 30.
[206]All-India Civil Rights Team, "After Bathe Massacre...". In Sevanan, the children also complained that police kicked them and pulled their ears during a raid.

common in villages where the landless agricultural labourers organised by the various *sangathans* [meetings] of the CPI(M-L) organisations have fought for wage increases and occupation of *gair mazarua* [government] land. In some villages the raids are very frequent. Jhunauti [Jehanabad district, Bihar] was subjected to at least twenty raids in the last two months. In Andhrachak, Jehanabad district, Bihar, there is one raid every week. Sevanan, Jehanabad district, Bihar, is subjected to at least two raids a week.[207]

### Raid in Andhrachak

Residents of Andhrachak spoke to Human Rights Watch representatives about a raid on their village on February 10, 1998. Some 300 police officers, including members of the Special Reserve Police Force,[208] surrounded fifty homes and arrested six people, all of whom were still in jail at the time of the interview on February 26, 1998. Ranjeet, a twenty-eight-year-old agricultural laborer, witnessed the arrest of his brother, father and cousin.

> The first time they came at 4:30 p.m., they didn't take anyone. They came into all the houses. They took my friend's torches, his tobacco box and Rs. 500 out of the money box. They ransacked all the rooms and broke the pots and doors. We ran because we were afraid of being beaten... They also beat my brother's wife with the butt of their gun. They hit her on her backside; she had to seek treatment. The second time they came it was 4:00 a.m. The people they arrested were also beaten with sticks. They were charged under Criminal Procedure Code 107 [preventive detention].[209] I went to jail to get them released. They said they would only give bail after [national parliamentary] elections. They say it is Rs. 1,000 (US$25) for bail. We will have to get a loan or a bond.[210]

---

[207] Ibid.

[208] The Special Reserve Police Force (SRPF) is an armed branch of the police that is called in during times of emergency. See also Chapter VI for the role of SRPF in a police firing on Dalits in Ramabai Colony, Bombay.

[209] The use of preventive detention provisions by the police as a means of harassing Dalits and Dalit activists is further described in Chapter VIII.

[210] Human Rights Watch interview, Jehanabad district, Bihar, February 26, 1998. Getting a loan or a bond, we were told, was financially crippling for families in which male members earned only three kilograms of rice a day plus one meal. Women earned rice but no meals.

The police told villagers upon arriving that they came in search of guns and that they suspected Naxalite activity in the area. But as sixty-year-old Sona Devi explained, "Where are we going to get guns from? We don't even have money for food, clothes or a home." Devi complained that the police never went to the landlords' houses: "They are the ones that have guns." She claimed that the Ranvir Sena was operational in Kayal, an adjacent village where Dalits laborers worked. "The Kayal people call the sena in to scare us and threaten us. We are afraid of them. They will kill us. They have already killed two Dalits in the field before... The Kayal village people tell police we are Naxalites, but no one goes and sees their Ranvir Sena activities."[211]

Devi also reported that nine to ten days before the police raid, Bhumihar men came to the village to threaten its residents. "They said if you touch us, harm us, or don't work in the fields, then we will send the Ranvir Sena to set fire to the villages and kill everyone." The villagers did not go to the police, explaining that they "are afraid of them also, they [the sena and the police] are all together."[212] Other women in the village claimed that members of the Sena had "misbehaved" with them. "They come in the night and beat the men and rape the women. It has happened many times. They beat the women too and rip their clothes off. The police don't do anything."[213]

### Raid in Jhunauti

The village of Jhunauti in Jehanabad district, Bihar, has over 190 Dalit households. Over one hundred Bhumihar families live adjacent to them in the same village. Since 1997, police have raided the village more than five times. A fifty-five-year-old Dalit agricultural laborer in the village described the raids to Human Rights Watch:

The raids take place mostly at night. Once it happened during the day. Two times they took people away; once they misbehaved with women;

---

Women also worked inside the landlords' homes but did not get paid for it. Even when working for government projects, like laying bricks or building construction, Dalits are paid with food and not with money. Human Rights Watch interviews, Jehanabad district, Bihar, February 26, 1998.

[211]Human Rights Watch interview with Sona Devi, Jehanabad district, Bihar, February 26, 1998.

[212]Ibid.

[213]Human Rights Watch interview with Andhrachak village women, Jehanabad district, Bihar, February 26, 1998.

usually they break everything and take our chickens. In December 1997 they came at 7:30 p.m., there were thirty-five to forty police. That is when they misbehaved with the women and broke everything. Everyone runs away when they come.[214]

The village school teacher, who was present during the December 1997 raid, explained the reason for it:

There is no Ranvir Sena in Jhunauti, but the police harass us. They found a gun at one laborer's house so they bothered all of us. In January 1998 they also went to Bhumihars for a raid. During the Kodihara "encounter,"[215] CPI(M-L) party people were killed. So they came here for a raid and then to the Bhumihars. In December during the bad episode [Bathe] they only came here... CPI(M-L)) stole a rifle from a landlord, which is what started the raid. But the party does not live here.[216]

The school teacher also asked the police why they were searching the village. They told him they were looking for rifles, guns, and Naxalites and proceeded to enter his house.

I said, "Why are you arresting me?" They said, "After we search the whole village we will leave you." They caught ten to twelve men. They were all eighteen to forty-five years in age. They asked one woman to name them all. She knew their names so she told them. They arrested five men, the younger ones. They said they were Naxalites. My son was one of them. He is twenty years old.[217]

His son was taken to jail with the others. They were then brought to Jehanabad court and charged under Indian Penal Code, Section 395, a *dacoity* charge which carries a maximum life sentence. Dacoity is defined under Section 391 as robbery committed by five or more persons. Thirty-eight days later, the court was asked for a bail order. The families had to pay Rs. 1,000 to Rs. 5,000

---

[214]Human Rights Watch interview, Jehanabad district, Bihar, February 26, 1998.
[215]See above.
[216]Human Rights Watch interview, Jehanabad district, Bihar, February 26, 1998.
[217]Human Rights Watch interview, Jehanabad district, Bihar, February 26, 1998.

(US$25 to $125) each and were forced to sell their chickens and belongings and to ask for contributions from the village. Most villagers earn only one and a half to two kilograms of rice per day as agricultural laborers. At the time of the interview, the dacoity case against them was still pending.

One woman was on her way to a neighbor's house when she was grabbed by a police officer. "Do you keep Naxalites in your house?" they asked her. "I cursed at them. I called them motherfuckers, and they removed my sari. I ran back home."[218] Forty-five-year-old Athi Basmatra Devi had Rs. 150 taken from her home, and twenty-year-old Kunti Kumari saw her husband being dragged away by the police. "He was in jail for thirty-eight days," she said. "He was innocent."[219]

Many villagers had left their homes out of fear of another raid. Most other villagers had little to say to the fact-finding team as they feared a backlash from the police. One resident explained, "The police harm us so much, that is why they are not talking to you. They beat down the innocent and we can never ask why. They say we are Naxalites. They are only after the Dalits. They do not to this with Bhumihars."[220]

### Extortion and looting

Police throughout India engage in extortion, motivated in part by their need to pay off debts incurred for securing their positions through bribes—a cycle that has been documented both by Indian civil rights organizations and by the government's National Police Commission reports.[221] In 1996 it was reported that police inspectors in Bihar were made to pay a bribe of Rs. 100,000 (US$2,500) before being recruited.[222] It is not anomalous, therefore, that raids by the police in

---

[218]Human Rights Watch interview with twenty-year-old agricultural laborer, Jehanabad district, Bihar, February 26, 1998.

[219]Human Rights Watch interview, Jehanabad district, Bihar, February 26, 1998.

[220]Ibid.

[221]*See*, for example, National Police Commission, "Corruption in Police," Chapter XXII, *Third Report of the National Police Commission* (New Delhi: Government of India, 1980), p. 28. Police also turn to extortion and other corrupt practices because of low salaries, lack of training, and de facto immunity from prosecution. Police in central Bihar frequently complain of "poor facilities [and] unpaid salaries...." Vajpayee, "Police was aware...," *Indian Express*. The low morale of the police, lack of discipline, lack of equipment, and the sophisticated weaponry of armed groups in the state have also been blamed for delayed police response to attacks on Dalits. Abdul Qadir, "Fear of fresh violence grips Jehanabad," *The Times of India*, December 5, 1997; Naidu, "Rise and rise...," *Hindustan Times*.

[222]Human Rights Watch interview with human rights activist, Jehanabad district, Bihar, February 25, 1998. See Chapter V for similar payment schemes in Tamil Nadu.

the aftermath of massacres have often been accompanied by looting and extortion. According to the ten-member team's report, on January 6, 1998, police raided the village of Makarpur in Jehanabad district, Bihar. The villagers mistook the police for the Ranvir Sena and began to run. Seven young men were arrested and, after three days of illegal detention, were released after paying a Rs. 5,500 (US$138) bribe. They were threatened with further detentions and beatings if they refused to pay the money.[223] In Nagwan village, Patna district, Bihar, two people were taken to the police station and threatened with being booked for a crime unless they paid Rs. 900 (US$22.50).[224]

In several villages, under the pretense of *kurki-japti* (attachment of movable property), police have seized the property of those "absconding" in criminal cases. In so doing, they followed none of the legal procedures for seizure, including presentation of a court order and list of materials to be seized, and seizing in the presence of two witnesses. As the report noted of the pattern of behavior:

> The material seized in this looting is of varied kind, and appears to be aimed at destroying the livelihood of people. Grain or rice stored in the house, all possible utensils, chairs, cots and tables, door frames, etc. are taken away. Buffaloes were taken away in Uber village in Jehanabad [district, Bihar]. Goats were also taken away in some villages... In Uber, not satisfied with having taken away the buffaloes, the police asked the householders to give them Rs. 100 (US$2.50) a day to feed the buffaloes.[225]

In some cases, police abandoned the pretense of seizure or attachment of property and engaged in outright looting. In Kodihara village in Patna district police stole jewelry, clothes, Rs. 2,000 (US$50), and consumables collected in preparation for a marriage from a villager's house.[226] The raids have had a devastating effect on the livelihood of villagers who earned two kilograms of rice or less than Rs. 25 (US$0.63) a day.

---

[223] All-India Civil Rights Team, "After Bathe Massacre...".
[224] Ibid.
[225] Ibid.
[226] Ibid.

## V. THE PATTERN OF ABUSE: SOUTHERN DISTRICT CLASHES IN TAMIL NADU AND THE STATE'S RESPONSE

No Dalit has faith in the police establishment... The southern clashes have been attempts of Dalit self-assertion and a reflection of their loss of faith.

— Christodas Gandhi, Tamil Nadu implementation officer for the Atrocities Act[227]

Caste clashes in the southern state of Tamil Nadu have predominantly involved two communities: the Thevars (a backward caste) and the Pallars (or Dalits). As has been the case in other states, Dalits in Tamil Nadu have long suffered from exploitative economic relationships and have frequently been the victims of violence. However, changes since the early 1990s have altered the economic relationship between the Thevars and the Pallars and have changed the contours of the conflict. Having benefited from the state's policy of reservations in education and from the income provided by relatives working abroad, the Pallars have become much less dependent on Thevar employment and have begun to assert themselves in the political arena. The Thevars have responded to this threat to their hegemony with violence. Dalits, too, have begun to fight back.

This chapter examines caste clashes in the state's southern districts between July 1995 and December 1998. Unlike the conflict in the eastern state of Bihar, the violence is often spontaneous and not the result of organized armed movements. Much as in the state of Bihar, however, the police have colluded with the caste Hindus to preserve the status quo and keep Dalits from peacefully claiming their rights. The police, many of whom are Thevars themselves, have conducted raids on Dalit villages ostensibly to search for Dalit militants. During these raids, police have assaulted villagers and detained many under preventive detention laws. Women in particular have been targeted.

According to the Indian government's 1996-1997 annual report for the Ministry of Human Affairs, caste-related incidents in 1996 in the southern state of Tamil Nadu increased by 34 percent over previous years. Out of 282 reported

---

[227]Human Rights Watch interview with Christodas Gandhi, honorable secretary, Adi Dravida/Tribal Welfare Department, and then-nodal officer under the Atrocities Act, Tamil Nadu, Madras, February 13, 1998. Under Rule 9 of the Scheduled Castes and Scheduled Tribes (Prevention of Atrocities) Rules, 1995, a nodal officer is responsible for coordinating the functioning and implementation of the Atrocities Act in his or her state.

incidents, 238 took place between scheduled castes and other backward communities. The main caste groups involved were the Thevars, Naidars, and Vanniyas (all backward castes) and the Adi Dravidas and Pallars (both scheduled castes or Dalits).[228]  The number of incidents between Pallars and Thevars increased again dramatically at the height of caste clashes in the southern districts of Tamil Nadu from April 1997 to December 1998. The nexus between Thevars, the police, and district officials in the affected areas was repeatedly reflected in violent search and raid operations in Dalit villages, in the forced displacement of thousands of Dalit villagers, often with the aid of district officials, and in the disproportionate number of Dalits arrested under preventive detention statutes during the clashes. Abuses against Dalits continued following a police raid on the Dalits of Gundupatti village in February 1998 and violent clashes between Dalits and Thevars from October to December 1998. According to the state government, at least 251 people died in caste violence between August 1995 and October 1998.[229]

Clashes in the southern districts of Tamil Nadu have largely been attributed to increased Pallar economic and political autonomy and the backlash against it. Since the mid-1990s, the Pallars have begun to support a new political leadership, unaligned to mainstream political parties, and promoted by two movements: the Dalit Panthers of India (DPI) Tamil Nadu, and the Devendra Kula Vellalar Federation (DKVF) led by Dr. K. Krishnaswamy, a member of the Tamil Nadu legislative assembly.[230]  In 1998 the DKVF became a political party and named itself Puthiya Tamalingam. These political movements have provided an organized platform for growing resistance to the still prevalent norms of "untouchability" in the state. Dalits have demanded equal treatment in temple festivals, have refused to carry out ritually demeaning tasks, have demanded access to public water sources, and have claimed an equal share of public goods and village properties. Thevars have responded by "clinging more resolutely to their caste status as a way of affirming their superiority."[231]  Government statistics from 1995 revealed that

---

[228]Ministry of Home Affairs, *Annual Report: 1996-97* (New Delhi: Government of India, 1998), pp. 6-7.

[229]"To avoid caste clashes, TN Govt proposes to remove all statues," *Hindustan Times*, October 23, 1998.

[230]The Dalit community in the southern districts mainly comprises Pallars who also refer to themselves as Devendra Kula Vellalars. Since the research for this report was completed, DPI changed its name to the Liberation Panthers.

[231]M. Pandian, "Elusive 'peace' in Tamil Nadu," *The Hindu*, May 30, 1997. Pandian is a researcher at the Madras Institute of Development Studies.

Thevars were the perpetrators in 91 percent of cases involving the coercive enforcement of "untouchability" practices.[232]

### Context of Clashes

Between July 1995 and June 1996, clashes between Thevars and Pallars resulted in large-scale destruction of property, loss of life on both sides, and the arrest of many Dalit youths under preventive detention laws like the Tamil Nadu Goondas Act[233] and the National Security Act, 1980.[234] In most cases, the usually spontaneous clashes originated over issues of land, the holding of protests and rallies, the use of village resources, or any Dalit attempt to defy the caste-based order. Typically, both sides were armed with stones or agricultural tools.

The cycle of violence began anew in late April 1997 when the government announced the creation of a new transport corporation in Virudhunagar district in the name of a Pallar community member (the Veeran Sundaralingam Transport Corporation, VSTC). Thevars opposed the proposal and, according to press reports, some were heard to remark, "How do you expect us to travel in a bus named after a Dalit? It is a personal affront to our manhood."[235] On May 1, 1997, VSTC was inaugurated; Thevars threw stones at the buses and refused to ride them.[236]

On May 2, Dalit leader Dr. Krishnaswamy was arrested and accused of sparking violence with his "inflammatory speeches."[237] Spontaneous protests erupted as news of his arrest spread through the region. Protesters staged several road blocks and, for the three days that Dr. Krishnaswamy remained in jail, "police resorted to firing, lathi-charges[238] and bursting tear gas shells to control agitating

---

[232]"TN caste clashes spark exodus," *The Telegraph*, December 20, 1995.

[233]The Tamil Nadu Goondas Act allows for the preventive detention of those considered to be "goondas" or habitual offenders. The state-specific legislation has come under attack by many human rights groups as a violation of due process and for the broad and discretionary powers that it assigns the police.

[234]For more on the preventive detention of Dalit youths and activists, and the National Security Act, see Chapter VIII.

[235]A. S. Panneerselvan, "On the Violence Threshold," *Outlook*, May 21, 1997.

[236]The decision to form VSTC was made by the previous government during the latter part of the 1995-1996 clashes. The ruling Dravidian Movement Party (Dravida Munnetra Kazhagam, DMK) decided to implement the decision after Dalit groups threatened protests.

[237]Panneerselvan, "On the Violence...," *Outlook*.

[238]The act of a charging a crowd using police canes or wooden batons.

Dalits."[239] Two Dalits were killed by police bullets. On May 7 three Thevars were killed by the police at Sivakasi in Virudhunagar district while protesting the arrest of two Thevar youths.[240]

In protest against police action on Thevars at Sivakasi, Thevars in Mansapuram village attempted to introduce coconut shells at tea stalls for Dalits to keep them from sharing tea tumblers used by caste Hindus. When Dalits resisted, Thevars torched and looted Dalit houses in Amachiyarpatti village. In Rengappanaikkanpatti Thevars vowed to make Dalits "dig pits for the burial of bodies of dominant castes."[241] The entire Dalit population of the village was later forcibly driven out, as Thevars set fire to their homes and fields.

In the months following the renaming of the transport corporation and Dr. Krishnaswamy's arrest, the districts of Theni, Madurai, Virudhunagar, Tirunelveli, and Tuticorin witnessed periodic eruptions of violence and the forced displacement of thousands of Dalits from their homes. Police and district officials treated the situation as a law and order problem, and under the guise of seeking out Dalit militant activists, conducted search and raid operations exclusively on Dalit villages. They arrested and assaulted hundreds of men and women as they looted their homes and destroyed material possessions. As discussed below, women were the primary victims.

A June 1997 fact-finding mission by the People's Union for Civil Liberties (PUCL), the country's largest civil rights organization, concluded that in caste clashes in Madurai district, "Dalits were the worst affected in terms of property loss and physical injuries sustained, like hand and leg fractures, due to violent attack[s] on them"; that police had filed many false cases against Dalits; and that "increased political consciousness amongst the Dalits... regarding their fundamental social, political and economic rights expressed in terms of demands for social equality [and] equitable distribution of resources" played a major role in the attacks against them.[242]

---

[239]People's Union for Civil Liberties, "Final Report of the PUCL-Tamil Nadu Team that Inquired into Caste Disturbances in Southern Districts of Tamil Nadu," (Madras: PUCL, 1997), pp. 3-4.
[240]Ibid.
[241] "Clashes in TN result of caste disparities: Report," *The Statesman* (Delhi), July 2, 1997.
[242]People's Union for Civil Liberties, "Final Report of the PUCL-Tamil Nadu Team...". Another investigative mission, conducted at the same time by a committee of writers and academics in the state, also concluded that "Dalit arrests far outnumber[ed] Maravar [Thevar] arrests" and that "the displacement and destruction of houses have taken place only in the Dalit habitats." "Clashes in TN...," *The Statesman*.

### Links between Thevars and state agents

The Thevars numerically outnumber other backward castes in the region. The Thevar Peravai (Thevar Front), the most active and organized of Thevar organizations, was until early 1998 led by retired Director General of Police (DGP) Pon Paramaguru. His successor, Dr. N. Sethuraman, was also the general secretary of Moovendar Munnetra Kazhagam, a political party launched by the All India Thevar Peravai in 1998.

During his tenure as DGP from 1972 to 1975, Paramaguru recruited many Thevars into the police force. J. Jayalalitha, leader of the All India Anna Dravida Munnetra Kazhagam party (AIADMK), was considered a "strong Thevar community supporter" during her five-year tenure as chief minister of the state from 1991 to May 1996.[243] Her support included extending influential political and police positions to members of the Thevar community—allowing them to further consolidate their power base.[244] N. Sasikala, Jayalalitha's aide and confidante and a Thevar community member, was also accused of "astutely promoting her caste."[245] Lawyers, human rights activists and the local press have noted that, as a result, a majority of the police force in the southern districts now "hails from [the Thevar] caste and, often, have been unable to overcome their caste affiliations."[246]

---

[243]Human rights interview with civil rights attorneys, Madurai district, Tamil Nadu, February 16, 1998.

[244]"Clashes in TN...," *The Statesman.*

[245]Panneerselvan, "On the Violence...," *Outlook.* In December 1996 Jayalalitha was arrested on corruption charges. The Directorate of Vigilance and Anti-Corruption has charged Jayalalitha and Sasikala with, *inter alia,* amassing approximately Rs 65.86 crores ( US$16.4 million, one crore equals 10 million rupees) in illegal assets during Jayalalitha's term as chief minister. "Probe reveals RS 65 cr amassed by Jaya," *Indian Express,* May 4, 1997. The two were also the main accused in the "TANSI" land scandal in which Jayalalitha allegedly used her official status as chief minister to purchase state-owned land far below market value, resulting in a Rs. 3 crores (US$750,000) loss to the state. "Proceedings against Jayalalitha in 'TANSI' case adjourned" *Indian Express,* August 27, 1998. As of February 1999, several charges were still pending, and she remained general secretary of AIADMK.

[246]Panneerselvan, "On the Violence...," *Outlook.* Human Rights Watch was told by several activists that police constables in the southern districts were made to pay Rs. 50,000 (US$1,250) to secure their posts. Human Rights Watch interviews, Bangalore, July 25, 1998; Human Rights Watch interviews with People's Watch, People's Union for Civil Liberties, and civil rights attorneys in Madurai district, Madurai and Madras, Tamil Nadu, February 1998. People's Watch is a Madurai-based NGO that works extensively on human

According to Dr. Krishnaswamy, though "atrocities against Dalits were institutionalised during the previous AIADMK regime," a 1996 shift in political power to the DMK party, led by M. Karunanidhi, did not result in a "change in the behaviour of the police."[247] Inspector General Vijay Kumar, former security officer under Jayalalitha's administration, was accused by human rights activists of using the police force to engineer attacks on Dalit villages during the 1997 clashes. Activists have also charged that the district collector (local government official) of Virudhanagar district, Rajagopal, a Brahmin native of Thevar-dominated Enjar village, supported the Thevar community during the 1997 clashes: "He committed all sorts of atrocities against Dalits, including lathi-charge and unnecessary shootings."[248] Rajagopal was also accused of forcing Dalits to abandon their houses.[249]

In June 1997 the state government responded to police excesses during the clashes by transferring large numbers of officers out of "sensitive" districts, without meting out any additional punishment. Chief Minister Karunanidhi ordered the transfers after noting "some disturbing trends in the functioning of the lower levels of police during the disturbances, particularly in the southern districts."[250]

### Economic context

In recent years the economic relationship between Thevars and Pallars (Dalits) has shifted notably. Like most Dalits in rural India, the Pallars traditionally were employed as agricultural laborers (on Thevar lands) and were paid less than minimum wage. In the early 1990s, Pallars began to enjoy minimal upward economic mobility, which reduced their dependency on Thevars. Pallars became able to own and farm their own lands or look elsewhere for employment.

A researcher at the Madras Institute of Development Studies attributes increased Pallar prosperity to two factors:

The first is the policy of reservations, which has been more effectively implemented in this state, more than other states. Reservations in education frees Dalits from land-based occupation. The relationship between the landlord and the laborer has given way to urban-based

---

rights research, documentation, and advocacy in Tamil Nadu and other southern states.
[247]Panneerselvan, "On the Violence...," *Outlook.*
[248]Human rights interview with civil rights attorneys, Madurai district, Tamil Nadu, February 16, 1998.
[249]"Clashes in TN...," *The Statesman.*
[250]"Major shake-up of police force," *The Hindu,* June 20, 1997.

occupations. The second reason is that many Dalits have been recruited by Gulf countries. They send their proceeds home, and their families are able to acquire land through this process. So feudal dependency has lessened.[251]

Marginal landowners themselves, Thevars have dealt with this new economic threat through caste mobilization:

> The main backward classes in the state, the Thevars, are opposed to the Dalits. They themselves are not an advanced community. They are landlords but not in a big sense. They are not advanced in education, but still they employed Dalits as laborers. Because of the move away from production sectors, Thevars now can only assert their power through caste pride. So it takes on paper dominance. Before, caste was deployed through land.[252]

The Dalit communities, for their part, have realized the political potential of their somewhat better economic status by becoming more organized in their demands. This has affected state-wide patterns of violence and reactions by state agents. For the first time, the Pallars have begun to resist their traditional mistreatment: politically, by contesting elections, and physically, by responding to violence with violence.

Some Dalit activists have argued that their people's armed response is necessary for self-preservation and economic survival. As Murugeswari, the first Dalit female president of the Kandamanur village council, Tamil Nadu, has stated:

> While both parties have indulged in violence, there is an essential difference. Dalits are fighting for their rights and Thevars are fighting to retain their hegemony. It would be cruel to equate the fight for livelihood to the arson [sic] to retain power on the basis of birth.[253]

Thevars argue that the Dalits are merely self-interested and provoke the clashes themselves. In an interview with Human Rights Watch, Thevar leader Dr. N. Sethuraman claimed that the violence was being instigated by militant Dalit

---

[251]Human Rights Watch interview with M. Pandian, Madras, February 13, 1998.
[252]Ibid.
[253]Panneerselvan, "On the Violence...," *Outlook.*

activists: the clashes, he asserted, ensured the survival of Dalit organizations and their ability to attract funds from foreign donors.

> Dalit-oriented NGOs are promoting hatred between the two communities. Foreign Christian organizations fund these Dalit organizations. Their intention is not to eradicate hatred but to perpetuate hatred so that their organization can survive. They induce violence, take photos and get money. They want the clash to continue so they can survive. It is a very negative attitude. I doubt whether their intentions are really Christian.[254]

Dr. N. Sethuraman led the Thevar procession through Desikapuram village minutes before the police surrounded the Dalit colony and conducted a violent search and raid operation. The incident is further described below.

According to Sethuraman, the practice of "untouchability" has been virtually eradicated in the state. But according to several human rights groups, government reports, and our own investigations, as of February 1998 "untouchability" was still practiced in various forms in most villages where Dalits were minorities. These forms include separate tea tumblers at tea shops and prohibitions on entering places of public worship or wearing shoes in the presence of upper castes.

Sethuraman also claimed that "Thevar minorities are being chased out of their lands and homes," a practice that he termed "reverse untouchability." He went on to add that "the same has not happened to Dalits in a single village."[255] But Human Rights Watch visited several southern district villages where Dalits had been pushed out of their homes by Thevars and, months later, were unable to return. We also visited several villages where social and economic boycotts against Dalits were still in effect and others where murders and large-scale displacement of Dalits had taken place.

**Melavalavu Murders**

In September 1996, the village of Melavalavu, in Madurai district, was declared a reserved constituency under Article 243D of the Indian constitution.[256] The declaration signaled that the Melavalavu *panchayat* (village council), which

---

[254]Human Rights Watch interview with Dr. N. Sethuraman, Madurai, February 18, 1998.
[255]Ibid.
[256]See Appendix A for article.

covers eight villages with approximately 1,000 Dalit families,[257] would have seats reserved for scheduled-caste candidates.[258] In June 1997, a group murder of elected Dalits by neighboring Thevars signaled that constitutionally mandated shifts in legal power to scheduled castes would not be tolerated by caste Hindus displaced from their once secure elected positions.

Several observers have attributed the violence in the village and the resulting tensions to a shift in power relations brought on by the government's mandate of reservation of panchayat seats for Dalits. Dr. George Mathew of the New Delhi Institute of Social Sciences visited the area along with two other researchers soon after the murders. He published his conclusions in an article in *The Hindu*:

> The murders of the Dalit leaders of Melavalavu Panchayat were clearly because "untouchability" was still ingrained in the social system. The economic conditions in the village were abysmal, but the power was concentrated in the hands of a privileged few. These people had hitherto enjoyed a hold over the common properties such as fish ponds, temple lands and forest produce and did not want to relinquish these privileges to the Panchayat Raj system run by the downtrodden... [T]he violence was basically a result of a shift in the power equations from the haves to the have nots.[259]

The article also noted that the leasing of the twenty-five fish ponds alone would fetch an income of Rs. 500,000 to Rs. 1,000,000 annually (US$12,500 to $25,000). The new *panchayati raj* system put control of such common properties

---

[257]"6 Dalits hacked to death in Madurai," *The Times of India* (Bombay), July 3, 1997. The Dalits in this area belong to the Pariah community.

[258]Articles 243D and 243T, inserted by the Constitution (Seventy-third Amendment) Act, 1992 and the Constitution (Seventy-fourth Amendment) Act, 1992, respectively, provide that in every panchayat and every municipality, seats shall be reserved for scheduled-caste and scheduled-tribe members in proportion to their representation in the population. Among the seats reserved for the scheduled castes and scheduled tribes, not less than one-third shall be reserved for women belonging to those castes or tribes. Additionally, no less than one-third of all seats in every panchayat and municipality shall be reserved for women. At least one-third of the total number of seats for the offices of the chairpersons at each level shall also be reserved for women, and all such seats shall be allotted by rotation to different constituencies.

[259]"Melavalavu violence due to shift in power equations," *The Hindu*, August 16, 1997.

in the hands of the panchayat—that is, in Dalit hands—since the 1997 elections.[260] In a separate article, Mathew referred to the killings as

> a serious attack on the institution of panchayati raj, which has the potential of changing the powerful rural groups. The new panchayats are perceived by the traditional powerful groups as a threat. Melavalavu and similar villages are paying a price for not holding the panchayat elections regularly and strengthening the foundations of democracy.[261]

The case of Melavalavu provides an example of the interaction of social forces, efforts at reform, violent reaction, and impunity. The announcement of reservations in Melavalavu in 1996 led to a threat of "economic sanctions" by the majority caste Hindu community should any Dalit file for the position of panchayat president. The sanction would effectively leave Dalits without employment or access to economic and social services in villages in that area. As reported in the Bombay-based daily, *Times of India*, "They were warned that they would lose their jobs as farmhands and not be allowed to graze cattle or draw water from wells located on 'patta' [unutilized] land held by the dominant castes."[262]

The elections, scheduled for October 1996, were subsequently canceled, as all three Dalit nominees withdrew their candidacy for fear of sanctions against the entire scheduled-caste electorate. When polling finally did take place in February 1997, the election was suspended after several incidents of booth capturing.[263] A thirty-five-year-old Dalit named Murugesan won the presidency in the third round of polling, which took place under heavy police protection and was boycotted by the dominant castes. He was, however, unable to perform his tasks as president:

---

[260]Ibid. Literally translating to "rule by five elders" the panchayati raj system was based on the traditional models of the village system for settling customary and local disputes. This model of governance was given up under the influence of the Westminster model. Since the 1950s, however, there has been a movement to revive the panchayati raj system in an effort to model a participatory and relevant polity and to return to village governance as a means of decentralizing development. In addition to continuing its role as a village governing body, the panchayats are also responsible for the implementation of several development programs. Institute of Social Sciences, *Panchayati Raj Update* (New Delhi), November 1995, p. 8.

[261]George Mathew, "The meaning of Melavalavu," *The Hindu*, September 30, 1997.

[262]"6 Dalits hacked...," *Times of India*.

[263]Booth capturing was described briefly, in the Bihar context, in Chapter IV.

neighboring Thevars physically prevented him from entering his office space at the panchayat building.[264]

Several village residents told Human Rights Watch about violence against Dalit voters during the elections:

> With police protection the election was held, but at the end of the day upper-caste people entered into the booth and threatened and stabbed one boy and beat both men and women and took away the ballot boxes and threw them into the well. Then again they declared elections after one week. In that one we elected Murugesan. There was heavy police protection.    Still the Amblakars [Thevars] boycotted the elections. Then Murugesan was not able to go to the office. Only during the swearing-in ceremony did he go to the office because he had a police escort.[265]

Murugesan's twenty-six-year-old widow, Manimegala, described the threats that her husband had received after winning the presidency:

> After he was elected he received as many as ten threatening letters from Thevars. He kept them all in his office and showed them all to the [district] collector. Once he showed one to me. The letter said that one day or another we will definitely cut off your head, and they did. The police did not arrest the main culprits. I keep four children alone. The government gave me employment in the highways department. I put tar on the roads. I get Rs. 1,500 [US$37.50] per month, but it is not enough for four children. The government gave Rs. 150,000 [US$3,750] in compensation, but the collector deposited it in the bank.[266]

On the day of the attack, June 30, 1997, Murugesan was returning from a visit to the collector's office to inquire about compensation for houses burned in an earlier incident. Kumar, an eyewitness who barely survived the attack himself, boarded the bus and sat next to Murugesan. The assault, Kumar told Human Rights Watch, was led by a Thevar named Ramar. Ramar and Alagarsamy, the former

---

[264]"6 Dalits hacked...," *Times of India*.   Human Rights Watch interview, Madurai district, Tamil Nadu, February 15, 1998.

[265]Human Rights Watch interviews, Madurai district, Tamil Nadu, February 15, 1998.

[266]Human Rights Watch interview with Manimegala, Madurai district, Tamil Nadu, February 15, 1998.

panchayat president, gave explicit instructions to their gang of Thevars to "kill all the Pariahs [Dalits]."[267]

> There were nearly forty of them. They were all Thevars. They stabbed Murugesan on the right side of his belly. It was a very long knife. From outside the bus Ramar instructed the Thevars to kill all the Pariahs. Among twelve, six were murdered on the spot. They pulled all six out of the bus and stabbed them on the road with bill hooks more than two feet long.[268] I hid myself under the seat and later hid in the crowd. Five Thevars joined together, put Murugesan on the ground outside the bus, and chopped off his head, then threw it in a well half a kilometer away. I saw it happen, I was hiding in the crowd. Some grabbed his hands, others grabbed his head, and one cut his head with a bill hook. They deliberately took the head and poured the blood on other dead bodies.[269]

When the attackers noticed his presence, Kumar was chased into the fields and cut with a bill hook on the back of his neck, his right underarm, and his finger but ultimately managed to escape by fleeing into the plantation fields of a Dalit village.[270]

Family members of the six murder victims received Rs. 150,000 (US$3,750) in compensation from the state government under the Scheduled Castes and Scheduled Tribes (Prevention of Atrocities) Act, 1989.[271] A total of twelve persons were arrested within a month of the incident.[272] However, eyewitnesses have

---

[267]Human Rights Watch interview with Kumar, Madurai district, Tamil Nadu, February 15, 1998. Activists in the area assert that Ramar had been involved in several other incidents in the past. According to the head of the Dalit Panthers of India, Tamil Nadu, "if he had been handled properly earlier, Melavalavu never would have happened." Human Rights Watch interview, Madras, February 13, 1998.

[268]A bill hook is an agricultural instrument with a hooked blade.

[269]Human Rights Watch interview with Kumar, Madurai district, Tamil Nadu, February 15, 1998.

[270]Ibid.

[271]Human Rights Watch interview, Madurai district, Tamil Nadu, February 15, 1998. "Minister visits Melavalavu," *The Hindu*, July 3, 1997. See Chapter X for more on the Atrocities Act.

[272]Melavalavu murders: twelve arrested," *The Hindu*, July 31, 1997. Two others surrendered in court and, according to an official press release, were charged under the National Security Act, 1980. Ibid.

claimed that the ringleaders were not among them. Those arrested were charged under sections 341, 307, and 302 of the Indian Penal Code for wrongful restraint, attempted murder, and murder, respectively, and under Section 3(1)(10) of the Atrocities Act, the act's least serious offense, for name-calling or insulting a Dalit person in a public place.

Kumar claimed that the police had an eyewitness and victim sign papers saying that one of the accused, named Sedhu, was innocent.[273] Human Rights Watch spoke to that witness, a forty-five-year-old agricultural laborer, who told us the following:

> The police told me to sign papers saying who the real culprit was, so I signed it. I signed a plain piece of paper. Mellur DSP [Deputy Superintendent of Police] Subramanium came here in a jeep and called for me and asked me why I put my signature on a white paper. "Someone got Rs. 50,000 [US$1,250] for it," he said, "did you get your share?" I said I got nothing from him. "You must have gotten Rs. 25,000 [US$625] at least," he said. I don't know what happened with the paper.[274]

A two-member team from the State Human Rights Commission visited the village in early August, five weeks after the killings. Hundreds of women testified to incidents of theft, the burning of Dalit houses, and stone-throwing at night. They also complained of their inability to go to work in the fields, of a lack of police protection, and that most of the men had fled the village out of fear.[275] Karupaia, Murugesan's older brother, organized a march on August 8, 1997 to protest the lack of action on the part of the police. Participants estimated the number of marchers at 3,000, both men and women. They named the principal culprits as Ramar, Alagarsami, Poniah, Baskarar, Andichami, Markandan, Duraipandian, Chandran, Selvam, Alagu, Vadivelu, Karanthamalai, Ranganathan, Chakarmurti, Chockanathar, Sedhu, Rajendran, and Jothi.

> When we approached the *taluk* [village block] office, the superintendent of police (SP) and other officials were there. From above the building,

---

[273]Human Rights Watch interview with Kumar, Madurai district, Tamil Nadu, February 15, 1998.

[274]Human Rights Watch interview, Madurai district, Tamil Nadu, February 15, 1998.

[275]"Human rights panel visits Melavalavu," *Indian Express*, August 6, 1997.

a red-colored cloth was thrown down. We were in two rows. A "country bomb" fell in the gap and exploded.[276] Everyone scattered. There are iron pieces from the bomb inside Karuppan's leg. Tirumavalavan, the leader of the Dalit Panthers of India who led the procession, was the intended target.[277]

Tirumavalavan proceeded to inform the SP that the people who threw the bomb had descended from the building and were getting away. Many pointed them out, but the police refused to arrest them. The marchers then started throwing stones. The SP ordered a lathi-charge on the procession, and many of the protesters were severely injured. The police arrested a total of thirty-six protesters and charged them under the Indian Explosives Act and under Indian Penal Code sections 147, 148, 323 and 436 for rioting, rioting with a deadly weapon, voluntarily causing hurt, and mischief by explosive substance.[278] They also arrested a member of DPI and held him responsible for setting off the bomb. Tirumavalavan expressed outrage at the police's failure to arrest "the main accused Ramar in the Melavalavu incident," while simultaneously "nabbing a DPI member and holding him responsible for the blast."[279]

On August 9, 1997, the thirty-six people arrested were sent to Madurai jail. They were held for forty-five days. Released on bail, they were required to check in twice a day at the Trichitown police station, over 125 kilometers from the village. At the time of Human Rights Watch's visit, the conditions had been modified to reporting once a day at nearby Mellur police station. According to Karupaia, the arrests were retaliatory:

> The police put false cases against us because we organized a procession. They wanted to teach us a lesson. The Section 436 charge [mischief by explosive substance] is still pending. One shop was burned but we did not do it. One hundred Thevars came behind us in the procession and set fire to a shop on the main road.[280]

---

[276]The term "country bomb" refers to a crudely manufactured bomb which, unlike a time bomb, requires direct ignition.

[277]Human Rights Watch interview with Karupaia, Madurai district, Tamil Nadu, February 15, 1998.

[278]Ibid.

[279]"Police cane dalit processionists," *The Hindu*, August 9, 1997.

[280]Human Rights Watch interview with Karupaia, Murugesan's older brother, Madurai district, Tamil Nadu, February 15, 1998.

Human Rights Watch spoke to a forty-year-old resident of Melavalavu who was arrested during the lathi-charge:

> I was in jail for forty-five days. My son was also arrested. After the arrest the police said that we looted the shops and set fire to them, but we never did any of those things. In the jail it is a routine practice to ask what cases you came in for, and then they give you blows with their lathis. It is an "admission beat." I was injured in the head and taken to the jail hospital. I was beaten two times with the lathi.[281]

The leader of DPI and Dr. Krishnaswamy have both charged that the "National Security Act as well as the [Tamil Nadu] Goondas Act were being grossly misused against the Dalits by the state government" and that several Dalits had been kept in preventive custody for many days.[282] In the months following the murders, concerned groups demanding appropriate action by the police organized several protests and marches. On July 10, 1997, members of the Social Action Movement, a grassroots NGO, demonstrated in front of the Madurai collectorate's office in order to highlight the plight of the villagers in the aftermath of the murders.[283] On July 23, 1997, DPI marched to demand the release of all Dalits arrested under the National Security Act in connection with the murders.[284]

By the end of September 1997, more than forty people had been charged in the Melavalavu murders case, while eleven had been formally accused but remained at large.[285] On November 24, 1997, DPI members marched again to urge the government to arrest those absconding in the murders and to demand a Central Bureau of Investigation (CBI)[286] inquiry into the case.[287]

Members of the Thevar Peravai, who organized a protest on October 28, 1997, also demanded a CBI inquiry. The then-vice president, Dr. N. Sethuraman,

---

[281]Human Rights Watch interview, Madurai district, Tamil Nadu, February 15, 1998.
[282]"Dalit leader promises 'peaceful' procession," *Indian Express*, August 4, 1997. For more on the preventive detention of Dalit activists, see Chapter VIII.
[283]"Govt's back-up measures lethargic in Melavalavu," *Indian Express*, July 10, 1997.
[284]"Tension in the air as Dalits take out a procession," *Indian Express*, July 24, 1997.
[285]"Chargesheet filed in Melavalavu murder case," *The Hindu*, September 27, 1997.
[286]CBI is a federal investigative agency that handles cases of corruption and cases of inter-state and other complicated crimes. CBI inquiries are often demanded in cases where local or state investigations are perceived to be biased or impartial.
[287]"Procession seeks arrest of accused in murders," *The Hindu*, November 25, 1997; "Dalit Panthers Iyakkam march peaceful," *Indian Express*, November 25, 1997.

claimed that innocent people had been arrested.[288]   When Human Rights Watch spoke to Dr. Sethuraman, now president of Thevar Peravai, about the incident, he claimed it had no basis in caste conflict:

> This is not a fight between Dalits and Thevars.  There's a lot of proof. It was a personal quarrel between the milk society president, a forward-caste member, and Murugesan, the Dalit president.  But they have sorted it out now, and the new president can now perform his duties without any problem.  The chief minister says that is a quarrel between Thevars and Dalits, but it is not.  We have asked for a CBI inquiry to bring these things out.[289]

When Human Rights Watch visited the village in February 1998, the bodies of the six murdered men were still buried in shallow graves in the village center as "a tribute befitting martyrs."[290]   The new Dalit panchayat president was again unable to perform his duties, and Thevars—in a concerted campaign to punish Dalits—had ceased to employ Dalits as laborers on their lands.  The Thevars also encouraged others to refrain from awarding farm work to Dalits.  Many Dalit students were also afraid to go to school for fear of further reprisal.[291]

Human Rights Watch spoke to the new panchayat president, Raja, who was six months into his term.  He claimed that the threats from Thevars had continued and that the police protection he received was inconsistent and insufficient to ward off another attack.  Five Dalit women, elected members of the panchayat, had also been unable to perform their duties.

> The office is in the caste Hindu area.  I am not allowed in the office.  So we have to hold meetings in our TV room here; it is a makeshift office. They are still threatening us.  They are watching and following me. Five Dalit women are members of the panchayat.  If the elected Dalit

---

[288]"Thevar Peravai march for CBI probe," *Indian Express*, October 29, 1997.

[289]Human Rights Watch interview with Dr. N. Sethuraman, Madurai district, Tamil Nadu, February 18, 1998.

[290]Human Rights Watch interview with Melavalavu resident, Madurai district, Tamil Nadu, February 15, 1998.

[291]"Dalits of Melavalavu treated as outcasts," *The Hindu*, July 12, 1997; Human Rights Watch interview, Madurai district, Tamil Nadu, February 15, 1998; "Govt's back-up measures lethargic in Melavalavu," *Indian Express*, July 10, 1997.

women go there, the upper caste would do some harm. If the women insist on going into the office, they will hit them. There is one police guard for me. He has a gun, but he puts it inside his bag. He only gives protection when I go to the taluk [village block] office. But any other time he doesn't give protection. He has joined the police of the other camp. Everything is paralyzed.[292]

Raja also explained the village's dire economic situation:

We got regular employment in their fields. Some Dalits have land, but most are landless laborers. Women received Rs. 12 [US$0.30] for six hours of work from the morning until the afternoon. Men received Rs. 25 [US$0.63] for six hours of work, but they do harder work using bigger instruments. The period after the elections they did not invite us for field work. Now the women work fifteen kilometers away, and most of the men went to Kerala [a neighboring state] and send money back.[293]

Thirty-four-year-old Gandhi also spoke of the difficulties faced by female agricultural laborers: "Prior to the elections I worked in this village. Now I go nearby to work on anyone's land... If you go near the landlords' houses and they are in a drunken mood, they misbehave with us, and we want to avoid that."[294]

The February 1998 national parliamentary elections brought a new wave of violence to the village: Thevars allegedly beat Dalit women in poll booths when the women went to cast their vote.[295] As of July 1998, Raja had still not received funds normally allocated to panchayat presidents for village development—leading human rights activists to believe that the local administration had yet to legitimize his presidency.[296] As of February 1999, the forty people arrested for the murders

---

[292]Human Rights Watch interview with Raja, Madurai district, Tamil Nadu, February 15, 1998.
[293]Ibid.
[294]Human Rights Watch interview with Gandhi, Madurai district, Tamil Nadu, February 15, 1998.
[295]Human Rights Watch interview with Raja, Madurai district, Tamil Nadu, February 15, 1998.
[296]Human Rights Watch interview with Henry Thiagaraj, Dalit Liberation Education Trust, Bangalore, July 25, 1998.

were out on bail, and no one had been prosecuted. Ramar, the person identified by eyewitnesses as the ringleader of the attack, was still at large.

## Displacement of Dalit Villagers

In villages where Dalits constitute a minority, caste clashes have led to large-scale displacements of Dalit communities. The displacement often follows an attack by neighboring caste Hindu villagers in which Dalits are assaulted and their houses are burned. In some cases, beyond ignoring repeated calls for protection, police have directly aided in the displacement. Dalit fields are then taken over by the majority caste Hindu communities while displaced villagers languish in makeshift homes on government property for months. Aside from distributing nominal amounts in compensation or promising construction of new houses, the local administration does little to ensure that the Dalits are able to return to their homes and fields, or to prosecute those responsible for the attacks. Two examples of displacement are described below.

### Mangapuram

The village of Mangapuram, part of Rajapalayam in Virudhunagar district, once housed 3,000 Thevar and 250 Pallar (Dalit) families. On March 7, 1996, upon returning from a conference organized by Dr. Krishnaswamy, several Pallars were assaulted by Thevars in this village. Following the attack, 150 Pallar houses were set on fire; a Pallar resident of the village was thrown into the fire and burned alive. Soon after the incident the Pallars rebuilt their houses and continued to reside in the village. Tensions in the village increased in May 1997 with the renaming of the transport corporation.[297] Escalating tensions led the Pallars to request police protection in early May 1997. Several police officers were deployed in the area as a result. On May 12, 1997, in renewed violence, Pallars destroyed several Thevar houses; ten were promptly arrested. Thevars retaliated on May 15 by throwing petrol bombs into the Pallar residential area.[298]

On June 9, 1997, Pallar villagers asked the district collector to provide them with adequate protection against future Thevar attacks. The collector was unsympathetic. On June 10, the deputy superintendent of police, a Thevar, attempted to force Pallars out of the village. On the same day, hundreds of Thevar

---

[297]See above. People's Watch, "Caste Clashes in Southern Districts - 1997: A detailed report" (Madurai: 1997), p. 81.
[298]Ibid.

villagers attacked the Pallars and set their houses on fire. As most of their houses had burned to the ground, the Pallars took refuge in nearby villages.[299]

In February 1998 Human Rights Watch visited the area where displaced Pallar families had taken shelter and where they remained eight months after the incident. An area just over three acres in size, literally adjacent to Mangapuram village, housed more than 350 people in 200 poorly constructed huts. An adjoining area housed over 200 people in seventy huts. Families with over four members, many with small children, were made to live in huts approximately thirty-five square feet in size. The small spheres of public space were used for cattle and makeshift latrines. Most families were left without a source of income, and there was little word from the government about returning them to their village. No action was taken against the Thevars responsible for the attacks or against police officials complicit in allowing the displacement to occur. Many villagers still bore scars, which they attributed to lathi attacks by police officers who took part in the displacement.

### Rengappanaikkanpatti

Before 1997 the village of Rengappanaikkanpatti, situated in Virudhunagar district, was a minority-Pallar, majority-Thevar village. The Thevars comprised nearly 400 families. Among the thirty Pallar families who lived there at the time, many owned agricultural lands and brick houses, a clear indication of their relative prosperity and reportedly a motivation for the attack. On June 13, 1996, when Dr. Krishnaswamy visited the village, Thevars threw stones at his vehicle and five days later disconnected street lights and threw bombs into the Pallar settlement. When the incident was reported to the sub-inspector of the Rajakularaman police station, he refused to register the complaint.[300]

On May 12, 1997, the Thevars of Rengappanaikkanpatti, together with Thevars from a nearby village, set fire to Pallar houses. The fire also destroyed farm lands, coconut groves, and motor pumps. After the attack, which lasted four hours, Pallars took refuge in the neighboring village of Sholapuram and asked the

---

[299]Ibid. Asking Pallars to vacate the village rather than taking action against the attackers has led prominent human rights organizations to accuse the DSP of being an "agent" of the Thevars. Human Rights Watch interview, Virudhunagar district, Tamil Nadu, February 15, 1998.

[300]Human Rights Watch interview, Virudhunagar district, Tamil Nadu, February 15, 1998; People's Watch, "Caste Clashes in Southern Districts - 1997...," p. 82.

government to provide them with housing facilities.[301] Human Rights Watch spoke to members of a family of eleven who were still residing on government property in Sholapuram village nine months after the attack. Dharmalingam, the seventy-five-year-old head of the family, stated:

> Nearly twenty houses were burned down. We were an easy target because we were a minority in the village. Only three houses were spared. Our house is still there; it's very strong. They stole the motor pump set and motor oil from the garden... We cannot go back to our house, they will beat us. We have our own field, four acres in all. But we won't go to the house. We had six rooms, a kitchen and a common room. Now look at us.[302]

At the time of the interviews, the family lived in a community hall that earlier had sheltered thirty Pallar families for the village. Valliamai, Dharmalingam's sixty-five-year-old wife, lamented, "We had such a big house but see our fate now. One of my grandsons is handicapped. The government had to give him a new wheelchair; even that they damaged."[303] Although the government gave the family Rs. 10,000 (US$250) in compensation, the amount covered very little of what they had lost. Dharmalingam registered a complaint with the police, but they did not take any action. The sub-inspector of the police station, a member of the Thevar community and the same officer who refused to register earlier complaints by Pallars against Thevars, instead filed a case against Dharmalingam, charging him with setting fire to the houses himself in order to bring false charges against others. Dharmalingam was held at the police station for four days.

At the time of our visit to the site, the family was building a house using their own funds; only people who lost thatch houses were given new ones. The others were told to return to the village. "But how can we go back?" Dharmalingam asked. His nineteen-year-old grandson, Dharmaraj, believed that the Thevars were threatened by the prosperity of their Dalit neighbors and were trying to take Pallar lands for themselves:

---

[301]Ibid.

[302]Human Rights Watch interview with Dharmalingam, Virudhunagar district, Tamil Nadu, February 15, 1998.

[303]Human Rights Watch interview with Valliamai, Virudhunagar district, Tamil Nadu, February 15, 1998.

Thevars had no lands. All thirty Dalit families had lands. In all houses one or two people from Dalit houses went to government postings [jobs]. They were jealous... We live on fertile lands. We had government postings so they were jealous. Most of us did not use reservations. We got it on our own merit.[304]

Displaced Pallar families have also been unable to cultivate the lands they left behind. As Dharmaraj explained, "After the rainy season we put paddy [rice] on the fields; but they are damaging our fields and don't let us go there. We put paddy again, but again they damaged it. They scold us whenever we go. They let loose their own cattle in the field. There is no police protection at all."[305] Despite the numerous attacks on Pallars in this area, the police have continually failed to heed calls for protection. If there were police protection, Dharmalingam argued, they would be able to go back to their house and their land. Instead, he said: "Whenever the police come to the village, they go to the Thevar area. The Thevars gave them chicken and other good meals. The sub-inspector belongs to the Thevar community, and most others also belong to that community."[306]

### Police Raids in the Southern Districts

In the aftermath of clashes in the southern districts, and under the guise of seeking out firearms and militant activists, police forces numbering in the hundreds conducted raids in Dalit villages. The pattern of the raids consisted of arbitrary arrests and assaults on Dalit men and women and often included looting and destruction of property. In some cases, police removed their badge numbers so villagers would not be able to identify and file cases against them.[307] Studies conducted by the Tamil Nadu Commission for Scheduled Castes and Scheduled Tribes in various southern district villages concluded that attacks on these villages were motivated by a desire to cripple Dalits economically by targeting obvious symbols of their newfound wealth. In an interview with Human Rights Watch, R. Balakrishnan, director of the commission, described the results of one such study:

---

[304]Human Rights Watch interview with Dharmaraj, Virudhunagar district, Tamil Nadu, February 15, 1998.
[305]Ibid.
[306]Human Rights Watch interview, Virudhunagar district, Tamil Nadu, February 15, 1998.
[307]Human Rights Watch interview with People's Watch, Bangalore, July 25, 1998.

I have done a study in Kodiyankulum and found that the theme of that attack was economy. Fans, TV sets, and blenders were broken. All signs of wealth earned from the Gulf were destroyed. They said they would break the economy and put them [Pallars] ten years back.[308]

The pattern of these police attacks was established with the raid on Kodiyankulum village in 1995.

### Kodiyankulum

Since 1980 the Dalits of Kodiyankulum village, in Tuticorin district, have benefited from the flow of funds from family members employed in Dubai, Kuwait, and the United States.[309] On August 31, 1995, a 600-member police force attacked the all-Dalit village in the presence of the superintendent of police and the district collector[310] and destroyed property worth hundreds of thousands of rupees.[311] In what appeared to be a premeditated attack, police destroyed consumer durables such as televisions, fans, tape-recorders, sewing machines, bicycles, agricultural implements, tractors and lorries, and also demolished food grain storages.  They made a bonfire of clothes and burned the passports and testimonials[312] of educated Dalit youth. The village post office was targeted,[313] and police allegedly poisoned the only village well.[314] A village elder claimed that "all through the operation, the policemen were showering abuse on us and made derogatory references to our caste, which only showed their deep-rooted

---

[308]Human Rights Watch interview with R. Balakrishnan, Madras, February 12, 1998.

[309]S. Viswanathan, "A village ruined: In Tamil Nadu, when the police went berserk," *Frontline*, September 20, 1995.

[310]People's Union for Civil Liberties, "Final Report of the PUCL-Tamil Nadu Team...," p. 2.

[311]Viswanathan, "A village ruined...," *Frontline*.

[312]Testimonials are documents attesting to one's educational and/or caste status. Without testimonials, it is difficult to gain access to jobs and government positions reserved for scheduled-caste members.

[313]Viswanathan, "A village ruined...," *Frontline*.

[314]V. R. Mani, "Centre seeks report on the police atrocities on Dalits," *The Sunday Times of India*, December 3, 1995.

prejudice."[315]  District collector Paneerselvam, accused of leading the raid, was subsequently transferred to Madras.[316]

The stated purpose of the raid was to capture Dalits allegedly involved in the murder of three Thevars in a nearby village two days earlier.[317] Many suspect that it was the "relative affluence of the Dalits that attracted the attention of the uniformed men. The idea, it appears, was to destroy their economic base, because the police feel the Kodiyankulum Dalits provide moral and material support to the miscreants in surrounding areas."[318]

Similar raids have taken place during the southern district clashes. Punduthai, a forty-five-year-old Pallar widow of Thevar-dominated Vanaltaiparam village, was stripped of all her valuables. At the time of the caste riots, "They entered the house and took all house things, dresses and everything. We kept quiet. We didn't say anything. If we said something we would get beaten or they would set fire to the house." Since the riots, Punduthai and her two children have relocated to a Pallar-dominant village.[319]  Two other clash-related raids are described below.

### Gundupatti

On February 26, 1998, in the village of Gundupatti, Dindigul district, some one hundred policemen and thirty policewomen, along with four truckloads of unidentified men thought to be affiliated with the ruling Dravida Munnetra Kazhagam (DMK) party, attacked Dalits and bonded laborers residing in two villages in Kookal Panchayat, a remote area of the Kodaikanal hills. Attackers reportedly looted and destroyed property and assaulted residents, including women, children and elderly persons. Kerosene was poured into stored food grains and grocery items. The attackers, including police personnel, reportedly urinated in cooking vessels. According to a local human rights organization, women were kicked and beaten, their clothing was torn, and police forced sticks and iron pipes into their mouths. The police attack, whose victims were predominantly women,

---

[315]Viswanathan, "A village ruined...," *Frontline.*
[316]The district collector of Tirunelveli district, also affected by the 1995 clashes, was also transferred. "TN caste clashes spark exodus," *The Telegraph*, December 20, 1995.
[317]Mani, "Centre seeks report...," *The Sunday Times of India.*
[318]Ibid. By "miscreants," the writer was referring to militant activists.
[319]Human Rights Watch interview, Madurai, February 18, 1998.

was apparently in retaliation for a decision made by residents of the Kookal Panchayat to boycott the national parliamentary elections.[320]

After conducting its own investigation into the incident, the National Commission for Women, a government agency, issued an enquiry report on the Gundupatti case. The report concluded that the police "took sides with a political faction," that the criminal force used against women was unwarranted, and that the actions of the police "ha[d] not advanced beyond the colonial concept of power and the subjects."[321]

> The police had a field day breaking open houses, pulling out people, beating them up and even violating their modesty, using criminal force on women and girls, pulling out their *mangla sutras* [marriage necklaces], abusing them with filthy language. They allegedly dragged women and arrested sixteen of them along with nine men. One woman's baby was thrown while they were starting off with their truck. The whole village made many entreaties to the police and then alone the child was allowed to be taken by the mother. In this state of terror and panic, one of the young pregnant women had a miscarriage on the road itself.[322]

The twenty-five men and women were then beaten in the police station and sent to jail after being taken before a magistrate. They remained in prison for

---

[320]Human Rights Watch telephone interview with People's Watch, March 1998; National Commission for Women, *National Commission for Women Enquiry Report on Gundupatti Case of Dindigul District, Tamil Nadu* (New Delhi: Government of India, 1998). The "boycott election" campaign is common to agrarian struggles throughout India, including the Naxalite movement in Andhra Pradesh. Those advocating the boycott see no political value in voting and do not believe that change can be brought about through the election process. Boycott campaigns have often resulted in violent reactions by governments that are afraid of losing large numbers of votes. In Andhra Pradesh in the early 1990s, the government brought in increasing numbers of police and paramilitary forces with each successive election, to intimidate the citizenry into voting. The pattern reached its climax during the 1994 Andhra Pradesh assembly elections when the government moved in paramilitary forces numbering in the tens of thousands to send the message that everyone must vote, regardless of the party they chose. "Political Campaigns," in *30 years of Naxalbari*, www.blythe.org/mlm/misc/india/cpiml/pwg/30years/part9.htm.

[321]National Commission for Women, *Enquiry Report on Gundupatti....*

[322]Ibid.

nearly a month. The People's Watch activist who initially brought this case to the attention of the National Commission for Women was later charged with dacoity.[323] In early September 1998 the One Man Commission of Enquiry appointed by the government of Tamil Nadu submitted its report on police excess to the state's chief minister. The report suggested compensation to the victims.

### Desikapuram

The same pattern of destruction was apparent during a raid on Desikapuram village in Virudhunagar district in June 1997. The arrest of Dalit leader Dr. Krishnaswamy on May 2, 1997 led to a staged roadblock by the village population, composed entirely of Pallars. On May 22 protesters were confronted by some 1,000 police officers, many of whom then proceeded to enter the village and search the houses. According to a People's Watch report, "The police had entered the village in the name of 'search,' damaged the houses and looted the jewels, money, watches and whatever they could pick up."[324] The next morning, some officers entered the village and demanded a total of Rs. 15,000 (US$375) from residents. On June 22, Thevar Peravai leader Dr. Sethuraman led a procession of eighteen cars, nineteen vans and several trucks through the affected areas. Two jeeps followed by a busload of police were also part of the procession. When the procession passed through Desikapuram, both sides started throwing stones at one another. The fighting escalated as Thevars began throwing sickles and setting fire to haystacks while Pallars damaged the Thevar vans with stones.[325]

Around 3:00 p.m. the police raided the village. Many villagers, including a total of nineteen women, were arrested during the raid: fifteen women were held for fifteen days and four for twenty-nine. Many of the men and women suffered fractured arms and legs as a result of the attack. In February 1998 Human Rights Watch spoke to villagers about their confrontations with the police. Muniamal, a forty-year-old agricultural laborer and mother of four, spoke to Human Rights Watch about the manner in which the police entered the village and the villagers' homes:

> They made a circle and surrounded the entire village. There were nearly a thousand or more. They entered the village. We locked our doors.

---

[323]Human Rights Watch interview with activist, Bangalore, July 25, 1998. Dacoity is defined under Indian Penal Code Section 391 as robbery committed by five or more persons.
[324]People's Watch, "Caste Clashes in Southern Districts - 1997...," p. 84.
[325]Ibid, p. 85.

They broke down the doors of my neighbor's house, where I was at the time. Nearly ten police entered my house. They broke the trunk that contained all our valuables. They took all the dresses and threw them out. My daughter's gold earrings, anklets of silver, my husband's watch, a chain and a ring, and a total of four pounds of gold. I went to my house and saw all the damage. The tube lights were damaged as was the fan.[326]

The police then arrested Muniamal in her house and demanded that she leave her four-year-old son behind. She refused, so they took her son as well. "They used vulgar words, caste names like *podivadi* and *pallachi* [caste name for prostitute]... Using a lathi they hit me on my thigh, shoulder, and on my back. I had big bruises."[327] Muniamal spent the night at the Rajapalayam North police station. She was given only ointment for her wounds, and not permitted to see a doctor. The next morning both men and women were taken by bus to the Rajapalayam government hospital. Although the men were treated for fractures, the women did not receive any treatment. The women were then taken to the Siviputur magistrate court, and the men were taken to Madurai central jail. They were charged collectively under the Tamil Nadu Public Properties (Prevention of) Destruction Act, 1992, and under Indian Penal Code sections 147 (rioting), 148 (rioting with a deadly weapon), 324 (causing hurt with dangerous weapons), and 307 (attempted murder). The public property charge was allegedly for setting fire to a Thevar van earlier in the day. Several eyewitnesses reported, however, that the police themselves had set the van on fire:

They blamed us for the van. We all saw that the police did it. I spent fifteen days in jail with my son. The one night we spent at the police station they gave no food, only water. They used vulgar words and beat me again with a lathi. They also beat us in the bus from the hospital to the magistrate, and then from the magistrate to the jail. The men went to Madurai central jail and the women to Nillakoti jail, which is far away. In the bus they threatened us, saying, "Do not tell anyone the police beat you. If you tell anyone, the Nillakoti jail will not accept you

---

[326]Human Rights Watch interview with Muniamal, Virudhunagar district, Tamil Nadu, February 15, 1998.
[327]Ibid.

and you will have to go to Trichi jail," which is very far away. So I was afraid and said nothing.[328]

Thirty-year-old Irulayee was also sent to jail with one of her three children:[329]

When they arrested me they grabbed me by my hair and dragged me out of the house. I have scars on my forearms and knees from the lathi beatings. Three police beat me and used vulgar caste language. I was beaten in my home, at the police station, and on the bus. I spent fifteen days in jail with my two-year-old daughter.[330]

In the same village, a twenty-five-year-old agricultural laborer described how the police took her daughter's earrings, three rings, and Rs. 300 [US$7.50] after breaking down her door.[331] She, too, was arrested:

I had to leave my children, a four-year-old girl who is still breast-feeding, and my eight-year-old boy. To get us on and off the bus to the police station, they shoved their lathis into our stomachs and backs. I was in jail for thirty-one days, sixteen days extra because of a technical mistake.[332]

An eighteen-year-old student named Muniamal, one of the few literate residents of the village, was punished for questioning the police as they were arresting women:

It was Sunday, so I was home from school. On the street a twenty-year-old girl named Ladha was arrested. I saw it happen and asked my neighbor why they were arresting women. The police shouted, "*Karuvachi,*" which means black girl. I said, "Don't call me that." He started using more vulgar words. He said, "What a bold pallachi

---

[328]Ibid.
[329]Ibid.
[330]Human Rights Watch interview with Irulayee, Virudhunagar district, Tamil Nadu, February 15, 1998.
[331]Human Rights Watch interview, Virudhunagar district, Tamil Nadu, February 15, 1998. Most women in the village earned only Rs. 15 (US$0.38) for a full day's work.
[332]Ibid.

[prostitute]!" I pleaded with him not to arrest me. I said, "I have to go to school tomorrow sir." They used the same vulgar words. "Why are you pallachis studying?" He then tied my hair to another girl's hair, Guruammal, she's fifteen. Then they started beating us on our backs with their lathis. I begged them to leave and not arrest us. My headmaster, Karnakaraj of the government higher secondary school, asked the police to release me. Still I was taken to the police station. Again I was beaten. They pulled off half my sari.[333]

Munusu, a twenty-five-year-old agricultural laborer who owned small amounts of land in the area, explained that he was looted twice, once by the Thevars earlier in the day and again by the police in the afternoon:

All people behind the [Thevar] procession came into the village. They damaged the houses, set fire, and looted the properties. The police were also there. Then at 11:00 a.m. they left. Then around 3:00 p.m. the police alone came... They surrounded the village and entered into the houses. They damaged the radios, fans, televisions, and took gold chains and other valuables.[334]

Munusu was also beaten and arrested by the police. He spoke to Human Rights Watch about his ill-treatment in custody:

I ran into my house and locked the doors and entrance. Nearly ten people were in my house. They pulled us all out and beat us with lathis. I sustained a fracture in my right leg. They put us in a police van and took us to Rajapalayam North police station. We stayed overnight. We got no food between 6:00 p.m. and 8:00 a.m. We were also beaten at the police station. Because my injury was serious, they did not beat us overnight, but then started again in the morning. Then they took five of us to the hospital. We did not get proper treatment. Then we were taken to court at 11:00 a.m. I couldn't walk, so I stayed in the vehicle.

---

[333]Human Rights Watch interview with Muniamal, Virudhunagar district, Tamil Nadu, February 15, 1998.
[334]Human Rights Watch interview with Munusu, Virudhunagar district, Tamil Nadu, February 15, 1998.

The magistrate had to come out to the van; everyone was covered with blood. I said, "We didn't do anything, and still the police beat us."[335]

Upon recording their statement, the magistrate remanded them to Madurai central jail at 3:00 p.m. They were not able to eat the food brought by their relatives until the morning after. Munusu described what he termed an "admission beat" upon entering jail:

> I waited in front of the jail gate from 3:00 p.m. to 7:30 p.m. The Madurai jail police were told that we indulged in violence and that we were from the Pallar community, so they beat us too. It was an admission beat. The police took two at a time into the latrine and beat us again with their lathis. They put everyone in jail except us five. We were taken to the hospital. We became unconscious from the beating. I had blood clots in my right leg.[336]

Munusu remained in the accident ward for six days and then in the hospital's jail ward for nine. After spending three further days in the central jail, he was released on bail with the help of a human rights organization. He required care in the Virudhunagar government hospital for the next two months. The district collector awarded him Rs. 15,000 (US$375) as relief, but no action was taken against the police.[337]

Fifty-year-old Kaddar Karai also recounted his experience in custody, which left him permanently disabled:

> They took us in a van to the police station. While I was getting down from the van they beat me on my right leg and arm with the back of their guns. There is now a metal plate with eight bolts in my leg. They also fractured bones on the right side of my forearm. I fell down immediately, and they carried me to the police station. My leg was completely broken.[338]

---

[335]Ibid.
[336]Ibid.
[337]Ibid.
[338]Human Rights Watch interview with Kaddar Karai, Virudhunagar district, Tamil Nadu, February 15, 1998.

Human Rights Watch viewed an x-ray of Kaddar Karai's shattered leg and the bolts that were keeping it in place. Despite the severity of his injures, he was kept at the police station overnight.

> I received no medicine and no water. I kept bleeding. In the morning I went to Rajapalayam hospital. They gave me a simple bandage but no treatment. The police took me to court. I stayed in the van. We were then sent to central jail. That night I was taken to the government hospital along with four others.[339]

Kaddar Karai remained in the hospital for seventy days. He is no longer able to walk or move from his cot without assistance. He received Rs. 15,000 (US$375) from the collector, but no action was taken against the police.[340]

In an interview with Human Rights Watch, Dr. N. Sethuraman, leader of the Thevar procession that instigated the attack, claimed that Desikapuram is a center for militant activity.

> These Dalit islands are used for anti-social activities like manufacturing bombs and militant training for unemployed youngsters. They hide culprits so the police cannot enter. If police want to enter they have to do it in the thousands. The police are not practicing tactical methods. They are brutal but not clever.[341]

The police's behavior during the raids was not indicative of a systematic search for armed activists. Rather, the attacks and assaults were characterized by large-scale destruction of property, leading many NGOs and government officials to believe that attacks by the Thevar-dominated police were motivated by personal caste affiliations.[342] As of December 1998 no action had been taken to prosecute the police responsible for these attacks.

---

[339]Ibid.
[340]Ibid.
[341]Human Rights Watch interview with Dr. N. Sethuraman, Madurai district, Tamil Nadu, February 18, 1998.
[342]Human Rights Watch interviews with People's Watch, Dalit Panthers of India, Government of Tamil Nadu Tribal Welfare Department, Tamil Nadu State Commission for Scheduled Castes and Scheduled Tribes, and Tamil Nadu State Human Rights Commission, in Madras and Madurai, Tamil Nadu, February 1998.

### Violence Against Dalit Women During the Southern District Clashes

Sexual oppression is intimately connected to land oppression. By keeping lower-caste women sexually subjugated, the upper castes control the men.

— Father Manuel Alphonse, All India Catholic University Federation (AICUF)[343]

As Dalit men migrate to cities in search of jobs, women are left to work as agricultural laborers in rural areas. Women "bear the brunt of attacks because they are stuck in these feudal arrangements."[344] As a result of escalating caste clashes, attacks on Dalit women, by state and private actors, have also escalated.

### Violence by private actors

On January 25, 1998, the Dalit colony of Veludavur village in Villapuram district was attacked by members of seven caste Hindu villages. The attack was allegedly perpetrated by the Vanniya caste and instigated by the Naidars (both backward castes). Tensions began with a government auction of common properties in the village, such as ponds and tamarind trees; the Dalits were demanding their right to participate. The same evening, Vanniyas entered and destroyed 400 Dalit huts. Many of the young Dalit men were in Andhra Pradesh at the time, cultivating sugarcane. Only women, children and the elderly were left

---

[343] Human Rights Watch interview, Madras, February 13, 1998.

[344] Human Rights Watch interview with Nicholas, an activist overseeing 120 villages for the Integrated Rural Development Society, a nongovernmental organization, Madras, February 14, 1998. The sexual abuse of Dalit women and girls is not limited to agricultural settings. In Villapuram district, close to fifty-eight stone quarry factories employ a majority of Dalit women between the ages of fifteen and twenty. Many come from miles away in search of employment. They work a minimum of twelve hours in day and night shifts; women and girls working at night are particularly vulnerable to attacks by factory owners and their sons: "Some are given concessions for performing sexually, they are given less work. Women are raped every night, but they don't talk about it, they have to get married later on. Dalit boys also work in these factories. They see what happens but are unable to oppose it." Human Rights Watch interview with S. Martin, Village Community Development Society, Madras, February 13, 1998.

in the village, and the women were particularly targeted. A social worker in the village claimed that there were "sexual attempts on many women, but they don't want to talk about it. Many are unmarried or their husbands are away. They fear the consequences if these things are revealed."[345] Over 700 families were displaced as a result of the attack. They took shelter in neighboring villages.[346]

Burnad Fatima of the Tamil Nadu Women's Forum (TNWF) explained the number of cases TNWF had come across in which women were targets of caste clashes:

> Any time any caste riots take place, there is immediate action against women and immediate raping. During last year's riots, a forty-year-old woman was gang raped. A seventy-year-old was dragged out of her house and stripped. In Anchipet a handicapped girl was thrown from her wheelchair which was then damaged. Innocent women are butchered, raped, and killed even though they are not directly responsible for any of the riots.[347]

TNWF and People's Watch members went on to describe another attack during the southern district clashes, and the lack of press attention to such cases:

> In Nammakal [district] a girl was gang raped, murdered, and then butchered. She belonged to the scavengers community.[348] The men belonged to the weaving community. They cut off her hand and leg and shaved her head. They then cut her head and put a stick into her private parts and then hung her head with the stick. Why are they driven to this extent? Because for them Dalits are nothing. They give

---

[345]Human Rights Watch interview with Nicholas of Integrated Rural Development Society, Madras, February 14, 1998. Nicholas organizes Dalits in the village. The key facts of this case have been investigated and independently verified by People's Watch whose findings corroborate our own.

[346]Ibid.

[347]Human Rights Watch interview with Burnad Fatima, Madras, February 14, 1998. TNWF has submitted cases to the National Commission for Women, the National Human Rights Commission, and the National Commission for Scheduled Castes and Scheduled Tribes.

[348]The term "scavengers" refers to those employed privately and by the state to clear feces from public and private latrines and carry them to dumping grounds and disposal sites. Scavengers also dispose of dead animals. For more on the practice of manual scavenging, see Chapter VII.

more respect to their animals... The papers are censored, they don't name the community, and they don't report the figures.[349]

A representative of the Rural Center for Women's Development in Tirunelveli district spoke to Human Rights Watch of instances of rape by landlords, other upper castes, and the police, "who always support the landlords... [W]omen never say anything because they are afraid and need employment. Also society would blame them. Even their husband would separate from them. I see it daily."[350]

Punduthai, a forty-five-year-old widow and mother of two, told Human Rights Watch that she had to leave her village to protect herself and her daughter from sexual abuse by Thevar men during the clashes.

In the village, the Thevars entered the house and had sexual intercourse with the Dalit women. They used force and committed rape. My husband died, so if I had stayed then the same things would happen to me. My daughter is also a mature girl. She is twenty years old. I was also worried about my daughter. I can't arrange her marriage. I left all the lands. This is the regular lot of the dominated persons. If there are any riots then all of them jointly rape; they gang rape. I hid in the hills at the time of the riots. We were afraid of these things, so we left.[351]

In November 1997 a twenty-two-year-old Dalit woman spoke up against the debt bondage of her husband and his family (Thevars are the dominant moneylenders and Dalits their primary borrowers).[352] As a result she was brutally beaten and sexually abused by a Vanniya landlord:

Her husband and father-in-law did not go to work for two days. The landlord came and asked why. He threatened and insulted her, and she

---

[349]Human Rights Watch interviews with TNWF and People's Watch, Madras, February 14, 1998.

[350]Human Rights Watch interview, Tirunelveli district, Tamil Nadu, February 17, 1998. The representative wished to remain anonymous.

[351]Human Rights Watch interview with Punduthai, Madurai, Tamil Nadu, February 18, 1998.

[352]Jayaraj Sivan, "Thevar-Dalit caste wars haunt southern TN," *Indian Express*, October 7, 1997.

said, "We are not living here under your mercy." The landlord went wild. He started beating her, he tore her blouse to pieces, touched her breast, hit her in the vagina and rolled her on the ground. There was no one to stop him.[353]

Due to disinterest, ignorance of proper procedure, or their own caste biases, the police failed to register or properly investigate many cases of attacks against women during the clashes. Only with pressure from organized women's and human rights groups has the issue been placed before national commissions. The recommendations of these commissions, however, are not binding under statutory law.

### Police torture of women/custodial violence

In addition to attacks by members of the upper castes, women are attacked by the police, security forces, and private militias or armies hired by Thevars.[354] Human Rights Watch spoke to many government officials, activists, and villagers in the Tamil Nadu region about police torture and custodial violence against women. C. V. Shankar, director for the Adi Dravida Tribal Welfare Department, of the state government of Tamil Nadu, explained:

We found that women are put in front in both communities and act as a buffer. This has resulted in police action against women. They are taken far away from their homes. Unless they were directly involved in violence, they should not be arrested. In some cases we felt that the arrests could have been avoided.[355]

H. Hanumanthappa, then-chairman of the National Commission for Scheduled Castes and Scheduled Tribes, added:

Once the police start raiding, the menfolk run away. Then they [police] make women the victims. The procedure they adopt is to take the child

---

[353]Human Rights Watch interview with S. Martin, Village Community Development Society, Madras, February 13, 1998.

[354]Human Rights Watch interview with Burnad Fatima of Tamil Nadu Women's Forum, Madras, February 14, 1998. See also Chapter IV for attacks on women by private militias in Bihar.

[355]Human Rights Watch interview with C. V. Shankar, Madras, February 13, 1998.

or wife so that the men come back. They feel that they are the masters of the situation. It has resulted in mass rapes.[356]

The police practice of taking family members as hostages in order to force their relatives to turn themselves in is a common occurrence in Tamil Nadu and other parts of the country.[357] Specific incidents of hostage-taking and custodial violence against women are described below.

Guruswamy Guruammal, a twenty-six-year-old agricultural laborer, suffered a miscarriage as a result of brutal beatings during a police raid on December 2, 1997. She is a resident of Chilaumbotti village of the southern district of Theni and earns Rs. 20 a day (US$0.50). The raid had preceded a planned visited by Dr. Krishanaswamy; posters had been distributed to announce his arrival. On December 2, one such poster was burned by Thevars in the district which led to a Pallar protest and road block. Police raided the village in response to the protests and assaulted many Dalits with their lathis.

> At 9:00 a.m. the police lathi-charged the villagers. Superintendent of Police Rajesh Das called me a pallachi, which is a caste name for prostitute. He then opened his pant zip. Sub-Inspector Arivanandam, who is from same community as me, was also there. Rajesh Das said, "Please stand, do not go," and other police scolded me. At 11:00 a.m. the sub-collector came. I told the collector that the superintendent of police had opened his zip and used a vulgar word. I also told him that they had broken my silver pot. The sub-collector said, "You go, I will deal with him." Das was angry that I had pointed him out.[358]

The police, numbering in the hundreds, returned early the next morning and again lathi-charged the village.

> They broke all the doors and arrested all the men in the village. Arivanandam and Rajesh Das said, "Where is Guruammal's house?" My husband hid under the cot. My mother was with me at the time. I

---

[356]Human Rights Watch interview with H. Hanumanthappa, New Delhi, March 10, 1998.
[357]Asia Watch (now Human Rights Watch), *Punjab in Crisis: Human Rights in India* (New York: Human Rights Watch, 1991), p. 36.
[358]Human Rights Watch interview with Guruswamy Guruammal, Madurai, February 18, 1998.

was in my night clothes. The police started calling me a prostitute. I replied, "Your wife is a prostitute." They beat me. I was four months pregnant at the time. He pulled me naked on the road for one hundred feet. I got injuries on my legs. There were two elderly witnesses, a woman and my grandfather. The police also beat the woman when she asked them to stop dragging me. She is sixty years old; her hand was fractured. There were two men police and two lady police. They brought me to the police van and took me to the office of the Theni superintendent of police. Fifty-three men had been arrested. One of them took off his *lungi* [wrap-around cloth] and gave it to me to cover myself. He was only wearing shorts after that.[359]

Guruammal begged the police at the station to help her. She explained that she was pregnant and in need of medical attention. In response, they called her names and mocked her for making such bold statements the day before. Eventually, Guruammal was transferred to the Trichi jail hospital, where she remained for twenty-five days. After ten days, she had a miscarriage. At the time of the interview, and as a result of being dragged and beaten by the police fists and guns, Guruammal was still visibly scarred on her neck, arms, legs, and abdomen.

She claimed that the police told her to testify that the raid on her village was in search of the illicit brewing of *arrack* (illicit liquor):

They said if you accept the fact that the raid was for arrack, then you will be released. They said, "If you don't say arrack, we will file charges against you." So these are the cases that were filed against me and the fifty-three men.[360]

Although Guruammal was attacked as punishment for speaking up against the police, many other women are punished for alleged crimes committed by their male

---

[359]Ibid.

[360]Ibid. According to press reports and human rights activists in the region, the southern districts are "believed to be dens of illicit liquor. The trade ensures a lucrative amount not only for the sellers but the police too. The Thevars... are the master of the trade in these districts. They engage Dalits for distilling arrack. The police-Thevars nexus ensures that the Dalits remain exploited. And any revolt is taken care of." Mayank Mishra, "Victims of dual oppression," *Business Standard* (Calcutta), December 28, 1995.

relatives. Activists from People's Watch and the Tamil Nadu Women's Forum explained the tactics employed by the police:

> The police enter houses and attack the women even though they should never search when the women are alone. The police are arresting women if either the husband or son is absconding. They take them into custody and rape them. Three years ago, in a slum nearby, a forty-three-year-old woman lost her husband. Her son was involved in a murder case. She was arrested along with her daughter and daughter-in-law. They were taken to the police station where the police raped the mother in front of the other women. They then brought her home and burned her in her hut.[361]

The activists also described a new tactic employed by the police of removing women's clothes and beating them from their knees to their shoulders, "because they know that women will not show others these parts."[362]

At a Madras conference on women's rights, held on April 28 and 29, 1995, dozens of Dalit and tribal women publicly came forward to testify about their experiences of custodial rape at the hands of Tamil Nadu police. The conference was sponsored by the Tamil Nadu Women's Forum and Asia Pacific Forum for Women, Law and Development. In many of the statements, women claimed that the police were searching for their male relatives when they first came upon them.

Pursuant to Section 160 of the Criminal Procedure Code, police conducting investigations are prohibited from questioning female witnesses at any place other than their residence. Women are often unaware of these laws, and their ignorance is exploited by the police. As she stated at the women's rights conference, Rangammal of Orathanadu village came into contact with the police when her husband was repeatedly arrested for selling arrack. One night, the police came to her house and forcibly took her to the police station.

> They said I should not be going home at that time and dragged me into the room, and three of them raped me repeatedly. I lost consciousness.

---

[361]Human Rights Watch interview with Burnad Fatima of Tamil Nadu Women's Forum, Madras, February 14, 1998.
[362]Ibid.

In the morning they allowed me to go with a warning that I should not reveal anything. Due to fear I remained silent.[363]

Vijaya from Coimbatore was approached by the police late in the night:

When I demanded to know where I was being taken, the police answered that I was providing food for [my brother] Vellaiyan... Since Vellaiyan was related to us the police caught hold [of] us like that... Later, one after another, five of them raped me repeatedly. I was unable to bear the pain since I was also a small girl... [T]he policemen said that I was pretending pain and I would even bear with another ten persons.[364]

The police had also taken Vijaya's parents into custody. "The police said if I promised not to reveal anything to anyone, they would release my parents, and I agreed to it."[365] Together with her aunt and mother, Vijaya arrived at the Anathapuram police station the next day.

The Sub-Inspector on duty was Krishnamoorthy. He said at least the Pondicherry police had raped and left [me] alive, if he telephoned the Dharmapuri police [they] would rape me and throw me [in] the canal... When we pleaded that we were uneducated and without any jobs, mostly engaged in manual works and needed justice, the Sub-Inspector threatened that he would have us beaten up if we further spoke. We had no other alternative but to return to the village.[366]

With the help of civil liberties groups, Vijaya approached the police again. After some days, she added, "women police took me to a doctor. They explained to the doctor that I was of low character, a prostitute, that I was spreading rumours to prevent the arrest of my brothers, etc. They then advised the doctor not to take my case serious[ly]."[367] Vijaya's family was soon approached by the police and

---

[363]Tamil Nadu Women's Forum, "First Day: Sharing by victims of violence," Conference on Women's Rights, April 28, 29, 1995, Madras, p. 15.
[364]Ibid., p. 2.
[365]Ibid., p. 5.
[366]Ibid., p. 6.
[367]Ibid., p. 7.

offered Rs. 150,000 (US$3,750) to drop the case. She did not accept the money. The police charged Vijaya's father with theft and took him into custody for ten days. He claimed that he was tortured, while the police claimed that Vijaya was threatening the police with a false case of rape so that her father would be released. Because none of the villagers were willing to step forward as witnesses, Vijaya was unable to pursue her case.[368]

In the village of Muthaandikuppam, South Arcot district, a husband filed a complaint against his wife, Vasantha, after a misunderstanding between the couple. On the night of March 21, 1994, Vasantha was forced to spend the night in the police station under the pretext that there were no women police available to escort her home. She was "gang raped by four constables and a sub-inspector of the same police station and [then] murdered. They attempted to dispose [of] the body but could not succeed. They spread a rumour that Vasantha committed suicide by hanging from the fan at the police rest room in the police station."[369] Community members, civil liberties groups, and political parties demanded appropriate, severe sanctions against the perpetrators. The Tamil Nadu government responded by temporarily suspending the constables involved.[370]

On February 21, 1995, twenty-year-old Poonkothai witnessed the rape and murder of her forty-eight-year-old mother by police who were searching for her brother. The incident took place around 7:00 a.m. when police arrived at Poonkothai's house looking for her brother Murthy: "They blamed my mother [for] hiding the whereabouts of my brother, who is suspected in a murder of a person found dead... near his house." Despite her mother's repeated denials, the police took both of them, along with Poonkothai's one-and-a-half-year-old daughter, to the Vannarapettai police station.

> We were beaten up severely and were tortured with abusive words and
> brutal attacks... One of the senior personnel ordered the others to use
> the "Punjab method" to elicit facts from my mother. They stripped my
> mother in front of me and took her inside... I repeatedly heard my
> mother groaning and pleading them not to torture her... With tears she
> was telling me that four men gang raped her and tortured her by

---

[368]Ibid., pp. 9-10.
[369]Ibid., p. 22. The testimony was given by Tamil Nadu Women's Forum.
[370]Ibid., pp. 22-23.

inserting the lathi in the vagina and beat[ing] her in her private parts.[371]

The police later brought her mother home, stuffed a piece of cloth in her mouth, poured petrol over her, and set her on fire. They left the scene soon thereafter. A neighbor intervened and took the mother to the hospital, where she later died. When Poonkothai's husband approached the police station to file a case, the police registered the death as a suicide. After many NGO protests, the police filed a First Information Report (FIR). Poonkothai's two neighbors, whose sons were also police suspects, and her two sisters-in-law were also taken into custody for several days and similarly tortured. One sister-in-law had just delivered a child.[372]

A report produced by the women's conference stated: "The drama usually played by police is just this. They come in search of the offenders and finding them absconding, whisk away the womenfolk to the police station and outrage their modesty."[373] The conference also concluded that atrocities committed on women by the police were increasing.[374]

**Renewed Clashes**

From October to December 1998, violent confrontations in the districts of Ramanathapuram, Pudukkottai, Perambalur, and Cuddalore signaled that caste clashes had not only continued but had spread to once-peaceful districts. In Ramanathapuram district, Thevars responded to a state-wide Dalit conference by organizing a rally on October 4, 1998. That afternoon, streams of lorries carrying Thevar youths were seen heading toward Ramanathapuram. On the way, several vehicles stopped at roadside villages and Thevars entered Dalit and Muslim hamlets throwing petrol bombs and ransacking houses. Two women were killed. Thevar youths claimed that they were provoked, allegedly by Dalits placing

---

[371]Ibid., p. 27.
[372]Ibid., pp. 28-29.
[373]Tamil Nadu Women's Forum, "Report of the Conference on Women's Rights are Human Rights at Madras, April 28-29, 1995," (Madras), p. 12.
[374]S. Viswanathan, "Caste-based mobilisation and violence," *Frontline*, November 6, 1998. Attacks on women to demoralize whole communities are not limited to Dalits. A woman interviewed by Human Rights Watch testified that when the police were looking for two of the four Thevar men who had raped her, they brought the two men's mothers into the police station: "The two accused had run away to Kerala. When both found out that their mothers were in this situation, they came back and surrendered." Human Rights Watch interview, Tirunelveli district, Tamil Nadu, February 17, 1998.

barriers on the road. As news of the attacks spread, Dalits retaliated. Despite all the violence, Koottamaippu—the Thevar coalition sponsoring the rally—was allowed to hold it. Among its demands: the repeal of the Scheduled Castes and Scheduled Tribes (Prevention of Atrocities) Act, 1989.[375]

Dalits and journalists throughout the affected areas have blamed the police and district administration for their failure to effectively respond to increasing tensions in the district arising from publicity for the conference. According to *Frontline*, a bi-monthly news magazine, "The police presence was minimal and vehicles were not being checked for weapons. This was in contrast to the intensive searches carried out by the police when Puthiya Tamalingam [a Dalit organization] held its rally on September 11."[376]

The situation remained volatile in the district for days afterwards. Police were given shoot-on-sight orders for arsonists, while a large contingent of the striking police force was rushed in.[377] Both sides also alleged harassment and torture by the police conducting raids under the pretext of searching for criminals and weapons.[378] According to People's Watch, the death toll on both sides reached fifteen.

On October 7, 1998, three days after the incident, state Governor Fathima Beevi called for an overhauling of the police system to prevent "police excess." The director general of the Bureau of Police Research and Development urged

---

[375]Ibid. The District Chamber of Commerce estimated that businesses in the district suffered a total loss of Rs. 3.5 crores (US$8.75 million). Three hundred shops were destroyed, several buses were damaged, and over one hundred street lamps were smashed. Ibid.

[376]Ibid. On August 6, 1997, over thirty all-Dalit organizations convened a rally in Madras to draw attention to attacks on Dalits in the state. According to an article in *Frontline* news magazine, "[t]he severe restrictions placed on the Dalit rally were in marked contrast to the attitude of the authorities to the several caste-based processions and rallies in the last few years in Tamil Nadu." The organizers of the rally, which culminated in the presentation of a memorandum on attacks to state Governor Fathima Beevi, declared that over 100,000 Dalits would participate. However, the preventive arrests of thousands of activists throughout the state prior to the rally and a 20,000-strong police presence ensured that only a few thousand would attend. Forces included policemen from the neighboring states of Karnataka and Andhra Pradesh as well as a company of the Rapid Action Force (an armed police force used in times of emergency). Vehicles bringing Dalits into the city were also detained at twenty-nine separate checkpoints for hours at a time. S. Viswanathan, "Extreme measures," *Frontline*, September 5, 1997.

[377]"Shoot-at-sight orders issued, situation tense in Ramanathapuram," *Financial Express*, October 5, 1998. The striking police force is Tamil Nadu's reserve police force that is used for emergencies and riot control.

[378]Viswanathan, "Caste-based mobilisation...," *Frontline*.

implementation of the National Police Commission recommendations, while the chairperson of the State Human Rights Commission recommended that police personnel should be made to undergo human rights awareness training every six months.[379] None of these recommendations had been implemented as of February 1999.

Just over a month after the violence in Ramanathapuram, caste tensions erupted in Thirunallur village in nearby Pudukkottai district. On November 19, 1998, three Dalit youths were stripped, tied to a tree, and beaten through the night. According to a press report, their "heads were tonsured, and they were also made to roll around the village temple in the presence of a large gathering which included their kith and kin. The next morning they were asked to leave the village."[380] The attack was part of a judgment handed down by twelve members of the all-caste Hindu local village council: the young men were being punished for marrying non-Dalit Hindu girls. Tensions remained high in the village for weeks following the beatings. Not until a month later were the culprits charged and the victims given part of their compensation, under the Scheduled Castes and Scheduled Tribes (Prevention of Atrocities) Act, 1989.[381]

On December 1, 1998, in a massive operation reminiscent of the 1995 police raid on Kodiyankulum village, 300 armed policemen entered the Dalit colony at Ogalur village in Perambalur district. Under the pretext of rounding up "anti-social elements," police reportedly entered over 1,000 homes and, using lathis and iron rods, attacked the residents. After causing extensive damage to their homes and property, police arrested sixty-nine Dalits. Among them were thirty-four women, some with babies in their arms and a few who were pregnant. The reported background to the attack was a dispute between the Dalits and the caste Hindus over a piece of temple land and the attempted sexual assault of a Dalit woman by a caste Hindu man in the village; the man accompanied the police during their attack. As of January 1999, the Dalit laborers were still unable to work in the caste Hindu fields and their children were unable to go to school.[382]

Another incident, reported by the news magazine *Frontline,* took place on December 16, 1998. In Puliyur village, Cuddalore district, a mob of caste Hindus (Vanniyas) numbering about 300 raided a Dalit settlement and attacked its residents with sticks and iron rods. Approximately 500 houses were ransacked and thirteen

---

[379]"Governor wants overhauling of police system," *The Hindu,* October 8, 1998.
[380]S. Viswanathan, "An act of humiliation," *Frontline,* January 29, 1999.
[381]Ibid.
[382]S. Viswanathan, "Rising tensions," *Frontline,* January 29, 1999.

Dalits seriously injured. The day before the attack, a Dalit funeral procession was stopped as it passed a Vanniya house. "In the melee that followed, the caste-Hindu resident was reportedly assaulted by a Dalit, who, it is said, had been slapped a day earlier for smoking in the presence of the caste-Hindu resident." In this case, smoking was a luxury to which the Dalits were not entitled in the presence of a caste Hindu.[383]

### Tamil Nadu Government-Appointed Commissions

State governments in India share a common history of appointing judicial commissions of inquiry to quell public outcries against police excesses during large-scale communal and caste clashes. Although these commissions do serve a political function, their findings, if and when released to the public, are frequently in favor of the state.[384] The Tamil Nadu experience is no exception to this rule.

As of December 1998 the state was one of five to have established a state human rights commission (SHRC). The commission's investigations into human rights abuses by the police and caste Hindus are, however, blocked if the state first appoints its own judicial commission of inquiry. Like the National Human Rights Commission, state human rights commissions are denied jurisdiction over an investigation if the matter is pending before "any commission duly constituted under any law for the time-being [sic] in force."[385] The state government of Tamil Nadu has exploited this provision by appointing its own commissions of inquiry before state human rights commission investigations get underway. States have little control over the investigations of statutory (human rights) commissions. Conversely, government-appointed commissions almost invariably find in favor of the state and the police. Those findings that go against the state are rarely implemented or made public.

---

[383]Ibid.

[384]One notable exception is the Srikrishna Commission established in response to the notorious 1992-1993 Bombay Riots which claimed the lives of 700 people, mostly Muslims, in the aftermath of the destruction of the Babri Masjid, a sixteenth-century mosque, in December 1992. The reports findings were presented to the government of Maharashtra on February 16, 1998, more than five years after the riots took place. The report determined that the riots were the result of a deliberate and systematic effort to incite violence against Muslims and singled out Shiv Sena leader Bal Thackeray and Chief Minister Manohar Joshi as responsible. The Shiv Sena-BJP government, however, refused to adopt the commission's recommendations and instead labeled the report "anti-Hindu." "Srikrishna report indicts Thackeray, Joshi," *Indian Express*, August 7, 1998.

[385]Protection of Human Rights Act, 1993, Sec. 36(1).

A Tamil Nadu government official explained that judicial commissions' findings "do not become public unless the government tables it with the legislature; findings that are against the state are often not tabled... By appointing its own commissions, the state government does not permit the State Human Rights Commission to do the investigation. It literally ties its hands."[386] The appointment of judicial commissions has become almost routine following caste clashes. The Justice Mohan Commission, for example, was appointed by the state government in July 1997 to look into recurring caste clashes and suggest measures to prevent them, but only "after the state government knew that the State Human Rights Commission was on the job."[387] The Justice Mohan Commission submitted its report in September 1998. In October 1998, Chief Minister Karunanidhi announced that not all the recommendations could be accepted.[388]

In another large-scale clash in Coimbatore in November 1997, Muslims shops and houses were burned down by Hindus, reportedly with support from the police. Before the SHRC could take up the investigation, the state appointed the Justice Gokulakrishnan Commission, and "[a]gain their hands were tied." During the southern district clashes of April to December 1997, police opened fire in two villages and attacked Dalit women in a third. Three commissions headed by three district judges were immediately appointed.[389] The director of People's Watch contends that "it has been the history of Dalit people that every commission of inquiry has gone against their interests." Another activist added that "the retired judges who are appointed always toe the line of the government."[390]

Given proper resources, state human rights commissions stand to play an important role in the protection of human rights. Because their investigations enjoy greater independence from the state than judicial commission investigations, the statutes under which they are formed need to be amended to ensure that judicial commissions cannot be appointed as a means of undermining their powers.

---

[386]Human Rights Watch interview, Madras, February 12, 1998.
[387]Ibid.
[388]"Meet will decide on caste rallies," *The Hindu*, October 24, 1998.
[389]Human Rights Watch interview with State Human Rights Commission member, Madras, February 12, 1998. A judicial commission of inquiry into the police firing of July 1997 in Ramabai Colony, Bombay, concluded in August 1998. The report was tabled with the state legislative assembly in December 1998. The commission held that the sub-inspector who ordered the firing was responsible for the deaths of ten Dalits. The state government suspended him as his punishment. For more on the Ramabai incident and the Gundewar Commission, see Chapter VI.
[390]Human Rights Watch interviews, Bangalore, July 26, 1998.

Moreover, the mandates of human rights commissions themselves need to be strengthened to ensure that their recommendations are binding and their findings are made public.

## VI.  THE RAMABAI KILLINGS

Fifty years of independence.  The salute of fifty bullets.  Ten Dalits murdered.  This is our independence.

— Poster in Ramabai colony[391]

Excessive use of force by members of the police is not limited to the rural areas that are largely the focus of previous chapters in this report.  Police abuse against the urban poor, slum dwellers, Dalits, and other minorities has included arbitrary detention, torture, extrajudicial executions, and forced evictions.[392]  Because they cannot afford to bribe the police, Dalits and other poor minorities are disproportionately represented among those detained and tortured in police custody.  Although the acute social discrimination characteristic of rural areas is less pronounced in cities, Dalits in urban areas, who make up the majority of bonded laborers and street cleaners, do not escape it altogether.  Many live in segregated colonies which have been targets of police raids.

This chapter describes a July 1997 incident in Bombay in which police opened fire on a crowd of Dalits protesting the desecration of a statue of Dr. B. R. Ambedkar in their settlement.  The firing, which killed ten and injured twenty-six, was in direct violation of international standards on the use of firearms by law enforcement officials and of Bombay Police Manual guidelines.  According to human rights groups and colony residents, the firing was unprovoked and caste-motivated.

### The Killings

On July 11, 1997, residents of Ramabai Ambedkar Nagar, a predominantly Dalit-populated urban colony in Bombay, woke up to find their statue of Dr.

---

[391]Writing on a poster in Ramabai colony (translated from Marathi).  The poster also included pictures and names of those killed during the police firing.
[392]See Human Rights Watch/Children's Rights Project, *Police Abuse and Killings of Street Children in India* (New York: Human Rights Watch, 1996). See also A. R. Desai, ed., *Repression and Resistance in India* (Delhi: Popular Prakashan Private, Ltd., 1990); A. R. Desai, *Expanding Governmental Lawlessness and Organized Struggles* (Delhi: Popular Prakashan Private, Ltd., 1991); and Indian People's Tribunal, "Forced Evictions - An Indian People's Tribunal Enquiry into the Brutal Demolitions of Pavement and Slum Dwellers' Homes," A report by Justice Hosbet Suresh, retired judge, Bombay High Court (Bombay: August 1995).

Ambedkar desecrated by a garland of sandals around his neck. The placing of shoes or sandals around the neck of the likeness of a person is taken as a sign of extreme disrespect and is usually an attempt to denigrate that person and his or her beliefs.[393] When residents complained of the desecration to Local Beat No. 5 Pantnagar Police, located ten feet away from the statue, they were told to lodge a complaint at the Pantnagar police station. By 7:00 a.m. the growing crowd began protesting and blocked the Eastern Express Highway in front of the colony. Within minutes, members of the Special Reserve Police Force (SRPF),[394] led by Sub-Inspector M. Y. Kadam, arrived in a van and stopped in front of the colony, hundreds of meters away from the statue and the protests on the highway. SRPF constables opened fire on pedestrians on the service road in front of the colony and later into alleys between colony houses. The firing lasted for ten to fifteen minutes and killed ten people. Most of the victims were shot above the waist. Sub-Inspector Kadam and his SRPF constables left soon after the firing, only to be replaced by the city police and other SRPF members.[395]

Four hours later, at 11:30 a.m., at a site 150 meters away from the firing and 300 meters away from the desecrated statute, an angry crowd set fire to a luxury bus. At 2:00 p.m. twenty to twenty-five police officers entered Ramabai colony, started spreading tear gas, and began lathi-charging residents in their homes. At 4:00 p.m. they lathi-charged again. By late afternoon, twenty-six people had been seriously injured, and Local Beat No. 5 had been destroyed by protesters.

Sub-Inspector Kadam, who ordered the firing, had a number of cases of "atrocities" against Dalits pending against him. Kadam's former supervisor and SRPF commandant Vasant Ingle had previously charged Kadam with being "anti-

---

[393] A fact-finding report by the National Alliance of People's Movements, a human rights NGO, explained the significance of the statue and the reaction brought on by its desecration: "To anyone who knows the symbolic importance of the Dr. Ambedkar statue for Dalit identity and the deep and ingrained relation the Dalits have with Dr. Ambedkar's ideology, to the role he and his leadership played in giving them self confidence and a place in human society–its socio-economic-political arena – the reaction (emotional) can be easily understood, justified, and rationalised." National Alliance of People's Movements, "A Report and Statement of Facts on the Incidents of Atrocity against Dalits in Ramabai Ambedkar Nagar, Mumbai (Bombay), on July 11, 1997," [no date].

[394] The Special Reserve Police Force (SRPF) is a branch of the police deployed in times of emergency for riot control.

[395] Indian People's Human Rights Commission, "Gunning Down Dalits: Police firing at Ramabai Ambedkar Colony, Mumbai on 11th July 1997" (Bombay); Human Rights Watch interviews, Bombay, February 2, 1998.

Dalit": he had accused Kadam of mistreating a subordinate for "casteist reasons" and had ordered his suspension for violating the Scheduled Castes and Scheduled Tribes (Prevention of Atrocities) Act, 1989.[396] Ingle has also charged that Kadam's excessive use of force in dealing with Ramabai residents was a direct result of his caste prejudice. Kadam has denied this charge.[397]

The Ramabai incident led to significant unrest throughout the state of Maharashtra, including rioting and social boycotts against protesting Dalits.[398] A two-member team of the Indian People's Human Rights Commission (IPHRC), a Bombay-based NGO, visited the districts of Nagpur, Amravati, Yavatmal, and Wardha in October 1997 to investigate violence against Dalits in the wake of disturbances related to protests against the Ramabai incident. According to an article in the *Times of India*, the team concluded that in various villages, "the police had abetted supporters of the ruling Shiv Sena-BJP alliances... in committing atrocities on Dalits and terrorising them" and that "the people owing allegiance to the ruling alliance parties had made determined efforts to terrorise and punish the Buddhists [converted Dalits] for having dared to protest against the shameful act of desecration of the Ambedkar statue."[399] According to IPHRC, such efforts included the stripping and parading of a Dalit woman in Karanja-Ghadge village in Wardha district. She was later reportedly framed for murder by the police after she complained of her ill-treatment.[400]

Soon after the firing, the Maharashtra state government appointed a commission of inquiry, headed by Justice S. D. Gundewar, to determine whether "the steps taken by the police to deal with the large crowd and to disperse it were adequate, in accordance with the procedure established for riot control," or if the force used was excessive. The commission was also asked to report on measures, general or specific, "which are required to be taken by the police and the administration to avoid such occurrence in the future."[401]

---

[396]"I had no tear gas shells, says SRPF sub-inspector," *Times of India,* July 20, 1997; "Govt. will not be dismissed despite pressure, feels CM," *Times of India,* July 16, 1997.
[397]Indian People's Human Rights Commission, "Gunning Down Dalits...," p. 36.
[398]"Dalit woman stripped and paraded naked, says IPHRC report," *The Times of India* (Bombay), November 1, 1997.
[399]Ibid.
[400]Ibid.
[401]"Notification of Commission of Inquiry (Hon'ble Shri Justice S.D. Gundewar) into desecration of Dr. Ambedkar Statue, Violence, Police Firing on 11th July 1997 at Ghatkopar, Mumbai," Bombay, 1997.

According to several eyewitness accounts and fact-finding reports, including that of the Indian People's Human Rights Commission, the National Alliance of People's Movements, and the Air Corporation SC/ST Employees Association,[402] the firing went on intermittently for at least fifteen minutes. In a statement of claim submitted before the Gundewar Commission of Inquiry, an eyewitness described the manner in which the police began firing. Before firing they "did not lathi-charge, burst tear gas shells, fire a few rounds in the air or... make any serious, positive efforts to disperse people" but instead, "in a designed manner, deliberately, intentionally opened fire on innocent masses."[403]

A senior-level official in the Bombay police department, who wished to remain anonymous, told Human Rights Watch he believed that the SRPF engaged in excessive use of force. This particular official did not believe that the firing was caste-motivated. He did, however, characterize members of the SRPF as "trigger-happy." He then added, "I would have shot at one, in the leg, to get the message across, not killed ten. They do commit excesses. They killed too many people. They sit around with nothing to do until they get called in, and then they overreact."[404]

In February 1998 Human Rights Watch visited Ramabai colony and spoke to many of its residents. Monk Kashyap, an eyewitness, told Human Rights Watch about the sequence of events in the early-morning firing:

> I heard screaming; I went out to see. It was early. I was standing outside about thirty meters away. They didn't shoot me, because I was wearing my monk's robe. They told me to leave. Everyone was sleeping. I saw forty or fifty people saying, "*Rasta roko*" ["block the road"]. Two police cars [city police] went straight through and did not stop. An SRPF van came. One or two protesters must have thrown stones at private cars. There were no shots above the head, just a direct shoot. First they hit Kaushaliyabhai Patare. The bullet went through her and hit the medical dispensary 150 meters away. She was forty-

---

[402]The association represents scheduled-caste and scheduled-tribe employees of Air India, Indian Airlines, and the Hotel Corporation of India.
[403]"Statement of Claim (Case)/Version on Behalf of Namdev Dam Ubale, Before the Commission of Inquiry (Hon'ble Shri Justice S.D. Gundewar) into Desecration of Dr. Ambedkar Statue Violence, Police Firing on 11th July, 1997 at Ghatkopar, Mumbai," Bombay, November 18, 1997, p. 12.
[404]Human Rights Watch interview, Bombay, February 5, 1998.

five. She died on the spot. I kept watching. They said, "Sadhu [monk], get out of here." I came inside but kept looking through the window. Sukhdev Kapadne was there. They grabbed him and put him in the car. Then they asked him who he was. He said he was a social worker and they told him to go. Then they shot him in the back. The bullet came out of his chest, and he fell forward. He was fifty years old.[405]

Monk Kashyap also witnessed the shooting of Sukhdev Kapadne, Kaushaliyabhai, Amar Dhanawade, Vilas Dodke, and Anil Garud, all of whom "died on the spot."[406] After the initial firing, police charged forward into the housing areas. Once they were fully inside the colony, the firing continued. Most residents were caught completely by surprise. One of the bullets hit Bablu Verma and killed him: "He trembled like a fish and died. If someone tried to help him they would shoot at him too. He was twenty-six years old."[407] Shridevi Giri was also injured by bullets. "I was hit in the arm twice," she said as she showed us her scars. Another woman stepped into the alley and saw her husband shot: "I was standing outside my door and saw the bullet hit my husband in the stomach."[408] Babu Phulekar was also standing in the alley and was also injured.

V. S. Khade, a prominent member of the community, confirmed the manner of attack: "They did not say anything. There was no lathi-charge, no tear gas, no bubble bullets, just a direct firing." Khade lost his nephew's son in the firing.

He used to stay with us more after his mother died in 1994. On that day he was going to work. The crowds wouldn't allow him to cross the highway. So he came back and told my wife and my daughter not to go outside. Then he went to inform his father, who was one kilometer away. Before he could get there he was shot and killed. His brother and uncle went to pick him up, but the police shouted, "Don't touch him or we'll shoot you too." I heard the shots. When I arrived he was already dead. He was only seventeen.[409]

---

[405]Human Rights Watch interview with Monk Kashyap, Bombay, February 2, 1998.
[406]Ibid.
[407]Ibid.
[408]Human Rights Watch interviews with Shridevi Giri and colony resident, Bombay, February 2, 1998.
[409]Human Rights Watch interview, Bombay, February 2, 1998.

Soon after the incident took place, colony residents proceeded to the Pantnagar police station to lodge a complaint against the police involved in the firing. The police refused to record or register a complaint.[410] By 11:00 a.m. all the bodies had been transported to the hospital, though none had been taken by the police. Colony residents described the scene later that day:

> There were hundreds of officers. They tried to keep everyone quiet. There was no firing and no lathi-charge. Then at 2:00 p.m. twenty to twenty-five police came in the colony and started spreading tear gas. They shouted, "Close your doors and windows and don't come out." People went back inside. One person was injured from the tear gas. He was burned from the thighs down. The police left soon thereafter, but people were still going to the hospital until 11:00 p.m. that night. Everyone who died died on the spot. On the spot they killed ten people.[411]

Milind, the nineteen-year-old tear gas victim, spoke to Human Rights Watch about his experience with the police before and after being burned:

> It was 6:00 a.m.; I was in my store. I had been working there for one or two months. Someone came and told me what had happened to the statue. I saw the garland of shoes. Someone said bring the dogs, bring the police. I heard it all. I came home because I was tired. At around 1:30 or 2:00 p.m., they threw tear gas next door. We heard the explosion and saw smoke, and I went outside. I stood outside, and they threw tear gas on me. I was only wearing a towel. I fell down. My legs were burning, and blood was coming out. My underwear and towel crumbled to the floor. My mother started screaming, "My son is dying, my son is dying." A police officer told her, "Get in the house or I will shoot you."[412]

According to Milind, a police officer put him in a van to take him to the hospital, where, after an hour and a half, the doctors stitched his wounds, and the

[410]Human Rights Watch interview with colony resident present at police station, Bombay, February 2, 1998.
[411]Human Rights Watch interviews with colony residents, Bombay, February 2, 1998.
[412]Human Rights Watch interview with Milind, Bombay, February 2, 1998.

police took him to the police station to "take his statement." Along with his parents, Milind arrived at the station at 6:00 p.m. As of 11:30 p.m. he had not eaten and was told that he would not be fed.

> I asked for water, and they said, "Drink your urine." They kicked out my parents at 2:30 a.m. and said, "Go home or you'll also be arrested." Then they threw me in the lock-up and started beating me. They shouted, "Ramabai people destroyed our police station. You won't get food or water." They started beating me with their sticks; on my back, on my legs. Blood started coming out of my legs. Inspector Marate came in. I told him what his officers were doing, and he called me a motherfucker. "Ramabai's people should be treated this way," he shouted. He was talking about Dalits. Then he slapped me and told me to go to sleep. I went to bed without any medicine or food.[413]

According to an article in the Bombay-based weekly, *Sunday Mid-Day*, the senior inspector of the Pantnagar police station, where Milind was held overnight, stated that Milind was "part of the mob which set the police *chowky* [booth] in Ramabai Colony on fire. To disperse the mob tear gas shells were fired, and he sustained leg injuries." He added that Milind was brought back to the police station after treatment and kept under detention until things "cooled out." "Why would we beat him when he was already injured?" he asked.[414]

The following afternoon Milind's parents arrived at the police station with a letter from Bharati Jadhav, Pantnagar's municipal councillor. Milind was released and admitted to the hospital, where he remained for one and a half months. His family paid for his treatment and his medicines. Although they did receive some money from local politicians, they received nothing from the government. He also did not get the job that the government had promised him as compensation. As Milind told Human Rights Watch, many others were left out as well:

> Many people were also hurt in the lathi-charge, but they got no money either. One person's head was split open, and one person went blind from a bullet fragment. They got nothing. No money for them, no job

---

[413]Ibid.
[414]"'Drink your urine' police tell riot victim," *Sunday Mid-Day*, July 13, 1997.

for them. [Only] the people whose family member died or who were shot got money and a job.[415]

At the time of the interview, Milind was studying in the tenth grade and was still looking for employment.

### National and International Standards on the Use of Firearms

The indiscriminate use of lethal force against unarmed demonstrators contravenes key provisions of the United Nations Basic Principles on the Use of Force and Firearms by Law Enforcement Officials, which *inter alia* states:

> Law enforcement officials, in carrying out their duty, shall, as far as possible, apply non-violent means before resorting to the use of force and firearms. Whenever the lawful use of force and firearms is unavoidable, law enforcement officials shall: (a) Exercise restraint in such use and act in proportion to the seriousness of the offence and the legitimate objective to be achieved; (b) Minimize damage and injury, and respect and preserve human life ....

With respect to the policing of unlawful assemblies, Article 13 of the Basic Principles dictates that, "in the dispersal of unlawful assemblies that are unlawful but non-violent, law enforcement officials shall avoid the use of force or, where that is not praticable, shall restrict such force to the minimum extent necessary." Article 14 adds that, "in the dispersal of violent assemblies, law enforcement officials may use firearms only when less dangerous means are not practicable and only to the minimum extent. Law enforcement officials shall not use firearms in such cases, except under conditions stipulated in principle 9." Principle 9 allows for the use of firearms in cases of self-defense or defense of others against the imminent threat of death or serious injury.

The Basic Principles also state that: "Governments shall ensure that arbitrary or abusive use of force and firearms by law enforcement officials is punished as a criminal offence under their law."[416]

---

[415]Human Rights Watch interview, Bombay, February 2, 1998.

[416]The Basic Principles were adopted by the Eighth United Nations Congress on the Prevention of Crime and the Treatment of Offenders on September 7, 1990. The United Nations General Assembly subsequently welcomed these principles in Resolution 45/121 and called on all governments to be guided by them. They constitute authoritative

Many of the steps taken by the Special Reserve Police were also in clear violation of the Bombay Police Manual provisions on riot control. Relevant provisions and the police's defense before the Gundewar Commission of Inquiry are outlined below. According to Rule No. 59 of the manual:

> It should be accepted as a cardinal principle that troops of armed police engaged in suppression of disorder should in no circumstances be brought into such close contact with a hostile mob which greatly outnumbers them as to lead to the risk of their being committed to hand-to-hand struggle. Apart from the danger of their being rushed or deprived of their arms, it is impossible in these circumstances to exercise adequate fire control and the effect of fire at such close quarters is, therefore, likely to be unnecessarily severe.

By its own admission, the state reserve police present at the scene brought itself into close contact with the crowd, fired shots in the air, and, according to several eyewitnesses and a fact-finding report, all but one person killed had bullet wounds above the waistline.[417] Even assuming that there was a "riotous mob" in need of control, SRPF forces seemed to have reversed the conventional riot control protocol. Rather than proceeding from a lathi-charge to tear gas, firing in the air, and firing below the waist, they first fired above the waist, then administered tear gas, and on two occasions in the afternoon (at 2:00 p.m. and later at 4:00 p.m.), lathi-charged residents in their homes after beating down their doors.[418] The lathi-charge included severe beatings of two women both of whom "bore the marks of lathi-charge on their hands and feet."[419]

In a statement of claim submitted on behalf of the police department to the Gundewar Commission of Inquiry, the police claimed that a total of fifty rounds were fired: four in the air and seven just north of the first firing.[420] They did not account for the remaining thirty-nine rounds. Witnesses have challenged the

---

guidelines for the promulgation of national legislation regulating the use of force and firearms.

[417] Air Corporation SC/ST Employees Association, "Memorandum of Report on Police Firing at Mata Ramabai Ambedkar Nagar, Ghatkopar, Mumbai," p. 8.

[418] Human Rights Watch interviews, Bombay, February 2, 1998.

[419] "Memorandum of Report on Police Firing...," p. 9.

[420] "Statement of Claim (Case)/On Behalf of Police Department, Before the Hon'ble Commission of Inquiry in the Matter of Police Firing at Ramabai Ambedkar Nagar/Eastern Express Highway (Pantnagar Police Station on 11.7.97)," Bombay, October 24, 1997, p. 10.

police's claim that only fifty rounds were fired. As Khade explained: "They fired for fifteen minutes... But ten people were killed and so many were injured. A few people were shot two or three times. So how could it be that only fifty bullets were fired?"[421]

The police's statement claims that a mob had set a luxury bus on fire and had stoned several tankers, and that an explosion of those tankers was imminent. According to the police, Sub-Inspector Kadam ordered one of his officers to fire warning shots in the air and upon realizing that the warning shots had no effect on the crowd, he "ordered his rifle section to aim and fire at arsonists and rioteers."[422] They claimed, however, that the firings had no effect on the "mob." During his deposition before the Gundewar Commission on February 18, 1998, Sub-Inspector Kadam admitted to ordering his subordinates to fire in the air, even though he was aware that the Police Manual prohibited such actions. When asked why he decided to ignore police procedures, Kadam replied that he had read in a newspaper that firing in the air was an effective way to disperse a mob.[423]

Rule No. 60 of the Bombay Police Manual, on the use of firearms in dispersing an unlawful assembly, instructs that whenever firing becomes "unavoidable to unruly mobs, it should be ensured that the aim is kept low and directed against the most threatening part of the crowd. Care should be taken not to fire upon persons separated from the crowd nor to fire over the heads of the crowd as thereby innocent persons may be injured. Under no circumstances, should firing in the air be resorted to as experience proves that this leads ultimately to greater loss of life." The rule goes on to state that "it is impossible to pick out and put out of action individual leaders of a mob" and that "ineffective fire against a really determined mob is likely to influence it further so that the attack will be pressed home and the police overwhelmed." Sub-Inspector Kadam disregarded explicit procedure and ordered his officers to "aim and fire at arsonists and rioteers." The police claimed that the situation was unavoidable and that Kadam's orders needed to be looked at "in light of the situation that [was] faced by the officers on the spot."[424]

Finally, in reference to medical aid during riots and disturbances, Rule 62 confers upon officers the obligation to "do the best they can do to provide medical aid to persons injured on such occasions and, when necessary to convey them to

---

[421]Human Rights Watch interview, Bombay, February 2, 1998.
[422]"Statement of Claim (Case)/On Behalf of Police Department," pp. 6-7.
[423]"I gave orders to fire in air, admits Kadam," *The Times of India*, February 19, 1998.
[424]"Statement of Claim (Case)/On Behalf of Police Department," p. 13.

hospitals as quickly as possible." None of the bodies that were taken to the hospital that day were taken by the police. Moreover, anyone attempting to administer aid to the injured was immediately ordered to step away or face the same consequences.

An amateur video of the events was submitted by the police as documentation of the department's claim that the firing was necessary to control a mob on its way to setting gas tankers on fire. The video, the police claimed, "vividly depicts the incidents of arson, the black billowing clouds emanating from the rear of the LPG [liquefied petroleum gas] tankers, the northward movement of the police party and subsequent arrival of fire brigade and dousing of fire."[425] The authenticity of the video, however, has been called into question. A human rights NGO that examined the video concluded that the tape was doctored. It pointed to the video's choppy editing and the presence of two different backgrounds for incidents that police claim took place at the same scene. Closer examination of the video, eyewitness reports, and NGO fact-finding missions all confirm that the burning of public property that the police use as justification for their actions at 7:00 a.m. in fact took place much later in the day at a site hundreds of meters away.

The Indian People's Human Rights Commission issued a scene-by-scene analysis of the two-minute video, exposing inconsistencies between shots.[426] Background scenes in the video provide evidence of two separate locales: Ramabai Colony and Nalanda Nagar, which is located some 150 meters away from Ramabai and approximately 300 meters away from the agitation around the statue.[427] Although a luxury bus was set on fire, this occurred at around 11:30 a.m., more than four hours after the Ramabai firing began. Moreover, according to eyewitnesses, two seemingly empty tankers were brought in by the police themselves and placed behind the burning bus in order to "hide their blunder" and to fabricate a defense to the firing.[428]

In its response to allegations received from the United Nations Special Rapporteur on Contemporary Forms of Racism, Racial Discrimination, Xenophobia and Related Intolerance, the government of India put forward the same defense:

---

[425]Ibid., p. 9.
[426]Indian People's Human Rights Commission, "Gunning Down Dalits...," Annexure IV.
[427]"Memorandum of Report on Police Firing...," p. 9.
[428]Ibid.

The gathering became violent and started damaging private and public property. It also tried to set fire to a LPG gas tanker. In order to discourage the mob from doing so (which otherwise would have resulted in extensive damage to human life and property) and for self-defence, the Police resorted to a "Cane-Charge" and subsequently, having failed to control the mob, opened fire. Unfortunately, 10 persons died and 24 persons were injured in the firing. 8 police personnel were also injured.[429]

The government also asserted that allegations such as those received pertaining to caste "do not fall within the mandate" of the special rapporteur.

On August 7, 1998, the Gundewar Commission report was presented to the Shiv Sena-Bharatiya Janata Party government.[430] In December 1998 the report was tabled in the state legislative assembly. The commission held Sub-Inspector Kadam responsible for an "unjustified, unwarranted and indiscriminate firing which [took place] without warning." It further recommended that the government terminate his services. The Shiv Sena-BJP government accepted the report and declared that Kadam would be suspended.[431] Many activists have protested the suspension and have demanded that Kadam be dismissed and charged with murder under Section 302 of the Indian Penal Code.[432] As of February 1999 he had not been charged. Given the police action and the resulting loss of life and injuries, it is incumbent upon the government of Maharashtra to prosecute officers responsible for the attack.

---

[429]Government of India, "Response of the Government of India to allegations received from the Special Rapporteur on the Contemporary Forms of Racism, Racial Discrimination, Xenophobia and Related Intolerance," June 19, 1998. The allegations were submitted by a coalition of NGOs based in India, the United States, Canada, and the United Kingdom.
[430]"Gundewar Commission report submitted," *Express News Service*, August 8, 1998.
[431]"Row in Maharashtra Houses over panel reports," *The Hindu*, December 31, 1998; "Gundewar panel blames SI for firing," *The Hindu*, December 25, 1998.
[432]"Dalits demand Kadam's dismissal," *Times of India*, January 1, 1999.

# VII. DISCRIMINATION AND EXPLOITATIVE FORMS OF LABOR

Allocation of labor on the basis of caste is one of the fundamental tenets of the caste system. Within the caste system, Dalits have been assigned tasks and occupations that are deemed ritually polluting for other caste communities. Throughout this report, Human Rights Watch has documented the exploitation of agricultural laborers who work for a few kilograms of rice or Rs. 15 to Rs. 35 (US$0.38 to $0.88) a day. A sub-group of Dalits is condemned to labor even more exploitative. An estimated forty million people in India, among them fifteen million children, are bonded laborers. A majority of them are Dalits. According to government statistics, an estimated one million Dalits are manual scavengers who clean public latrines and dispose of dead animals; unofficial estimates are much higher. In India's southern states, thousands of Dalit girls are forced into prostitution before reaching the age of puberty.

Bondage is passed on from one generation to another. Scavenging and prostitution are hereditary occupations of "untouchable" castes. Dalits face discrimination when seeking other forms of employment and are largely unable to escape their designated occupation even when the practice itself has been abolished by law. In violation of their basic human rights, they are physically abused and threatened with economic and social ostracism from the community for refusing to carry out various caste-based tasks.

## Bonded Labor

"Bonded labor" refers to work in slave-like conditions in order to pay off a debt. Due to the high interest rates charged and the abysmally low wages paid, the debts are seldom settled. Bonded laborers are frequently low-caste, illiterate, and extremely poor, while the creditors/employers are usually higher-caste, literate, comparatively wealthy, and relatively more powerful members of the community.[433] The Bonded Labour System (Abolition) Act, 1976 abolishes all agreements and obligations arising out of the bonded labor system. It aims to release all laborers from bondage, cancel any outstanding debt, prohibit the creation of new bondage agreements, and order the economic rehabilitation of

---

[433]For more on bonded labor in South Asia, including recommendations for the release and rehabilitation of bonded laborers, see Human Rights Watch/Asia, *The Small Hands of Slavery: Bonded Child Labor in India* (New York: Human Rights Watch, 1996); and Human Rights Watch/Asia, *Contemporary Forms of Slavery in Pakistan* (New York: Human Rights Watch, 1995).

freed bonded laborers by the state.[434] It also punishes attempts to compel persons
into bondage with a maximum of three years in prison and a Rs. 2,000 (US$50)
fine.[435] However, the extent to which bonded laborers have been identified,
released, and rehabilitated in the country is negligible.

Most agricultural laborers interviewed for this report were paid between Rs.
15 and Rs. 25 (US$0.38 to $0.63), or two to three kilograms of rice, per day, well
below the minimum wage prescribed in their state.[436] Women were consistently
paid less than men. Many laborers owed debts to their employers or other
moneylenders. Under the Bonded Labour System (Abolition) Act, 1976, payment
of less than minimum wage for the purposes of working off a debt amounts to
bondage. The act's definition of the "bonded labour system" includes "any system
of forced, or partly forced labour under which a debtor enters, or has, or is
presumed to have, entered, into an agreement with the creditor to the effect that

> (v) by reason of his birth in any particular caste or community, he would
> (1) render, by himself or through any member of his family, or
> any person dependent on him, labour or service to the creditor,
> or for the benefit of the creditor, for a specified period or for an
> unspecified period, either without wages or for nominal
> wages....[437]

Nominal wages are defined as wages which are less than

> (a) the minimum wages fixed by the Government, in relation to the
> same or similar labour, under any law for the time being in force; and
> (b) where no such minimum wage has been fixed in relation to any form
> of labour, the wages that are normally paid, for the same or similar
> labour to the labourers working in the same locality.[438]

---

[434]The Bonded Labour System (Abolition) Act, 1976, Sec. 4, 5, 6 and 14.

[435]Ibid., Sec. 16.

[436]Minimum wages prescribed for agricultural laborers vary from state to state and, with the
exception of Haryana and Punjab, typically range from Rs. 30 to Rs. 40 (US$0.75 to $1.00)
a day.

[437]Bonded Labour System (Abolition) Act, 1976, Sec. 2.

[438]Ibid. Even in cases where interviewees were earning the prescribed minimum wage, their
earnings did not amount to a subsistence or "living wage," a right that is guaranteed under
Article 43 of the Indian constitution.

## Caste and Employment Discrimination

In traditional Indian society, the fourfold varna theory describes a broad functional division of labor. Though the caste system has not prevented occupational mobility for caste Hindus, many "untouchable" communities have been forced to continue their occupations as leather workers, disposers of dead animals, or manual scavengers, and to perform other tasks deemed too ritually polluting for upper castes.

The constitutional abolition of "untouchability" meant that caste Hindus could no longer force Dalits to perform any "polluting" occupation. Yet sweeping, scavenging, and leatherwork are still the monopoly of the scheduled castes, whose members are threatened with physical abuse and social boycotts for refusing to perform demeaning tasks. Migration and the anonymity of the urban environment have in some cases resulted in upward occupational mobility among Dalits, but the majority continue to perform their traditional functions. A lack of training and education, as well as discrimination in seeking other forms of employment, have kept these traditions and their hereditary nature alive.[439]

### Manual scavenging

Manual scavenging is a caste-based occupation. Dalit manual scavengers exist under different caste names throughout the country, such as the Bhangis in Gujarat, the Pakhis in Andhra Pradesh, and the Sikkaliars in Tamil Nadu. Members of these communities are invariably placed at the very bottom of the caste hierarchy, and even the hierarchy of Dalit sub-castes. Using little more than a broom, a tin plate, and a basket, they are made to clear feces from public and private latrines and carry them to dumping grounds and disposal sites. Though long outlawed, the practice of manual scavenging continues in most states.

Those working for urban municipalities are paid Rs. 30 - 40 a day (less than US$1), and those working privately are paid Rs. 5 (US$0.13) a month for each house they clean. Even those working for municipalities rarely get paid and are offered little health benefits for a job that entails many health hazards. In cities scavengers are actually lowered into filthy gutters in order to unclog them; they are fully immersed in human waste without any protective gear. In Bombay, children made to dive into manholes have died from carbon monoxide poisoning. In many communities, in exchange for leftover food, scavengers are also expected to remove dead animal carcasses and deliver messages of death to the relatives of

---

[439]See generally, Rama Sharma, *Bhangi, Scavenger in Indian Society: Marginality, Identity and Politicization of the Community* (New Delhi: M. D. Publications Pvt. Ltd., 1995).

their upper-caste neighbors. Their refusal to do so can result in physical abuse and ostracism from the community.

A social worker in the Dhandhuka taluk of Ahmedabad district, Gujarat, explained the relevance of caste to this work:

> Bhangis are the section of Dalits that do this work. The funds come from the government. In villages, the cleaners and who they clean for are always divided by caste... At all levels, villages and municipalities, Bhangis are the workers and they always work for upper castes.[440]

In a 1997 report, the National Commission for Safai Karamcharis claimed that manual scavengers are "totally cut off from the mainstream of progress" and are "still subjected to the worst kind of oppression and indignities. What is more pathetic is the fact that manual scavenging is still largely a hereditary occupation. *Safai karamcharis* are no doubt the most oppressed and disadvantaged section of the population."[441] The commission is a statutory body set up pursuant to the National Commission for Safai Karamcharis Act, 1993. Safai karamcharis are defined as those persons engaged in, or employed for, manually carrying human excreta or any sanitation work.

Martin Macwan is founder-director of Navsarjan, an NGO that has led the campaign to abolish manual scavenging in the western state of Gujarat. In an interview with Human Rights Watch he claimed that when Navsarjan had attempted to rehabilitate scavengers it was difficult to find alternative employment for them, and even more difficult to convince scavengers that they were able to take on, or were "worthy of performing," different occupations.[442]

Members of the Bhangi community in Gujarat are paid by state municipalities to clean the gutters, streets, and community dry latrines. In an article in *Frontline*, a safai karamchari of Paliyad village, Ahmedabad district, complained that in the rainy season, the "water mixes with the faeces that we carry in baskets on our heads, it drips onto our clothes, our faces... When I return home, I find it difficult to eat food. The smell never leaves my clothes, my hair. But in the summer there

---

[440]Human Rights Watch interview, Ahmedabad district, Gujarat, July 23, 1998.

[441]National Commission for Safai Karamcharis, *The Role of the National Commission for Safai Karamcharis in Liberation and Rehabilitation of Safai Karamcharis and their Dependents* (New Delhi: Government of India, 1997), p. 1.

[442]Human Rights Watch interview with Martin Macwan, New York, October 15, 1998.

is often no water to wash your hands before eating. It is difficult to say which [season] is worse."[443]

Human Rights Watch spoke to members of the Bhangi community in Gujarat's Ahmedabad district. The Bhangis lived in a residential area called Bhangivas separate from the Dharbars, Rajputs, and Vanniyas who constitute the caste Hindus in the area. The Bhangis were primarily employed as manual scavengers. They were also responsible for removing dead cats and dogs and were given Rs. 5 (US$0.13) or small amounts of food for doing so.

Forty-year-old Manju, a manual scavenger employed by the urban municipality, described her daily routine and wages:

> In the morning I work from 6:00 a.m. to 11:00 a.m. cleaning the dry latrines. I collect the feces and carry it on my head to the river half a kilometer away seven to ten times a day. In the afternoon I clean the gutters. Another Bhangi collects the rubbish from the gutters and places it outside. Then I come and pick it up and take it one kilometer away. My husband died ten years ago since then I have been doing this. Today I earn Rs. 30 a day (US$0.75). Nine years ago I earned Rs. 16 (US$0.40), then Rs. 22 (US$0.55), and for the last two years it has been Rs. 30. But the payments are uncertain. For the last two months we have not received anything. Every two months they pay, but there is no certainty. We are paid by the Nagar Palika municipality chief officer.[444]

Like many others, Manju's health had suffered as a result of her occupation: "I have often gotten sick: fevers, headaches, breaking and spraining hands and feet, fatigue, and dizziness. It is all dirty work."[445] Several other Bhangi women interviewed complained of similar ailments. Most looked considerably older than their stated age. In addition to the abovementioned diseases of the poor, manual scavengers also tend to suffer from respiratory infections, gastrointestinal disorders, and trachoma, a chronic contagious bacterial conjunctivitis commonly resulting in blindness. Human Rights Watch spoke to several workers with vision problems and to sixty-five-year-old Bachubhai Chaganbhai, who suffered from tuberculosis. He claimed that the illness was due to "working as a cleaner. I used to clean open

---

[443]Mari Marcel Thekaekara, "A continuing social outrage," *Frontline*, Oct. 4–17, 1997, quoting Leelaben of Paliyad village.
[444]Human Rights Watch interview with Manju, Ahmedabad district, Gujarat, July 23, 1998.
[445]Ibid.

latrines. Because of this work I am sick. I stopped working five years ago and have been sick with TB ever since."[446]

Because Bachubhai was a "permanent" worker, he received Rs. 1,500 (US$37.50) pension per month. He used to earn Rs. 2,000 (US$50) a month, or approximately Rs. 65 (US$1.63) a day. Activist Martin Macwan explained that

> [b]eing permanent means that you have an appointment letter. You also get health benefits but not much; you get to visit government dispensaries, which are not in good shape. But the state government has to give grants to the state municipalities depending on the number of permanents that are employed, so the municipalities try to keep them as casual laborers instead. But the number of hours they work is usually the same.[447]

Despite the similarity in work and hours spent, casual laborers are paid only Rs. 34 (US$0.85) a day while permanent laborers were paid Rs. 80 (US$2). Most casual laborers never achieve permanent status, even after years of employment. Leelaben, another scavenger interviewed by Human Rights Watch, had been cleaning the latrines in Birla High School for over twenty years, "Still they have not made me permanent," she said. "I used to get paid Rs. 15 (US$0.38) a month, now I get paid Rs. 200 (US$5) a month."[448]

The situation of private workers, mostly women working in upper-caste households, is even bleaker. In the Bhangivas residential area, in July 1998, there were a total of thirty private workers; the rest were employed by the municipality. Many private workers were paid only Rs. 3 (US$0.08) a day.[449]

An activist in the southern state of Andhra Pradesh, who has been working for the rehabilitation of cleaning workers for the past fourteen years, described a similar pay scale in his state:

---

[446]Human Rights Watch interview with Bachubhai Chaganbhai, Ahmedabad district, Gujarat, July 23, 1998.

[447]Human Rights Watch interviews with group of manual scavengers, Ahmedabad district, Gujarat, July 23, 1998.

[448]Human Rights Watch interview with Leelaben, Ahmedabad district, Gujarat, July 23, 1998.

[449]Human Rights Watch interviews with group of manual scavengers, Ahmedabad district, Gujarat, July 23, 1998.

Dalit survivors of a Ranvir Sena massacre in Laxmanpur-Bathe, Jehanabad district, Bihar, on December 1, 1997. The survivors' family members were among the sixty-one people killed. See Chapter IV. February 1998 © Human Rights Watch.

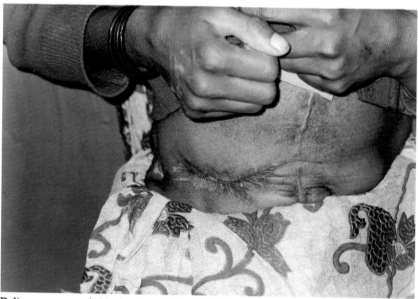

Dalit woman wounded in the Laxmanpur-Bathe massacre. She was shot in the stomach but survived after extensive surgery. February 1998 © Human Rights Watch.

Monument erected in Laxmanpur-Bathe by a Marxist-Leninist group. The monument shows the names of those killed in the massacre. Several Marxist-Leninist groups, or "Naxalites," have engaged in a militant struggle to achieve higher wages and more equitable land distribution in the state of Bihar. February 1998 © Human Rights Watch.

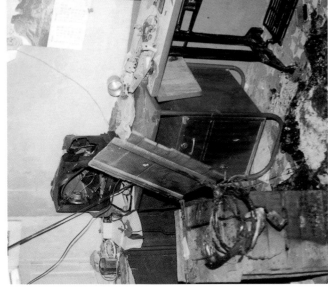

A Dalit home in Muthusamypuram village, Virudhunagar district, Tamil Nadu. Relatively prosperous Dalits were targeted in raids by Thevars (caste Hindus) and the police during the southern district clashes in Tamil Nadu between 1995 and 1998. See Chapter V.

© People's Watch.

Landowners and members of the Ranvir Sena in Ekwari village, Bhojpur district, Bihar. February 1998.

© Human Rights Watch.

Shallow graves in Melavalavu village, Madurai district, Tamil Nadu. Following the election of a Dalit to the village council presidency, members of a higher-caste group murdered six Dalits in June 1997, including the elected council president, whom they beheaded. See Chapter V. February 1998 © Human Rights Watch.

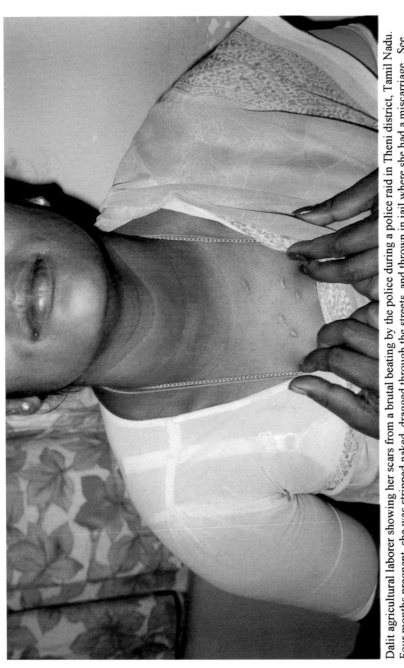

Dalit agricultural laborer showing her scars from a brutal beating by the police during a police raid in Theni district, Tamil Nadu. Four months pregnant, she was stripped naked, dragged through the streets, and thrown in jail where she had a miscarriage. See Chapter V. February 1998 © Human Rights Watch.

A tea stall in Ahmedabad district, Gujarat. Dalits are made to wash and use separate tea tumblers than those used by non-Dalits. July 1998 © Human Rights Watch.

Dalit slum in an urban municipality in Gujarat. July 1998 © Human Rights Watch.

Dalit manual scavenger in Ananthapur municipality, Andhra Pradesh. Manual scavenging is a caste-based occupation in which workers clear feces from public and private latrines and dispose of dead animals with their bare hands. See Chapter VII.
© Bejawada Wilson.

Statue of Dr. B. R. Ambedkar, revered Dalit leader, in Ramabai Colony, Bombay. On July 11, 1997 a protest against the statue's desecration led to police firing on Dalit colony residents, killing ten and injuring twenty-six. See Chapter VI.
February 1998 © Human Rights Watch.

Poster with names and portraits of those killed in Ramabai Colony. The poster, translated from Marathi, reads: "Fifty years of independence. The salute of fifty bullets. Ten Dalits murdered. This is our independence." February 1998 © Human Rights Watch.

Private cleaners receive Rs. 5 to 10 a month for each house they clean [US$0.12 to $0.25]. They clean up to ten to fifteen houses a day, many of which have six or more family members. Those employed by urban municipalities are paid Rs. 2,000 to Rs. 2,500 [US$50 - $63] a month but are only paid once every four to six months. Some are permanent, and some are casual. There are no health benefits, no gloves, no masks, no utensils. The majority are women.[450]

A survey conducted by Safai Karmachari Andolan, an NGO movement for the elimination of manual scavenging, found over 1,650 scavengers in ten districts in Andhra Pradesh. Many were also engaged in underground sewage work. The survey also revealed that 98 percent of manual scavengers in the state belonged to scheduled castes.[451]

A third category of cleaning workers are responsible for cleaning the railway systems. In Andhra Pradesh they are paid Rs. 300 (US$7.50) a month with very few benefits. In Gujarat, they are paid Rs. 12 (US$0.30) a day "for unlimited hours of work. They are told they can stop working when the train comes, but in India you never know when the train will come."[452]

An activist working with the Sikkaliar (Dalit) community of Tamil Nadu described the community's economic exploitation and the tasks that its members are forced to perform. His village had 200 Thevar families. Seventy Sikkaliar families lived in a separate government-built colony. Those who worked as scavengers and removed dead animals from the village received Rs. 150 (US$3.75) per month for their services.[453]

Social discrimination against scavengers is rampant. Most scavengers live in segregated rural colonies and are unable to make use of common resources. According to an Andhra Pradesh activist:

In one toilet there can be as many as 400 seats which all have to be manually cleaned. This is the lowest occupation in the world, and it is

---

[450]Human Rights Watch interview with Bejawada Wilson, Safai Karmachari Andolan, Bangalore, July 26, 1998.
[451]Ibid.
[452]Human Rights Watch interview with Martin Macwan, Navsarjan, Ahmedabad, July 23, 1998.
[453]Human Rights Watch interview with Manibharati, Coordinator, Navjeevan Trust, Madurai district, Tamil Nadu, February 17, 1998.

done by the community that occupies the lowest status in the caste system. Even other scheduled-caste people won't touch the safai karamcharis [cleaning workers]. It is "untouchability" within the "untouchables," yet nobody questions it.[454]

Human Rights Watch was taken to various tea stalls to witness the separate tea tumbler system in which scavengers are made to wash and handle their own tumblers so that glasses reserved for caste Hindus are not "polluted."

When we are working, they ask us not to come near them. At tea canteens, they have separate tea tumblers and they make us clean them ourselves and make us put the dishes away ourselves. We cannot enter temples. We cannot use upper-caste water taps. We have to go one kilometer away to get water.[455]

Despite their appalling work conditions, manual scavengers are unable to demand higher wages or sanitary instruments for use in the collection of human excreta: "When we ask for our rights from the government, the municipality officials threaten to fire us. So we don't say anything. This is what happens to people who demand their rights."[456] According to Macwan, in Ranpur town, Ahmedabad district, women who arrived late for work were made to clean men's urinals as punishment, "even if the men were still inside."[457] Another social worker active in Gujarat added that Bhangis were forced to deliver messages of death to upper-caste family relatives; "They will be boycotted and beaten so they cannot say no."[458]

Human Rights Watch spoke to an activist working to organize Sikkaliars in the Theni district of southern Tamil Nadu. He works with fifty Sikkaliar families in a Thevar-dominated area. The interview revealed that apart from having to perform degrading tasks, the Sikkaliars are also subject to physical and sexual abuse as well as restrictions on their right to vote.

---

[454]Human Rights Watch interview with Bejawada Wilson, Bangalore, July 26, 1998.
[455]Human Rights Watch interview, Ahmedabad district, Gujarat, July 23, 1998.
[456]Human Rights Watch interview, Ahmedabad district, Gujarat, July 23, 1998.
[457]Human Rights Watch interview with Martin Macwan, Ahmedabad district, Gujarat, July 23, 1998.
[458]Human Rights Watch interview with Bhimjibhai Sonarai, Navsarjan social worker, Ahmedabad district, Gujarat, July 23, 1998.

Sikkaliars have to bury the Thevars' dead animals, and women have to collect waste. They only get meals for their work, even for burying animals. Sometimes Sikkaliars take the dead animal's meat and divide it among themselves. The Thevars harass women laborers, particularly young ladies. Once a girl attains puberty, she is harassed by Thevar men. If anyone opposes it, they will be severely punished. Sikkaliars depend on Thevars, and because there is no other support they often leave for other villages out of fear when fighting occurs. They are doing scavenger work as well as [agricultural] laborer work for which they are paid less than minimum wage. They clean the latrines, the bathrooms, the drains, and they do cremation work. If not they are severely punished by the Thevars. The children are not able to go to school.[459]

The activist also described how Dalits are unable to freely exercise their constitutionally guaranteed right to vote. During the February 1998 elections, Sikkaliars were forced to vote according to the demands of the Thevar community or risk losing the little income they had: "Because Thevars are in the majority, they will come inside the voting booth and tell them who to vote for. If they don't act according to instructions, then they don't get employment, or they will be beaten."[460]

Thevars treat Sikkaliars as slaves so they can utilize them as they wish. They exploit them sexually and make them dig graveyards for high-caste people's burials. They have to take the death message to Thevars. These are all unpaid services. Maybe they give them Rs. 10 [US$0.25] for the message. There are also very meager wages for grave digging.

---

[459]Human Rights Watch interview with Manibharati, Coordinator for the NGO Navjeevan Trust, Madurai district, Tamil Nadu, February 17, 1998.

[460]Ibid. During the 1998 national parliamentary elections, political parties in the Baghpat constituency in the northern state of Uttar Pradesh alleged that in several villages, no other castes except those belonging to the incumbent member of parliament were allowed to vote. "Ajit Singh's foes fear massive booth capturing," *Rediff On the Net*, February 11, 1998. www.redifindia.com/news/1998/feb/11bagh.htm. For more on election-related violence against Dalits, see chapters IV and V. For more on booth capturing, see Chapter IV.

Still they have to do these things or they will be thrown out of the village.[461]

The activist referred to the women in his village as "sexual slaves" and claimed that Thevar men frequently enter Dalit houses at night to rape the women: "Dalit people have anger against Thevar people in mind. Thevars use their women, but Dalits cannot do anything."[462] According to R. Balakrishnan, director of the Tamil Nadu chapter of the National Commission for Scheduled Castes and Scheduled Tribes, the raping of Dalit women exposes the hypocrisy of the caste system: "No one practices untouchability when it comes to sex."[463]

### The relationship between scavenging and debt bondage

When interviewed in early 1998, thirty-year-old Parsotambhai, a mother of three in Ahmedabad district, Gujarat, earned Rs. 10 (US$0.25) a month for each house she cleaned. She also received small amounts of food once a day and complained that there was too much work.[464] Others voiced similar complaints:

> They give one person too much work so they have to take their family members, even their children, at night to finish the work; otherwise they would get fired. It takes four people to do the work that they give one person. None of the children are really studying. Girls sometimes study up to fifth standard, boys up to seventh.[465]

Given the insignificant amounts of remuneration and the need to engage several family members in work assigned to one, it comes as little surprise that many families borrow money from their upper-caste neighbors and consequently going into bondage. Their poverty is so acute that Macwan has even documented

---

[461]Human Rights Watch interview with Manibharati, Madurai district, Tamil Nadu, February 17, 1998.

[462]Ibid.

[463]Human Rights Watch interview with R. Balakrishnan, Madras, February 13, 1998.

[464]Human Rights Watch interview with Parsotambhai, Ahmedabad district, Gujarat, July 23, 1998.

[465]Human Rights Watch interviews with group of manual scavengers, Ahmedabad district, Gujarat, July 23, 1998. "Standard" equals grade.

a Bhangi practice of separating non-digested wheat from buffalo dung to make *chappatis* (flat bread).[466] One scavenger commented:

> There is no health care, no benefits from the government. We
> cannot live on what we get paid, but we have to. We also have
> to take loans from the upper caste. They charge 10 percent in
> interest per month. We have no clothes, no soap, no wages, and
> no payments on time.[467]

### Failure to implement protective legislation

The Employment of Manual Scavengers and Construction of Dry Latrines (Prohibition) Act, 1993 punishes the employment of scavengers or the construction of dry (non-flush) latrines with imprisonment for up to one year and/or a fine as high as Rs. 2,000 (US$50).[468] Offenders are also liable to prosecution under the Scheduled Castes and Scheduled Tribes (Prevention of Atrocities) Act, 1989. In 1992 the government launched a national scheme that called for the identification, training, and rehabilitation of safai karamcharis throughout the country.

According to the National Commission for Safai Karamcharis, the progress "has not been altogether satisfactory." As a result it has benefited only "a handful of safai karamcharis and their dependents. One of the reasons for unsatisfactory progress of the Scheme appears to be inadequate attention paid to it by the State Governments and concerned agencies."[469] When confronted with the existence of manual scavenging and dry latrines within their jurisdiction, state governments often deny their existence altogether or claim that a lack of water supply prevents states from constructing flush latrines.[470] This despite the fact that

---

[466]Human Rights Watch interview with Martin Macwan, Ahmedabad district, Gujarat, July 23, 1998.

[467]Human Rights Watch interview, Ahmedabad district, Gujarat, July 23, 1998.

[468]See Appendix D for full text of the act.

[469] National Commission for Safai Karamcharis, *The Role of the National Commission for Safai Karamcharis in Liberation and Rehabilitation of Safai Karamcharis and their Dependents* (New Delhi: Government of India, 1997), p. 4.

[470]In 1995 the Gujarat-based NGO Navsarjan initiated legal action on behalf of thirty-five safai karamcharis in Ranpur town, Ahmedabad district, charging government officials with negligence in allowing the outlawed practice of manual scavenging to continue. In an affidavit the state government responded by claiming that the practice no longer existed in the state. In 1998 the Gujarat High Court described as "unfortunate" the government's actions in filing a false affidavit denying the prevalence of the practice. Human Rights

a sum of Rs. 4,640,000,000 (US$116 million) was allocated to the scheme under the government's Eighth Five Year Plan.[471] Activists claim that the resources, including government funds, exist for construction and for the rehabilitation of scavengers; what is lacking is the political will to do so. Members of the National Commission for Safai Karamcharis consider it imperative that the commission be "vested with similar powers and facilities as are available to the National Commission for Scheduled Castes and Scheduled Tribes."[472] Currently the commission only has advisory powers and no authority to summon or monitor cases.

### The Devadasi System: Ritualized Prostitution[473]

The practice of *devadasi*, in which a girl, usually before reaching the age of puberty, is ceremoniously dedicated or married to a deity or to a temple, continues in several southern states including Andhra Pradesh and Karnataka. Literally meaning "female servant of god," devadasis usually belong to the Dalit community. Once dedicated, the girl is unable to marry, forced to become a prostitute for upper-caste community members, and eventually auctioned into an urban brothel. The age-old practice continues to legitimize the sexual violence and discrimination that have come to characterize the intersection between caste and gender. The patrons of the devadasis

> are generally from the higher castes because those from the devadasis own castes are too poor to afford to [pay] for the rituals... In many cases a patron kept many girls and the number of girls used to be a yard stick of the status of that man. This system of patronage has given way to [a system of] commercial prostitution in the populated big cities.[474]

---

Watch interview with Martin Macwan, founder-director of Navsarjan, New York, October 15, 1998.

[471] National Commission for Safai Karamcharis, *The Role of the National Commission...*, pp. 2-4.

[472] Ibid., p. 8. For more on the National Commission for Scheduled Castes and Scheduled Tribes, see Chapter X.

[473] Devadasis are also known by the names *jogati* and *basavi*. See also Nagendra Kumar Singh, *Divine Prostitution*, (New Delhi: A. P. H. Publishing Corporation, 1997).

[474] Ruth Manorama, "Dalit Women Perspective," presented at the Global Gathering on Women Under Racism and Casteism, 1992.

Activists involved in the Dalit women's movement explain that the nexus between caste and forced prostitution is quite strong and that the devadasi system is no exception. Most Indian girls and women in India's urban brothels come from lower-caste, tribal, or minority communities. Like other forms of violence against women, ritualized prostitution, activists believe, is a system "designed to kill whatever vestiges of self-respect the untouchable castes have in order to subjugate them and keep them underprivileged."[475] By keeping Dalit women as prostitutes, and by tying prostitution to bondage in rural areas, upper-caste men reinforce their declaration of social and economic superiority over the lower castes.

According to the Ambedkar Centre for Justice and Peace, a Canada-based NGO:

> Thousands of untouchable female children (between 6 and 8 years) are forced to become maidens of God (Devadasis, Jogins, a Hindu religious practice in Andhra Pradesh, Karnataka State, Maharashtra, Orissa State, to mention only a few). They are taken from their families, never to see them again. They are later raped by the temple priest and finally auctioned secretly into prostitution and ultimately die from AIDS. It is estimated by NGOs that 5,000 to 15,000 girls are auctioned secretly every year.[476]

In an interview with Human Rights Watch, the head of an NGO active in Karnataka explained that in her state the girl is offered to the Goddess Yellamma in a village ceremony:

> Earlier it was for priests, but now it is for high-caste men. They used to live in the temples... now anyone can use them including lorry drivers... Dreadlocked hair is taken as a sign from the Goddess Yellamma that the girl is meant to be a devadasi. In a festival, a marriage ceremony takes place between the girl and god. The eldest lady of the devadasi community ties the mangal sutra [marriage necklace]. In some ceremonies the girl was

---

[475]Ruth Manorama, "Dalit Women...".
[476]Yogesh Varhade, "International Advocacy and the Role of the United Nations and Civil Society," Ambedkar Centre for Justice and Peace, Presidential address, Conference '98, June 6, 1998, p. 3.

paraded almost naked. The girl is then given some money but still works in the fields. She lives separately in the village and is used by all the men, including Dalit men.[477]

In 1992 the Karnataka state government passed the Karnataka Devadasi (Prohibition of Dedication) Act and called for the rehabilitation of devadasi women. Like many laws aimed at protecting women and lower castes, the act suffers from a lack of enforcement. Moreover, the police themselves have been known to use devadasis. As the Karnataka activist explained, the law works to the disadvantage of women because it criminalizes their actions and not the actions of their patrons. Police will even go so far as to demand sex as a bribe: "They will threaten to file charges under the act if the woman says no."[478] Their perceived status in society, as women who are supposed to serve men sexually, also makes it more difficult for devadasis to approach the police for help: "When a devadasi is raped, it is not considered rape. She can be had by any man at any time."[479]

In reviewing India's third periodic report to the U.N. Human Rights Committee, submitted under Article 40 of the International Covenant on Civil and Political Rights (ICCPR) in July 1997, the Human Rights Committee regretted "the lack of national legislation to outlaw the practice of Devadasi, the regulation of which is left to the states," and added that "it appears that the practice continues and that not all states have effective legislation against it." The committee emphasized that the practice was incompatible with the ICCPR and recommended that "all necessary measures be taken urgently" toward its eradication.[480]

---

[477]Human Rights Watch interview with Jyothi Raj, Rural Education and Development Society, Bangalore, July 26, 1998.
[478]Ibid.
[479]Ibid.
[480]Consideration of Report by India to the Human Rights Committee, CCPR/C/79/Add.81, August 4, 1997.

## VIII.  THE CRIMINALIZATION OF SOCIAL ACTIVISM

With [few] or no amendments to the Indian Penal Code, 1870,
the Criminal Procedure Code, 1930, and the Indian Evidence
Act, 1872, the same laws that were used by the British to keep
the Indians down are now being used by the upper castes to keep
the Dalits down.

— Dalit attorney[481]

It is generally known that false criminal cases are sometimes
engineered merely for the sake of making arrests to humiliate
and embarrass some specified enemies of the complainant, in
league with the police for corrupt reasons.

— National Police Commission, Government of India[482]

In violation of the right to equal protection before the law, as guaranteed
by Article 14 of the constitution and Article 26 of the International Covenant on
Civil and Political Rights, local police routinely abuse vaguely worded provisions
of the Indian Penal Code, the Criminal Procedure Code, and various preventive
detention statutes to thwart attempts by Dalits to demand their legal rights.  The
arbitrary detention of Dalits and treatment of Dalit men and women in custody are
also clear violations of laws governing police conduct.

State agents have acted directly and forcefully against those attempting to
claim their rights.  Dalit activists throughout the country face charges as
"terrorists," "threats to national security," and "habitual offenders."  Many have to
spend much of their income on lawyers' fees or anticipatory bail.  Dalit activists
are frequently charged under the National Security Act, 1980, the Indian
Explosives Act, 1884, and even the Terrorism and Anti-Disruptive Activities Act
(TADA).[483]  The most common charges under the Indian Penal Code include

---

[481]Human Rights Watch interview with Dalit attorney, Madurai, Tamil Nadu, February 16,
1998.

[482]National Police Commission, "Corruption in Police," Chapter XXII, *Third Report of the
National Police Commission* (New Delhi: Government of India, 1980), p. 31.

[483]The National Security Act, 1980, allows for a person to be detained for up to twelve
months in order to prevent him or her from acting in any manner that is prejudicial to the
security of the state government or to the maintenance of public order.  TADA, also a widely

sections 147 and 148 on rioting and rioting with a deadly weapon; Section 341 for wrongful restraint; sections 323 and 324 for voluntarily causing hurt; sections 302 and 307 for murder and attempted murder; and Section 427 for mischief. Provisions of the Criminal Procedure Code are also used to detain Dalit activists and deter them from organizing Dalit community members.

The criminalization of social activism in India is a pattern that has been previously documented by Human Rights Watch.[484] Dalits are easy targets for the police. With little knowledge of their rights, limited access to attorneys, and no money for hearings or bail, they often languish in prison even for minor offenses. This section briefly outlines the rights of the accused upon arrest and the treatment of Dalit activists in the states of Tamil Nadu, Maharashtra, Gujarat and Karnataka.

**Rights of the Accused**

When an accused is arrested, he or she has the right to: be informed of the reasons for the arrest;[485] see the warrant if arrested under a warrant;[486] consult a lawyer of his or her choice;[487] appear before the nearest magistrate within twenty-four hours;[488] and be told whether he or she is entitled to be released on bail.[489]

---

criticized security law, permitted among other things, the use in trial of coerced confessions. The law prohibited any act that questioned the integrity of India, thereby criminalizing free speech. In response to increasing domestic pressure, the central government allowed the law to lapse in May 1995 although detention of persons under TADA continues for offenses allegedly committed before the law lapsed—a practice that authorities reportedly abuse through the spurious backdating of violations. Those newly detained join thousands of others who continue to be held under a provision authorizing their continued detention, even though the law itself is no longer in force.

[484]*See*, for example, Asia Watch, "Before the Deluge: Human Rights Abuses at India's Narmada Dam," *A Human Rights Watch Report*, vol. 4, no. 15, June 1992; Human Rights Watch/Asia, "Memorandum to World Bank President James Wolfensohn from Human Rights Watch/Asia concerning World Bank projects in the Singrauli region of India," April 16, 1998.

[485]Constitution of India, Art. 22; Criminal Procedure Code, Sec. 50.

[486]Criminal Procedure Code, Sec. 75.

[487]Constitution of India, Art. 22.

[488]Ibid. Section 57 of the Criminal Procedure Code adds, "no police officer shall detain in custody a person arrested without warrant for a longer period than under all the circumstances of the case is reasonable, and such period shall not, in the absence of a special order of a Magistrate under section 167, exceed twenty-four hours exclusive of time necessary for the journey from the place of arrest to the Magistrate's Court."

[489]Criminal Procedure Code, Sec. 50.

Section 163 of the Criminal Procedure Code prohibits any officer from making any threat or promise for the purpose of obtaining a statement from a witness or an accused.   Causing harm to obtain a confession or to obtain information regarding an offense is also punishable by up to ten years imprisonment under Section 330 of the Indian Penal Code.  Police torture of an accused is a violation of the detainee's fundamental rights to life and liberty guaranteed under articles 20 and 21 of the constitution.[490]  Nevertheless, police torture persists.  Several Supreme Court cases have also determined that victims of police torture are entitled to compensation.[491]

### D. K. Basu v. State of West Bengal

In December 1996 the Supreme Court established detailed instructions for proper police procedure to be followed by the police in cases of arrest or detention. These requirements, as articulated in *D. K. Basu v. State of West Bengal*, include:

- Police personnel carrying out arrests and handling the interrogation of an arrestee must wear accurate, visible and clear identification and name tags giving their designations.  The particulars of all personnel who handle interrogations must be recorded in a register.

- The police officer carrying out the arrest must prepare a memo of arrest at the time of arrest; this memo must be attested by a witness who may be either a member of the family of the arrestee or a responsible person of the locality where the arrest has been made.

- The person arrested or detained shall be entitled to have a friend, relative or other person known to him, or having an interest in his welfare, informed as soon as practicable.

- The arrestee should, when he or she so requests, be medically examined at the time of arrest, and major injuries, if any are present on his or her body, must be recorded in a memo.  The inspection memo should be

---

[490]See also Chapter X for applicable provisions of the International Covenant of Civil and Political Rights.
[491]See generally, P. D. Mathew, *What You Should Know About the Police* (New Delhi: Indian Social Institute, 1996), pp. 30-38.

signed by both the arrestee and by the police officer concerned, and a
copy should be given to the arrestee.

- The arrested person should undergo a medical examination by a trained
  doctor every forty-eight hours of his or her detention in custody.

- The arrestee should be permitted to meet his or her lawyer during
  interrogation.[492]

The Supreme Court has given weight to the enforceability of these
instructions—which are in line with international guidelines for the treatment of
persons under arrest or detention[493]—by adding that those in violation of these
directions would be liable for contempt.[494] As illustrated in chapters IV and V on
the pattern of abuse in rural Bihar and Tamil Nadu, respectively, police officers and
other state agents have generally disregarded proper procedure in arresting Dalits,
subjecting them to physical abuse and torture. The arrest of Dalit activists on
falsified charges has also been a common occurrence.

Human Rights Watch spoke to many Dalit lawyers and NGOs with legal
aid divisions in Tamil Nadu, Andhra Pradesh, Karnataka, and Maharashtra. Many
claimed that defending Dalits against false charges constituted most of their
workload. Prominent activist Henry Thiagaraj of the Dalit Liberation Education
Trust explained:

> Most of [our] legal people go to court to get anticipatory bail for
> false arrests of Dalits... The police will file the FIR [first
> information report] in such a way to say that the Dalit went to
> pick a fight. They take complaints only from upper-caste
> people. Then they say that the Dalits created the conflict, that
> they are contributing to communal violence. Then they ask the
> magistrate to pass an order that they should stay fifty kilometers

---

[492]D. K. Basu v. State of West Bengal (Writ Petition CRL No. 539 of 1986).
[493]See, for example, United Nations Basic Principles for the Treatment of Prisoners,
Adopted and Proclaimed by General Assembly resolution 45/111 of 14 December 1990.
[494]National Human Rights Commission, Annual Report 1996-1997 (New Delhi: Government
of India, 1998), pp. 20-21.

away from the village. The women and children who remain behind end up starving and living in fear.[495]

A team of Dalit attorneys in southern Tamil Nadu who represent Dalits in the Rajapalayam and Sriviliputhur districts added the following on the role of corruption:

> If there is a fight between Dalits and upper castes in which a Dalit is attacked or property is damaged, and if he chooses to go to the police station, the police officer, usually an upper-caste fellow, will refuse to do an FIR, saying that his [the Dalit's] version is false. Conversely, the Dalit gets charged by the people he is accusing. In all police stations, all work can only be done with the aid of a lot of money. Even for FIRs or arresting an accused, bribes are needed. Dalit people are penniless, and the police are also influenced by caste.[496]

**False Arrests During the Tamil Nadu Southern District Clashes**
Apart from specific offenses, the police also customarily arrest large numbers of people under preventive arrest laws. This practice may be linked to caste tensions in various ways. For example, according to the Dalit attorneys interviewed, in Tamil Nadu, Dalits are often charged under the Tamil Nadu Public Properties (Prevention of) Destruction Act, 1992. During a June 1997 police raid on Desikapuram village, Virudhunagar district, dozens of Dalit men and women were arrested and charged under the Public Properties Act for allegedly setting fire to a Thevar van. Several eyewitnesses reported, however, that the police themselves had set the van on fire.[497] Charges under the Public Properties Act are non-bailable; those arrested under the act spend a minimum of one month in prison. The police also charge them with non-bailable Indian Penal Code offenses. With the more minor charges, "they have to be released within seven to ten days. But

---

[495]Human Rights Watch interview with Henry Thiagaraj, Madras, February 14, 1998.
[496]Human Rights Watch interview with Dalit attorneys, Madurai, Tamil Nadu, February 16, 1998.
[497]For more on the police raid, see Chapter V.

in cases of murder or charges under the Public Properties Act, it could be three months or more."[498]

In another case, police spread an even wider net to criminalize those caste Hindus that did not toe the police line. After a caste Hindu attack on the Dalit colony of Veludavur, Villapuram district, in January 1998, police arrested twenty-three people under the Atrocities Act. The arrests, activists claimed, were meant to punish those caste Hindus who did not endorse the attack: "They arrested high-caste people who weren't involved, to punish non-Dalits who did not support the attacks."[499] Affected villagers named fifteen aggressors in the FIR, but only three of the fifteen named were arrested. The rest of the detainees, those not named in the FIR, could be arrested because of the police practice of adding "and others" to the ends of the names of the accused. "Then they can arrest anyone they want," one activist said, "usually, this is how it works."[500] On the basis of the FIR—which concerned a caste Hindu attack—the police went on to arrest four Dalits who did not belong to the village, charging them with attempted murder under Section 307 of the Indian Penal Code and under the Public Properties Act for allegedly carrying petrol pumps. Two of the detainees were members of the Dalit Panthers of India.[501]

Tirumavalavan is the head of the Dalit Panthers of India (DPI) for Tamil Nadu. DPI is a nonviolent awareness-raising and organizing movement concentrating primarily on women's rights and land issues and claims. Since the mid-1990s, DPI has helped to promote a new Dalit political leadership in Tamil Nadu, unaligned to mainstream political parties. Its platform includes demands for land to Dalits for living and for cultivation, for the inclusion of Dalits in government land auctions, and for implementation of the Atrocities Act. Tirumavalavan has been involved in many protests against government inaction in Dalit murder cases, such as the Mellavalavu murders described in Chapter V. He told Human Rights Watch about the following incident.

In early October 1997 an armed group of caste Hindus entered the village of Nantiswaramangalam. Six Dalit youths were taken back to the assailants' village, tied to a tree, and beaten. The attack was reportedly triggered by a Dalit resident's attempt to draw water from the village water pond. When the police

---

[498]Human Rights Watch interview with Dalit attorneys, Madurai, Tamil Nadu, February 16, 1998.
[499]Human Rights Watch interview with Nicholas of Integrated Rural Development Society, and other activists, Madras, February 14, 1998.
[500]Ibid.
[501]Ibid.

arrived, they released the youths but did not register a case under the Atrocities Act. After DPI's involvement, the police booked a case under Section 3(1)(10) for name-calling, the least serious offense under the Atrocities Act.[502] The district administration suggested that the police initiate "peace talks" between the communities, but no action was taken. According to Tirumavalavan, "The government usually tries to make a compromise in these cases but does not take action against caste Hindu people."[503] Violence continued in the village for more than a week and included further beatings, arson, and physical and sexual assaults on women. A DPI member who attempted to intervene and call for peace talks was severely beaten by caste Hindus and admitted to the hospital for head injuries after being struck with a sickle. Dalit residents were soon forced to leave their village and sought refuge in the neighboring village of Sholadurum. More than a month later the district administration had done nothing to get them back to their homes.[504]

Increasing tensions in the area led to a staged roadblock in the first week of November 1997. Buses were burned, for which thirty people, all Dalits, were arrested. Of those thirty, five were arrested under the National Security Act, 1980, and two were below fifteen years of age. Tirumavalavan claimed that they were not involved in the burning of buses. He explained that the arrests were examples of a typical police pattern:

> They were picked up in their house, and all thirty are still in jail. The two underage people are no longer being charged under the National Security Act but they are still in jail because of pressure from the community. But you cannot arrest below fifteen years of age. The police gave their age as nineteen, but we proved that they were under fifteen. The police have to catch someone so they indiscriminately arrest. A lot of others burn buses and destroy property but only Dalits get arrested. When there is any public law and order problem they come to Dalit homes.[505]

---

[502]For more on non-registration of Atrocities Act cases and the use of Section 3(1)(10), see Chapter X.

[503]Human Rights Watch interview with Tirumavalavan, Madras, February 13, 1998.

[504]Ibid.

[505]Ibid. The key facts of this case have been investigated and independently verified by People's Watch whose findings corroborate our own.

Tirumavalavan himself has been arrested numerous times. He told Human Rights Watch that he and other members of his movement are targeted by the police for organizing Dalits to claim their rights:

> We are very pessimistic because the government is dominated by the high castes. They immobilize people. I am often arrested under Indian Penal Code sections 153(a) [for promoting enmity between different groups] and 120(b) [for criminal conspiracy], and also under the Sedition Act and the National Security Act. When I speak in a public meeting they disperse the meeting. In late 1992 I was abducted by the police in a jeep. They said the superintendent of police wanted to meet me. Another accusation is that we are called extremist Naxalite groups. We are a powerful group, so we are automatically linked with Naxalites. We are not underground. We boycott elections. We do not advocate violence. We just organize Dalits to emancipate their slavery.[506]

The Sedition Act, embodied under Indian Penal Code Section 124A, reads as follows:

> Whoever by words, either spoken or written, or by signs, or by visible representation, or otherwise, brings or attempts to bring into hatred or contempt, or excites or attempts to excite disaffection towards, the Government established by law in India, shall be punished with imprisonment for life, to which fine may be added, or with imprisonment which may extend to three years, to which fine may be added....[507]

In 1962 the Supreme Court held that Section 124A—though susceptible to abuse by state agents—was not in violation of the constitutional right to free speech found under Article 19(1)(a).[508] The court added that it is only when the words have "the pernicious tendency or intention of creating public disorder or

---

[506]Ibid. For more on Naxalites, see chapters III and IV.
[507]Indian Penal Code, Sec. 124A.
[508]*Kedar Nath*, AIR 1962 SC 955.

disturbance of law and order that the law steps in."[509] However, as with the police's propensity to abuse vaguely worded provisions of the Indian Penal Code and Criminal Procedure Code, the law has been used to prohibit peaceful meetings and protests, in clear violation of Article 19 of the constitution which guarantees freedom of speech and a right to peaceful assembly.

According to a Dalit activist working in Tirunelveli and Tuticorin districts, Tamil Nadu, many "young, educated youths" were also detained under the Tamil Nadu Goondas Act during the southern district clashes in 1997.[510] A goonda is defined as a habitual criminal, usually associated with a criminal gang.

Human Rights Watch interviews with activists in Maharashtra, Gujarat, and Tamil Nadu revealed that the National Security Act, 1980 is also commonly used against Dalit protesters and organizers. One activist exclaimed, "Organizing untouchables is a threat to national security?"[511] The act allows the central and state governments to make orders to detain a person with a view to "preventing him from acting in any matter prejudicial to the defence of India, the relations of India with foreign powers, or the security of India," or with a view to "preventing him from acting in any manner prejudicial to the security of the State Government, or from acting in any manner prejudicial to the maintenance of public order...".[512] Upon obtaining confirmation from an advisory board under Section 12 of the act, a person may be detained for up to twelve months.[513]

## Maharashtra Case Studies

Human Rights Watch spoke with several activists working to train Dalits in the registration of Atrocities Act cases in the "atrocity-prone" Marathwada region of eastern Maharashtra. Several were suffering a legal backlash as a result of their activism.

Shankar Pawar works among Dalits in the Andhra Pradesh-Karnataka-Maharashtra border region. In 1993 he was detained under Criminal Procedure Code Section 151 for fifteen days for organizing Dalits to demand their due share

---

[509]Indian Penal Code, Sec. 124A, Comments.

[510]Human Rights Watch interview with Bharathan, Programme Coordinator, Navjeevan Trust, Madurai district, Tamil Nadu, February 17, 1998. Navjeevan Trust is an NGO that campaigns against child labor and trains local panchayat leaders.

[511]Human Rights Watch interview with Vivek Pandit, Usgaon, Maharashtra, January 29, 1998.

[512]The National Security Act, 1980, Sec. 3.

[513]Ibid., Sec. 13.

of auctioned temple lands.[514] Under Section 151, "a police officer knowing of a design to commit any cognizable offence may arrest, without orders from the Magistrate and without a warrant, the person so designing, if it appears to such officer that the commission of the offence cannot otherwise be prevented." Although sub-section (2) of Section 151 does not allow for the detention to exceed twenty-four hours, in the state of Maharashtra the section has been amended to allow for detention up to fifteen days. After his detention, Pawar was jailed for fifty-two days and concurrently tried under the National Security Act. Only after his case was pleaded before three High Court judges was he released.[515]

Datta Khandagale is a social worker in Chorakali village, Usmanabad district, Maharashtra. He works with fifty Dalit families who are segregated from the majority caste Hindus in the village. In September 1992, Khandagale asked the police to register an Atrocities Act case against upper castes who had instituted a social boycott against Dalit villagers. The boycott was in retaliation for the Dalits' attempt to enter a village temple for prayer. As they entered, the upper-caste villagers began to throw stones and, as a result, one woman's head was cut open. When Khandagale approached the police with a complaint, the police responded, "You're the one making trouble in the village, increasing tensions between communities," and then proceeded to file a Criminal Procedure Code Section 107 case against him. Section 107 allows the police to preventively detain any person "likely to commit a breach of the peace of disturb the public tranquility." Nine Dalits were arrested, including Khandagale. Because they could not pay the bond, they remained in jail for five days.[516]

The harassment did not end with the police. After his release, Khandagale was approached by local politicians in his district. He was told, "If you don't [drop] the case [Atrocities Act case] it will be bad for you." Other politicians followed suit: "They said you should reject the case. We said, 'No, we can't.' Then they threatened the other eight and said, 'If you don't leave the case alone, we will kill you.'" The politicians were accompanied by ten to fifteen police during their visit. The other eight arrestees eventually dropped the case.

---

[514]Human Rights Watch interview with Shankar Pawar, Usgaon, Maharashtra, January 29, 1998.
[515]Human Rights Watch interview with Vivek Pandit, Samarthan, Usgaon, Maharashtra, January 29, 1998.
[516]Human Rights Watch interview with Datta Khandagale, Usgaon, Maharashtra, January 29, 1998.

Khandagale was later summoned by the Superintendent of Police (SP) of Usmanabad district. When he arrived he found over twenty upper-caste villagers in the SP's office.

> In front of them he scolded me and said, "Why are you causing trouble and agitating the Dalits?" "You fool," he said, "Why are you creating trouble between the two groups?" I asked him not to swear at me and said, "You are threatening the people that need your protection, and you are insulting me in front of them [upper-caste villagers]." Then he kicked me out of the office. I came home and wrote down everything that happened and sent him the letter. I asked, "If you talk against me and pressure me in front of the upper caste then what's to keep them from killing me?"[517]

He also sent the letter to the Ministry of Home Affairs. The SP eventually apologized for his behavior, but the upper castes continued with their threats. Only after appeals to the chief minister was Khandagale granted police protection, which continued for three years. Police presence also put an end to the upper-caste social boycott in the village, and the village temple is now open to all Dalits. Khandagale is the only one who goes in, "[t]he others are too afraid."[518] The woman who sustained head injuries from the 1992 stone throwing was ultimately persuaded to drop all charges. In 1994, the water supply to the temple was disrupted. The upper-caste villagers attributed the problem to the presence of "untouchables" in the temple. At the time of the Human Rights Watch interview in January 1998, Khandagale continued to be harassed by the police and threatened by upper-caste villagers for his organizing activities.

Vivek Pandit of the NGO Samarthan, who has provided legal literacy training to these and other Maharashtra activists, had seventeen charges pending against him as of December 1998. At one point, he had to appeal to the High Court to get back his passport, it had been impounded by the state government to keep him from leaving the country.[519] In an interview with Human Rights Watch, Pandit claimed that the district administration and the police were using laws to

---

[517]Ibid.
[518]Ibid.
[519]Human Rights Watch interview with Vivek Pandit, Bombay, February 4, 1998.

"torture and stamp out Dalit leaders."[520] Pandit has been actively involved in the case of a man named Digambar who, at the time of his interview with Human Rights Watch, was fighting an externment (banishment) order from his village "for creating a nuisance and disrupting law and order." Upon receiving his externment notice, Digambar sent a thirteen-point response to district officials. Portions of the response, translated from Marathi, are provided below:

> I am a scheduled-caste youth working for my people. I am organizing scheduled castes as per fundamental rights guaranteed under the constitution, including the right to freedom of association. Because of my work, some casteist elements are bound to get angry. I have never committed any crimes of a serious nature. You are a representative of the state and have a duty to protect scheduled castes under the constitution. Instead, how can you issue [a notice against] me? The government has to abide by law and not get pressurized by the upper caste. Officers are violating fundamental rights, and now you are too. My duty is to uphold these rights. I am going to mobilize and organize against offenses. If the cases I have registered are false, where is the proof?.. Kindly withdraw the notice.[521]

At the time of the interview, Digambar was awaiting the district administration's response.

## Other Case Studies

During our investigations, Human Rights Watch came across several other cases of police harassment of NGO activists, ranging from periodic police visits, to arrests and charges of aiding and abetting in various crimes or interfering in police investigations.

V. T. Rajshekar is the editor of *Dalit Voice*, India's most widely circulated Dalit journal. Prior to running the journal, he was a journalist with *Indian Express* for twenty-five years. Rajshekar has often come under attack for his writings. In

---

[520]Human Rights Watch interview with Vivek Pandit, Usgaon, Maharashtra, January 29, 1998.
[521]Human Rights Watch interview with Digambar, Usgaon, Maharashtra, January 29, 1998; Human Rights Watch interview with Vivek Pandit, Bombay, February 4, 1998.

1986 his passport was impounded because of "anti-Hinduism writings outside of India." The same year, he was arrested in Bangalore under TADA:

> The police came from Chandigarh and arrested me and took me to the Chandigarh jail for an editorial I wrote in *Dalit Voice*. Another writer who republished the editorial was also arrested. Then they came to me. After fifteen days, after much Dalit agitation, I was released with an apology.[522]

In addition to TADA, Rajshekar has also been arrested under the Sedition Act and under the Indian Penal Code for creating disaffection between communities—all for his writings. He has also endured attempts on his life and has been placed on the Home Ministry's "dangerous persons list."[523]

Gilbert Rodrigo, a member of the Tamil Nadu-based NGO Legal Resources for Social Action told Human Rights Watch that he was "visited" by members of the police special branch each year. They inquire about the sources of his organization's funding and how the money is spent.[524] Nicholas, a member of the Integrated Rural Development Society, who organizes Dalits in Tamil Nadu to register cases under the Atrocities Act, has been charged three times under Section 107 of the Indian Penal Code for aiding and abetting Dalits in their alleged crimes. According to Nicholas, the use of Section 107 "is an attempt by the state to divert us from our work. You have to go very far for the hearings. They make you run around. It is mental torture."[525] Martin Macwan and his team of 180 social workers provide legal aid and training to Dalits in Gujarat. His organization, Navsarjan, has also led a state-wide campaign to abolish the practice of manual scavenging. Many of his team members have been charged under the Criminal Procedure Code for disturbing police investigations.[526]

---

[522]Human Rights Watch interview with V. T. Rajshekar, Bangalore, February 7, 1998.
[523]Ibid.
[524]Human Rights Watch interview with Gilbert Rodrigo, Madras, February 14, 1998.
[525]Human Rights Watch interview with Nicholas, Madras, February 13, 1998.
[526]Human Rights Watch interview with Martin Macwan, Ahmedabad, July 23, 1998.

# IX. ATTACKS ON DALIT WOMEN: A PATTERN OF IMPUNITY

Singularly positioned at the bottom of India's caste, class, and gender hierarchies, largely uneducated and consistently paid less than their male counterparts, Dalit women make up the majority of landless laborers and scavengers, as well as a significant percentage of the women forced into prostitution in rural areas or sold into urban brothels.[527] As such, they come into greater contact with landlords and enforcement agencies than their upper-caste counterparts. Their subordinate position is exploited by those in power who carry out their attacks with impunity.

Throughout this report, Human Rights Watch has documented the use of sexual abuse and other forms of violence against Dalit women as tools by landlords and the police to inflict political "lessons" and crush dissent and labor movements within Dalit communities. In Laxmanpur-Bathe, Bihar, women were raped and mutilated before being massacred by members of the Ranvir Sena in 1997; in Bihar and Tamil Nadu, women have been beaten, arrested, and sometimes tortured during violent search and raid operations on Dalit villages in recent years. Like other Indian women whose relatives are sought by the police, Dalit women have also been arrested and raped in custody as a means of punishing their male relatives who are hiding from the police. As very young women, they are forced into prostitution in temples under the devadasi system.

Cases documented by India's National Commission for Women, by local and national nongovernmental women's rights organizations, and by the press, reveal a pattern of impunity in attacks on women consistent with our findings. In all cases of attacks on women documented in this report, the accused state and private actors escaped punishment; in most cases, attacks were neither investigated nor prosecuted. Until recently, the plight of Dalit women has also been neglected by various political movements. As explained by Ruth Manorama, head of the newly constituted National Federation for Dalit Women:

> Dalit women are at the bottom in our community. Within the women's movement, Dalit issues have not been taken seriously. Within the Dalit movement, women have been ignored. Caste, class, and gender need to be looked at together. Dalit women

---

[527]Human Rights Watch interview with T. K. Chaudary, Joint Commissioner of Police, Mumbai (Bombay) Police, February 5, 1998.

have contributed to this discourse... Women's labor is already undervalued; when she is a Dalit, it is nil... The atrocities are also much more vulgar.[528]

Other activists echo the notion that women are hit the hardest in everyday life and during caste clashes. One activist told Human Rights Watch, "Sexual violence is linked to debt bondage in rural areas."[529] Another commented on the need to give priority to women's cases:

Making women eat human defecation, parading them naked, gang rapes, these are women-specific crimes. Gang rapes are mostly of Dalit women. These cases should be given top priority, requiring immediate action and immediate punishment.[530]

This chapter examines some of the constitutional, statutory, and international treaty protections afforded to women in India. It then offers several case studies to illustrate the government's failure to prosecute cases of rape and the manner in which differential rates of prosecution are compounded by corruption and caste and gender bias, even at the trial level.

**Women and the Law**

### India's constitution
Article 14 of India's constitution ensures equality by providing that: "The State shall not deny to any person equality before the law or the equal protection of the laws within the territory of India." Article 15(1) provides that the "State shall not discriminate against any citizen on grounds only of religion, race, caste, sex, place of birth or any of them," while articles 16(1) and 16(2) prohibit discrimination in general, and gender discrimination in matters of public

---

[528]Human Rights Watch interview with Ruth Manorama, Bangalore, July 25, 1998. The National Federation for Dalit Women is a secular, democratic organization with representatives from twenty-seven Indian states and union territories. It represents the first major effort to nationalize the Dalit women's movement.
[529]Human Rights Watch interview, Bangalore, July 25, 1998.
[530]Ibid.

employment. To promote equality, Article 15(3) provides that the state is free to make "any special provision for women and children."

Part IV of the constitution lists the Directive Principles of State Policy, including Article 39(b) of the constitution which provides that the state direct its policy toward ensuring equal pay for equal work for men and women. Section (a) of the same article provides that the state shall, in particular, direct its policy toward securing that citizens, men and women equally, have the right to an adequate means of livelihood. Section (c) requires that the state secure the health of workers, men and women, and ensure that children are not abused, and citizens are not forced by economic necessity to enter vocations that are unsuited to their age and strength. Finally, Article 44 of the constitution, asks that the state strive to introduce a uniform civil code for citizens so that varying religious codes do not dictate the personal laws governing women's lives. These provisions cannot be enforced in the state through courts as they are a "directive principles" of state policy.[531]

### Penal and criminal codes

In recognizing the history of police abuse against women, amendments to the Indian Penal Code and Criminal Procedure Code afford women a variety of legal protections in their dealings with state agents. For instance, when a woman is searched upon arrest, it must be done by a female officer with "strict regard to decency and modesty."[532] A police officer has no power to compel a woman or a child below the age of fifteen to appear in a police station to obtain information from her, and must instead visit the place in which the informant resides.[533] When searching a place occupied by a person sought to be arrested, if the place is

---

[531]See also Chapter V for a discussion of constitutional amendments allowing for increased representation of women and of scheduled caste and scheduled tribe members, in panchayats (village councils) and urban municipalities. Many have viewed these amendments as an important opportunity to solidify women's participation in the political process and in the decisions that affect their communities and lives most intimately. The Parliament, along with several non- and intergovernmental organizations, has been training women elected into panchayats. As the "panchayat maintains the social justice in the area... [w]omen members play a very important role against the violence and atrocities inflicted on women. [These amendments are seen as] a turning point in the patriarchal system." "Women in Panchayats," Project Progress Report, UNIFEM, p. 4.

[532]P. D. Mathew, *What You Should Know About the Police* (New Delhi: Indian Social Institute, 1996), p. 10.

[533]Ibid., p. 24.

occupied by a female (not being the person to be arrested) the police must give notice to her before entering that she has the liberty to withdraw.[534]

The Indian Penal Code also provides for stricter punishments when the crime of rape is committed in custody. Section 376 states that the crime of rape, when committed by a private actor, is punishable by a minimum of seven to ten years and a maximum of life imprisonment. Under subsection (2), the rape is punishable by "rigorous imprisonment" for a term of ten years to life if it is committed by a police officer against a woman in his custody (or in the custody of a police officer subordinate to him), or on the premises of his police station or a station house.

### Convention on the Elimination of All Forms of Discrimination against Women, 1979

Under Article 2 of the International Convention on the Elimination of All Forms of Discrimination against Women, states parties are required to "establish legal protection of the rights of women on an equal basis with men and to ensure through competent national tribunals and other public institutions the effective protection of women against any act of discrimination." They must also "refrain from engaging in any act or practice of discrimination against women and to ensure that public authorities and institutions shall act in conformity with this obligation."[535] Women are also entitled to equal remuneration and protection of health and safety in working conditions.[536]

With respect to the situation of rural women, the convention requires states parties to take into account the "significant roles which rural women play in the economic survival of their families, including their work in the non-monetized sectors of the economy," and to, "take all appropriate measures to ensure the application of the provisions of this Convention to women in rural areas."[537]

---

[534]Ibid., p. 11.

[535]Convention on the Elimination of All Forms of Discrimination against Women, adopted and opened for signature, ratification and accession by U.N. General Assembly Resolution 34/180 of December 18, 1979 (entered into force September 3, 1981), Art. 2, (c, d). India ratified the convention on July 9, 1993. See Chapter X for the applicability of other international conventions to the situation of Dalits.

[536]Ibid., Art. 11 (1).

[537]Ibid., Art. 14.

## Failure to Prosecute Rape Cases

Beginning with the lodging of the First Information Report (FIR) at the local police station through to the judge's opinion, should a case reach that far, women in India are faced with daunting obstacles in prosecuting cases of rape. If a woman is poor, belongs to a lower caste, and lives in a rural area, it is even more difficult for her to gain access to the justice system. Those who are able to pursue cases of sexual assault have to battle entrenched biases at every stage of the process: with the police, the doctors,[538] the judges, and even their own families.

Even if the police agree to file the FIR, they often fail to efficiently and deliberately collect the necessary evidence. Witnesses, should they exist, rarely agree to come forward to testify or corroborate the victim's statement for fear of retribution from the perpetrators, who are often in positions of relative power in the community. If the case manages to get filed and investigated despite these obstacles, then new problems arise when the woman goes before a judge whose gender biases and caste affiliations can greatly influence the judgment in the case.

For the reasons outlined above, and because of low reporting, conviction in rape cases is uncommon. From 1989 to 1993, reported crimes against women in India increased by 25.2 percent. At the same time, the National Crime Records Bureau's 1994 report revealed that convictions for crimes against women were minimal.[539]

> Out of the total (rape) cases in which trials were completed, 41.5 percent ended in conviction during 1990, 34.2 percent in 1991 and 33.8 percent in 1992 and 30.3 percent in 1993. Thus the acquittal percentage is showing an upward trend over the years. The rate of disposal of cases in courts was 23.9 percent in 1992

---

[538]When a thirty-seven-year-old woman was gang raped in Amina Nagar, a slum area in Jogeshwari, Bombay, she was refused a proper medical examination when taken to the hospital. The doctor was afraid of even broaching the subject for fear of legal liability: "How can we routinely do a rape check-up when a case of assault on a woman is reported? It is such a delicate subject." As quoted in Rupande Panala, "When a Poor Woman Gets Raped," *Manushi* (New Delhi) Sept. - Oct. 1990, p. 36. The police also hastily turned her away and shouted, "Do you know the meaning of rape?" They then recorded the incident as a case of outraging a woman's modesty, a bailable offense under Section 354 of the Indian Penal Code, punishable with just one year's imprisonment. Both the police and the doctors reportedly said: "If it was a young girl with injuries on her breast, we would suspect rape." Ibid., pp. 35-36.

[539]Sakshi, "Gender and Judges: A Judicial Point of View," (New Delhi, 1996), p. 8.

and 16.8 percent in 1993. On an average, 80 percent of the cases remained pending for trial. This is a disquieting status.[540]

The average conviction rate for rape has also been consistently lower than the less serious crimes of burglary and theft.[541]

In addition to compiling testimony on cases of rape by the police and during caste clashes, Human Rights Watch also interviewed several victims of rape on their experience with the legal system. Two illustrative cases are outlined below. Also included is the well-known case of Bhanwari Devi—whose rapists were acquitted on a judge's reasoning that "an upper-caste man could not have defiled himself by raping a lower-caste woman."[542]—and other cases illustrating gender bias at the trial level.

### M. Meena

M. Meena is a twelve-year-old Dalit girl; her name has been changed to protect her identity. She was raped in September 1997 by a twenty-one-year-old Thevar man in a southern district of Tamil Nadu.[543] Successful prosecution of her case was thwarted when the accused paid bribes to the police. Because of Meena's young age, Human Rights Watch obtained details of her rape and subsequent experience with the police largely from interviewing a social worker who had been active in her case; we then met with Meena to confirm the reports. The social worker described the incident:

> On her way home from a local store, a Thevar boy named Karuppaswami called Meena over on the pretext that she would help him pick something up. She refused and kept going. He then showed her a bill hook and threatened her.[544] He pulled her to a nearby tree, undressed her, and raped her. She was unconscious and could not walk. Some people took her home and called the Manur police station. The police said to come and file a report. So they took her there and gave a complaint. The

---

[540]National Crime Records Bureau (Ministry of Home Affairs), *Crime in India 1994*, as quoted in Sakshi, "Gender and Judges: A Judicial Point of View" (New Delhi, 1996), p. 9.
[541]Ibid.
[542]"In Brief: Recent Rape Cases," in *Kali's Yug* (New Delhi), November 1996, p. 20.
[543]The Thevars are a powerful "backward caste" in Tamil Nadu. For more on Thevars, see Chapter V. For more on backward castes generally, see Chapter III.
[544]A bill hook is an agricultural instrument with a hooked blade.

Thevar people also went to the police station and gave Rs. 10,000 (US$250) to the police and threatened the girl's father not to divulge the facts or the family would face dire consequences.[545]

As a result of pressure from the rapist's family, the police filed a case under Section 75 of the Madras City Police Act—instead of sections 375 and 376 of the Indian Penal Code for rape and punishment for rape. Section 75 of the Police Act refers to creating a nuisance in a public place and carries a fine as its punishment. With the help of the social worker, Meena's parents again approached the police to file a rape case.

The next day I went to the village and saw the girl. She was in bad condition. She had a fever, and she was unconscious. I talked to the parents and said, "Let's go to the police and government hospital." We took the girl to the superintendent of police's (SP) office. We only saw him at 5:00 p.m. Then the SP said that he will call the police to file a case and asked us to take the girl to a government hospital at High Ground Paliangotti. I was with them the whole time. The doctors refused to do a check-up without an FIR. We then took her in a van and came back to the police station. There was no inspector there. The police refused to register an FIR. At 11:00 p.m. the inspector came and registered an FIR. He then sent the police constable with us to the hospital. At 12:30 a.m. we reached the hospital. They did the check-up. At 10:00 a.m. the next morning we took her to court. The magistrate asked to admit her in the hospital. She was there for ten days. The police collected her panties. There were blood stains on it. She recovered and went back to school.[546]

After much persistence, Meena's parents were finally able to register a case of rape under Section 376 of the Indian Penal Code. However, the police refused to simultaneously register the case under the Atrocities Act. The accused

---

[545]Human Rights Watch interview with Vijayakumari, Society for Rural Development Trust, Managing Trustee, Tirunelveli district, Tamil Nadu, February 17, 1998.
[546]Ibid.

spent forty-five days in jail and was subsequently released on bail. In December 1997, soon after his release, he physically assaulted the husband of the social worker who had been helping Meena with her case. According to the social worker, "The rapist and his relatives blocked and damaged my husband's vehicle with their van and beat him. We went back and beat one of those boys, and they filed a case against us. But we also filed a case in a different police station."[547] As of December 1998 no charges had been filed in the rape case, and the accused remained out on bail.

### R. Chitra

In 1996, twenty-six-year-old R. Chitra (also an alias) of Kammapatti village, Tirunelveli district, southern Tamil Nadu, was gang raped by Thevars from a neighboring village. After much public pressure from residents of her village, the police took up the case, but despite her positive identification of the rapists, and despite many eyewitnesses to the event, they ultimately dropped the investigation. Chitra told Human Rights Watch of her experience with the Thevars:

> It happened one and a half years ago. Another girl named Savariammal and I went to the forest for grass for our goats. There is a dilapidated building in the forest. Behind that building, four persons hid themselves... The four people came out and said "Where are you coming from?" I said I am from Kammapatti. They asked my village name, so they knew I was a Dalit. They left and went five steps ahead. When they passed, me and my friend started gathering our goats and prepared to leave. The men were holding bill hooks in their hands, and we knew it was not a safe place to be. All of a sudden, one man turned around and grabbed my hand. I tried to resist them for two hours. Among the four, one hid and the remaining three boys took turns. They had weapons, I only had a stick. They then took away my stick so I had no defense... Some other people from that village saw the struggle but did not come close, because the men had weapons. Three men raped me. It lasted for an hour. There was no bleeding, but there were bruises all over. When one committed penetration, the other two stood by and watched. In turn they all raped me. The fourth one was

---

[547]Ibid.

hiding and saw the whole thing. I had bruises all over, on my chest, my hip. My skin was torn and full of nail marks. I was hurt because I was trying to escape.[548]

After a failed attempt to commit suicide by pouring kerosene on her body and setting herself on fire, Chitra was convinced by her family to go to the police. She did not know her rapists but recognized that they were Thevars from a neighboring village. She was also able to provide the police with details on their clothing, their appearance, and their age: "I gave an oral complain, and the constable reduced it to writing. That was the only time they were sympathetic."[549] The day of her suicide attempt, Chitra visited the Tirunelveli government hospital, where four female doctors examined her and collected specimens. She also handed over to police the clothes she had been wearing when raped. Despite the strength of the evidence, the police told her brothers to persuade her not to register a complaint. But her brothers were persistent, and most of the residents of her Dalit-dominant village insisted that the police arrest the accused. They argued that if "anything was committed by Dalits, the police do not allow it, so why are they allowing this?"[550] The day after the rape, the police arrested two persons and presented them for identification. The following day Chitra's brother complained to the deputy superintendent of police that the two remaining accused had not been arrested. After the police took the mothers of the two absconding men to the police station, they too surrendered.[551]

So I identified all four. The sub-inspector recorded my statement. The police also talked to Savariammal, the girl who was with me. She said she saw it happen but did not know the identity of the people. But she must have known. She simply kept away from saying the truth. She was probably threatened. All surrounding villages belong to Thevars. The police arrested and remanded them to Koilpatti jail. I went for the line-up in

---

[548]Human Rights Watch interview with R. Chitra, Tirunelveli district, Tamil Nadu, February 17, 1998.
[549]Ibid.
[550]Ibid.
[551]For more information on the practice of police hostage-taking of women whose male relatives are hiding from the authorities, see Chapter V.

front of the magistrate. They put eighteen persons in a row. They put the four among them. Even then I identified them.[552]

After many promises of state compensation for Chitra, the money never came. Despite initial cooperation from the police, the case never went to trial. Chitra was not even informed if the culprits were arrested after she identified them: "I don't know how many days they were in jail. I haven't been contacted again by the police." She was denied access to her own medical records. "The doctors said they have to give them to police and they will send them to court."[553] For social and monetary reasons, Chitra's family has been unwilling and unable to pursue the case. "My family is afraid to proceed because of their reputation," she explained. "The FIR should be there. I was never invited to court to depose, so I think the trial was not held. I didn't go again... We don't have money for an advocate, and we cannot travel frequently to court. Even if I decide to pursue I have to get permission from my mother and brothers."[554]

### Caste and Gender Bias in the Courts

The lack of law enforcement leaves many Dalit women unable to approach the legal system to seek redress. Women are often also unaware of the laws; their ignorance is exploited by their opponents, by the police, and, as illustrated by the cases below, by the judiciary. Even when cases are registered, the lack of appropriate investigation, or the judge's own caste and gender biases, can lead to acquittal, regardless of the availability of evidence or witnesses. The failure to successfully prosecute cases of rape also allows for crimes against women to continue unabated, and in the caste context, encourages the use of rape as a tool to punish and silence Dalit communities.[555]

---

[552]Human Rights Watch interview with R. Chitra, Tirunelveli district, Tamil Nadu, February 17, 1998.
[553]Ibid.
[554]Ibid.
[555]For more on rape as a tool of political repression see *The Human Rights Watch Global Report on Women's Human Rights* (New York: Human Rights Watch, 1995); Asia Watch (now Human Rights Watch), *The Human Rights Crisis in Kashmir: A Pattern of Impunity* (New York: Human Rights Watch, 1993); Human Rights Watch/Africa, *Shattered Lives: Sexual Violence during the Rwandan Genocide and its Aftermath* (New York: Human Rights Watch, 1996); Americas Watch (now Human Rights Watch), *Untold Terror: Violence Against Women in Peru's Armed Conflict* (New York: Human Rights Watch, 1992).

### Bhanwari Devi

Bhanwari Devi's case is a typical example of the influence of caste bias on the justice system and the inability of lower-caste women to obtain redress. It is also a striking example of rape as a weapon of retaliation used to punish and silence women's rights advocates. The nature of the district judge's opinion sounded many alarms, and the case itself was taken up by several women's rights organizations in north India.

Bhanwari Devi joined the Rajasthan Government's Women's Development Programme (WDP), called Sathin, in 1985 as a grassroots worker.[556] In April 1992 she reported the child marriage of the one-year-old daughter of Ram Karan Gurjar to WDP authorities. The police came to the village and tried to stop the marriage, but the family proceeded with the ceremony in secret. On September 22, 1992, in the presence of her husband, Bhanwari was gang raped by members of the Gurjar family in retaliation for her intervention in the child marriage. Upon approaching the police, Bhanwari was told, however, that she was too old and unattractive to merit the attentions of young men.

The trial judge acquitted the accused on the reasoning that "rape is usual committed by teenagers, and since the accused are middle-aged and therefore respectable, they could not have committed the crime. An upper-caste man could not have defiled himself by raping a lower-caste woman."[557] Those accused of raping Bhanwari also enjoyed political support. BJP leader Kanhaiya Lal Meena reportedly organized a rally in support of the accused.[558] As of February 1999, Bhanwari was still in court appealing the acquittal.

Bhanwari's case, and in particular the manner in which it was handled by the police and the courts, is not an isolated incident. Cases at all levels have the potential to be influenced by the judge's personal perceptions of caste and gender that are brought to bear in determining the credibility of evidence or the likelihood of guilt. The case material that follows, though not specific to the report, is intended to illustrate the atmosphere of prejudice that Dalit women face—both as Dalits and as women. These biases are pervasive all the way to the top of the legal system. The few cases that manage to reach the Supreme Court still do not escape these deep-seated prejudices.

---

[556] "In Brief: Recent Rape Cases," p. 20.

[557] Ibid.

[558] K. S. Tomar, "Atrocities against Rajasthan women on the rise: Report," *The Hindustan Times*, May 28, 1998.

### Shri Satish Mehra v. Delhi Administration and Another

Gender bias that blames women for the actions of men also persists at the Supreme Court level. In *Shri Satish Mehra v. Delhi Administration and Another*, a July 1996 case of the rape of a three-year-old girl by her father, the Supreme Court concluded that there lacked sufficient evidence to proceed to trial and pointed to the "seemingly incredulous nature of the accusations against a father that molested his infant child." The court instead accused the mother of leveling false accusations to take revenge on her husband for an unhappy marriage.[559]

The opinion added that the judge presiding over the case prior to the Supreme Court appeal ought not to have overlooked the peculiar circumstances of the case, including the fact that the accused's wife found their marital life to be "extremely painful and unhappy from the very inception" and that she had accused him of being an alcoholic and prone to inflicting severe physical violence.[560] Based on these circumstances, the Supreme Court concluded that the wife's "attitude to the petitioner, even de hors the allegation involving the child, was vengeful."[561] As in the Bhanwari Devi case, despite the legal basis it claimed for the decision, the court only briefly touched on evidentiary matters and seemed instead to be motivated by its professed disbelief that such crimes could actually take place.

### Suman Rani *(Prem Chand and Another v. State of Haryana)*

As described in Chapter V, Dalit women are frequent victims of custodial rape. Section 376(2) of the Indian Penal Code mandates minimum sentences for state agents who rape women in their custody. Other loopholes in the law, however, allow the judiciary to sidestep mandatory sentencing. In the famous Suman Rani custodial rape case, the Supreme Court refused to apply the minimum ten-year sentence to the police officers charged because of the victim's "questionable character." The court's opinion quoted a medical officer who testified that the "victim girl [was] used to frequent intercourse and parturition and there was no mark of violence of sexual assault on any part of her body." The opinion further added:

> [T]he victim Suman Rani was a woman of questionable character and easy virtue with lewd and lascivious behavior and

---

[559]In the Supreme Court of India, Criminal Appellate Jurisdiction, Criminal Appeal No. 1385 of 1995, p. 6.
[560] Criminal Appeal No. 1385 of 1995, p. 6.
[561] Ibid.

that the very fact that this girl had not complained of the alleged rape said to have been committed at [the] police station by these two appellants to anyone till [five days after the incident] shows that the present version is not worthy of acceptance.[562]

The court ultimately held that the peculiar facts of the case, coupled with the conduct of the victim, did not warrant the imposition of the minimum ten-year sentence.[563] The court instead invoked the proviso to Section 376(2), which allows for the judge to use his discretion in reducing the minimum sentence, and cut the sentence in half.

---

[562] 1989 Supp (1) SCC, p. 287.

[563] In a rape case in the state of Karnataka, decided by the Supreme Court in October 1983, the sentence was also reduced to less than what was provided by law. In a letter to the chief justice dated October 27, 1993, women's organizations noted that gender bias was pervasive at all levels of the judiciary that seeks to blame the victim for the crimes committed against her. References in the judgment to the victim's character, her clothes, and her behavior were severely criticized, as was the categorization of rape as an "act of passion," and of the criminals as "victims of sexual lust." The letter also noted that the Karnataka judgment blamed the girl because "she agreed to share a room with the two men." "Some judgments which reflect a similar patriarchal and Gender Biased approach towards victims of rape," (New Delhi: 1996), obtained from attorney Kirti Singh, All-India Democratic Women's Association.

# X. FAILURE TO MEET DOMESTIC AND INTERNATIONAL LEGAL OBLIGATIONS TO PROTECT DALITS

The practice of "untouchability," other caste-based discrimination, violence against Dalit men, women, and children, and other abuses documented in this report are in violation of numerous domestic and international laws. A body of international human rights conventions, domestic legislation, and constitutional provisions collectively impose on the government of India a duty to guarantee certain basic rights to the Dalit population and to punish those who engage in caste-based violence and discrimination.

Other chapters of this report describe the pattern of state complicity in attacks on Dalit community members. This chapter outlines the government's legal obligations and the manner in which state complicity extends to the non-registration of cases against caste Hindus, including the government's failure to implement the Scheduled Castes and Scheduled Tribes (Prevention of Atrocities) Act, 1989. A brief description of the government's two-pronged strategy to improve the socio-economic status of scheduled castes and to provide them with legal protection in the form of social welfare legislation is also provided. Like the Atrocities Act, the strategy has been undermined by a lack of political will to ensure its implementation. The government of India has failed to provide Dalits with the most basic of constitutional guarantees described below.

## India's Obligations under Domestic Law

The Constitution of India proclaims the decision of the Constituent Assembly (which framed the constitution) to provide social, political, and economic justice for all. To this end the constitution has several provisions to protect scheduled castes and to improve their position. The constitution affects social justice in two ways. First, it confers rights on men and women alike, through "fundamental rights" which can be enforced by the courts. Second, it directs the states to implement "directive principles of state policy." Although these are not enforceable in Indian courts, they are declared to be fundamental in the governance of the country and as such have moral and political value.

### Scheduled castes and the constitution

Article 17 of the constitution abolishes the practice of "untouchability" and punishes the enforcement of any disability arising out of the practice. Article 21 guarantees the right to life and liberty. The Indian Supreme Court has interpreted this right to include the right to be free from degrading and inhuman treatment, the right to integrity and dignity of the person, and the right to speedy

179

justice.[564] When read with Article 39A on equal justice and free legal aid, Article 21 also encompasses the right to legal aid for those faced with imprisonment and those too poor to afford counsel.[565]

Article 23 prohibits traffic in human beings and other similar forms of forced labor. Since the majority of bonded laborers belong to scheduled castes, Article 23 is especially significant for them.[566] Similarly, Article 24 provides that no child under the age of fourteen shall work in any factory or mine or engage in any hazardous employment. Again a majority of children engaged in bonded labor in such hazardous industries are scheduled caste members. Article 45 charges that the state shall endeavor to provide free and compulsory education for all children until they reach the age of fourteen, while Article 43 calls on the state to secure to all workers, agricultural, industrial or otherwise, a living wage and conditions of work ensuring a decent standard of life.

Article 46 comprises both development and regulatory aspects and stipulates that: "The State shall promote with special care the educational and economic interests of the weaker sections of the people, and in particular, of the Scheduled Castes and the Scheduled Tribes, and shall protect them from social injustice and forms of exploitation." As the article falls under the category of directive principles and not fundamental rights, it cannot be enforced by the state's courts. Article 15(4) empowers the state to make any special provisions for the advancement of any socially and educationally backward classes of citizens, or for scheduled castes and scheduled tribes. This particular provision was incorporated into the constitution through the Constitution (First Amendment) Act, 1951 and has enabled several states to reserve seats for scheduled castes and scheduled tribes in educational institutions, including technical, engineering, and medical colleges. It has also paved the way for reservations in police forces.

Article 330 provides reservations for seats for scheduled castes and scheduled tribes in the Lok Sabha (the House of the People), while Article 332 provides for reservations in the state legislative assemblies. Article 334 originally stipulated that the above two provisions would cease to have effect after a period of ten years from the commencement of the constitution. This article has since

---

[564]See S. K. Singh, *Bonded Labour and the Law* (New Delhi: Deep and Deep Publications, 1994), pp. 48–51.

[565]*Hussainara v. State of Bihar*, AIR 1979 SC 1369, 1377; *Khatri v. State of Bihar*, AIR 1981 SC 928; *Suk Das v. Arunachal Pradesh*, AIR 1986 SC 991; *Ranchod v. State of Gujarat*, AIR 1974 SC 1143.

[566]The Bonded Labour System (Abolition) Act, 1976 was passed pursuant to this article.

been amended four times, extending the period by ten years on each occasion. The provision is now set to expire in January 2000.

Through Article 16(4) the state is empowered to make "any provision for the reservation of appointments or posts in favour of any backward class of citizens which, in the opinion of the State, is not adequately represented in the services under the State." The claims of scheduled castes and scheduled tribes, as per Article 335, shall also be taken into consideration, consistent with maintaining efficiency of administration, in the making of appointments services and posts in connection with the union or of a state.

In addition to constitutional provisions, the government of India has pursued a two-pronged approach to narrowing the gap between the socio-economic status of the scheduled caste population and the national average: one prong involves regulatory measures which ensure that the various provisions to protect their rights and interests are adequately implemented, enforced and monitored; the second focuses on increasing the self-sufficiency of the scheduled caste population through financial assistance for self-employment activities through development programs to increase education and skills.[567]

The protective component of this strategy includes the enforcement of those legal provisions that make up the Protection of Civil Rights Act, 1955, and the Scheduled Caste and Scheduled Tribe (Prevention of Atrocities) Act, 1989; of other state and central government laws; and of "positive discrimination" through reservations in the arenas of government employment and higher education. These protective measures are monitored by the National Commission for Scheduled Castes and Scheduled Tribes. The development measures for the educational, social, and economic upliftment of scheduled castes are administered by the Ministry of Welfare through the state governments.[568]

### The National Commission for Scheduled Castes and Scheduled Tribes

The National Commission for Scheduled Castes and Scheduled Tribes is a body set up pursuant to Article 338 of the Indian constitution. It has been entrusted with the responsibility of ensuring that the safeguards and protections that have been given to scheduled castes and tribes are implemented. As part of the National Commission, the Commission on Atrocities Against Scheduled Castes and

---

[567]Ministry of Welfare, *Annual Report 1995-1996* (New Delhi: Government of India, 1996), p. 8.

[568]Ibid. The provision of finances to members of scheduled castes and scheduled tribes for self-employment activities is administered through the National Scheduled Castes and Scheduled Tribes Finance and Development Corporation.

Scheduled Tribes oversees implementation of the Prevention of Atrocities Act, 1989, and the Protection of Civil Rights Act, 1955, though does not have a statutory responsibility to do so. The commission both receives complaints and proactively investigates matters that come to its attention through news reports or by any other means. Under the constitution the commission has the powers of a civil court and can call on anyone for evidence to ensure that the laws are being implemented. The commission lacks the powers of a criminal court, however, and therefore cannot enforce its findings.[569]

### The Protection of Civil Rights Act, 1955

With an eye to eradicating pervasive discrimination practiced against scheduled-caste members, the central government enacted the Protection of Civil Rights Act, 1955 (PCR Act) to enforce the abolition of "untouchability" under Article 17 of the constitution. The PCR Act punishes offenses that amount to the observance of "untouchability." These include, *inter alia*, prohibiting entry into places of worship, denying access to shops and other public places, denying access to any water supply, prohibiting entry into hospitals, refusing to sell goods or render services, and insulting someone on the basis of his or her caste.[570]

In 1973 the Protection of Civil Rights Cell was established to respond to a lack of convictions under the PCR Act.[571] According T. K. Chaudary, the inspector general of police for the PCR cell in Maharashtra from 1992 to 1996, and current Joint Commissioner of Police, Mumbai (Bombay) Police:

> Until 1973 there was no conviction. It was all at the whims and fancies of police officers. They only took action if the person belonged to the right caste. So in order to streamline the act, the cell came into place. From 1975 onwards they played a coordinating role. They had no power of their own but made sure some cases were registered and the some complaints were heard; still there were hardly any convictions... witnesses turned hostile.[572]

---

[569]In the socio-economic context, the commission also has the responsibility of ensuring that scheduled caste development is taking place; it constantly monitors and reviews with state governments and ministries the implementation of their programs and policies.

[570]The Protection of Civil Rights Act, 1955, Sec. 3, 4, 5, 6 and 7.

[571]Since the promulgation of the Atrocities Act in 1989, the cell has shifted its focus to atrocities cases.

[572]Human Rights Watch interview, Bombay, February 5, 1998.

Chaudary added, "Society as a whole never accepted the PCR Act. No one ever thought that name-calling wouldn't be okay. Ill-treatment was very common."[573] The act was also vulnerable to abuse. "It was easy to make an allegation that someone was called by his or her caste name."[574]

### The Scheduled Castes and Scheduled Tribes (Prevention of Atrocities) Act, 1989

The greatest deficiency of the Protection of Civil Rights Act was the fact that abuses against Dalits were not limited to name-calling or denial of entry into public spaces: violence was a defining characteristic of the abuse. Thirty-four years after the introduction of the PCR Act, the Scheduled Castes and Scheduled Tribes (Prevention of Atrocities) Act, 1989, was enacted to bring these other forms of abuse to an end. "In the Atrocities Act... the complainant is given more weight... There are also stringent provisions against the police for negligence."[575]

The promulgation of the act itself was an acknowledgment by the central government that abuses, in their most dehumanizing form, continue to take place

---

[573] Ibid.

[574]The Atrocities Act has attracted similar accusations of misuse, including allegations that cases are filed simply as a means of collecting state compensation, as prescribed under the Prevention of Atrocities Rules, 1995, or to harass upper-caste members of rival political parties. The most widely "misused" provision, it is claimed, is the one concerning the use of derogatory language against Dalits. Critics of the act point to the high proportion of cases registered under this provision; human rights activists point to police refusal to register cases or solely registering cases under this provision, even when the crime reported is far more violent and severe (see below).
    In 1997 in the state of Uttar Pradesh, the Bharatiya Janata Party, known for its upper-caste base, called for repealing the legislation altogether on the claim that members of the lower-caste dominant Bahujan Samaj Party (BSP) had been instigated to file cases under the act against their upper-caste political opponents. The instigation, they claimed, came from then-Chief Minister Mayawati, a Dalit politician. "Left wants all-party meet on SC, ST Act," *The Hindu*, September 25, 1997. Proponents of the act reacted by highlighting the deplorable situation of scheduled castes and scheduled tribes in the state and by criticizing any state government that took the position that "a Central [government] enactment on a sensitive subject such as the protection of SCs/STs should not be implemented with vigour [simply] to suit the political convenience of the ruling [BJP] party." Madhav Godbole, "Making a mockery of the law," *The Hindu*, October 21, 1997. See below for attempts to withdraw cases under the act en masse in the state of Maharashtra.

[575]Human Rights Watch interview with T. K. Chaudary, Bombay, February 5, 1998.

against Dalits throughout the country. The Tamil Nadu nodal (implementation) officer for the Atrocities Act explained to Human Rights Watch:

> The Atrocities Act is very stringent. It is needed to eradicate the practice, not just control it. It is the second phase of the Protection of Civil Rights Act which is very soft. The 1989 [Atrocities] Act is grounded in the understanding that scheduled castes are being subjected to violence, not just the practice of "untouchability." There was a long period of dialogue before its enactment.  After forty years of India, people began to acknowledge that violence continued to be perpetrated and it needed to be stopped. The act presumes that if a non-scheduled-caste member harms a scheduled-caste member then it is because of the culpable mind of "untouchability" [a belief in the inferiority of lower castes]. They don't have to utter the caste name in the 1989 act; any humiliation is an offense.[576]

A list of offenses under the act provides a glimpse into the forms that such violence can take, several of which have been documented in this report. Section 3(1) stipulates that the following acts, when committed by a person who is not a member of a scheduled caste or a scheduled tribe, are atrocities and thereby punishable by a term of six months to five years with a fine.

- Forcing a member of a Scheduled Caste or Scheduled Tribe to drink or eat any inedible or obnoxious substance (Section 3(1)(i));

- Acting with intent to cause injury, insult or annoyance to any member of a Scheduled Caste or Scheduled Tribe by dumping excreta, waste matter, carcasses or any other obnoxious substance in his premises or neighbourhood (Section 3(1)(ii));

- Forcibly removing clothes from the person of a member of a Scheduled Caste or Scheduled Tribe, or parading him naked or with painted face or

---

[576]Interview with Christodas Gandhi, Tamil Nadu Nodal Officer for the Atrocities Act, Madras, February 13, 1998. Gandhi has since been replaced as nodal officer.

body, or committing any similar act which is derogatory to human dignity (Section 3(1)(iii));

- Wrongfully occupying or cultivating any land owned by, or allotted to, or notified by any competent authority to be allotted to, a member of a Scheduled Caste or Scheduled Tribe, or getting the land allotted to him transferred (Section (3)(1)(iv));

- Wrongfully dispossessing a member of a Scheduled Caste or Scheduled Tribe from his land or premises, or interfering with the enjoyment of his rights over any land, premises, or water (Section 3(1)(v));

- Compelling or enticing a member of a Scheduled Caste or Scheduled Tribe to do "beggar" or other similar forms of forced or bonded labour, other than any compulsory service for public purposes imposed by the Government (Section (3)(1)(vi));

- Forcing or intimidating a member of a Scheduled Caste or a Scheduled Tribe not to vote or to vote [for] a particular candidate or to vote in a manner other than that provided by law (Section (3)(1)(vii));

- Corrupting or fouling the water of any spring, reservoir, or any other source ordinarily used by members of the Scheduled Castes or the Scheduled Tribes so as to render it less fit for the purpose for which it is ordinarily used (Section (3)(1(xiii));

- Denying a member of a Scheduled Caste or a Scheduled Tribe any customary right of passage to a place of public resort or obstructing such members so as to prevent him from using or having access to a place of public resort to which other members of public or any section thereof have a right to use or access to (Section 3(1)(xiv));

- Forcing or causing a member of a Scheduled Caste or a Scheduled Tribe to leave his house, village, or other place of residence (Section 3(1)(xv)).

The act also punishes public servants for committing any of the enumerated offenses. Specific offenses are also designed to protect Dalit and tribal women. Specifically, Sections 3(1)(xi) and 3(1)(xii) criminalize the assault or use of force on any woman belonging to a scheduled caste or scheduled tribe, "with the intent to dishonour or outrage her modesty," and the use of a position of dominance to exploit a scheduled caste or scheduled tribe woman sexually.

Section 3(2) of the act prohibits, *inter alia*, the fabrication of false evidence in cases against members of scheduled castes or scheduled tribes and defines punishments for public servants who commit any of the offenses enumerated in Section 3. In addition to providing for stricter punishments for various offenses, the act also imposes certain positive duties on state and central governments to ensure proper implementation of the act.[577] Many of these duties are listed under Section 21 which, among other things, provides that the central government shall, every year, send to both houses of parliament a report on the measures taken by the center and the states in pursuance of the provisions of the act. The section also includes guidelines for:

- Providing legal aid to victims;

- Making provisions for travel and maintenance expenses for witnesses and victims;

- Providing prompt economic and social rehabilitation to victims;

- Appointing officers for initiating or exercising supervision over prosecutions under the act;

- Identifying areas where Dalits would be subject to periodic or large scale atrocities, and;

- Setting up citizens committees to assist the government in the formulation and implementation of measures under the act.

Offenses under the act are cognizable—an officer can arrest without a warrant—and non-bailable. Provisions of the Criminal Procedure Code regarding anticipatory bail do not apply.[578] Property can also be attached, sold, or forfeited

---

[577]Articles 17 and 46 of the constitution, on the abolishment of "untouchablility" and the promotion of educational and economic interests of scheduled castes, respectively, also become enforceable in courts of law through the enactment of the Atrocities Act. Vivek Pandit, "A Handbook on Prevention of Atrocities (Scheduled Castes and Scheduled Tribes)," A Vidhayak Sansad Publication, December 1995, p. 11.

[578]The Supreme Court of India has held that the denial of anticipatory bail is constitutional.

to recover fines imposed by the court. When serious crimes such as rape, murder, or assault are proved, the punishments meted out are much greater than those provided for under the Indian Penal Code.

In 1995 the government of India enacted accompanying rules for the Atrocities Act. The rules set out the amounts of, and timetables for, state-allotted compensations for victims of various crimes defined under the act. Rules 16 and 17 call for the constitution of state and district-level vigilance and monitoring committees comprising official and non-official members. The committees are responsible for reviewing, *inter alia,* implementation of the act, prosecution of cases, victim relief and rehabilitation, and the role of different officers and agencies charged with the act's implementation. The Atrocities Act, and its accompanying rules, could go far in promoting justice and human rights among members of scheduled castes and scheduled tribes, but only if they are properly implemented and those whom the act is meant to protect are made aware of its existence and the rights that they possess. A full text of the act, and the accompanying rules, are provided in the appendix.

### Failure to Implement the Scheduled Castes and Scheduled Tribes (Prevention of Atrocities) Act, 1989

> It is a great irony that we try to implement the act through an agency that is perceived as an agency of oppression.
> — Christodas Gandhi, then-Tamil Nadu implementation officer for the Atrocities Act[579]

> Higher-caste police already have a biased mind. They assume that complaints of [Dalits] are made up or bogus. It is with this mentality that they investigate. Any person who has already presumed something as wrong will ultimately prove the case wrong to prove him or herself right.
> — Dalit district superintendent of police[580]

Although a potentially powerful piece of legislation, the Scheduled Castes and Scheduled Tribes (Prevention of Atrocities) Act, 1989 is hampered by the

---

[579]Human Rights Watch interview with Christodas Gandhi, Madras, February 13, 1998.
[580]Quoted in Navsarjan, "Atrocities on Dalits in Gujarat. One Document and its Evaluations," (Ahmedabad: 1997).

police's lack of willingness to register offenses or their ignorance of the terms of the act itself. Under Indian law, a police officer is bound to enter in the station diary all reports brought to him concerning all cognizable and non-cognizable offenses. Failure to do so, or entering a report that was not made to him, is punishable under Section 177 of the Indian Penal Code. In most cases, however, the offending officer escapes punishment. The police take on the role of the judiciary and determine the merits of the case even before pursuing investigations. Cases at all levels are influenced by caste bias, corruption and ignorance of procedures under the Atrocities Act.

The functions of the Indian police are governed by the Indian Police Act, 1861, the Code of Criminal Procedure, 1973, the Indian Penal Code, 1860, the Indian Evidence Act, 1832, the Constitution of India, and other state acts. The government of India has known about the extent of police corruption in the registration of cases at least since 1979 when the National Police Commission issued a devastating indictment of police behavior. Two decades later, none of the police commission's recommendations have been adopted, and police continue to detain, torture, and extort money from Dalits without much fear of punishment.[581] Police often escape liability for their own abuses of Dalits and are rarely punished for their negligence in the non-registration of caste-related cases. Even when cases are registered, the absence of special courts to try them (see below) can delay conviction for up to three to four years. Some state governments, including those of Maharashtra and Uttar Pradesh, have come under upper-caste pressure to repeal the legislation altogether.

---

[581]Under a section titled "Corruption in Police," the National Police Commission's report published the following findings:

> The scope of corruption and allied malpractices arise at several stages in the day to day working of the police. A few typical situations are listed below: (1) Bribe demanded and received for registering a case and proceeding with investigation. (2) Bribe connected with arrest or non-arrest of accused and release or non-release on bail... (4) Extorting money by threatening persons, particularly the ill-informed and weaker sections of society, with conduct of searches, arrests and prosecution in court on some charge or the other... (6) Fabricating false evidence during investigations of cases and implicating innocent persons or leaving out guilty persons on *mala fide* considerations... (12) Bribery at the stage of recruitment to police.

National Police Commission, "Corruption in Police," Chapter XXII, *Third Report of the National Police Commission* (New Delhi: Government of India, 1980), p. 26.

### Non-registration of cases

Wherever the Atrocities Act is not used properly, it is because there is no knowledge, no strength, so it has failed. It is a tool. On its own it will not be implemented. The use of Atrocities Act as a tool has changed people's lives. There are hundreds of cases I can quote.

— Vivek Pandit, Maharashtra activist[582]

Most beneficiaries of the Atrocities Act know neither the content of the act nor which agencies are responsible for its implementation. In an interview with Human Rights Watch, the then-chairman of the National Commission for Scheduled Castes and Scheduled Tribes asserted, "Many states do not even have translated copies of the act or the rules. Station-house officers do not even know of its existence."[583] In many instances, however, even knowledge of proper procedures has not led to registration or investigation of cases. Because offenses under the Atrocities Act are non-bailable, the mere registration of certain offenses can result in fifteen to twenty days in jail for the accused. An activist in Tamil Nadu explained, "If any case comes under the Atrocities Act, the accused will go straight to jail without any bail. So caste Hindus cleverly use the police to avoid putting cases under the act."[584] Police manipulate First Information Reports [FIRs] and charge sheets, charging the accused under sections of the Indian Penal Code or under lesser offenses of the Atrocities Act. As explained by C. V. Shankar, director for the Adi Dravida Tribal Welfare Department, government of Tamil Nadu, the non-registration of Atrocities Act cases is deliberate:

They are biased because of their own caste. The police in general try to avoid registration. They want to settle cases with compensation. There are many power politics at the local level. Unless there is public pressure, the police administration tends to side with landowning communities that have political clout. A scheduled-caste person is therefore at the mercy of landlords

---

[582]Human Rights Watch interview with Vivek Pandit, director of NGO Samarthan, Usgaon, Maharashtra, January 29, 1998.
[583]Human Rights Watch interview with H. Hanumanthappa, New Delhi, March 11, 1998.
[584]Human Rights Watch interview with Chandra Bose, Sivagangal Monitoring and Vigilance Committee, Madurai, February 18, 1998.

because there are police pressures and other pressures to compromise the case.[585]

Part of that pressure arises from the exigencies of police corruption: "Whoever gives more money gets their side of the case registered. In more serious cases, they may have to register the case but then subsequent investigations get thwarted."[586] An activist working in over sixty villages in Tamil Nadu described the nexus between the police and upper-caste communities:

> The police consider Dalits to be their enemies. They don't register cases. They just say, "Don't fight anymore. After all, they [caste Hindus] are taking care of you; they are giving you employment. They made a mistake, let it go." And in so doing, the Dalits are usually persuaded to let the case go. In rare cases where they make an FIR, they will turn it around in the charge sheet and say that after investigation, they found that the FIR was not true. This is all to try and help the accused escape.[587]

Under Indian law if a police officer suspects the commission of an offense, he is obligated to investigate the facts and circumstances of the case. The officer must then send a report and a copy of the FIR to the magistrate empowered to take cognizance of the offense. If the officer-in-charge of the police station believes that there are insufficient grounds for investigation, then the reasons for non-investigation must be communicated to the complainant.[588] In the case of a cognizable offense, if the police officer does not take action on the basis of an FIR, the aggrieved person can submit a complaint to the magistrate having jurisdiction to take cognizance of the offense.[589] Despite these stringent procedures, Dalits generally hesitate to approach the police with their complaints. According to National Commission Chairman Hanumanthappa, "Scheduled caste people hesitate because they feel vulnerable. Even if they do report something, there is a tendency

---

[585]Human Rights Watch interview, Madras, February 13, 1998.

[586]Human Rights Watch interview with People's Union for Civil Liberties, Madras, February 12, 1998. For more on monetary pressures on the police, see Chapter IV.

[587]Human Rights Watch interview with Mr. Martin, Village Community Development Society, Madras, February 13, 1998.

[588]P. D. Mathew, *What You Should Know About the Police* (New Delhi: Indian Social Institute, 1996), p. 24.

[589]Ibid., p. 26.

not to register the case. Many times the station-house officer simply chases them away."[590]

Due to the diligent efforts of many Dalit activists and lawyers in the past several years, police have begun to register more cases under the Atrocities Act but often only as a result of immense public pressure. Increases in registration, however, have not resulted in increased convictions. A Dalit lawyer who has been practicing in Tamil Nadu for seventeen years asserted that in his experience only 2 percent of cases end in conviction. "The investigating officers are upper-caste," he said, "and the accused pay large amounts to judges to get an acquittal in the case."[591] The lack of convictions is a reflection of police and judicial corruption, of deficiencies in the investigation process, and of a lack of special courts to try Atrocities Act cases. Each is discussed in turn below.

### Police investigations and use of witnesses

In Tamil Nadu, from 1992 to 1997, some 750 cases of atrocities against Dalits were registered annually by the state police. However, the number of convictions secured by protection of civil rights cells established in each district to implement the Atrocities Act was very low. From 1992 to 1997 only four out of 1,500 cases led to a conviction, despite the fact that in 1997, as many as 118 villages were considered by the government to be "atrocity-prone."[592] Police officers have attributed the problem to the lack of a supporting unit to investigate reported crimes (the PCR cell in each district is headed only by an inspector of police) and to the fact that "most police personnel come to the cells either because they are facing action for delinquency or inefficiency, or as punishment for refusing to toe the line of their political bosses."[593] One senior official complained, "With the PCR cells seen as a dumping ground of bad elements in the Police Department, how do you expect us to perform well?"[594]

A lack of witnesses can also hamper an investigation—they either do not exist or are unwilling to come forward out of fear or economic vulnerability. According to T. K. Chaudary, "They would lose wages for the day, so they cannot come to testify."[595]

---

[590]Human Rights Watch interview, New Delhi, March 11, 1998.

[591]Human Rights Watch interview with Dalit attorney, Madurai, February 16, 1998.

[592]Radha Venkatesan, "Cells to protect SCs flounder in Tamil Nadu," *Indian Express* (Bombay), June 15, 1997.

[593]Ibid.

[594]Ibid.

[595]Human Rights Watch interview, Bombay, February 5, 1998.

These cases take place in the privacy of rural areas where there are no witnesses available. The demand of Indian criminal law is that a witness must be available to prove the crime. Indian law does not accept circumstantial evidence easily. That is the basic crux of the matter. Also there is great distrust toward the investigating officer. Good persons do not come forward to become witnesses, only those who can be influenced by the police.[596]

Local police biases are mirrored at the judicial level. Should a case even reach the trial level, the judge's own caste affiliations can color his or her perception of witness credibility: "Judges issue an opinion in favor of the accused because they belong to the same caste."[597] R. Balakrishnan, director of the Tamil Nadu chapter of the National Commission for Scheduled Castes and Scheduled Tribes, explained the obstacles at the trial level:

The implementing authorities are biased. Caste is inherited, and personal prejudices are put to use. Police don't take the job voluntarily; it is always thrust upon them. At the judicial level at least 90 to 95 percent of cases receive no punishment. I have studied many judgments and have seen that there is a tendency to accept evidence only from non-scheduled caste/scheduled tribe people. I have studied fifty to sixty cases; invariably the judge concluded that scheduled caste/scheduled tribe [SC/ST] evidence is not valid because they are an interested party. To attribute a pattern to a community is a prejudice in and of itself. That itself is an atrocity. They do not give weight to SC/ST evidence, but it is too much to expect evidence from a non-SC/ST when the victim is a Dalit. That is the dichotomy: if they did come forward, we would not need the act.[598]

---

[596]Ibid.

[597]Human Rights Watch interview, H. Hanumanthappa, New Delhi, March 11, 1998. See Chapter IX for caste and gender bias in the prosecution of rape cases.

[598]Human Rights Watch interview with R. Balakrishnan, Madras, February 13, 1998.

### Lack of special courts and special prosecutors

Even when cases are registered, there is no court to try them. No cases have gone to trial, so there are no convictions. Aside from paltry amounts from the prime minister's relief fund, no compensation is given in the registered cases, as is required by the 1995 rules.

— Bharathan, NGO activist[599]

The backlog of cases is largely due to a lack of special courts and special prosecutors. Pursuant to the act, each revenue district within each state must designate a special court for the trial of such offenses. According to lawyers with the People's Union for Civil Liberties (Tamil Nadu), almost all Atrocities Act cases go to regular sessions courts, which are already overburdened with original and appellate jurisdiction over district-level civil and criminal cases. Terrorism and Anti-Disruptive Activities Act (TADA) cases are also being sent to these courts.[600] According to a PUCL attorney:

One court has so many nomenclatures. The whole purpose of a speedy trial is defeated. Even with all these new cases, not a single extra typewriter is added. In reality there is no special court. Half the day goes into calling names, calling civil court matters, dealing with civil and criminal appeals, interim orders, and bail applications.[601]

An activist who runs a legal aid organization in Gujarat claims that Atrocities Act cases can take up to three years to reach trial while all others "take only one year. Existing sessions courts are named as special courts, existing public prosecutors are named as special public prosecutors. Cases take so long that people are forced to compromise."[602] Chairman Hanumanthappa confirmed that the problem persisted throughout the country: "In practice, sessions courts are

---

[599]Human Rights Watch interview with Bharathan, programme coordinator for Navjeevan Trust, Madurai district, Tamil Nadu, February 17, 1998.

[600]For a description of TADA, see Chapter VIII.

[601]Human Rights Watch interview with Sudha Ramalingam, People's Union for Civil Liberties, Madras, February 12, 1998.

[602] Human Rights Watch interview with Martin Macwan of Navsarjan, Ahmedabad, July 23, 1998.

designated as special courts. They are already overburdened. More than judges, special prosecutors are required. There should be exclusive special courts."[603]

In 1997 and 1998 four special courts were created in Tamil Nadu, in the districts of Madurai, Tirunelveli, Trichi, and Kumbakanam, to try Atrocities Act cases. Human Rights Watch spoke to the judge assigned to the Madurai district court, which at the time was handling cases from five districts; hundreds of cases had already been transferred to his court. Compensation in these cases was handled by the district collector and the district magistrate, not by the court itself. Without more special courts to share the caseload, the judge explained, the rate at which cases were tried would remain slow. Because of the length of time it takes to reach trial, and because of the severity of punishments under the act, the judge added that the accused were attempting to compromise cases by influencing witnesses, most of whom were already afraid to come forward for fear of the consequences: "I can depose only one or two cases a week. It takes so long that people are starting to compromise the case."[604]

Unless special courts are established in each revenue district in each state, and unless witnesses feel protected by the police, the backlog of cases will continue, and increases in case registration will not result in increased convictions. All states should ensure establishment of these courts and appoint special prosecutors for trying cases that arise under the act.

### Under-reporting of Atrocities Act cases: the Gujarat experience
An investigation conducted by Navsarjan, an NGO that has been working with Dalits in Gujarat since 1989, exposed the under-reporting of Atrocities Act cases and the biases of officers charged with its implementation. The study covered eleven "atrocity-prone" districts between 1990 and 1993 and showed that 36 percent of atrocities cases were not registered under the Atrocities Act. Moreover, in 84.4 percent of cases where the act was applied, cases were registered under the provision for name-calling (Section 3(1)(10)). That is, in many cases the actual and violent nature of abuses was concealed.[605]

---

[603]Human Rights Watch interview with H. Hanumanthappa, New Delhi, March 11, 1998.
[604]Human Rights Watch interview with Kandasamy Pandian, special court judge, Madurai district, Tamil Nadu, February 18, 1998.
[605]Navsarjan, "Atrocities on Dalits...". The study cross-checked police data with data from NGOs and the Social Welfare Ministry to calculate disparities in registration. Navsarjan also documented the time it took between reporting of incidents and ensuing police action. The average amount of elapsed time between registration of murder cases to police action was 121.2 hours, for rape cases, 532.9 hours.

Martin Macwan, founder and director of Navsarjan, told Human Rights Watch that the under-reporting continues to be a problem in his state and throughout the country. "The police say, 'Give me the complaint in writing,' and the complainant leaves. They take the writing as an application and do the preliminary inquiry but do not make it into an FIR. Without an FIR, the case cannot be registered."[606] Macwan added that apart from personal caste biases, this phenomenon could also be explained by pressures on the police to keep reported crime rates low in their jurisdictions. In the four years studied, police records showed that atrocities were up by 90 percent (both due to increased reporting and increased incidents),[607] yet police reports also reflected that the general crime rate was down by 1.35 percent.[608]

The police see their primary duty as the maintenance of law and order. An increased crime rate sends the message that they are not doing their job and can often lead to suspensions, demotions, and other punishments.[609] To keep up the facade of lower crime rates, police send information on only a portion of cases to district headquarters.[610] Under-reporting at the district level gets reflected in state-level statistics and presumably gets even more diluted at the national level. Ultimately, "there is no system for getting authentic information, and the public has no way of counter-checking the information that is there."[611]

The Navsarjan study also interviewed ninety-eight police officers of all ranks in the eleven districts surveyed, on their knowledge of and attitude toward the Atrocities Act. Dalits constituted a minority of the officers interviewed. Several deputy superintendents of police (DSP) in charge of implementing the act viewed the act as an obstacle between caste communities. "Because of the act,"

---

[606]Human Rights Watch interview with Martin Macwan, Ahmedabad, Gujarat, July 21, 1998.

[607]61.56 percent of the increased atrocities were due to "social reasons": "untouchability" practices and upper-caste reaction to Dalit attempts to share public resources and walk on public ways. Some 19 percent were land and labor-related disputes. Navsarjan, "Atrocities on Dalits...".

[608]Ibid.

[609]Human Rights Watch interviews with investigating officers for the National Human Rights Commission, New Delhi, March 10, 1998; C. V. Shankar, director for the Adi Dravida Tribal Welfare Department, Government of Tamil Nadu, Madras, February 13, 1998; and T. K. Chaudary, Joint Commissioner of Police, Mumbai (Bombay) Police, Bombay, February 5, 1998.

[610]Human Rights Watch interview with Martin Macwan, Navsarjan, Ahmedabad, Gujarat, July 21, 1998.

[611]Ibid.

one officer said, "Dalits have become more powerful, thus having an adverse impact on society." Another added that "Dalits are dependent on non-Dalits for economic reasons. Because of this act they are spoiling their own chances of employment." One DSP even complained, "We high-caste pay income tax which goes to the social welfare department that pays Dalits and they are the ones who make us accused and put us behind bars."[612] According to the survey, 75 percent of DSPs charged that Dalits were misusing the act and filing false cases for monetary gain. A Dalit superintendent of police rejected that assertion, saying, "Almost all laws are misused, but this act is for harijans [Dalits] and has direct provisions for stringent punishment. Therefore even a little misuse creates uproar in society."[613] Such uproar is best illustrated by the Maharashtra experience described below.

### Attempts to repeal the Atrocities Act: the Maharashtra experience

That the Atrocities Act is perceived as a serious threat to upper-caste interests was readily apparent in the state of Maharashtra where, in 1995, a promise to repeal the act became a centerpiece of the Shiv Sena party's electoral campaign. Caste-based violence is common in parts of rural Maharashtra.[614] In September 1995 the Maharashtra state government began withdrawing over 1,100 cases registered under the act, alleging that many of the cases were false and registered out of personal bias.[615] The stated goal of the drastic move, which began in 1994, was to "promote communal harmony."[616] On January 14, 1994, the state government renamed a university in Marathwada, eastern Maharashtra, as Dr. Ambedkar University. The renaming led to rioting and abuses by caste Hindus in the community. Many cases were registered under the Atrocities Act in the aftermath of the riots. In the week following the renaming, at least four Dalits were

---

[612]Navsarjan, "Atrocities on Dalits...".

[613]Ibid.

[614]In February 1993, a Dalit *kotwal* (village guard) named Ambadas Savne took shelter against the wall of a temple. He was accosted by caste Hindus chanting inside the temple, who claimed that he had rendered the structure "unholy" by touching its walls. As summary punishment for his perceived transgression he was stoned to death at the temple's footsteps. Human Rights Watch interview with Maharashtra activist who attempted to register Savne's case under the Atrocities Act, New York, October 22, 1998.

[615]"All cases under Atrocities Act being withdrawn," *The Times of India*, September 20, 1995.

[616] "A blunted weapon?" *The Hindu*, April 3, 1994.

stabbed, Dalit huts and shops were burned in seven villages, and statues of Dr. Ambedkar were desecrated throughout the region.[617]

The withdrawal of cases by then-Chief Minister Manohar Joshi was in fulfillment of a promise made by Shiv Sena chief Bal Thackeray during his election campaign in Marathwada.[618] The government also announced its intention to ask the central government to amend the act to limit its potential "abuse."[619] But the move to simultaneously withdraw so many cases was an illegal one. Section 321 of the Criminal Procedure Code requires the court's consent for any case to be withdrawn from prosecution. Attempts to circumvent a piece of central legislation also raise fundamental questions about the state government's constitutional responsibility.[620]

Despite the withdrawal of so many cases, a tremendous backlog in Atrocities Act cases remained in the state's court system. According to the Protection of Civil Rights cell in Maharashtra, as of 1996, the average age of a case registered under the act was more than five years. A 1996 PCR cell report stated that of the 875 cases registered under the act in 1994, 692 were still pending at the investigation level. In 1993, of the 1,921 cases registered, 1,918 were still pending. In 1992 a total of 1,449 cases were registered under the Atrocities Act and the Protection of Civil Rights Act; 1,066 remained unsettled in the courts. In the same year, only eleven people were convicted under the Atrocities Act.[621]

As a senior official within the PCR cell observed, such delay "defeats the purpose of promulgation of such welfare legislation."[622] The PCR cell has repeatedly asked the Home Ministry to form special courts in the state to clear the backlog. As of December 1998, none had been established.

The Atrocities Act was enacted in part to increase convictions against those accused of caste abuses who would otherwise escape conviction under the

---

[617]Jyoti Punwani, "Govt. move defeats aim of Prevention of Atrocities Act," *The Times of India* (Bombay), September 26, 1995.

[618]Ibid. Marathwada is a region in eastern Maharashtra.

[619]"All cases under Atrocities Act being withdrawn," *The Times of India*, September 20, 1995.

[620]Under the constitution, Parliament has the power to make laws for the whole of or any part of the territory of India (except Jammu and Kashmir), which state governments are then obligated to enforce.

[621]Sumedha Raikar, "Huge backlog of cases of atrocities on Scheduled Castes, Scheduled Tribes," *Indian Express* (Bombay), 1996.

[622]Ibid. The article also reports that lack of government permission for the prosecution of public servants also blocks the trying of cases against them.

Indian Penal Code. The withdrawal of cases ensured that "no one [would] take the law seriously anymore." Its purpose was effectively subverted.[623] NGOs working in the area also raised similar concerns: "Once this law becomes toothless it would become difficult for the Dalits to survive in the vicious rural setting."[624]

Human Rights Watch spoke with Vivek Pandit, head of the NGO Samarthan and an activist credited with securing registration of many cases in Maharashtra since 1991. Pandit has seen written instructions by state officials not to implement certain provisions of the Atrocities Act, particularly provisions related to physical abuse and land alienation.

> In Maharashtra, the election campaign was run on a promise to repeal the act. They tried to withdraw 1,128 atrocities cases. Samarthan kept the pressure on. I personally presented the case before the National Commission for Scheduled Castes and Scheduled Tribes. But the state government's resolution to repeal cases won't do it. Each case has to go through formal proceedings. They are throwing smoke in the constituency's eyes and saying that they are going to repeal it because of the "false cases" being registered. But there is not a single false case. We have the documents for each and every case. By saying that they are going to withdraw, they are sending the message to the police not to register the cases and that they are in favor of the upper castes.[625]

With the aim of eradicating "untouchability" and deterring the increased incidence of crimes against Dalits throughout the country, states should make a concerted effort to ensure full implementation of the Atrocities Act. Attempts to withdraw cases and delays in setting up special courts and appointing special prosecutors send the wrong message to implementing agencies and effectively subvert the stated aims of the act. Without immediate action, the Atrocities Act, like many other pieces of social welfare legislation, will remain a paper tiger.

---

[623]"A blunted weapon?" *The Hindu*, April 2, 1994, quoting a senior official familiar with civil rights cases.
[624]Ibid., quoting NGO workers.
[625]Human Rights Watch interview with Vivek Pandit, Bombay, January 29, 1998.

## India's Obligations under International Law

The abuses documented in this report are in violation of the international human rights treaties outlined below. As a party to these treaties, India is obligated to comply with their provisions. The Committee on the Elimination of Racial Discrimination (CERD) and the Human Rights Committee (HRC), monitoring bodies under the United Nations International Convention on the Elimination of All Forms of Racial Discrimination and the International Covenant on Civil and Political Rights, respectively, have both expressed concern over the severe social discrimination still practiced against members of scheduled castes and scheduled tribes. Both committees have also recommended measures that can be taken to ameliorate the situation.[626]

### International Convention on the Elimination of All Forms of Racial Discrimination, 1965

In the concluding observations of its forty-ninth session held in August 1996, as it reviewed India's tenth to fourteenth periodic reports under the convention, the Committee on the Elimination of Racial Discrimination (CERD) affirmed that "the situation of Scheduled Castes and Scheduled Tribes falls within the scope of" the International Convention on the Elimination of All Forms of Racial Discrimination, 1965.[627] Article 6 of the convention provides that state parties shall "assure to everyone within their jurisdiction effective protection and remedies, through the competent national tribunals and other State institutions, against any acts of racial discrimination which violate his human rights and fundamental freedoms contrary to this Convention, as well as the right to seek from such tribunals just and adequate reparation or satisfaction for any damage suffered as a result of such discrimination."[628]

The committee added that the provisions of Article 6 are mandatory and that "the State party [should] continue to and strengthen its efforts to improve the effectiveness of measures aimed at guaranteeing to all groups of the population, and especially to the members of the Scheduled Castes and Scheduled Tribes, the

---

[626]See also Chapter IX for a discussion of the Convention on the Elimination of All Forms of Discrimination against Women, 1979.

[627]Consideration of Report by India to the Committee on the Elimination of Racial Discrimination, CERD/C/304/Add.13, September 17, 1996. See Appendix E for full text of the committee's report.

[628]International Convention on the Elimination of All Forms of Racial Discrimination, 660 U.N.T.S. 195, entered into force Jan. 4, 1969, Art. 6. India ratified the convention on December 3, 1968.

full enjoyment of their civil, cultural, economic, political and social rights, as mentioned in article 5 of the Convention."[629] It recommended that:

- special measures be taken by the authorities to prevent acts of discrimination towards persons belonging to the scheduled castes and tribes, and in the case where such acts have been committed, to conduct thorough investigations, to punish those found responsible and provide just and adequate reparation to the victims;

- a continuing campaign be undertaken to educate the Indian population on human rights, in line with India's constitution and with universal human rights instruments, including the International Convention on the Elimination of All Forms of Racial Discrimination, and aimed at eliminating the institutionalized thinking of the high-caste and low-caste mentality;

- legal provisions be adopted to make it "easier for individuals to seek from the courts just and adequate reparation or satisfaction for any damage suffered as a result of acts of racial discrimination, including acts of discrimination based on belonging to caste or a tribe."[630]

**International Covenant on Civil and Political Rights, 1966**
In July 1997 the sixtieth session of the Human Rights Committee considered India's third periodic report submitted under Article 40 of the International Covenant on Civil and Political Rights (ICCPR). The committee made the following observations pertaining to caste:

The Committee notes with concern that, despite measures taken by the Government, members of scheduled castes and scheduled tribes, as well as the so-called backward classes and ethnic and

---

[629]Consideration of Report by India to the Committee on the Elimination of Racial Discrimination, CERD/C/304/Add.13, September 17, 1996.
[630]Ibid.

national minorities continue to endure severe social discrimination and to suffer disproportionately from many violations of their rights under the Covenant, *inter alia,* inter-caste violence, bonded labour and discrimination of all kinds. It regrets that the *de facto* perpetuation of the caste system entrenches social differences and contributes to these violations. While the Committee notes the efforts made by the State party to eradicate discrimination:

> it recommends that further measures be adopted, including education programmes at national and state levels, to combat all forms of discrimination against these vulnerable groups, in accordance with articles 2, paragraph 1, and 26 of the Covenant.[631]

In addition to the violations outlined above, Articles 7, 9, 14, and 26 of the ICCPR are of particular relevance to the abuses documented in this report. Article 7 prohibits the use of torture, or cruel, inhuman or degrading treatment or punishment. The right to liberty and security of person is guaranteed by Article 9 and includes freedom from arbitrary arrest and detention, entitlement to a trial within a reasonable time or to release, and compensation for victims of unlawful arrest or detention. Illegal arrests and detentions are by definition "arbitrary"; such acts can also be arbitrary if not in conformity with international standards of human rights and procedural fairness, regardless of specific provisions of domestic law.

While noting India's reservation to Article 9, the Human Rights Committee commented that this reservation, "does not exclude, *inter alia*, the obligation to comply with the requirement to inform promptly the person concerned of the reasons for his or her arrest."

The committee also added that:

> preventive detention is a restriction of liberty imposed as a response to the conduct of the individual concerned, that the decision as to continued detention must be considered as a

---

[631]Consideration of Report by India to the Human Rights Committee, CCPR/C/79/Add.81, August 4, 1997. See Appendix F for full text of the committee's report.

determination falling within the meaning of article 14, paragraph 1, of the Covenant, and that proceedings to decide the continuation of detention must, therefore, comply with that provision. Therefore:

> the Committee recommends that the requirements of article 9, paragraph 2, of the Covenant be complied with in respect of all detainees. The question of continued detention should be determined by an independent and impartial tribunal constituted and operating in accordance with article 14, paragraph 1, [the right to equality before all courts and tribunals] of the Covenant. It further recommends, at the very least, that a central register of detainees under preventive detention laws be maintained and that the State party accept the admission of the International Committee of the Red Cross to all types of detention facilities, particularly in areas of conflict.[632]

Finally, Article 26 of the ICCPR guarantees the right to equal protection before the law and prohibits discrimination on any ground including, among others, race, sex, religion, political or other opinion, social origin, birth, or other status.[633]

### International Covenant on Economic, Social and Cultural Rights, 1966

Article 7 of the International Covenant on Economic, Social and Cultural Rights (ICESCR) provides that state parties shall "recognize the right of everyone to the enjoyment of just and favorable conditions of work." These include "fair wages and equal remuneration for work of equal value without distinction of any kind," and "safe and healthy work conditions."[634]

---

[632]Ibid.

[633]International Covenant on Civil and Political Rights, G.A. Res. 2200 (XXI), 21 U.N. GAOR Supp. (No. 16), U.N. Doc A/6316 (1966) (entered into force March 23, 1976). India acceded to the convention on April 10, 1979.

[634]International Covenant on Economic, Social and Cultural Rights, G.A. Res. 2200 (XXI), 21 U.N. GAOR Supp. (No. 16), U.N. Doc. A/6316 (entered into force January 3, 1976). India acceded to the convention on April 10, 1979.

### Convention Against Torture and Other Cruel, Inhuman, or Degrading Treatment or Punishment, 1984

Succumbing in part to pressure from domestic human rights NGOs and the National Human Rights Commission, India signed the Convention Against Torture and Other Cruel, Inhuman, or Degrading Treatment of Punishment on October 14, 1997. The provisions of the convention will become binding upon its ratification.

The convention defines torture as:

> [A]ny act by which severe pain or suffering, whether physical or mental, is intentionally inflicted on a person for such purposes as obtaining from him or a third person information or a confession, punishing him for an act he or a third person has committed or is suspected of having committed, or intimidating or coercing him or a third person, or for any reason based on discrimination of any kind, when such pain or suffering is inflicted by or at the instigation of or with the consent or acquiescence of a public official or other person acting in an official capacity.[635]

Severe beatings of Dalit men and women by the police documented in this report fall well within this definition. Indian police routinely employ torture techniques in police stations, lock-ups, and detention centers throughout the country. The sexual abuse of women by state agents in a custodial setting amounts to torture if the agent uses force, the threat of force, or other means of coercion to compel a woman to engage in sexual intercourse.[636] If the agent uses force or coercion to engage in sexual touching of prisoners, including aggressively squeezing, groping, or prodding women's genitals or breasts, and the acts cause severe physical and mental suffering, that too would amount to torture.

---

[635]United Nations Convention Against Torture and Other Cruel Inhuman or Degrading Treatment or Punishment, Part I, Article I (1).

[636]In 1992 the U.N. Special Rapporteur on Torture noted, "Since it was clear that rape or other forms of sexual assault against women in detention were particularly ignominious violations of the inherent dignity and the right to physical integrity of the human being, they accordingly constituted an act of torture." U.N. Doc. E/CN.4/1992/SR.21, para. 35. Report by the Special Rapporteur, P. Koojimans, appointed pursuant to Commission on Human Rights resolution 1985/33, U.N. Doc. E/CN.4/1986/15 (February 19, 1986), p. 29.

Acts that do not rise to the level of torture or cruel or inhuman treatment may nevertheless be classified as degrading treatment, which is defined as treatment that causes or is intended to cause gross humiliation or an insult to a person's dignity.[637] The prohibition on degrading treatment also extends to the use of demeaning language where the employment of such language is intended to dehumanize and weaken an incarcerated person.[638]

### Convention on the Rights of the Child, 1989, and Forced Labour Convention, 1930

Finally, the Convention on the Rights of the Child, 1989 (CRC) and the Forced Labour Convention, 1930 mandate protections that are particularly relevant for bonded laborers. Article 32 of CRC dictates that states parties recognize the "right of the child to be protected from economic exploitation and from performing any work that is likely to be hazardous or... be harmful to the child's health or physical, mental, spiritual, moral or social development."[639] Similarly, the International Labour Organisation (ILO) Forced Labour Convention requires signatories to "suppress the use of forced or compulsory labour in all its forms in the shortest period possible."[640] In 1957, the ILO explicitly incorporated debt bondage and serfdom within its definition of forced labor.[641]

---

[637]In the *Greek Case*, the European Commission on Human Rights defined degrading treatment as that which "grossly humiliates one before others or drives him to act against his will or conscience." *Greek Case*, 1969 Yearbook of European Convention on Human Rights, p. 186 (1969).

[638]*Greek Case*, 1969 Yearbook of European Convention on Human Rights, pp. 462-3 (1969). For more information on the applicability of the Torture Convention to custodial abuse of women, *see* Human Rights Watch/Women's Rights Division, "Nowhere to Hide: Retaliation Against Women in Michigan State Prisons," *A Human Rights Watch Report*, Vol. 10, No. 2 (G), September 1998, pp. 14-17.

[639]Convention on the Rights of the Child, G.A. Res. 44/125, U.N. GAOR, 44th Session, Supp. No. 49, U.N. Doc. A/44/736 (1989) (entered into force September 2, 1990).

[640]Forced Labour Convention (No. 29), 1930, adopted at Geneva, June 28, 1930, as modified by the Final Articles Revision Convention, adopted at Montreal, October 9, 1946.

[641]International Labour Organisation, *Conventions and Recommendations 1919-1966* (Geneva: ILO, 1966), p. 891. The ILO also passed the Abolition of Forced Labour Convention (No. 105) in 1957; India, however, chose not to sign this convention.

## XI. CONCLUSION

As this report demonstrates, more than 160 million people in the "world's largest democracy" remain at risk of systematic human rights violations on the basis of the caste into which they are born. Despite the fact that India constitutionally abolished the practice of "untouchability" in 1950, the practice continues in the constitution's fiftieth year, and violence has become a defining characteristic of the abuse. In 1989 India enacted the Scheduled Castes and Scheduled Tribes (Prevention of Atrocities) Act to prevent and punish state and private actors for abuses against Dalits, to establish special courts for the trial of such offenses, and to provide for the rehabilitation and relief of the victims. However, without a serious and sustained commitment to implementing constitutional safeguards and other national and international legal protections, human rights abuses in their most degrading forms will continue against scheduled-caste community members.

As documented throughout this report, the response of state administrations to incidents of caste violence amounts to a failure to ensure equal protection under the law and exposes a pattern of complicity and collusion on behalf of police and local officials. Despite ambitious calls for action by central and state governments in the aftermath publicity of massacres and police raids, the Indian authorities have shown little commitment to resolving the root causes of caste conflicts. In Bihar, Tamil Nadu, and other states where massacres and large-scale police attacks on Dalits in rural and urban settings continue to take place, state administrations should act swiftly and without bias to bring offending state and private actors to justice. They must heed calls for protection from Dalit communities and work to address those issues of inequity that are at the heart of the class-caste conflict. To dismiss the violence as purely a "law and order" concern, or to depict it as the inevitable consequence of ancient feuds between caste Hindus and Dalits, or between the haves and the have-nots, is misleading and irresponsible. Such a characterization erroneously suggests that the state has no protective role to play, or that the state itself has not contributed to the abuse.

At the same time, other forms of human rights violations should not go unaddressed. The false arrests and detentions of social activists are insidious, as they punish those members of the population who attempt to peacefully and democratically claim their rights and protect the rights of others. The exploitation of agricultural laborers and the rigid assignment of demeaning occupations on the basis of caste keeps Dalits in a position of economic and physical vulnerability. The triple burden of caste, class, and gender effectively ensures that Dalit women are the furthest removed from legal protections. Only with the honest implementation of laws designed to protect agricultural laborers and abolish manual scavenging and forced prostitution, and the systematic prosecution of those responsible for attacks on Dalit men and women, can the process of attaining economic and physical security begin.

The Scheduled Castes and Scheduled Tribes (Prevention of Atrocities) Act has the potential to bring about social change by sending the message that human rights violations against scheduled-caste members will not go unpunished. The implementation of the Atrocities Act and other legislation, however, depends largely on the ability and willingness of the police to follow proper procedure and overcome caste biases, economic hurdles, and other obstacles. More than twenty years ago, the Indian government set up the National Police Commission to examine the causes of police abuse and police negligence. The commission's 1980 eight-volume report, which followed a series of similar reports by state-level commissions, is a comprehensive account of police brutality and corruption, providing serious recommendations to address the problems. It documents deficiencies in training, salaries, and the de facto immunity from punishment that police continue to enjoy.

Civil rights activists and attorneys in India have argued that even partial implementation of the reports' detailed recommendations would substantially curb police abuses and improve their overall performance. The importance of implementing the recommendations was reiterated in a recent Supreme Court judgment.[642] Despite repeated calls for reform from former Home Minister Indrajit Gupta, the National Human Rights Commission, and civil rights activists, little action has been taken. Without an immediate and comprehensive commitment to police reform, abuses against the countries lowest castes, and indeed against all marginalized communities, will continue. India's emerging human rights discourse, and the innovative work of the women's movement and the Dalit movement, are already helping to generate solutions to the problem of police corruption and caste issues generally. The Indian government should solicit the participation of these local groups and of the international community in tackling the problem.

The government of India has also consistently refused to allow relevant U.N. bodies, including working groups and special rapporteurs, to gain access to the country. Simultaneously, the difficulty of slotting caste-based abuses into standard categories of human rights violations, as well as the prevalence of constitutional and legislative protections at the national-level, have allowed for

---

[642]"Governor wants overhauling of police system," *The Hindu*, October 8, 1998.

these abuses to escape international scrutiny.    As a signatory to several international human rights conventions, India is obligated to abide by their provisions.

The Indian government should enlist the support of the United Nations, multilateral financial institutions, India's trading partners, and national and international nongovernmental organizations to eradicate the pervasive problem of caste-based abuse. It should also place a priority on strengthening institutional mechanisms aimed at addressing issues of violence and discrimination. In 1997 India celebrated its fiftieth anniversary of independence from British rule. In 1998 the world celebrated the fiftieth anniversary of the Universal Declaration of Human Rights. The Indian government should mark these occasions by dismantling a system that in practice relegates millions of people to a lifetime of violence, servitude, segregation, and discrimination, all on the basis of caste.

**Article 14. Equality before law.** -The State shall not deny to any person equality before the law or the equal protection of the laws within the territory of India.

**Article 15. Prohibition of discrimination on grounds of religion, race, caste, sex or place of birth. -**

(1) The State shall not discriminate against any citizen on grounds only of religion, race, caste, sex, place of birth or any of them.

(2) No citizen shall, on grounds only of religion, race, caste, sex, place of birth or any of them, be subject to any disability, liability, restriction or condition with regard to-
(a) access to shops, public restaurants, hotels and places of public entertainment; or
(b) the use of wells, tanks, bathing ghats, roads and places of public resort maintained wholly or partly out of State funds or dedicated to the use of the general public.

(3) Nothing in this article shall prevent the State from making any special provision for women and children.

(4) Nothing in this article or in clause (2) of article 29 shall prevent the State from making any special provision for the advancement of any socially and educationally backward classes of citizens or for the Scheduled Castes and the Scheduled Tribes.

**Article 16. Equality of opportunity in matters of public employment. -**

(1) There shall be equality of opportunity for all citizens in matters relating to employment or appointment to any office under the State.

(2) No citizen shall, on grounds only of religion, race, caste, sex, descent, place of birth, residence or any of them, be ineligible for, or discriminated against in respect of, any employment or office under the State.

(4) Nothing in this article shall prevent the State from making any provision for the reservation of appointments or posts in favour of any

backward class of citizens which, in the opinion of the State, is not adequately represented in the services under the State.

**Article 17. Abolition of Untouchability.** -"Untouchability" is abolished and its practice in any form is forbidden. The enforcement of any disability arising out of "Untouchability" shall be an offence punishable in accordance with law.

**Article 19. Protection of certain rights regarding freedom of speech, etc. -**

(1) All citizens shall have the right-
(a) to freedom of speech and expression;
(b) to assemble peaceably and without arms;
(c) to form associations or unions;
(d) to move freely throughout the territory of India;
(e) to reside and settle in any part of the territory of India; [and]
(g) to practise any profession, or to carry on any occupation, trade or business.

(2) Nothing in sub-clause (a) of clause (1) shall affect the operation of any existing law, or prevent the State from making any law, in so far as such law imposes reasonable restrictions on the exercise of the right conferred by the said sub-clause in the interests of the sovereignty and integrity of India, the security of the State, friendly relations with foreign States, public order, decency or morality, or in relation to contempt of court, defamation or incitement to an offence.

(3) Nothing in sub-clause (b) of the said clause shall affect the operation of any existing law in so far as it imposes, or prevent the State from making any law imposing, in the interest of the sovereignty and integrity of India or public order, reasonable restrictions on the exercise of the right conferred by the said sub-clause.

(4) Nothing in sub-clause (c) of the said clause shall affect the operation of any existing law in so far as it imposes, or prevent the State from making any law imposing, in the interests of the sovereignty and integrity of India or public order or morality, reasonable restrictions on the exercise of the right conferred by the said sub-clause.

(5) Nothing in sub-clauses (d) and (e) of the said clause shall affect the operation of any existing law in so far as it imposes, or prevent the State from making any law imposing, reasonable restrictions on the exercise of any of the rights conferred by the said sub-clauses either in the interests of the general public or for the protection of the interests of any Scheduled Tribe.

(6) Nothing in sub-clause (g) of the said clause shall affect the operation of any existing law in so far as it imposes, or prevent the State from making any law imposing, in the interests of the general public, reasonable restrictions on the exercise of the right conferred by the said sub-clause, and, in particular, nothing in the said sub-clause shall affect the operation of any existing law in so far as it relates to, or prevent the State from making any law relating to,-

(i) the professional or technical qualifications necessary for practising any profession or carrying on any occupation, trade or business, or

(ii) the carrying on by the State, or by a corporation owned or controlled by the State, of any trade, business, industry or service, whether to the exclusion, complete or partial, of citizens or otherwise.

**Article 20. Protection in respect of conviction for offences. -**

(1)No person shall be convicted of any offence except for violation of a law in force at the time of the commission of the Act charged as an offence, nor be subjected to a penalty greater than that which might have been inflicted under the law in force at the time of the commission of the offence.

(2) No person shall be prosecuted and punished for the same offence more than once.

(3) No person accused of any offence shall be compelled to be a witness against himself.

## Article 21. Protection of life and personal liberty. -

(1) No person shall be deprived of his life or personal liberty except according to procedure established by law.

## Article 23. Prohibition of traffic in human beings and forced labour. -

(1) Traffic in human beings and begar and other similar forms of forced labour are prohibited and any contravention of this provision shall be an offence punishable in accordance with law.

(2) Nothing in this article shall prevent the State from imposing compulsory service for public purposes, and in imposing such service the State shall not make any discrimination on grounds only of religion. race, caste or class or any of them.

## Article 24. Prohibition of employment of children in factories, etc. -

No child below the age of fourteen years shall be employed to work in any factory or mine or engaged in any other hazardous employment.

## Article 39. Certain principles of policy to be followed by the State. -

The State shall, in particular, direct its policy towards securing-

(a) that the citizens, men and women equally, have the right to an adequate means of livelihood;
(b) that the ownership and control of the material resources of the community are so distributed as best to subserve the common good;
(c) that the operation of the economic system does not result in the concentration of wealth and means of production to the common detriment;

## Article 43. Living wage, etc., for workers. -

The State shall endeavour to secure, by suitable legislation or economic organisation or in any other way, to all workers, agricultural, industrial or otherwise, work, a living wage, conditions of work ensuring a decent standard of life and full enjoyment of leisure and social and cultural opportunities and, in particular, the State shall endeavour to promote cottage industries on an individual or co-operative basis in rural areas.

### Article 44. Uniform civil code for the citizens. -

The State shall endeavour to secure for the citizens a uniform civil code throughout the territory of India.

### Article 45. Provision for free and compulsory education for children. -

The State shall endeavour to provide, within a period of ten years from the commencement of this Constitution, for free and compulsory education for all children until they complete the age of fourteen years.

### Article 46. Promotion of educational and economic interests of Scheduled Castes, Scheduled Tribes and other weaker sections. -

The State shall promote with special care the educational and economic interests of the weaker sections of the people, and, in particular, of the Scheduled Castes and the Scheduled Tribes, and shall protect them from social injustice and all forms of exploitation.

### Article 51A: Fundamental Duties. -

It shall be the duty of every citizen of India—

> (e) to promote harmony and the spirit of common brotherhood amongst all the people of India transcending religious, linguistic and regional or sectional diversities; to renounce practices derogatory to the dignity of women.

### Article 243D. Reservation of seats. -

> (1) Seats shall be reserved for-
> > (a) the Scheduled Castes; and
> > (b) the Scheduled Tribes, in every Panchayat and the number of seats so reserved shall bear, as nearly as may be, the same proportion to the, total number of seats to be filled by direct election in that Panchayat as the population of the Scheduled

Castes in that Panchayat area or of the Scheduled Tribes in that Panchayat area bears to the total population of that area and such seats may be allotted by rotation to different constituencies in a Panchayat.

(2) Not less than one-third of the total number of seats reserved under clause (1) shall be reserved for women belonging to the Scheduled Castes or, as the case may be, the Scheduled Tribes,

(3) Not less than one-third (including the number of seats reserved for women belonging to the Scheduled Castes and the Scheduled Tribes) of the total number of seats to be filled by direct election in every Panchayat shall be reserved for women and such seats may be allotted by rotation to different constituencies in a Panchayat.

(4) The offices of the Chairpersons in the Panchayats at the village or any other level shall be reserved for the Scheduled Castes the Scheduled Tribes and women in such manner as the Legislature of a State may, by law, provide:

Provided that the number of offices of chairpersons reserved for the Scheduled Castes and the Scheduled Tribes in the Panchayats at each level in any State shall bear, as nearly as may be, the same proportion to the total number of such offices in the Panchayats at each level as the population of the Scheduled Castes in the State or of the Scheduled Tribes in the State bears to the total population of the State:

Provided further that not less than one-third of the total number of offices of Chairpersons in the Panchayats at each level shall be reserved for women:

Provided also that the number of offices reserved under this clause shall be allotted by rotation to different Panchayats at each level.

**Article 243T. Reservation of seats. -**

(1) Seats shall be reserved for the Scheduled Castes and the Scheduled Tribes in every Municipality and the number of seats so reserved shall

bear, as nearly as may be, the same proportion to the total number of seats to be filled by direct election in that Municipality as the population of the Scheduled Castes in the Municipal area or of the Scheduled Tribes in the Municipal area bears to the total population of that area and such seats may be allotted by rotation to different constituencies in a Municipality. (2) Not less than one-third of the total number of seats reserved under clause (1) shall be reserved for women belonging to the Scheduled Castes or as the case may be the Scheduled Tribes,

(3) Not less than one-third (including the number of seats reserved for women belonging to the Scheduled Castes and the Scheduled Tribes) of the total number of seats to be filled by direct election in every Municipality shall be reserved for women and such seats may be allotted by rotation to different constituencies in a Municipality.

(4) The officers of Chairpersons in the Municipalities shall be reserved for the Scheduled Castes, the Scheduled Tribes and women in such manner as the Legislature of a State may, by law, provide.

(5) The reservation of seats under clauses (1) and (2) and the reservation of offices of Chairpersons (other than the reservation for women) under clause (4) shall cease to have effect on the expiration of the period specified in Article 334.

(6) Nothing in this Part shall prevent the Legislature of a State from making any provision for reservation of seats in any Municipality or offices of Chairpersons in the Municipalities in favour of backward class of citizens.

**Article 330. Reservation of seats for Scheduled Castes and Scheduled Tribes in the House of the People. -**

(1) Seats shall be reserved in the House of the People for-
(a) the Scheduled Castes;
(b) the Scheduled Tribes except the Scheduled Tribes in the autonomous districts of Assam; and
(c) the Scheduled Tribes in the autonomous districts of Assam.

(2) The number of seats reserved in any State or Union territory for the Scheduled Castes or the Scheduled Tribes under clause (1) shall bear, as nearly as may be, the same proportion to the total number of seats allotted to that State or Union territory in the House of the People as the population of the Scheduled Castes in the State or Union territory or of the Scheduled Tribes in the State or Union territory or part of the State or Union territory, as the case may be, in respect of which seats are so reserved, bears to the total population of the State or Union territory.

(3) Notwithstanding anything contained in clause (2), the number of seats reserved in the House of the People for the Scheduled Tribes in the autonomous districts of Assam shall bear to the total number of seats allotted to that State a proportion not less than the population of the Scheduled Tribes in the said autonomous districts bears to the total population of the State.

**Article 332. Reservation of seats for Scheduled Castes and Scheduled Tribes in the Legislative Assemblies of the States. -**

(1) Seats shall be reserved for the Scheduled Castes and the Scheduled Tribes, except the Scheduled Tribes in the autonomous districts of Assam, in the Legislative Assembly of every State.

(2) Seats shall be reserved also for the autonomous districts in the Legislative Assembly of the State of Assam.

(3) The number of seats reserved for the Scheduled Castes or the Scheduled Tribes in the Legislative Assembly of any State under clause (1) shall bear, as nearly as may be, the same proportion to the total number of seats in the Assembly as the population of the Scheduled Castes in the State or of the Scheduled Tribes in the State or part of the State, as the case may be, in respect of which seats are so reserved, bears to the total population of the State.

(3A) Notwithstanding anything contained in clause (3), until the taking effect, under article 170 , of the readjustment, on the basis of the first census after the year 2000, of the number of seats in the Legislative Assemblies of the States of Arunachal Pradesh, Meghalaya, Mizoram and

Nagaland, the seats which shall be reserved for the Scheduled Tribes in the Legislative Assembly of any such State shall be,-

(a) if all the seats in the Legislative Assembly of such State in existence on the date of coming into force of the Constitution (Fifty-seventh Amendment) Act, 1987 (hereafter in this clause referred to as the existing Assembly) are held by members of the Scheduled Tribes, all the seats except one;

(b) in any other case, such number of seats as bears to the total number of seats, a proportion not less than the number (as on the said date) of members belonging to the Scheduled Tribes in the existing Assembly bears to the total number of seats in the existing Assembly.

(3B) Notwithstanding anything contained in clause (3), until the re-adjustment, under article 170, takes effect on the basis of the first census after the year 2000, of the number of seats in the Legislative Assembly of the State of Tripura, the seats which shall be reserved for the Scheduled Tribes in the Legislative Assembly shall be, such number of seats as bears to the total number of seats, a proportion not less than the number, as on the date of coming into force of the Constitution (Seventy-second Amendment) Act, 1992, of members belonging to the Scheduled Tribes in the Legislative Assembly in existence on the said date bears to the total number of seats in that Assembly.

(4) The number of seats reserved for an autonomous district in the Legislative Assembly of the State of Assam shall bear to the total number of seats in that Assembly a proportion not less than the population of the district bears to the total population of the State.

(5) The constituencies for the seats reserved for any autonomous district of Assam shall not comprise any area outside that district.

(6) No person who is not a member of a Scheduled Tribe of any autonomous district of the State of Assam shall be eligible for election to the Legislative Assembly of the State from any constituency of that district

**Article 334. Reservation of seats and special representation to cease after [fifty years]. -**

Not withstanding anything in the foregoing provisions of this Part, the provisions of this Constitution relating to-
    (a) the reservation of seats for the Scheduled Castes and the Scheduled Tribes in the House of the People and in the Legislative Assemblies of the States; and
    (b) the representation of the Anglo-Indian community in the House of the People and in the Legislative Assemblies of the States by nomination, shall cease to have effect on the expiration of a period of [fifty years] from the commencement of this Constitution:
        Provided that nothing in this article shall affect any representation in the House of the People or in the Legislative Assembly of a State until the dissolution of the then existing House or Assembly, as the case may be.

**Article 335. Claims of Scheduled Castes and Scheduled Tribes to services and posts. -**

The claims of the members of the Scheduled Castes and the Scheduled Tribes shall be taken into consideration, constantly with the maintenance of the efficiency of administration, in the making of appointments to services and posts in connection with the affairs of the Union or of a State.

No. 33 of 1989

[11th September, 1989]

An Act to prevent the commission of offences of atrocities against the members of the Scheduled Castes and the Scheduled Tribes, to provide for Special Courts for the trial of such offences and for the relief and rehabilitation of the victims of such offences and for matters connected therewith or incidental thereto.

Be it enacted by Parliament in the Fortieth Year of the Republic of India as follows:-

## CHAPTER I
## PRELIMINARY

**1. Short title, extent and commencement-**

(1) This Act may be called the Scheduled Castes and the Scheduled Tribes (Prevention of Atrocities) Act, 1989.

(2) It extends to the whole of India except the State of Jammu and Kashmir.

(3) It shall come into force on such date as the Central Government may, by notification in the Official Gazette, appoint.

**2. Definitions-**

(1) In this Act, unless the context otherwise requires,-

(a) "atrocity" means an offence punishable under Section 3;

(b) "Code" means the Code of Criminal Procedure, 1973 (2 of 1974);

(c) "Scheduled Castes and Scheduled Tribes" shall have the meanings assigned to them respectively under clause (24) and clause (25) of Article 366 of the Constitution;

(d) "Special Court" means a Court of Session specified as a Special Court in section 14;

(e) "Special Public Prosecutor" means a Public Prosecutor specified as a Special Public Prosecutor or an advocate referred to in section 15;

(f) words and expressions used but not defined in this Act and defined in the Code or the Indian Penal Code (45 of 1860) shall have the meanings assigned to them respectively in the Code, or as the case may be, in the Indian Penal Code.

(2) Any reference in this Act to any enactment or any provision thereof shall, in relation to an area in which such enactment or such provision is, not in force, be construed as a reference to the corresponding law, if any, in force in that area.

## CHAPTER II
## OFFENCES OF ATROCITIES

**3. Punishments for offences of atrocities-**

(1) Whoever, not being a member of a Scheduled Caste or a Scheduled Tribe, -

(i) forces a member of a Scheduled Caste or a Scheduled Tribe to drink or eat any inedible or obnoxious substance;

(ii) acts with intent to cause injury, insult or annoyance to any member of a Scheduled Caste or a Scheduled Tribe by dumping excreta, waste matter, carcasses or any other obnoxious substance in his premises or neighborhood;

(iii) forcibly removes clothes from the person of a member of a Scheduled Caste or a Scheduled Tribe or parades him naked or with painted face or body or commits any similar act which is derogatory to human dignity;

(iv) wrongfully occupies or cultivates any land owned by, or allotted to, or notified by any competent authority to be allotted to, a member of a Scheduled Caste or a Scheduled Tribe or gets the land allotted to him transferred;

(v) wrongfully dispossesses a member of a Scheduled Caste or a Scheduled Tribe from his land or premises or interferes with the enjoyment of his rights over any land, premises or water;

(vi) compels or entices a member of a Scheduled Caste or a Scheduled Tribe to do 'begar' or other similar forms of forced or bonded labor other than any compulsory service for public purposes imposed by Government;

(vii) forces or intimidates a member of a Scheduled Caste or a Scheduled Tribe not to vote or to vote to a particular candidate or to vote in a manner other than that provided by law;

(viii) institutes false, malicious or vexatious suit or criminal or other legal proceedings against a member of a Scheduled Caste or a Scheduled Tribe;

(ix) gives any false or frivolous information to any public servant and thereby causes such public servant to use his lawful power to the injury or annoyance of a member of a Scheduled Caste or a Scheduled Tribe;

(x) intentionally insults or intimidates with intent to humiliate a member of a Scheduled Caste or a Scheduled Tribe in any place within public view;

(xi) assaults or uses force to any woman belonging to a Scheduled Caste or a Scheduled Tribe with intent to dishonor or outrage her modesty;

(xii) being in a position to dominate the will of a woman belonging to a Scheduled Caste or a Scheduled Tribe and uses that position to exploit her sexually to which she would not have otherwise agreed;

(xiii) corrupts or fouls the water of any spring, reservoir or any other source ordinarily used by members of the Scheduled Caste or the Scheduled Tribes so as to render it less fit for the purpose for which it is ordinarily used;

(xiv) denies a member of a Scheduled Caste or a Scheduled Tribe any customary right of passage to a place of public resort or obstructs such member so as to prevent him from using or having access to a place of public resort to which other members of public or any section thereof have a right to use or access to;

(xv) forces or causes a member of a Scheduled Caste or a Scheduled Tribe to leave his house, village or other place of residence, shall be punishable with imprisonment for a term which shall not be less than six months but which may extend to five years and with fine.

(2) Whoever, not being a member of a Scheduled Caste or a Scheduled Tribe,-

(i) gives or fabricates false evidence intending thereby to cause, or knowing it to be likely that he will thereby cause, any member of a Scheduled Caste or a Scheduled Tribe to be convicted of an offence which is capital by the law for the time being in force shall be punished with imprisonment for life and with fine; and if an innocent member of a Scheduled Caste or a Scheduled Tribe be convicted and executed in consequence of such false or fabricated evidence, the person who gives or fabricates such false evidence, shall be punished with death;

(ii) gives or fabricates false evidence intending thereby to cause, or knowing it to be likely that he will thereby cause, any member of a Scheduled Caste or a Scheduled Tribe to be convicted of an offence which is not capital but punishable with imprisonment for a term of seven years or upwards, shall be punishable with imprisonment for a term which shall not be less than six months but which may extend to seven years or upwards and with fine; (iii) commits mischief by fire or any explosive substance intending to cause or knowing it to be likely that he will thereby cause damage to any property belonging to a member of a Scheduled Caste or a Scheduled Tribe shall be punishable with imprisonment for a term which shall not be less than six months but which may extend to seven years and with fine;

(iv) commits mischief by fire or any explosive substance intending to cause or knowing it to be likely that he will thereby cause destruction of any building which is ordinarily used as a place of worship or as a place for human dwelling or as a place for custody of the property by a member of a Scheduled Caste or a Scheduled Tribe, shall be punishable with imprisonment for life and with fine;

(v) commits any offence under the Indian Penal Code (45 of 1860) punishable with imprisonment for a term of ten years or more against a person or property on the ground that such person is a member of a Scheduled Caste or a Scheduled Tribe or such property belongs to such member, shall be punishable with imprisonment for life and with fine;

(vi) knowingly or having reason to believe that an offence has been committed under this Chapter, causes any evidence of the commission of that offence to disappear with the intention of screening the offender from legal punishment, or with that intention gives any information respecting the offence which he knows or believes to be false, shall be punishable with the punishment provided for that offence; or

(vii) being a public servant, commits any offence under this section, shall be punishable with imprisonment for a term which shall not be less than one year but which may extend to the punishment provided for that offence.

**4. Punishment for neglect of duties-**

Whoever, being a public servant but not being a member of a Scheduled Caste or a Scheduled Tribe, wilfully neglects his duties required to be performed by him under this Act, shall be punishable with imprisonment for a term which shall not be less than six months but which may extend to one year.

**5. Enhanced punishment for subsequent conviction-**

Whoever, having already been convicted of an offence under this Chapter is convicted for the second offence or any offence subsequent to the second offence, shall be punishable with imprisonment for a term which shall not be less than one year but which may extend to the punishment provided for that offence.

**6. Application of certain provisions of the Indian Penal Code-**

Subject to the other provisions of this Act, the provisions of section 34, Chapter III, Chapter IV, Chapter V, Chapter V-A, section 149 and Chapter XXIII of the Indian Penal Code (45 of 1860), shall, so far as may be, apply for the purposes of this Act as they apply for the purposes of the Indian Penal Code.

**7. Forfeiture of property of certain persons-**

(1) Where a person has been convicted of any offence punishable under this Chapter, the Special Court may, in addition to awarding any punishment, by order in writing, declare that any property, movable or immovable or both, belonging to the person which has been used for the commission of that offence, shall stand forfeited to Government.

(2) Where any person is accused of any offence under this Chapter, it shall be open to the Special Court trying him to pass an order that all or any of the properties, movable or immovable or both, belonging to him, shall, during the period of such trial, be attached, and where such trial ends in conviction, the property so attached shall be liable to forfeiture to the extent it is required for the purpose of realization of any fine imposed under this Chapter.

## 8. Presumption as to offences-

In a prosecution for an offence under this Chapter, if it is proved that –

(a) the accused rendered any financial assistance to a person accused of, or reasonably suspected of committing, an offence under this Chapter, the Special Court shall presume, unless the contrary is proved, that such person had, abetted the offence;

(b) a group of persons committed an offence under this Chapter and if it is proved that the offence committed was a sequel to any existing dispute regarding land or any other matter, it shall be presumed that the offence was committed in furtherance of the common intention or in prosecution of the common object.

## 9. Conferment of powers-

(1) Notwithstanding anything contained in the Code or in any other provision of this Act, the State Government may, if it considers it necessary or expedient so to do,-

(a) for the prevention of and for coping with any offence under this Act, or

(b) for any case or class or group of cases under this Act, in any district or part thereof, confer, by notification in the Official Gazette, on any officer of the State Government, the powers exercisable by a police officer under the Code in such district or part thereof or, as the case maybe, for such case or class or group of cases, and in particular, the powers of arrest, investigation and prosecution of persons before any Special Court.

(2) All officers of police and all other officers of Government shall assist the officer referred to in sub-section (1) in the execution of the provisions of this Act or any rule, scheme or order made thereunder.

(3) The provisions of the Code shall, so far as may be, apply to the exercise of the powers by an officer under sub-section (1).

## CHAPTER III
## EXTERNMENT

**10. Removal of person likely to commit offence-**

(1) Where the Special Court is satisfied, upon a complaint or a police report that a person is likely to commit an offence under Chapter II of this Act in any area included in 'Scheduled Areas' or 'Tribal areas' as referred to in Article 244 of the Constitution, it may, by order in writing, direct such person to remove himself beyond the limits of such area, by such route and within such time as may be specified in the order, and not to return to that area from which he was directed to remove himself for such period, not exceeding two years, as may be specified in the order.

(2) The Special Court shall, along with the order under sub-section (1), communicate to the person directed under that sub-section the grounds on which such order has been made.

(3) The Special Court may revoke or modify the order made under sub-section (1), for the reasons to be recorded in writing, on the representation made by the person against whom such order has been made or by any other person on his behalf within thirty days from the date of the order.

**11. Procedure on failure of person to remove himself from area and enter thereon after removal-**

(1) If a person to whom a direction has been issued under Section 10 to remove himself from any area-

(a) fails to remove himself as directed; or

(b) having so removed himself enters such area within the period specified in the order, otherwise than with the permission in writing of the Special Court under sub-section (2), the Special Court may cause him to be arrested and removed in police custody to such place outside such area as the Special Court may specify.

(2) The Special Court may, by order in writing, permit any person in respect of whom an order under section 10 has been made, to return to the area from which he was directed to remove himself for such temporary period and subject to such conditions as may be specified in such order and may require him to execute a bond with or without surety for the due observation of the conditions imposed.

(3) The Special Court may at any time revoke any such permission.

(4) Any person who, with such permission, returns to the area from which he was directed to remove himself shall observe the conditions imposed and at the expiry of the temporary period for which he was permitted to return or on the revocation of such permission before the expiry of such temporary period shall remove himself outside such area and shall not return thereto within the unexpired portion specified under Section 10 without a fresh permission.

(5) If a person fails to observe any of the conditions imposed or to remove himself accordingly or having so removed himself enters or returns to such area without fresh permission the Special Court may cause him to be arrested and removed in police custody to such place outside such area as the Special Court may specify.

**12. Taking measurements and photographs, etc. of persons against whom order under section 10 is made-**

(1) Every person against whom an order has been made under Section 10 shall, if so required by the Special Court, allow his measurements and photographs to be taken by a police officer.

(2) If any person referred to in sub-section (1) when required to allow his measurements or photographs to be taken, resists or refuses to allow the taking of such measurements or photographs, it shall be lawful to use all necessary means to secure the taking thereof.

(3) Resistance to or refusal to allow the taking of measurements or photographs under sub-section (2) shall be deemed to be an offence under section 186 of the Indian Penal Code (45 of 1860).

(4) Where an order under section 10 is revoked, all measurements and photographs (including negatives) taken under sub-section (2) shall be destroyed or made over to the person against whom such order is made.

**13. Penalty for non-compliance of order under section 10-**

Any person contravening an order of the Special Court made under Section 10 shall be punishable with imprisonment for a term which may extend to one year and with fine.

## CHAPTER IV
## SPECIAL COURTS

**14. Special Court-**

For the purpose of providing for speedy trial, the State Government shall, with the concurrence of the Chief Justice of the High Court, by notification in the Official Gazette, specify for each district a Court of Session to be a Special Court to try the offences under this Act.

**15. Special Public Prosecutor-**

For every Special Court, the State Government shall, by notification in the Official Gazette, specify a Public Prosecutor or appoint an advocate who has been in practice as an advocate for not less than seven years, as a Special Public Prosecutor for the purpose of conducting cases in that Court.

## CHAPTER V
## MISCELLANEOUS

**16. Power of State Government to impose collective fine-**

The provisions of Section 10-A of the Protection of Civil Rights Act, 1955 (22 of 1955) shall, so far as may be, apply for the purposes of imposition and realization of collective fine and for all other matters connected therewith under this Act.

**17. Preventive action to be taken by the law and order machinery-**

(1) A District Magistrate or a Sub-divisional Magistrate or any other Executive Magistrate or any police officer not below the rank of a Deputy Superintendent of Police may, on receiving information and after such enquiry as he may think necessary, has reason to believe that a person or a group of persons not belonging to the Scheduled Castes or the Scheduled Tribes, residing in or frequenting any place within the local limits of his jurisdiction is likely to commit an offence or has threatened to commit any offence under this Act and is of the opinion that there is sufficient ground for proceeding, declare such an area to be an area prone to atrocities and take necessary action for keeping the peace and good behavior and maintenance of public order and tranquillity and may take preventive action.

(2) The provisions of Chapters VIII, X and XI of the Code shall, so far as may be, apply for the purposes of sub-Section (1).

(3) The State Government may, by notification in the Official Gazette, make one or more schemes specifying the manner in which the officers referred to in sub-Section (1) shall take appropriate action specified in such scheme or schemes to prevent atrocities and to restore the feeling of security amongst the members of the Scheduled Castes and the Scheduled Tribes.

**18. Section 438 of the Code not to apply to persons committing an offence under the Act-**

Nothing in Section 438 of the Code shall apply in relation to any case involving the arrest of any person on an accusation of having committed an offence under this Act.

**19. Section 360 of the Code and the provisions of the Probation of Offenders Act not to apply to persons guilty of an offence under the Act-**

The provisions of Section 360 of the Code and the provisions of the Probation of Offenders Act, 1958 (20 of 1958) shall not apply to any person above the age of eighteen years who is found guilty of having committed an offence under this Act.

**20. Act to override other laws-**

> Save as otherwise provided in this Act, the provisions of this Act shall have effect notwithstanding anything inconsistent therewith contained in any other law for the time being in force or any custom or usage or any instrument having effect by virtue of any such law.

**21. Duty of Government to ensure effective implementation of the Act-**

> (1) Subject to such rules as the Central Government may make in this behalf, the State Government shall take such measures as may be necessary for the effective implementation of this Act.

> (2) In particular, and without prejudice to the generality of the foregoing provisions, such measures may include,-

>> (i) the provision for adequate facilities, including legal aid, to the persons subjected to atrocities to enable them to avail themselves of justice-

>> (ii) the provision for travelling and maintenance expenses to witnesses including the victims of atrocities, during investigation and trial of offences under this Act;

>> (iii) the provision for the economic and social rehabilitation of the victims of the atrocities;

>> (iv) the appointment of officers for initiating or exercising supervision over prosecutions for the contravention of the provisions of this Act;

>> (v) the setting up of committees at such appropriate levels as the State Government may think fit to assist that Government in formulation or implementation of such measures;

>> (vi) provision for a periodic survey of the working of the provisions of this Act with a view to suggesting measures for the better implementation of the provisions of this Act;

(vii) the identification of the areas where the members of the Scheduled Castes and the Scheduled Tribes are likely to be subjected to atrocities and adoption of such measures so as to ensure safety for such members.

(3) The Central Government shall take such steps as may be necessary to co-ordinate the measures taken by the State Governments under sub-Section (1).

(4) The Central Government shall, every year, place on the table of each House of Parliament a report on the measures taken by itself and by the State Governments in pursuance of the provisions of this Section.

## 22. Protection of action taken in good faith-

No suit, prosecution or other legal proceedings shall lie against the Central Government or against the State Government or any officer or authority of Government or any other person for anything which is in good faith done or intended to be done under this Act.

## 23. Power to make rules-

(1) The Central Government may, by notification in the Official Gazette, make rules for carrying out the purposes of this Act.

(2) Every rule made under this Act shall be laid, as soon as may be after it is made, before each House of Parliament, while it is in session for a total period of thirty days which may be comprised in one session or in two or more successive sessions, and if before the expiry of the session immediately following the session or the successive sessions aforesaid, both Houses agree in making any modification in the rule or both Houses agree that the rule should not be made, the rule shall thereafter have effect only in such modified form or be of no effect, as the case may be; so, however, that any such modification or annulment shall be without prejudice to the validity of anything previously done under that rule.

## APPENDIX C: The Scheduled Castes and Scheduled Tribes (Prevention of Atrocities) Rules, 1995

G.S.R. 316 (E), dated 31st March, 1995.- In exercise of the powers conferred by sub-Section (1) of Sec. 23 of the Scheduled Castes and the Scheduled Tribes (Prevention of Atrocities) Act. 1989 (33 of 1989), the Central Government hereby makes the following rules, namely:

**1. Short title and commencement.-**

(1) These rules may be called the Scheduled Castes and the Scheduled Tribes (Prevention of Atrocities) Rules, 1995.

(2) They shall come into force on the date of their publication in the Official Gazette.

**2. Definitions.-**

In these rules. unless the context otherwise requires,-

(a) "Act" means the Scheduled Castes and the Scheduled Tribes (Prevention of Atrocities) Act, 1989 (33 of 1989).

(b) "dependent", with its grammatical variations and cognate expressions, includes wife, children, whether married or unmarried, dependent parents, widowed sister, widow and children of pre-deceased son of a victim of atrocity;

(c) "identified area" means such area where State Government has reason to believe that atrocity may take place or there is an apprehension of re-occurrence of an offence under the Act or an area prone to victim of atrocity;

(d) "Non-Government Organization" means a voluntary organization engaged in the welfare activities relating to the scheduled castes and the scheduled tribes and registered under the Societies Registration Act.- 1860 (21 of 1860) or under

any law for the registration of documents of such
Organization for the time being in force;

(e) "Schedule" means the Schedule annexed to these rules;

(f) "Section" means Section of the Act;

(g) "State Government", in relation to a Union territory, means
the Administrator of that Union territory appointed by the
President under Art. 239 of the Constitution;

(h) words and expressions used herein and not defined but
defined in the Act shall have the meanings respectively assigned
to them in the Act.

## 3. Precautionary and preventive measures.-

With a view to prevent atrocities on the Scheduled Castes and the
Scheduled Tribes the State Government shall,-

(i) identify the area where it has reason to believe that atrocity
may take place or there is an apprehension of reoccurrence of an
offence under the Act ;

(ii) order the District Magistrate and Superintendent of Police
or any other officer to visit the identified area and review the law
and order situation;

(iii) if deem necessary, in the identified area cancel the arm
licenses of the persons, not being member of the Scheduled
Castes or Scheduled Tribes, their near relations, servants or
employees and family friends and get such arms deposited in the
Government Armory;

(iv) seize all illegal fire-arms and prohibit any illegal
manufacture of fire-arms;

(v) with a view to ensure the safety of person and property, if deem necessary, provide arms licenses to the members of the Scheduled Castes and the Scheduled Tribes;

(vi) constitute a high power State-level committee, district and divisional level committees or such number of other committees as deem proper and necessary for assisting the Government in implementation of the provisions of the Act.

(vii) set up a vigilance and monitoring committee to suggest effective measures to implement the provisions of the Act;

(viii) set up Awareness Centers and organize Workshops in the identified area or at some other place to educate the persons belonging to the Scheduled Castes and the Scheduled Tribes about their rights and the protection available to them under the provisions of various Central and State enactments or rules, regulations and schemes framed thereunder;

(ix) encourage Non-Government Organizations for establishing and maintaining Awareness Centers and organizing Workshops and provide them necessary financial and other sort of assistance;

(x) deploy special police force in the identified area;

(xi) by the end of every quarter, review the law and order situation, functioning of different committees, performance of Special Public Prosecutors, Investigating Officers and other Officers responsible for implementing the provisions of the Act and the cases registered under the Act.

**4. Supervision of prosecution and submission of report.-**

(1) The State Government on the recommendation of the District Magistrate shall prepare for each District a panel of such number of eminent senior advocates who has been in practice for not less than seven years, as it may deem necessary for conducting cases in the Special Courts. Similarly, in consultation with the Director-Prosecution in charge

of the prosecution, a panel of such number of Public Prosecutors as it may deem necessary for conducting cases in the Special Courts, shall also be specified. Both these panels shall be notified in the Official Gazette of the State and shall remain in force for a period of three years.

(2) The District Magistrate and the Director of prosecution in charge of the prosecution shall review at least twice in a calendar year, in the month of January and July, the performance of Special Public Prosecutors so specified or appointed and submit a report to the State Government.

(3) If the State Government is satisfied or has reason to believe that a Special Public Prosecutor so appointed or specified has not conducted the case to the best of his ability and with due care and caution, his name may be, for reasons to be recorded in writing, denotified.

(4) The District Magistrate and the Officer-in-charge of the prosecution at the District level, shall review the position of cases registered under the Act and submit a monthly report on or before 20th day of each subsequent month to the Director of Prosecution and the State Government. This report shall specify the actions taken/proposed to be taken in respect of investigation and prosecution of each case.

(5) Notwithstanding anything contained in sub-rule (1) the District Magistrate or the Sub-Divisional Magistrate may, if deem necessary or if so desired by the victim of atrocity engage an eminent Senior Advocate for conducting cases in the Special Courts on such payment of fees as he may consider appropriate.

(6) Payment of fee to the Special Public Prosecutor shall be fixed by the State Government on a scale higher than the other panel advocates in the State.

**5. Information to Police Officer in-charge of a Police Station.-**

(1) Every information relating to the commission of an offence under the Act, if given orally to an officer in-charge of a police station shall be reduced to writing by him or under his direction. and be read over to the informant, and every such information, whether given in writing or reduced to writing as aforesaid, shall be signed by the persons giving it,

and the substance thereof shall be entered in a book to be maintained by that police station.

(2) A copy of the information as so recorded under sub-rule (1) above shall be given forthwith, free of cost, to the informant.

(3) Any person aggrieved by a refusal on the part of an officer in charge of a police station to record the information referred in sub-rule (1) may send the substance of such information, in writing and by post, to the Superintendent of Police concerned who after investigation either by himself or by a police officer not below the rank of Deputy Superintendent of Police, shall make an order in writing to the officer in-charge of the concerned police station to enter the substance of that information to be entered in the book to be maintained by the police station.

**6. Spot inspection by officers.-**

(1) Whenever the District Magistrate or the Sub-Divisional Magistrate or any other executive Magistrate or any police officer not below the rank of Deputy Superintendent of Police receives an information from any person or upon his own knowledge that an atrocity has been committed on the members of the Scheduled Castes or the Scheduled Tribes within his jurisdiction he shall immediately himself visit the place of occurrence to assess the extent of atrocity, loss of life, loss and damage to the property and submit a report forthwith to the State Government.

(2) The District Magistrate or the sub-Divisional Magistrate or any other executive Magistrate and the Superintendent of Police, Deputy Superintendent of Police after inspecting the place or area on the spot,-

> (i) draw a list of victims, their family members and dependents entitled for relief;
>
> (ii) prepare a detailed report of the extent of atrocity, loss and damage to the property of the victims;
>
> (iii) order for intensive police patrolling in the area;

(iv) take effective and necessary steps to provide protection to the witnesses and other sympathizers of the victims;

(v) provide immediate relief to the victims.

**7. Investigating Officer.-**

(1) An offence committed under the Act shall be investigated by a police officer not below the rank of a Deputy Superintendent of Police. The investigating officer shall be appointed by the State Government, Director-General of Police, Superintendent of Police after taking into account his past experience, sense of ability and justice to perceive the implications of the case and investigate it along with right lines within the shortest possible time.

(2) The investigating officer so appointed under sub-rule (1) shall complete the investigation on top priority within thirty days and submit the report to the Superintendent of Police who in turn will immediately forward the report to the Director-General of Police of the State Government.

(3) The Home Secretary and the Social Welfare Secretary to the State Government, Director of Prosecution the officer-in-charge of Prosecution and the Director-General of Police shall review by the end of every quarter the position of all investigations done by the investigating officer.

**8. Setting up of the Scheduled Castes and the Scheduled Tribes Protection Cell.-**

The State Government shall set up a Scheduled Castes and the Scheduled Tribes Protection Cell at the State headquarter under the charge of Director of Police, Inspector-General of Police. This Cell shall be responsible for,-

(i) conducting survey of the identified area;

(ii) maintaining public order and tranquillity in the identified area;

(iii) recommending to the State Government for deployment of special police force or establishment of special police post in the identified area;

(iv) making investigations about the probable causes leading to an offence under the Act;

(v) restoring the feeling of security amongst the members of the Scheduled Castes and the Scheduled Tribes;

(vi) informing the nodal officer and special officer about the law and order situation in the identified area;

(vii) making enquiries about the investigation and spot inspections conducted by various officers;

(viii) making enquiries about the action taken by the Superintendent of Police in the cases where an officer in-charge of the police station has refused to enter an information in a book to be maintained by that police station under sub-rule (3) of rule 5;

(ix) making enquiries about the wilful negligence by a public servant;

(x) reviewing the position of cases registered under the Act, and

(xi) submitting a monthly report on or before 20th day of each subsequent month to the State Government, nodal officer about the action taken proposed to be taken, in respect of the above.

## 9. Nomination of Nodal Officer.-

The State Government shall nominate a nodal officer of the level of a Secretary to the Government preferably belonging to the Scheduled Castes or the Scheduled Tribes, for coordinating the functioning of the District Magistrates and Superintendent of Police or other officers authorized by them investigating officers and other officers responsible for implementing the provisions of the Act. By the end of the every quarter, the nodal officer shall review,-

(i) the reports received by the State Government under sub-rules (2) and (4) of rule 4, rule 6, Cl. (xi) of rule 8.

(ii) the position of cases registered under the Act;

(iii) law and order situation in the identified area;

(iv) various kinds of measures adopted for providing immediate relief in cash or kind or both to the victims of atrocity or his or her dependent;

(v) adequacy of immediate facilities like rationing, clothing, shelter, legal aid, travelling allowance, daily allowance and transport facilities provided to the victims of atrocity of his/her dependents;

(vi) performance of non-Governmental organizations, the Scheduled Castes and the Scheduled Tribes Protection Cell, various committees and the public servants responsible for implementing the provisions of the Act.

**10. Appointment of a Special Officer.-**

In the identified area a Special Officer not below the rank of an Additional District Magistrate shall be appointed to co-ordinate with the District Magistrate, Superintendent of Police or other officers responsible for implementing the provisions of the Act, various committees and the Scheduled Castes and the Scheduled Tribes Protection Cell.

The Special Officer shall be responsible for:

(i) providing immediate relief and other facilities to the victims of atrocity and initiate necessary measures to prevent or avoid re-occurrence of atrocity;

(ii) setting up an awareness center and organizing workshop in the identified area or at the District headquarters to educate the persons belonging to the Scheduled Castes and the Scheduled Tribes about their rights and the protection available to them under the provisions of various Central and State enactments or rules and schemes, etc. framed therein;

(iii) coordinating with the non-governmental organizations and providing necessary facilities and financial and other type of assistance to non-governmental organizations for maintaining centers or organizing workshops.

**11. Travelling allowances, daily allowance, maintenance expenses and transport facilities to the victim atrocity, his or her dependent and witnesses.–**

(1) Every victim of atrocity or his/her dependent and witnesses shall be paid to and for rail fare by second class in express / mail/ passenger train or actual bus of taxi fare from his / her place of residence or actual bus or taxi fare from his /her place of residence or place of stay to the place of investigation or hearing of trial of an offence under the Act.

(2) The District Magistrate or the Sub-Divisional Magistrate or any other Executive Magistrate shall make necessary arrangements for providing transport facilities or reimbursement of full payment thereof to the victims of atrocity and witnesses for visiting the investigating officer, Superintendent of Police/Deputy Superintendent of Police, District Magistrate or any other Executive Magistrate.

(3) Every woman witness, the victim of atrocity or her dependent being a woman or a minor, a person more than sixty years of age and a person having 40 per cent or more disability shall be entitled to be accompanied by an attendant of her/ his choice. The attendant shall also be paid travelling and maintenance expenses as applicable to the witness or the victim of atrocity when called upon during hearing, investigation and trial of an offence under the Act.

(4) The witness, the victim of atrocity or his/her dependent and the attendant shall be paid daily maintenance expenses for the days he/she is away from the place of his/her residence or stay during investigation, hearing and trial of an offence, at such rates but not less than the minimum wages, as may be fixed by the State Government for the agricultural laborers.

(5) In additional to daily maintenance expenses the witness' the victim of atrocity (or his/her dependent) and the attendant shall also be paid diet expenses at such rates as may be fixed by the State Government from time to time.

(6) The payment of travelling allowance, daily allowance, maintenance expenses and reimbursement of transport facilities shall be made immediately or not later than three days by the District Magistrate or the Sub-Divisional Magistrate or any other Executive Magistrate to the victims, their dependents/attendant and witnesses for the days they visit the investigating officer or in-charge police station or hospital authorities or Superintendent of Police, Deputy Superintendent of Police or District Magistrate or any other officer concerned or the Special Court.

(7) When an offence has been committed under Sec. 3 of the Act, the District Magistrate or the Sub-Divisional Magistrate or any other Executive Magistrate shall reimburse the payment of medicines, special medical consultation, blood transfusion, replacement of essential clothing, meals and fruits provided to the victim(s) of atrocity.

## 12. Measures to be taken by the District Administration.-

(1)The District Magistrate and the Superintendent of Police shall visit the place or area where the atrocity has been committed to assess the loss of life and damage to the property and draw a list of victim, their family members and dependents entitled for relief.

(2) Superintendent of Police shall ensure that the First Information Report is registered in the book of the concerned police station and effective measures for apprehending the accused are taken.

(3) The Superintendent of Police, after spot inspection, shall immediately appoint an investigation officer and deploy such police force in the area and take such other preventive measures as he may deem proper and necessary.

(4) The District Magistrate or the Sub-Divisional Magistrate or any other Executive Magistrate shall make arrangements for providing immediate relief in cash or in kind or both to the victims of atrocity, their family

members and dependents according to the scale as in the schedule annexed to these Rules (Annexure-I read with Annexure-II). Such immediate relief shall also include food, water, clothing, shelter, medical aid, transport facilities and other essential items necessary for human beings.

(5) The relief provided to the victim of the atrocity or his /her dependent under sub-rule (4) in respect of death, or injury to, or damage to property shall be in addition to any other right to claim compensation in respect thereof under any other law for the time being in force.

(6) The relief and rehabilitation facilities mentioned in sub-rule (4) above shall be provided by the District Magistrate or the Sub-Divisional Magistrate or any other Executive Magistrate in accordance with the scales provided in the Schedule annexed to these rules.

(7) A report of the relief and rehabilitation facilities provided to the victims shall also be forwarded to the Special Court by the District Magistrate or the Sub-Divisional Magistrate or the Executive Magistrate or Superintendent of Police. In case the Special Court is satisfied that the payment of relief was not made to the victim or his/her dependent in time or the amount of relief or compensation was not sufficient or only a part of payment of relief or compensation was made, it may order for making in full or part the payment of relief or any other kind of assistance.

**13. Selection of Officers and other State Members for completing the work relating to atrocity.-**

(1) The State Government shall ensure that the administrative officers and other staff members to be appointed in an area prone to atrocity shall have the right aptitude and understanding of the problems of the Scheduled Castes and posts and police station.

(2) It shall also be ensured by the State Government that persons from the Scheduled Castes and the Scheduled Tribes are adequately represented in the administration and in the police force at all levels, particularly at the level or police posts and police station.

## 14. Specific responsibility of the State Government.-

The State Government shall make necessary provisions in its annual budget for providing relief and rehabilitation facilities to the victims of atrocity. It shall review at least twice in a calendar year, in the month of January and July the performance of the Special Public Prosecutor specified or appointed under Sec. 15 of the Act, various reports received, investigation made and preventive steps taken by the District Magistrate, Sub-Divisional Magistrate and Superintendent of Police, relief and rehabilitation facilities provided to the victims and the reports in respect of lapses on behalf of the concerned officers.

## 15. Contingency Plan by the State Government.-

(1) The State Government shall prepare a model contingency plan for implementing the provisions of the Act and notify the same in the Official Gazette of the State Government. It should specify the role and responsibility of various departments and their officers at different levels, the role and responsibility of Rural/ Urban Local Bodies and Non-Government Organizations. Inter alia this plan shall contain a package of relief measures including the following:

(a) scheme to provide immediate relief in cash or in kind or both;

(b) allotment of agricultural land and house-sites;

(c) the rehabilitation packages;

(d) scheme for employment in Government or Government undertaking to the dependent or one of the family members of the victim;

(e) pension scheme for widows, dependent children of the deceased, handicapped or old age victims of atrocity;

(f) mandatory compensation for the victims;

(g) scheme for strengthening the socioeconomic condition of the victim;

(h) provisions for providing brick/stone masonry house to the victims;

(i) such other elements as health care, supply of essential commodities, electrification, adequate drinking water facility, burial/cremation ground and link roads to the Scheduled Castes and the Scheduled Tribes.

(2) The State Government shall forward a copy of the contingency plan or a summary thereof and a copy of the scheme, as soon as may be, to the Central Government in the Ministry of Welfare and to all the District Magistrates, Sub-Divisional Magistrates, Inspectors-General of Police and Superintendents of Police.

**16. Constitution of State-level Vigilance and Monitoring Committee.-**

(1) The State Government shall constitute high power vigilance and monitoring committee of not more than 25 members consisting of the following:

(i) Chief Minister/Administrator-Chairman (in case of a State under President's Rule Governor-Chairman).

(ii) Home Minister, Finance Minister and Welfare Minister-Members (in case of a State under the President's Rule Advisors-Members);

(iii) all elected Members of Parliament and State Legislative Assembly and Legislative Council from the State belonging to the Scheduled Castes and the Scheduled Tribes- Members

(iv) Chief Secretary, the Home Secretary, the Director-General of Police, Director/ Deputy Director, National Commission for the Scheduled Castes and the Scheduled Tribes- Members;

(v) the Secretary in-charge of the welfare and development of the Scheduled Castes and the Scheduled Tribes- Convener.

(2) The high power vigilance and monitoring committee shall meet at least twice in a calendar year, in the month of January and July to review the implementation of the provisions of the Act, relief and rehabilitation facilities provided to the victims and other matters connected therewith, prosecution of cases under the Act, rule of different officers/agencies responsible for implementing the provisions of the Act and various reports received by the State Government.

**17. Constitution of District Level Vigilance and Monitoring Committee.-**

(1) In each district within the State, the District Magistrate shall set up a vigilance and monitoring committee in his district to review the implementation of the provisions of the Act, relief and rehabilitation facilities provided to the victims and other matters connected therewith, prosecution of cases under the Act, role of different officers /agencies responsible for implementing the provisions of the Act and various reports received by the District Administration.

(2) The district level vigilance and monitoring committee shall consist of the elected Members of the Parliament and State Legislative Assembly and Legislative Council, Superintendent of Police, three-group 'A' Officers, Gazetted Officers of the State Government belonging to the Scheduled Castes and the Scheduled Tribes, not more than 5 non-official members belonging to the Scheduled Castes and the Scheduled Tribes and not more than 3 members from the categories other than the Scheduled Castes and the Scheduled Tribes having association with Non-Government Organizations. The District Magistrate and District Social Welfare Officer shall be Chairman and Member-Secretary respectively.

(3) The district level committee shall meet at least once in three months.

**18. Material for Annual Report.-**

The State Government shall every year before the 31st March, forward the report to the Central Government about the measures taken for implementing provisions of the Act and various schemes/plans framed by it during the previous calendar year.

ANNEXURE I
Schedule

[See rule 12 (4)]

**Norms for Relief Amount**

| Name and Section Number of Offense | Minimum Amount of Relief |
|---|---|
| 1. Drink or eat inedible or obnoxious substance [Sec. 3 (1)(i)]<br><br>2. Causing injury insult or annoyance [Sec. 3 (1)(ii)]<br><br>3. Derogatory Act [Sec. 3 (1)(iii)] | Rs. 25,000 or more depending upon the nature and gravity of the offense to each victim and also commensurate with the indignity, insult and defamation suffered by the victim. Payment to be made as follows: 25% when the chargesheet is sent to the court; 75% when accused are convicted by the lower court. |
| 4. Wrongful occupation or cultivation of land. etc. [Sec. 3 (1)(iv)]<br><br>5. Relating to land, premises and water [Sec. 3 (1)(v)] | At least Rs. 25,000 or more depending upon the nature and gravity of the offense. The land/premises/water supply shall be restored where necessary at Government cost. Full payment to be made when chargesheet is sent to the Court. |
| 6. Begar or forced of bonded labor [(Sec. 3 (1)(vi)] | At least Rs. 25,000 to each victim. Payment of 25% at First Information Report stage and 75% on conviction in the lower court. |
| 7. Relating to right to franchise [Sec. 3 (1)(vii)] | Up to Rs. 20,000 to each victim depending upon the nature and gravity of offense. |
| 8. False, malicious or vexatious legal proceedings [Sec. 3 (1)(viii)]<br><br>9. False and frivolous information [Sec. 3 (1)(ix)] | Rs. 25,000 or reimbursement of actual legal expenses and damages whichever is less after conclusion of the trial of the accused. |

| | |
|---|---|
| 10. Insult, intimidation and humiliation [Sec. 3 (1)(x)] | Up to Rs. 25,000 to each victim depending upon the nature of the offense. Payment of 25% when chargesheet is sent to the court and the rest on conviction. |
| 11. Outraging the modesty of a woman [Sec. 3 (1)(xi)]<br><br>12. Sexual exploitation of a woman [Sec. 3 (1)(xii)] | Rs. 50,000 to each victim of the offense. 50% of the amount may be paid after medical examination and remaining 50% at the conclusion of the trial. |
| 13. Fouling of water [Sec. 3 (1)(xiii)] | Up to Rs. 1,00,000 or full cost of restoration of normal facility, including cleaning when the water is fouled. Payment may be made at the stage as deemed fit by District Administration. |
| 14. Denial of customary rights of passage [Sec. 3 (1)(xiv)] | Up to Rs. 1,00,000 or full cost of restoration of right of passage and full compensation of the loss suffered, if any. Payment of 50% when chargesheet is sent to the court and 50% on conviction in lower court. |
| 15. Deserting one from their place of residence [Sec. 3 (1)(xv)] | Restoration of the site/right to stay and compensation of Rs. 25,000 to each victim and reconstruction of the house at Govt. cost, if destroyed. To be paid in full when chargesheet is sent to the lower court. |
| 16. Giving false evidence [Sec. 3(2)(i) and (ii)] | At least Rs. 1,00,000 or full compensation of the loss or harm sustained. 50% to be paid when chargesheet is sent to Court and 50% on conviction by the lower court. |

| 17. Committing offences under the Indian Penal Code punishable with imprisonment for a term of 10 years or more [Sec. 3(2)] | At least Rs. 50,000 depending upon the nature and gravity of the offense to each victim and or his dependents. The amount would vary if specifically provided for otherwise in the Schedule. |
|---|---|
| 18. Victimization at the hands public servant [Sec. 3 (2)] | Full compensation on account of damages or loss or harm sustained. 50% to be paid when chargesheet is sent to the Court and 50% on conviction by lower court. |
| 19. Disability.<br>(a) 100% incapacitation.<br>    (i) Non-earning member of a family. | -At least Rs. 1,00,000 to each victim of offense. 50% on FIR and 25% at chargesheet and 25% on conviction by the lower court. |
|     (ii) Earning member of a family. | -At least Rs. 2,00,000 to each victim of offense. 50% to be paid on FIR/medical examination stage, 25% when chargesheet sent to court and 25% at conviction in lower. |
| (b) Where incapacitation is less than 100%. | -The rates are laid down in (i) and (ii) above shall be reduced in the same proportion, the stages of payment also being the same. However, not less than Rs. 15,000 to a non-earning member and not less than Rs. 30,000 to an earning member of the family. |
| 20. Murder/Death<br>(a) Non-earning member of a family. | -At least Rs. 1,00,000 to each case. Payment of 75% after postmortem and 25% on conviction by the lower court. |
| (b) Earning member of a family. | -At least Rs. 2,00,000 to each case. Payment of 75% after postmortem and 25% on conviction by the lower court. |

| 21. Victim of murder, death, massacre, rape, mass rape and gang rape, permanent incapacitation and dacoity. | In addition to relief amount paid under above items, relief may be arranged within three months of date of atrocity as follows:<br>(i) Pension to each widow and/or other dependents of deceased SC/ST at Rs. 1,000 per month, or employment to one member of the family of the deceased, or provision of agricultural land, a house, if necessary by outright purchase.<br>(ii) Full cost of the education and maintenance of the children of the victims. Children may be admitted to the Ashram Schools/residential schools.<br>(iii) Provision of utensils, rice, wheat, dals, pulses, etc. for a period of three months. |
| --- | --- |
| 22. Complete destruction/ burnt houses. | Brick/stone masonry house to be constructed or provided at Government cost where it has been burnt or destroyed. |

**APPENDIX D: The Employment of Manual Scavengers and Construction of Dry Latrines (Prohibition) Act, 1993**

(No. 46 of 1993)*

[5th June, 1993]

An Act to provide for the prohibition of employment of manual scavengers as well as construction or continuance of dry latrines and for the regulation of construction and maintenance of water-seal latrines and for matters connected therewith or incidental thereto.

WHEREAS fraternity assuring the dignity of the individual has been enshrined in he Preamble to the Constitution;

AND WHEREAS article 47 of the Constitution, inter alia, provides that the State shall regard raising the standard of living of its people and the improvement of public health as among its primary duties;

AND WHEREAS the dehumanizing practice of manual scavenging of human excreta still continues in many parts of the country;

AND WHEREAS the municipal laws by themselves as a measure for conversion of dry latrines into water-seal latrines and prevention of construction of dry latrines are not stringent enough to eliminate this practice;

AND WHEREAS it is necessary lo enact a uniform legislation for the whole of India for abolishing manual scavenging by declaring employment of manual scavengers for removal of human excreta an offence and thereby ban the further proliferation of dry latrines in the country;

AND WHEREAS it is desirable for eliminating the dehumanizing practice of employment of manual scavengers And for protecting and improving the human environment to make it obligatory to convert dry latrines into water-seal latrines or to construct water-seal latrines in new construction;

AND WHEREAS Parliament has no power to make laws for the States with respect to the matters aforesaid, except as provided in article 249 and 250 of the Constitution.

AND WHEREAS in pursuance of clause (1) of article 252 of the Constitution, resolutions have been passed by all the Houses of the Legislature of the States of Andhra Pradesh, Goa, Karnataka, Maharashtra, Tripura and West Bengal that the matters, aforesaid should be regulated in those State by Parliament by law;

Be it enacted by Parliament in the Forty-fourth Year of the Republic of India as follows:-

## CHAPTER I

## PRELIMINARY

**1. Short title, application and commencement.-**

(1) This Act may be called the Employment of Manual Scavengers and Construction of Dry Latrines (Prohibition) Act, 1993.

(2) It applies in the first instance to the whole of the States of Andhra Pradesh, Goa, Karnataka, Maharashtra, Tripura and West Bengal and to all the Union territories and it shall also apply to such other States which adopts this Act by resolution passed in that behalf under clause (1) of Article 252 of the Constitution.

(3) It shall come into force in the States of Andhra Pradesh, Goa, Karnataka, Maharashtra, Tripura and West Bengal and in the Union territories on such date as the Central Government may, by notification, appoint and in any other State which adopts this Act under clause (1) of Article 252 of the Constitution, on the date of such adoption.

**2. Definitions.-**

In this Act, unless the context otherwise requires,-

(a) "area", in relation to any provision of this Act, means such area as the State Government may, having regard to the requirements of that provision, specify by notification;

(b)"building" means a house, out-house stable, latrine, urinal, sheet house, hut, wall (other than a boundary wall) or any other structure whether made of masonry, bricks, wood, mud, metal or other material;

(c) "dry latrines" means a latrine other than a water-seal latrine;

(d) "environment" includes water, air and land and the inter-relationship which exist among and between water, air and land and human beings, other living creatures, plants, ro-organism and property;

(e) "environmental pollutant" means any solid, liquid or gaseous substance present in such concentration as may be, or tend to be, injurious to environment;

(f) "environmental pollution" means the presence in the environment of any environmental pollutant;

(g) "Executive Authority" means an Executive Authority appointed under sub-Section (1) Section 5;

(h) "HUDCO" means the Housing and Urban Development Corporation Limited, a Government company registered by that name under the Companies Act, 1956;

(i) "latrine" means a place set apart for defecation together with the structure comprising such place, the receptacle therein for collection of human excreta and the fittings and apparatus, if any, connected therewith;

(j) "manual scavenger" means a person engaged in or employed for manually carrying human excreta and the expression "manual scavenging" shall be construed accordingly;

(k) "notification" means a notification published in the official Gazette;

(l) "prescribed" means prescribed by rules made under this Act;

(m) "State Government", in relation to a Union territory, means the Administrator thereof appointed under Article 239 of the Constitution;

(n) "water-seal latrine" means a pour-flush latrine, water flush latrine or a sanitary latrine with a minimum water-seal of 20 milimetres diameter in which human excreta is pushed in or flushed by water.

## CHAPTER II

### PROHIBITION OF EMPLOYMENT OF MANUAL SCAVENGERS, ETC.

**3. Prohibition of employment of manual scavengers etc.-**

(1) Subject to sub-Section (2) and the other provisions of this Act, with effect from such date and in such area as the State Government may, by notification, specify in this behalf, no person shall-

(a) engage in or employ for or permit to be engaged in or employed for any other person for manually carrying human excreta; or

(b) construct or maintain a dry latrine.

(2) The State Government shall not issue a notification under sub-Section (1) unless-

(i) it has, by notification, given not less than ninety days' notice of its intention to do so;

(ii) adequate facilities for the use of water-seal latrines in that area exist; and

(iii) it is necessary or expedient to do so for the protection and improvement of the environment or public health in that area.

**4. Power to exempt.-**

The State Government may, by a general or special order published in the Official Gazette, and upon such conditions, if any, as it may think fit to impose, exempt any area, category of buildings or class of persons from any provisions of this Act or from any specified requirement contained in this Act or any rule, order, notification or scheme made thereunder or dispense with the observance of any such requirement in a class or classes of cases, if it is satisfied that compliance with such provisions or such requirement is or ought to be exempted or dispensed with in the circumstances of the case.

## CHAPTER III

## IMPLEMENTING AUTHORITIES AND SCHEMES

**5. Appointment of Executive Authorities and their powers and functions.-**

(1) The State Government may, by order published in the Official Gazette, appoint a District Magistrate or a Sub-Divisional Magistrate, as an Executive Authority to exercise jurisdiction within such area as may be specified in the order and confer such powers and impose such duties on him, as may be necessary to ensure that the provisions of this Act are properly carried out and the Executive Authority may specify the officer or officers, subordinate to him, who shall exercise all or any of the powers, and perform all or any of the duties, so conferred or imposed and the local limits within which such powers or duties shall be carried out by the officer or officers so specified.

(2) The Executive Authority appointed under sub-Section (1) and the officer or officers specified under that sub-Section shall, as far as practicable, try to rehabilitate and promote the welfare of the persons who were engaged in or employed for as manual scavengers in any area in respect of which a notification under sub-Section (1) of Section 3 has been issued by securing and protecting their economic interests.

## 6. Power of State Government to make schemes.-

(1) The State Government may, by notification, make one or more schemes for regulating conversion of dry latrines into, or construction and maintenance of, water-seal latrines, rehabilitation of the persons who were engaged in or employed for as manual scavengers in any area in respect of which a notification under sub-Section(1) of Section 3 has been issued in gainful employment and administration of such schemes and different schemes may be made in relation to different areas and for different purposes of this Act:

> Provided that no such schemes as involving financial assistance from the HUDCO shall be made without consulting it.

(2) In particular, and without prejudice to the generality of the foregoing power, such schemes may provide for all or any of the following matters, namely:-

> (a) time-bound phased programme for the conversion of dry latrines into water-seal latrines;

> (b) provisions of technical or financial assistance for new or alternate low cost sanitation to local bodies or other agencies;

> (c) construction and maintenance of community latrines and regulation of their use on pay and use basis;

> (d) construction and maintenance of shared latrines in slum areas or for the benefit of socially and economically backward classes of citizens;

> (e) registration of manual scavengers and their rehabilitation;

> (f) specification and standards of water-seal latrines;

> (g) procedure for conversion of dry latrines into water-seal latrines;

(h) licensing for collection of fees in respect of community latrines or shared latrines.

## 7. Power of State Government to issue directions.-

Notwithstanding anything contained in any other law but subject to the other provisions of this Act, the State Government may, in the exercise of its powers and performance of its functions under this Act, issue directions in writing to any person, officer or local or other authority and such person, officer or a local or other authority shall be bound to comply with such directions.

## 8. Executive authorities, inspectors, officers and other employees of such authorities to be public servants.-

All Executive Authorities, all officers and other employees of such authorities including the officers authorized under sub-Section (1) of Section 5, all inspectors appointed under sub-Section (1) of Section 9 and all officers and other employees authorized to execute a scheme or order made under this Act, when acting or purporting to act in pursuance of any provisions of this Act or the rules or schemes made or orders or directions issued thereunder, shall be deemed to be public servants within the meaning of Section 21 of the Indian Penal Code (45 of 1860).

## 9. Appointment of inspectors and their powers of entry and inspection.-

(1) The State Government may, by notification, appoint such persons as it may think fit to be inspectors for the purposes of this Act, and define the local limits within which they shall exercise their powers under this Act.

(2) Every inspector within the local limits of jurisdiction of an Executive Authority shall be subordinate to such authority.

(3) Subject to any rules made in this behalf by the State Government, an inspector may, within the local limits of his jurisdiction, enter, at all reasonable times, with such assistance as he considers necessary, any place for the purpose of-

(a) performing any of the functions of the Executive Authority entrusted to him;

(b) determining whether and if so in what manner, any such functions are to be performed or whether any provisions of this Act or the rules, orders or schemes made thereunder or any notice, directions or authorization served, made, given or granted under this Act is being or has been complied with;

(c) examining and testing any latrine or for conducting an inspection of any building in which he has reasons to believe that an offense under this Act or the rules, orders or schemes made thereunder has been or is being or is about to be committed and to prevent or mitigate environmental pollution.

**10.  Power of Executive Authority to prevent environmental pollution in certain cases.-**

(1) On receipt of information with respect to the fact or apprehension of any occurrence of contravention of the provisions of Section 3, whether through intimation by some person or on a report of the inspector or otherwise, the Executive Authority shall, as early as practicable, besides taking any other action under this Act, direct the owner or occupier of the promises to take such remedial measures, as may be necessary, within such reasonable time as may be specified therein and in case the owner or occupier, as the case may be, fails to comply with such directions, cause such remedial measures to be taken as are necessary to prevent or mitigate the environmental pollution at the cost of such owner or occupier of the premises.

(2) The expenses,  if any, incurred by the Executive Authority with respect to the remedial measures referred to in sub-Section (1), together with interest at such rate as the State Government may specify from the date when a demand for the expenses is made until it is paid, may be recovered by such authority or agency from the person concerned as arrears of land revenue or of public demand.

**11. Duty of HUDCO to extend financial assistance in certain cases.-**

(1) Notwithstanding anything contained in its Memorandum of Association or Articles of Association or schemes for the grant of loans for housing and urban development, it shall be the duty of HUDCO to extend, in suitable cases, financial assistance for the implementation of such schemes for the construction of water-seal latrines as may be made under Section 6.

(2) The financial assistance referred to in sub-Section (1) may be extended by HUDCO on such terms and conditions (including on easy and concessional rates of interest) and in such manner as it may think fit in each case or class of cases.

**12. Power to levy fee.-**

Any order or scheme which the State Government is empowered to make under this Act may notwithstanding the absence of any express provision to that effect, provide for levy of fees in respect of-

(a) community latrines constructed under a scheme on pay and use basis; or

(b) shared latrines constructed under a scheme; or

(c) supply of copies or documents of orders or extracts thereof; or

(d) licensing of contractors for construction of water-seal latrines; or

(e) any other purpose or matter fit involving rendering of service by any officer, committee, or authority under this Act or any rule, direction, order or scheme made thereunder:

Provided that the State may, if it considers necessary so to do, in the public interest, by general or special order published in the Official Gazette, grant exemption on

such grounds as it deems fit from the payment of any such fee either in part or in full.

## 13. Constitution of committees.-

(1) The Central Government may, by notification, constitute

(a) one or more Project Committees for appraising of the schemes for the construction of water-seal latrines in the country;

(b) one or more Monitoring Committees to monitor the progress of such schemes;

(c) such other committees for such purposes of the Act and with such names as the Central Government may deem fit.

(2) The composition of the committees constituted by the Central Government, the powers and functions thereof, the terms and conditions of appointment of the members of such committees and other members connected therewith shall be such as the Central Government may prescribe.

(3) The members of the committee under sub-Section (1) shall be paid such fees and allowances for attending the meetings as may be prescribed.

(4) The State Government may, by notification, constitute-

(a) one or more State Co-ordination Committees for co-ordinating and monitoring of the programmes for the construction of water-seal latrines in the State and rehabilitation of the persons who were engaged in or employed for as manual scavengers in any area in respect of which a notification under sub-Section (1) of Section 3 has been issued

(b) such other committees for such purpose of the Act and with such names as the State Government may deem fit.

(5) The composition of the committees constituted by the State Government the powers and functions thereof, the terms and conditions of the members of such committees and other matters connected therewith shall be such as the State Government may prescribe.

(6) The members of the committees under sub-Section (4) shall be paid such fees and allowances for attending the meetings as may be prescribed.

## CHAPTER IV

## PENALTIES AND PROCEDURE

### 14. Penalty for contravention of the provisions of the Act and rules, orders, directions and schemes.-

Whoever fails to comply with or contravenes any of the provisions of this Act, or the rules or schemes made or orders or directions issued thereunder, shall, in respect of each such failure or contravention be punishable with imprisonment for a term which may extend to one year or with fine, which may extend to two thousand rupees, or with both; and in case the failure or contravention continues, with additional fine which may extend to one hundred rupees for every day during which such failure or contravention continues after the conviction for the first such failure or contravention.

### 15. Offenses by companies.-

(1) If the person committing an offense under this Act is a company, the company as well as every person in charge of, and responsible to, the company for the conduct of its business at the time of the commission of the offense, shall be deemed to be guilty of the offence and shall be liable to be proceeded against and punished accordingly:

Provided that nothing contained in this sub-Section shall render any such person liable to any punishment, if he proves that the offence was committed without his knowledge or that he had exercised all due diligence to prevent the commission of such offence.

(2) Notwithstanding anything contained in sub-Section (1), where an offence under this Act has been committed by a company and it is proved that the offence has been committed with the consent or contrivance of, or that the commission of the offence is attributable to any neglect on the part of any director, manager, managing agent or such other officer of the company, such director, manager, managing agent or such other officer shall also be deemed to be guilty of that offence and shall be liable to be proceeded against and punished accordingly.

**Explanation.**- For the purposes of this Section.-

(a) "company" means any body corporate and includes a firm or other association of individuals; and

(b)"director", in relation to a firm, means a partner in the firm.

**16. Offences to be cognizable.**- Notwithstanding anything contained in the Code of Criminal Procedure, 1973, every offence under this Act shall be cognizable.

**17. Provision in relation to jurisdiction.-**

(1) No Court inferior to that of a Metropolitan Magistrate or a Judicial Magistrate of the first class shall try any offence under this Act.

(2) No prosecution for any offence under this Act shall be instituted except by or with the previous sanction of the Executive Authority.

(3) No Court shall take cognizance of any offence under this act except upon a complaint made by a person generally or specially authorized in this behalf by the Executive Authority.

**18. Limitation of prosecution.-**

No Court shall take cognizance of an offence punishable under this Act unless the complaint thereof is made within three months from the date on which the alleged commission of the offence came to the knowledge of the complaint.

# CHAPTER V

## MISCELLANEOUS

### 19. Information, reports or returns.-

The Central Government may, in relation to its functions under this Act, from time to time, require any person, officer, State Government or other authority to furnish to it, any prescribed authority or officer any reports, returns, statistics, accounts and other information as may be deemed necessary and such person, officer, State Government or other authority, as the case may be, shall be bound to do so.

### 20. Protection of action taken in good faith.-

No suit, prosecution or other legal proceedings shall lie against the Government or any officer or other employee of the Government or any authority constituted under this Act or executing any scheme made under this Act or any member, officer or other employee of such authority or authorities in respect of anything which is done or intended to be done in good faith in pursuance of this Act or the rules or schemes made, or the orders or directions issued, thereunder.

### 21. Effect of other laws and agreements inconsistent with the Act.-

(1) Subject to the provisions of sub-Section (2), the provisions of this Act, the rules, schemes or orders made thereunder shall have effect notwithstanding anything inconsistent therewith contained in any enactment other than this Act, customs tradition, contract, agreement or other instrument.

(2)If any act or omission constitutes an offence punishable under this Act and also under any other Act, then, the offender found guilty of such offence shall be liable to be punished under the other Act and not under this Act.

## 22. Power of Central Government to make rules.-

(1) The Central Government may, by notification, make rules to carry out the provisions of this Act.

(2) Without prejudice to the generality of the foregoing power, such rules may provide for all or any of the following matters, namely:-

(i) the composition of the Project Committees, Monitoring Committees and other committees constituted by the Central Government under sub-Section (1) of Section 13, the powers and functions thereof, the number of members and their terms and conditions of appointment and other matters connected therewith;

(ii) the fees and allowances to be paid to the members of the committees constituted under sub-Section (1) of Section 13.

(3) Every rule made by the Central Government under this Act shall be laid, as soon as may be after it is made, before each House of Parliament, while it is in session, for a total period of thirty days which may be comprised in one session or in two or more successive sessions, and if, before the expiry of the session immediately following the session or the successive sessions aforesaid, both Houses agree in making any modification in the rule or both Houses agree that the rule should not be made, the rule shall thereafter have effect only in such modified form or be of no effect, as the case may be; so however that any such modification shall be without prejudice to the validity of anything previously done under that rule.

## 23. Power of State Government to make rules-

(1) The State Government may, by notification, make rules, not being a matter for which the rules are or required to be made by the Central Government, for carrying out the provisions of this Act.

(2) Without prejudice to the generality of the foregoing power, such rules may provide for all or any of the following matters, namely:-

(i) the composition of the State Co-ordination Committees and other committees constituted by the State Government under sub-Section (4) of Section 13, the powers and functions thereof, the number of members and their terms and conditions of appointment and other matters connected therewith;

(ii) the fees and allowances to he paid to the members of the committees constituted under sub-Section (4) of Section 13;

(iii) any other matter which is required to be, or may be prescribed.

(3) Every rule and every scheme made by the State Government under this Act shall be laid, as soon as may be after it is made, before the State Legislature.

**24. Power to remove difficulties.-**

(1) If any difficulty arises in giving effect to the provisions of this Act, the Central Government may, by order published in the Official Gazette, make such provisions, not inconsistent with the provisions of this Act, as may appear to it to be necessary or expedient for the removal of the difficulty:

Provided that no such order shall be made in relation to a State after the expiration of three years from the commencement of this Act in that State.

(2) Every order made under this Section shall, as soon as may be after it is made, be laid before each House of Parliament.

**APPENDIX E: Committee on the Elimination of Racial Discrimination Concluding Observations on Caste**

COMMITTEE ON THE ELIMINATION OF RACIAL DISCRIMINATION

Forty-ninth session

CONSIDERATION OF REPORTS SUBMITTED BY STATES PARTIES UNDER ARTICLE 9 OF THE CONVENTION

**Concluding observations of the Committee on**

**the Elimination of Racial Discrimination**

**India 1/**

17 September 1996

CERD/C/304/Add.13.

1. At its 1161st, 1162nd and 1163rd meetings, held on 7 and 8 August 1996 (see CERD/C/SR.1161-1163), the Committee on the Elimination of Racial Discrimination considered the tenth to fourteenth periodic reports of India (CERD/C/299/Add.3) and adopted, at its 1182nd meeting, held on 22 August 1996, the following concluding observations.

**A. Introduction**

2. The Committee expresses its appreciation for the opportunity to resume its dialogue with the State party on the basis of its tenth to fourteenth periodic reports. It regrets the brevity of the report, all the more so since 10 years have passed since the previous report was submitted. It also regrets that the report does not provide concrete information on the implementation of the Convention in practice; it furthermore regrets that the report and the delegation claim that the situation of the scheduled castes and scheduled tribes does not fall within the scope of the Convention.

3. The Committee notes that the State party has not made the declaration provided for in article 14 of the Convention. Some of the members of the Committee requested that the possibility of making such a declaration be considered.

**B. Factors and difficulties impeding the implementation of the Convention**

4. It is noted that India is a large multi-ethnic and multicultural society. It is also noted that the extreme poverty of certain groups in the population, the system of castes and the climate of violence in certain parts of the country are among the factors which impede the full implementation of the Convention by the State party.

**C. Positive aspects**

5. The leading role played by India in the struggle against racial discrimination and apartheid at the international level is welcomed by the Committee. The Committee also acknowledges the far-reaching measures adopted by the Government to combat discrimination against members of scheduled castes and scheduled tribes.

6. The demographic data on the composition of the population and on the representation of various communities in the public service at the central and state level of government provided by the delegation during the meetings are welcomed.

7. The broad functions and powers of the recently established National Commission on Human Rights, as defined by the Protection of Human Rights Act (1993), which include the capacity to inquire into complaints of violations of human rights, to intervene in any proceeding involving allegations of violation of human rights pending before a court, to review constitutional and legal safeguards, to study treaties and other international instruments on human rights, to recommend measures for their effective implementation and to spread human rights literacy among the population, are welcomed by the Committee. It is noted with interest that the Commission encourages the states within the federation to create human rights commissions, as well as tribunals dealing specifically with human rights.

8. The Committee takes note of the plurality of newspapers and the mass media, and their awareness of human rights problems. The Committee holds that they play an important role in the implementation of the International Convention on the Elimination of All Forms of Racial Discrimination.

9. Note is also taken of the procedure of public interest litigation adopted by the Supreme Court, which affords the possibility to anyone, and not only to the victims of human rights violations, to seek redress from the court by any means, even by means of a postcard.

10. Articles 15(i) and 15(ii) of the Constitution of India, prohibiting all forms of discrimination by the State and its agents, or between individuals, including discrimination based on race and castes, as well as article 153, paragraphs (a) and (b), and article 505 of the Penal Code, which prohibit actions that promote disharmony, hatred, feelings of enmity and ill-will on grounds of race or religion, are found to be mainly in conformity with article 2, paragraph 1, of the Convention.

11. The Committee welcomes the statement in the State party's report to the effect that no organization which promotes and incites racial discrimination can legally exist in India and that the Constitution and the laws in this regard make it clear that the State party will take all necessary measures within the law to prevent activities and propaganda which promote and incite racial discrimination.

12. The lapse of the Terrorist and Disruptive Activities (Prevention) Act (TADA), which applied in parts of the north-eastern part of the country and in Jammu and Kashmir, under which the right to personal security of some members of ethnic and religious minorities living in those areas was often reported to be violated by security forces, is welcomed.

13. The importance accorded by the authorities to education as a means to spread awareness of human rights and literacy among the population and to struggle against all forms of discrimination, in particular racial discrimination, as well as the activities of the National Commission on Human Rights and the inclusion of human rights in the training of law enforcement officials, are welcomed.

## D. Principal subjects of concern

14. Noting the declaration in paragraph 7 of the report, reiterated in the oral presentation, the Committee states that the term "descent" mentioned in article 1 of the Convention does not solely refer to race. The Committee affirms that the situation of the scheduled castes and scheduled tribes falls within the scope of the Convention. It emphasizes its great concern that within the discussion of the report, there was no inclination on the side of the State party to reconsider its position.

15. The Committee is seriously concerned that the Kashmiris, as well as other groups, are frequently treated, on account of their ethnic or national origin, in ways contrary to the basic provisions of the Convention.

16. Clause 19 of the Protection of Human Rights Act prevents the National Commission on Human Rights from directly investigating allegations of abuse involving the armed forces. This is a too broad restriction on its powers and contributes to a climate of impunity for members of the armed forces. Moreover, it is regretted that the Commission is debarred from investigating cases of human rights violation that occurred more than a year before the making of the complaint.

17. The absence of information on the functions, powers and activities of the National Commission on Scheduled Castes and Scheduled Tribes and of the National Commission on Minorities makes it impossible to assess whether these Commissions have a positive impact upon the enjoyment of human rights and fundamental freedoms by members of the groups in question. 18. It is regretted that no information has been provided to the Committee on the effective implementation of the penal provisions referred to in paragraph 10 above. In this regard, concern is expressed at numerous reports of acts of discrimination based on race, colour, descent or national or ethnic origin, although it was stated that no such case has yet been brought before the courts; this leads the Committee to wonder whether individuals are sufficiently informed about their rights.

19. The lack of concrete information on the legal provisions in force to prohibit organizations which incite and promote racial discrimination and hatred, and to punish members of such organizations in accordance with article 4 of the Convention, as well as on their application in practice, including eventual court decisions, is regretted. This is most serious in view of widespread violence against certain minorities actively sponsored by extremist organizations that have not been declared illegal.

20. The lack of information on the text of the Directive Principles of State Policy of the Constitution relating to the promotion of social, economic and cultural rights, and on measures to give them effect, makes any evaluation of the implementation of article 5 of the Convention more difficult.

21. Regrets are expressed that the National Security Act and, in some areas of India, the Public Safety Act, remain in force.

22. It is noted with concern that the denial of the equal enjoyment of political rights, as provided for in article 5 (c) of the Convention, has led to an increase of violence, in particular in Jammu and Kashmir.

23. It is noted that although constitutional provisions and legal texts exist to abolish untouchability and to protect the members of the scheduled castes and tribes, and although social and educational policies have been adopted to improve the situation of members of scheduled castes and tribes and to protect them from abuses, widespread discrimination against them and the relative impunity of those who abuse them point to the limited effect of these measures. The Committee is particularly concerned at reports that people belonging to the scheduled castes and tribes are often prevented from using public wells or from entering cafés or restaurants and that their children are sometimes separated from other children in schools, in violation of article 5 (f) of the Convention.

24. The Committee regrets that certain communities do not enjoy representation in proportion to their size.

25. Although it is noted that the Supreme Court and the high courts have the jurisdiction to award compensation to victims of human rights violations, including in the field of racial discrimination, concern is expressed that there exists no specific statute providing for the right of individuals to seek from the courts just and adequate reparation or satisfaction for any damage suffered as a result of acts of racial discrimination, as required by article 6 of the Convention.

## E. Suggestions and recommendations

26. The Committee recommends that the State party continue and strengthen its efforts to improve the effectiveness of measures aimed at guaranteeing to all groups of the population, and especially to the members of the scheduled castes and scheduled tribes, the full enjoyment of their civil, cultural, economic, political and social rights, as mentioned in article 5 of the Convention. In this regard, the Committee recommends that the next report to be submitted by the State party contain full and detailed information on the legislative aspects and the concrete implementation of the Directive Principles of the State Policy of the Constitution.

27. The Committee recommends that special measures be taken by the authorities to prevent acts of discrimination towards persons belonging to the scheduled castes and scheduled tribes, and, in cases where such acts have been committed, to

conduct thorough investigations, to punish those found responsible and to provide just and adequate reparation to the victims. In this regard, the Committee particularly stresses the importance of the equal enjoyment by members of these groups of the rights to access to health care, education, work and public places and services, including wells, cafés or restaurants.

28. The Committee recommends that clause 19 of the Protection of Human Rights Act be repealed to allow inquiries of alleged abuses committed by members of the armed and security forces to be conducted by the National Commission on Human Rights and that the Commission be enabled to look into complaints of acts of racial discrimination that occurred more than a year before the filing of the complaint.

29. The Committee recommends that the next periodic report of the State party include information on the powers and functions, as well as on their effective implementation, of the National Commission on Scheduled Castes and Scheduled Tribes and of the National Commission on Minorities.

30. The Committee also recommends that the Government provide in its next periodic report information, including the number of complaints lodged and sentences passed, about the implementation in practice of the legal provisions prohibiting acts of racial discrimination and organizations which promote and incite racial discrimination, in accordance with articles 2 and 4 of the Convention.

31. The Committee recommends a continuing campaign to educate the Indian population on human rights, in line with the Constitution of India and with universal human rights instruments, including the International Convention on the Elimination of All Forms of Racial Discrimination. This should be aimed at eliminating the institutionalized thinking of the high-caste and low-caste mentality.

32. The Committee reaffirms that the provisions of article 6 of the Convention are mandatory and that the Government of India should adopt legal provisions making it easier for individuals to seek from the courts just and adequate reparation or satisfaction for any damage suffered as a result of acts of racial discrimination, including acts of discrimination based on belonging to a caste or a tribe. 33. The Committee suggests that the State party ensure wide publicity, as far as possible in the official and state languages, to its tenth to fourteenth reports and to the present concluding observations.

34. The Committee recommends that the State party ratify at its earliest convenience the amendments to article 8, paragraph 6, of the Convention, adopted by the fourteenth meeting of States parties.

35. The Committee recommends that the State party's next periodic report, due on 4 January 1998, be a comprehensive report and that it address all the points raised in these concluding observations.

1/ The comments of the Government of India were submitted to the Committee on the Elimination of Racial Discrimination pursuant to article 9, paragraph 2, of the Convention and are reprinted in annex IX to the annual report of the Committee (A/51/18).

**APPENDIX F: Human Rights Committee Concluding Observations on Caste**

Concluding observations of the Human Rights Committee: India. 04/08/97. CCPR/C/79/Add.81. (Concluding Observations/Comments)

HUMAN RIGHTS COMMITTEE CONSIDERATION OF REPORTS SUBMITTED BY STATES PARTIES UNDER ARTICLE 40 OF THE COVENANT

Concluding observations of the Human Rights Committee

India

1. The Committee considered the third periodic report of India (CCPR/C/76/Add.6) at its 1603rd to 1606th meetings on 24 and 25 July 1997 and subsequently adopted, at its 1612th meeting (sixtieth session), held on 30 July 1997, the following observations.

A. Introduction

2. The Committee welcomes the third periodic report of India, although it regrets the delay in submitting it to the Committee. While noting that the report provides comprehensive information on the constitutional and legislative norms applicable in India in the field of human rights, and makes reference to the Committee's previous comments during consideration of the State party's second periodic report, as well as to a number of court decisions, the Committee regrets the lack of information therein on difficulties encountered in implementing the provisions of the Covenant in practice. The delegation acknowledged in some measure these difficulties and it provided the Committee with detailed and comprehensive written and oral information in the course of the consideration of the report. In this regard, the Committee appreciates the cooperation which India has thus extended to the Committee in the discharge of its mandate.

3. The information submitted by a wide range of non-governmental organizations also assisted the Committee in its understanding of the human rights situation in the State party.

## B. Factors and difficulties affecting the implementation of the Covenant

4. The Committee recognizes that terrorist activities in the border states, which have caused the death and injury of thousands of innocent people, force the State party to take measures to protect its population. It stresses, however, that all measures adopted must be in conformity with the State party's obligations under the Covenant.

5. It notes, moreover, that the size of the country, its huge population, the massive poverty and the great disparities in the distribution of wealth among various social groups affect the advancement of rights. The persistence of traditional practices and customs, leading to women and girls being deprived of their rights, their human dignity and their lives, and to discrimination against members of the underprivileged classes and castes and other minorities, and ethnic, cultural and religious tensions constitute impediments to the implementation of the Covenant.

## C. Positive aspects

6. The Committee notes with satisfaction the existence of a broad range of democratic institutions and a comprehensive constitutional and legal framework for the protection of human rights. The Committee also welcomes frequent references to provisions of international human rights instruments by the courts, in particular the Supreme Court.

7. The Committee welcomes the establishment of the National Human Rights Commission in 1993 and the respect which the Government of India accords to its recommendations. The Committee notes that the Commission has been given powers, limited though these are, under the Protection of Human Rights Act, to inquire into complaints of human rights violations, to intervene in court proceedings involving allegations of human rights violations or otherwise dealing with human rights issues, to review constitutional and legal norms and the conformity of laws with international human rights instruments, to make specific recommendations to the Parliament and other authorities and to undertake activities in the field of human rights education. It also welcomes the recent setting up of human rights commissions in six states, including Punjab and Jammu and Kashmir, and of human rights courts in several other states of the Union.

8. The Committee also welcomes the establishment of the National Commission for Scheduled Castes and Scheduled Tribes and the National Commission for Women in 1992, and the National Commission for Minorities in 1993. These commissions have initiated some improvements, in particular in the levels of education and in the representation of the various groups concerned within elected bodies and other authorities.

9. The Committee welcomes the lapse, in 1995, of the Terrorist and Disruptive Activities Act (TADA), under which members of the security and armed forces enjoyed special powers in the use of force, arrest and detention. It also welcomes the related review of cases under this Act, following which a number of cases were dropped, and the directives given by the Supreme Court to deal with questions of bail under the TADA, though a number of cases still require to be dealt with.

10. The Committee has noted that positions in elected bodies are reserved for members of scheduled castes and tribes and that a constitutional amendment has reserved one third of the seats in elected local bodies (Panchayati Raj) for women. The Committee also notes the introduction of a bill to reserve one third of the seats for women in the Federal Parliament and in state legislatures.

11. The Committee welcomes the restoration of elected legislatures and governments in all states within the Union, including Punjab and Jammu and Kashmir, as well as the holding of federal parliamentary elections in April-May 1996. In addition, the Committee welcomes the constitutional amendment giving a statutory basis to Panchayati Raj - village self-rule institutions - and the enactment of the Panchayati Raj (Extension to Scheduled Areas) Act of 24 December 1996, which are designed to increase participation in the conduct of public affairs at the community level.

12. The Committee further welcomes the declared intention of the Government to introduce legislative measures to further freedom of information.

D. Subjects of concern and the Committee's recommendations

13. The Committee, noting that international treaties are not self-executing in India:

recommends that steps be taken to incorporate fully the provisions of the Covenant in domestic law, so that individuals may invoke them directly before the courts. The Committee also recommends that consideration be given by the authorities to ratifying the Optional Protocol to the Covenant, enabling the Committee to receive individual communications relating to India.

14. The Committee, noting the .reservations and declarations made by the Government of India to articles 1, 9, 13, 12, 19, paragraph 3, 21 and 22 of the Covenant:

> invites the State party to review these reservations and declarations with a view to withdrawing them, so as to ensure progress in the implementation of the rights contained in those articles, within the context of article 40 of the Covenant.

15. The Committee notes with concern that, despite measures taken by the Government, members of scheduled castes and scheduled tribes, as well as the so-called backward classes and ethnic and national minorities continue to endure severe social discrimination and to suffer disproportionately from many violations of their rights under the Covenant, *inter alia,* inter-caste violence, bonded labour and discrimination of all kinds. It regrets that the *de facto* perpetuation of the caste system entrenches social differences and contributes to these violations. While the Committee notes the efforts made by the State party to eradicate discrimination:

> it recommends that further measures be adopted, including education programmes at national and state levels, to combat all forms of discrimination against these vulnerable groups, in accordance with articles 2, paragraph 1, and 26 of the Covenant.

16. While acknowledging measures taken to outlaw child marriages (Child Marriages Restraint Act), the practice of dowry and dowry related violence (Dowry Prohibition Act and the Penal Code) and sati - self-immolation of widows - (Commission of Sati (Prevention) Act), the Committee remains gravely concerned that legislative measures are not sufficient and that measures designed to change the attitudes which allow such practices should be taken. The Committee is also concerned that giving male children preferred treatment persists, and deplores that practices such as foeticide and infanticide of females continue. The Committee further notes that rape in marriage is not an offence and that rape committed by a husband separated from his wife incurs a lesser penalty than for other rapists. The Committee therefore recommends:

that the Government take further measures to overcome these problems and to protect women from all discriminatory practices, including violence. Additional information should be provided in the State party's next periodic report on the functions, powers and activities of the National Commission for Women.

17. The Committee is concerned that women in India have not been accorded equality in the enjoyment of their rights and freedoms in accordance with articles 2, paragraph 1, 3 and 26 of the Covenant. Nor have they been freed from discrimination. Women remain under-represented in public life and at the higher levels of the public service, and are subjected to personal laws which are based on religious norms and which do not accord equality in respect of marriage, divorce and inheritance rights. The Committee points out that the enforcement of personal laws based on religion violates the right of women to equality before the law and non-discrimination. Therefore:

> it recommends that efforts be strengthened towards the enjoyment of their rights by women without discrimination and that personal laws be enacted which are fully compatible with the Covenant.

18. The Committee remains concerned at the continuing reliance on special powers under legislation such as the Armed Forces (Special Powers) Act, the Public Safety Act and the National Security Act in areas declared to be disturbed and at serious human rights violations, in particular with respect to articles 6, 7, 9 and 14 of the Covenant, committed by security and armed forces acting under these laws as well as by paramilitary and insurgent groups. The Committee, noting that the examination of the constitutionality of the Armed Forces (Special Powers) Act, long pending before the Supreme Court is due to be heard in August 1997, hopes that its provisions will also be examined for their compatibility with the Covenant. In this respect, bearing in mind the provisions of articles 1, 19 and 25 of the Covenant:

> the Committee endorses the views of the National Human Rights Commission that the problems in areas affected by terrorism and armed insurgency are essentially political in character and that the approach to resolving such problems must also, essentially, be political, and emphasizes that terrorism should be fought with means that are compatible with the Covenant.

19. The Committee regrets that some parts of India have remained subject to declaration as disturbed areas over many years - for example the Armed Forces (Special Powers) Act has been applied throughout Manipur since 1980 and in some areas of that state for much longer - and that, in these areas, the State party is in effect using emergency powers without resorting to article 4, paragraph 3, of the Covenant. Therefore:

> the Committee recommends that the application of these emergency powers be closely monitored so as to ensure its strict compliance with the provisions of the Covenant.

20. The Committee expresses concern at the lack of compliance of the Penal Code with article 6, paragraphs 2 and 5, of the Covenant. Therefore:

> the Committee recommends that the State party abolish by law the imposition of the death penalty on minors and limit the number of offences carrying the death penalty to the most serious crimes, with a view to its ultimate abolition.

21. The Committee notes with concern that criminal prosecutions or civil proceedings against members of the security and armed forces, acting under special powers, may not be commenced without the sanction of the central Government. This contributes to a climate of impunity and deprives people of remedies to which they may be entitled in accordance with article 2, paragraph 3, of the Covenant. Therefore:

> the Committee recommends that the requirement of governmental sanction for civil proceedings be abolished and that it be left to the courts to decide whether proceedings are vexatious or abusive. It urges that judicial inquiries be mandatory in all cases of death at the hands of the security and armed forces and that the judges in such inquiries, including those under the Commission of Enquiry Act of 1952, be empowered to direct the prosecution of security and armed forces personnel.

22. The Committee regrets that the National Human Rights Commission is prevented by clause 19 of the Protection of Human Rights Act from investigating directly complaints of human rights violations against the armed forces, but must request a report from the central Government. The Committee further regrets that

complaints to the Commission are subject to a one-year time limit, thus preventing the investigation of many alleged past human rights violations. Therefore:

> the Committee recommends that these restrictions be removed and that the National Human Rights Commission be authorized to investigate all allegations of violations by agents of the State. It further recommends that all states within the Union be encouraged to establish human rights commissions.

23. The Committee expresses concern at allegations that police and other security forces do not always respect the rule of law and that, in particular, court orders for habeas corpus are not always complied with, particularly in disturbed areas. It also expresses concern about the incidence of custodial deaths, rape and torture, and at the failure of the Government of India to receive the United Nations Special Rapporteur on the question of torture and other cruel, inhuman or degrading treatment or punishment. Therefore:

> while the Committee welcomes the requirement by the National Human Rights Commission that all such alleged incidents be reported and investigated, and that all post-mortem examinations be taped, it recommends:

>> (a) The early enactment of legislation for mandatory judicial inquiry into cases of disappearance and death, ill-treatment or rape in police custody;

>> (b) The adoption of special measures to prevent the occurrence of rape of women in custody;

>> (c) The mandatory notification of relatives of detainees without delay;

>> (d) That the right of detainees to legal advice and assistance and to have a medical examination be guaranteed;

>> (e) That priority be given to providing training and education in the field of human rights to law enforcement officers, custodial officers, members of the security and armed forces, and judges

and lawyers, and that the United Nations Code of Conduct for Law Enforcement Officials be taken into account in this regard.

24. The Committee regrets that the use of special powers of detention remains widespread. While noting the State party's reservation to article 9 of the Covenant, the Committee considers that this reservation does not exclude, *inter alia*, the obligation to comply with the requirement to inform promptly the person concerned of the reasons for his or her arrest. The Committee is also of the view that preventive detention is a restriction of liberty imposed as a response to the conduct of the individual concerned, that the decision as to continued detention must be considered as a determination falling within the meaning of article 14, paragraph 1, of the Covenant, and that proceedings to decide the continuation of detention must, therefore, comply with that provision. Therefore:

the Committee recommends that the requirements of article 9, paragraph 2, of the Covenant be complied with in respect of all detainees. The question of continued detention should be determined by an independent and impartial tribunal constituted and operating in accordance with article 14, paragraph 1, of the Covenant. It further recommends, at the very least, that a central register of detainees under preventive detention laws be maintained and that the State party accept the admission of the International Committee of the Red Cross to all types of detention facilities, particularly in areas of conflict.

25. The Committee notes with concern that, although the Terrorist and Disruptive Activities (Prevention) Act has lapsed, 1,600 people remain in detention under its provisions. Therefore:

the Committee recommends that measures be taken to ensure either the early trial of these people or their release. It is also concerned that there are legislative proposals to reintroduce parts of the Act and that this could lead to further violations of the Covenant.

26. The Committee expresses concern at the overcrowding and poor health conditions and sanitation in many prisons, the inequality of treatment of prisoners and the lengthy periods of pre-trial detention, all of which are incompatible with articles 9 and 10, paragraph 1, of the Covenant. Therefore:

the Committee, while welcoming the initiative to give the central Government a greater role in the administration and management of prisons, recommends that measures be taken to reduce overcrowding, to release those who cannot be given a speedy trial and to upgrade prison facilities as quickly as possible. In this respect, the Committee recommends that attention be given to the United Nations Standard Minimum Rules for the Treatment of Prisoners.

27. Concerning court procedure:

the Committee urges the institution of reforms to the procedure of the courts to ensure a speedy trial of those charged with offences, prompt hearing in civil cases and similar urgency in hearing appeals.

28. The Committee expresses its concern at reports that fines have been imposed, without a hearing, on communities in areas declared disturbed. Therefore:

the Committee recommends that the imposition of such fines be prohibited.

29. The Committee expresses concern at the extent of bonded labour, as well as the fact that the incidence of this practice reported to the Supreme Court is far higher than is mentioned in the report. The Committee also notes with concern that eradication measures which have been taken do not appear to be effective in achieving real progress in the release and rehabilitation of bonded labourers. Therefore:

the Committee recommends that a thorough study be urgently undertaken to identify the extent of bonded labour and that more effective measures be taken to eradicate this practice, in accordance with the Bonded Labour System (Abolition) Act of 1976 and article 8 of the Covenant.

30. The Committee expresses concern at reports of forcible repatriation of asylum seekers, including those from Myanmar (Chins), the Chittagong Hills and the Chachmas. Therefore:

the Committee recommends that, in the process of repatriation of asylum seekers or refugees, due attention be paid to the provisions of the Covenant and other applicable international norms.

31. The Committee deplores the high incidence of child prostitution and trafficking of women and girls into forced prostitution, and it regrets the lack of effective measures to prevent such practices and to protect and rehabilitate the victims. The Committee also regrets that women who have been forced into prostitution are criminalized by the Immoral Trafficking Prevention Act and, further, that article 20 of the Act puts the burden of proof on a woman to prove that she is not a prostitute, which is incompatible with the presumption of innocence. Therefore:

> the Committee recommends that the application of this law to women in the situation described be repealed and that measures be taken to protect and rehabilitate women and children whose rights have been violated in this way.

32. The Committee further regrets the lack of national legislation to outlaw the practice of Devadasi, the regulation of which is left to the states. However, it appears that the practice continues and that not all states have effective legislation against it. The Committee emphasizes that this practice is incompatible with the Covenant. Therefore:

> the Committee recommends that all necessary measures be taken urgently to eradicate the practice of Devadasi.

33. The Committee expresses its concern at the plight of street children and at the reported high level of violence against children within society. It is particularly concerned at reports of child mutilation. Therefore:

> the Committee recommends that urgent measures be taken to address the problem of violence against children and that specific mechanisms be set up for the protection of children.

34. The Committee expresses concern that, despite actions taken by the State party, there has been little progress in implementing the Child Labour (Prohibition and Regulation) Act of 1986. In this respect:

> the Committee recommends that urgent steps be taken to remove all children from hazardous occupations, that immediate steps be taken to implement the recommendation of the National Human Rights Commission that the constitutional requirement that it should be a fundamental right for all children under 14 to have free and compulsory

education be respected, and that efforts be strengthened to eliminate child labour in both the industrial and rural sectors. The Committee also recommends that consideration be given to establishing an independent mechanism with effective national powers to monitor and enforce the implementation of laws for the eradication of child labour and bonded labour.

35. Concerning the periodic report:

the Committee draws to the attention of the Government of India the provisions of paragraph 6 (a) of the guidelines regarding the form and content of periodic reports from States parties, and requests that, accordingly, its next period report, due on 31 December 2001, should contain material which responds to all these concluding observations. The Committee further requests that these concluding observations be widely disseminated among the public at large in all parts of India.

## APPENDIX G: Relevant United Nations Forms and Addresses

## Special Rapporteur on Violence against Women, its Causes and Consequences

### CONFIDENTIAL

### VIOLENCE AGAINST WOMEN

### INFORMATION FORM

**INFORMER:**

Name of person/organization:

Address:

Fax/Tel/e-mail:

**VICTIM(S):**

Name:

Address:

Date of birth:

Nationality:

Sex:

Occupation:

Ethnic background (if relevant):

Marital status:

**THE INCIDENT**

Date:                    Time:                 Location/country:

Number of assailants:

Are the assailant(s) known to the victim?

Description of the assailant(s) (include any identifiable features):

Description of the incident:

Does the victim believe she was specifically targeted because of gender? If yes, why?

Has the incident been reported to the relevant State authorities?

If so, which authorities and when?

Actions taken by the authorities after the incident:

**WITNESSES:**

Were there any witnesses?

Name/age/relationship/contact address:

**PLEASE RETURN TO THE SPECIAL RAPPORTEUR ON VIOLENCE AGAINST WOMEN CENTRE FOR HUMAN RIGHTS**

**UNITED NATIONS**

**1211 GENEVA 10, SWITZERLAND**

**(FAX:(41-22) 917-02-12)**

Reprinted from http://www.unhchr.ch/html/menu2/7/b/women/womform.htm

## MODEL QUESTIONNAIRE TO BE COMPLETED BY PERSONS ALLEGING ARBITRARY ARREST OR DETENTION

### I. Identity of the person arrested or detained

1.    Family name:

2.    First name:

3.    Sex:     (Male)     (Female)

4.    Birth date or age (at the time of detention):

5.    Nationality/Nationalities:

6.        (a) Identity document (if any):

          (b) Issued by:

          (c) On (date):

          (d) No.:

7.    Profession and/or activity (if believed to be relevant to the arrest/detention):

8.    Address of usual residence:

### II. Arrest

1.   Date of arrest:

2.   Place of arrest (as detailed as possible):

3.   Forces who carried out the arrest or are believed to have carried it out:

4.   Did they show a warrant or other decision by a public authority?

     (Yes)        (No)

5.  Authority who issued the warrant or decision:

6.  Relevant legislation applied (if known):

**III. Detention**

1.  Date of detention:

2.  Duration of detention (if not known, probable duration):

3.  Forces holding the detainee under custody:

4.  Places of detention (indicate any transfer and present place of detention):

5.  Authorities that ordered the detention:

6.  Reasons for the detention imputed by the authorities:

7.  Relevant legislation applied (if known):

**IV.** Describe the circumstances of the arrest and/or the detention and indicate precise reasons why you consider the arrest or detention to be arbitrary:

**V.** Indicate internal steps, including domestic remedies, taken especially with the legal and administrative authorities, particularly for the purpose of establishing the detention and, as appropriate, their results or the reasons why such steps or remedies were ineffective or why they were not taken:

**VI.** Full name and address of the person(s) submitting the information (telephone and fax number, if possible):

Date: .................................................
Signature:..................................................................

This questionnaire should be addressed to the Working Group on Arbitrary Detention, Centre for Human Rights, United Nations Office at Geneva, 8-14 avenue de la Paix, 1211 Geneva 10, Switzerland, fax No. (022) 9170123.

a/ A separate questionnaire must be completed for each case of alleged arbitrary arrest or detention. As far as possible, all details requested should be given. Nevertheless, failure to do so will not necessarily result in the inadmissibility of the communication.

b/ For the purpose of this questionnaire, "arrest" refers to the initial act of apprehending a person. "Detention" means and includes detention before, during and after trial. In some cases, only Section II, or Section III may be applicable. None the less, whenever possible, both Sections should be filled in.

c/ Copies of documents that prove the arbitrary nature of the arrest or detention, or help to better understand the specific circumstances of the case, as well as any other relevant information, may also be attached to this questionnaire.

d/ If a case is submitted to the Working Group by anyone other than the victim or his family, such person or organization should indicate authorization by the victim or his family to act on their behalf. If, however, the authorization is not readily available, the Working Group reserves the right to proceed without the authorization. All details concerning the persons(s) submitting the information to the Working Group, and any authorization provided by the victim or his family, will be kept confidential.

Reprinted from

http://www.unhchr.ch/html/menu2/7/b/arb_det/ardintro.htm#question

## COMMUNICATIONS UNDER EXTRA-CONVENTIONAL MECHANISMS

Country and thematic mechanisms which are extra-conventional have no formal complaints procedures, differing in that regard from certain treaty-based bodies, namely: *Human Rights Committee, Committee against Torture, and Committee on the Elimination of Racial Discrimination* (please refer to Individual complaints Section on the aforementioned bodies).

The activities of the country and thematic mechanisms are based on communications received from various sources (the victims or their relatives, local or international NGO's, etc.) containing allegations of human rights violations. Such communications may be submitted in various forms (e.g. letters, faxes, cables) and may concern individual cases as well as details of situations of alleged violations of human rights.

With regard to the submission of communications to the extra-conventional mechanisms, there is no differentiation between country-oriented and thematic mechanisms. Both require the same minimum criteria, namely:

- identification of the alleged victim(s);
- identification of the perpetrators of the violation;
- identification of the person(s) or organization(s) submitting the communication (anonymous communications are, therefore, not admissible);
- detailed description of the circumstances of the incident in which the alleged violation occurred.

Other details pertaining to the alleged specific violation, may be required for the relevant thematic mechanism, (e.g. past and present places of detention of the victim; any medical certificate issued to the victim, identification of witnesses to the alleged violation; any measures undertaken to seek redress locally, etc.)

In principle, communications will not be considered if they are also submitted under *ECOSOC resolution 1503* and/or the *Optional Protocol of the International Covenant on Civil and Political Rights.*

As a general rule, communications containing abusive language or which are obviously and patently politically-motivated are not considered. Communications should describe the facts of the incident and the relevant details referred to above, clearly and concisely.

In order to facilitate the examination of reported violations, a questionnaire was drawn up on several thematic mechanisms and is made available to persons wishing to report cases of alleged violations to these mechanisms. In addition, some country-oriented rapporteurs may also use questionnaires in order to facilitate their task, particularly in the context of field missions. It should, however, be noted that communications are considered even when they are not submitted in the form of a questionnaire.

Reprinted from http://www.unhchr.ch/html/menu2/8/ex_conv.htm

| Procedure/ Mandate | Examining Body or Expert(s) | Address |
|---|---|---|
| "1503" | Sub-Commission on Prevention of Discrimination and Protection of Minorities | **Sub-Commission on Prevention of Discrimination and Protection of Minorities** c/o Support Services Branch, Office of the High Commissioner for Human Rights, United Nations Office at Geneva, 8-14 avenue de la Paix, 1211 Geneva 10, Switzerland |
| Optional Protocol to the International Covenant on Civil and Political Rights | Human Rights Committee | **Human Rights Committee** c/o Office of the High Commissioner for Human Rights, United Nations Office at Geneva, 8-14 avenue de la Paix, 1211 Geneva 10, Switzerland |
| Article 22 of the Convention against Torture and Other Cruel, Inhuman or Degrading Treatment or Punishment | Committee against Torture | **Committee against Torture** c/o Office of the High Commissioner for Human Rights, United Nations Office at Geneva, 8-14 avenue de la Paix, 1211 Geneva 10, Switzerland |
| Article 14 of the International Convention on the Elimination of All Forms of Racial Discrimination | Committee on the Elimination of Racial Discrimination | **Committee on the Elimination of Racial Discrimination** c/o Office of the High Commissioner for Human Rights, United Nations Office at Geneva, 8-14 avenue de la Paix, 1211 Geneva 10, Switzerland |

| Procedure/ Mandate | Examining Body or Expert(s) | Address |
|---|---|---|
| Extrajudicial, summary or arbitrary execution | Special Rapporteur on Extrajudicial, Summary or Arbitrary Executions | **Special Rapporteur on Extrajudicial, Summary or Arbitrary Executions** c/o Office of the High Commissioner for Human Rights, United Nations Office at Geneva, 8-14 avenue de la Paix, 1211 Geneva 10, Switzerland |
| Violence against women | Special Rapporteur on violence against women, its causes and consequences | **Special Rapporteur on Violence against Women** c/o Office of the High Commissioner for Human Rights, United Nations Office at Geneva, 8-14 avenue de la Paix, 1211 Geneva 10, Switzerland FAX: (41-22) 917-0092 |
| Arbitrary Detention | Working Group on Arbitrary Detention | **Working Group on Arbitrary Detention** c/o Office of the High Commissioner for Human Rights, United Nations Office at Geneva, 8-14 avenue de la Paix, 1211 Geneva 10, Switzerland FAX: (41-22) 917-0123 |

# XIII WORLDS

Other titles by the same author

*XIII Winters*

# XIII WORLDS

## PURSUING RUGBY LEAGUE
## AROUND THE GLOBE

Edited by Dave Hadfield

MAINSTREAM
PUBLISHING

EDINBURGH AND LONDON

First published in Great Britain in 1996 by
MAINSTREAM PUBLISHING COMPANY (EDINBURGH) LTD
7 Albany Street
Edinburgh EH1 3UG

ISBN 1 85158 759 4

A catalogue record for this book is available from the British
Library

Typeset in Sabon
Printed and bound in Great Britain by Butler & Tanner Ltd, Frome

# Contents

# Introduction

It was one of the buzz-phrases that accompanied the upheaval of Super League's troubled birth that Rugby League would, if the revolution took place, acquire a 'global vision'. This book is a celebration of the fact that, in some quarters at least, it has always had one, albeit one often fogged by the parochialism and myopia which have held it back for a hundred years. On the face of it, a sports enthusiast partly motivated by a desire to travel should pick another sport. As our critics never tire of reminding us, there have been, until recently, only five Test-playing countries. Rugby League might have been played at both ends of the world, from Cumbria to Christchurch, but it has not often been played at many places in between. That might be a convenient generalisation but, as this collection of writings sets out to show, it is only part of the truth.

The problem with the code's attempts to expand worldwide has not simply been one of inertia. The more characteristic rhythm has been that of a cycle of optimism, confusion and neglect. In countless parts of the world – but including Italy, South Africa and the USA in this volume – locally based enthusiasts have been encouraged to start operations and been promised every assistance. The pages of the game's trade press have been full of glowing prognoses of future growth and prosperity. A game or two has taken place. Then comes stage two; it turns out not to be quite as easy as that, and doubts set in over whether it can really be justified to put time and energy – not to mention money – into distant and sometimes fanciful projects when Batley can't pay their milk bill. It is a long-running argument, this one between the parochial and the international, and it is one

7

which the charity-begins-at-home faction usually wins. Because of that, much of this book is devoted to what might have been in some of the countries where Rugby League has taken root and, however briefly, begun to flower. It is also about what can still be achieved in diverse locations all over the earth's surface.

Most of all, though, it is a series of snapshots of an extraordinary range of places and circumstances amid which Rugby League has been a guest, if not always a permanent settler. In each case, what we are presenting is an outsider's view. None of the chapters is written by a native, or even a long-term resident of the country in question. They are all, by their very nature, impressionistic and highly personal. If there are any common threads among them, the first is a sense of delight and discovery which comes with exploring something largely unknown through the medium of a game which is, to all of the contributors, as familiar and close a companion as our own families. Another note which recurs throughout is the respect and affection in which we hold those individuals – and it almost always is individuals – who throw themselves into the often quixotic task of spreading the game of Rugby League. They are a much-maligned bunch, particularly among those international big-wigs of the code who talk a good game on expansion but who, in reality, do not like to stray too far from their five-star hotels or get their hands dirty. Just to get involved in the business of trying to establish a new game in alien territory implies a degree of monomania that can make some pioneers hard work as well as hard workers. But they are a special breed, whatever their failings, and I hope that the sections of this book which deal with their efforts are a fitting tribute to them.

There are other chapters, of course, that deal with parts of the world – like Australia, at one end of the scale of international prestige, and Papua New Guinea, at the other – where Rugby League has not only survived but thrived. The delights of visiting these countries lie in the interplay of the familiar and the unfamiliar. The circumstances in which the game is played might be wildly different from anything the incomer might have experienced at home but, at the heart of it, there is this game which seems to hit very much the same buttons for those who watch it and participate in it.

That is something else I have noticed on re-reading the various contributions to XIII Worlds: the way that the distinctions between observer and participant are frequently so blurred that they become meaningless, like colonial boundaries in Central Africa. Rugby League is small enough for people to criss-cross between various levels of involvement without having their passports stamped. Thus the writers in this collection have been variously engaged in spectating, playing, coaching, administering, reporting, generally pissing it up and every conceivable combination of these activities. There is no one who can be said confidently to wear only one hat; Rugby League does not lend itself to such neat compartmentalisation.

When I first discovered Rugby League at the age of 11, one of the features of it that attracted me to it was the way that my contemporaries who had been born to it had a heightened sense of attachment to their town, their team and their game that was missing from a family like mine which had already lived all over the country. There is no denying that this strong sense of where we come from is one of the game's most abiding strengths. But that would be worth little without the counterbalance of itchy feet. Almost despite itself, the game has always been fascinated by what is over the next hill. Perhaps, like the tribes in central New Guinea, we are not sure that there is anything there at all. This book sets out to show that there is, and to capture something of its flavour.

In the filing cabinets at *Open Rugby*, we found a yellowing copy of the *Rugby League Gazette* from September 1950, in which Harry Sunderland, perhaps the most energetic promoter of international expansion that the code has produced, recounts a world tour from which he had just returned convinced that the time was right to get America involved in the game. He writes,

> At the present moment it is merely a dream – just as the plans of the late A.H. Baskerville, G.W. Smith, Lance B. Todd and others were dreams when they organised their pioneering tour of England in 1907. It was a 'dream' when we planned to show a sample of our game to the Frenchmen in the Stade Pershing in Paris in 1933, and it was a dream when the men who met in October 1928 decided to take the Rugby League Cup Final to Wembley in May 1929.

Turn the pages and you find Tom Longworth of the *News Chronicle* arguing that there was 'plenty to do here yet, Harry!' He continued,

> Let us do something nearer home before we think about going to sunny California. Let us make the sunshine come to our own grounds. Let us expand in 'Dear Old ENGLAND' before we think any more about California.

In the same issue, we have 'Mancunian' asking, 'Are the Italians really necessary?' These are the same arguments that have been rumbling on in the letters page of *The Rugby Leaguer* and in the Rugby League Council ever since. Nobody will be surprised to find which side of the debate this book favours.

In my own case, I have to hold both hands up and admit to a healthy dollop of self-interest. Quite apart from the belief that it is essential for the long-term health and vitality of the game, the reason I want the most stirring and satisfying of sports to be played in more parts of the world is that I want to go and see it there. I have, as people who spend 50 weeks of the year in Bolton constantly remind me, already been pretty lucky in that regard. There are still one or two omissions, however, which trigger the occasional unworthy pang of envy. I have been to most of the Pacific island nations described by Trevor Hunt but, by a masterpiece of planning, always managed to miss the BARLA tour by a day or two. Morocco was one of my first destinations, as a teenaged weekend hippy heavily influenced by the Incredible String Band and Crosby, Stills and Nash's (without Young at that stage, I think, but with a lead singer from Salford) 'Marrakesh Express', but I have not yet managed to return to watch Rugby League on the king's birthday.

And then there is the Milwaukee question. I'm still outraged with myself for having missed that experience, but I must have been in a sceptical frame of mind at the time, because I had grave doubts over it taking place at all and decided to do the caring, sharing thing by taking the family on holiday instead. Bulgaria is supposed to be warm and pleasant at that time of the year, so much of the first day was spent trying to convince the family for whom I had made such a major sacrifice that their initial impression of the misnamed Sunny Beach as a windswept hell-hole was erroneous. When a tree blew down in the garden of the restaurant in which we were huddling that night, I gave up on that line of argument. There is a moral in that somewhere – although I should add that I had an intriguing conversation with a bar-owner who was keenly interested in staging a Rugby League match on the field behind his establishment. From such small acorns . . . but you could say the same thing about the tree that came crashing down.

A number of thanks are due to those who, in their various ways, have propped up the rotting timber of this particular enterprise and held it roughly upright despite the roaring storms of deadlines missed and timetables jettisoned. Our editors at Mainstream, Avril Gray and Cathy Mineards, have been understanding and flexible, while Neil Tunnicliffe has again performed above and beyond any reasonable call of duty. Apart from his own chapters and his continuing role as Minister with Infinitely Expandable Portfolio at Rugby League headquarters, Neil has taken care of the crucial knocking-into-shape phase of production. This makes him the only resident of Harrogate who can truly be said to have a dirty, manual job. I would also like to thank the other contributors, even those who turned in manuscripts which looked as though they had been at sea in a bottle for some months after being scratched on old parchment with a twig. Not inappropriate to the subject matter, you might say, but it ensured that Tunnicliffe's job became dirtier and more manual as the weeks went on.

I have never minded travelling alone – indeed, there are those with whom I have travelled who say that it is the only way I should do it – but much of the pleasure of exploring new places comes from doing so with like-minded companions. In that case, I am in the debt of fellow-travellers with whom I made some of the journeys described in my own sections of this book – people like Peter Ward, John Huxley, Dave Part, Mel Woodward, Trevor Gibbons, Harry Edgar, Mick Smyth and the members, both playing and social, of Bolton Rugby League Club.

If I am to dedicate the book to one person, though, it must be my late uncle – or mother's cousin's husband, to be precise – Rowland Newsome. He died last year after a long life into which he packed more travel than seemed feasible; indeed, I'm at a loss to think of a part of the world that he didn't manage to see at some stage. He got off to a good start by running off to sea in his teens, although by the time I knew him, he had dropped anchor in that famed seaport of Altrincham. As a youth not much different in age from his when he had first gone to sea, I used to marvel at the contents of the big chest on the landing, with its bits and bats from China, Japan, the South Seas and – in one or two cases, I suspected – Altrincham market. His was the early influence that put travel well up on my agenda, and he was eventually as fascinated by my wanderings as I had been by his.

11

He knew little about Rugby League, but he recognised a good excuse when he saw one, and this collection is a small tribute to his memory.

DAVE HADFIELD
Departure lounge, Bolton International Airport
June 1996

# The Rough and Smooth Guide

## Dave Hadfield

I think it was Zsa-Zsa Gabor who said: 'I've been rich and I've been poor. Rich is better.' Ms Gabor would not normally be regarded as an authority on Australian Rugby League but, when it comes to the contrast between watching it the hard way and the easy way, like a poor man or like a rich man, she has put the ball over the black dot. I've done it both ways; easy is better – or, at least, easier.

Nobody, apart from a few handfuls of dispossessed aboriginals, can be truly poor in Australia. For one thing, the country is too rich in resources to allow it. For another, you can live on fresh air. If you had to choose somewhere in the world to be of relatively modest means, it would have to be a place where food is cheap and plentiful and where you need the minimum of clothing and heating. A clean singlet and a pair of shorts, and you can be indistinguishable from a bloke who might have millions. For a while I thought I was living next to poor people in a flat – bafflingly called a 'unit' in Australia – in Bondi, but I based that assumption solely on the way that they wore no shoes in winter. But then the warm weather came, and the whole unit of them switched overnight into the thick suede and sheepskin footwear known at the time as 'ugg boots.' They weren't poor; they were just stupid.

Most people in Australia are not stupid, but they are undeniably lucky. If they happen to come from Sydney or Brisbane, they really have won the double roll-over jackpot in the National Lottery of life. Not only do they dwell in cities which must be among the most habitable anywhere in the world, they also have Rugby League. They have Rugby League under blue skies; they have Rugby League on the back pages of all the newspapers. They have prawns the size of your forearm. They have it all. Lucky bastards.

Until quite recently, it was pretty difficult to share in this luck. As a Rugby League man, the one reliable way to drink from Australia's overflowing cup was to be an outstanding British player. The timing had to be right; 1970, when we had a few outstanding players, was just about perfect. I recall Malcolm Reilly telling me that, when he first signed for Manly, the club installed him in the Manly Pacific Hotel directly facing the Steyne Beach – not the modern building that stands there now, but the original, considerably more evocative verandahed structure. He mentally compared the scene in front of him with the one in Allerton Bywater and could hardly believe his good fortune. Lucky bastard.

There are approximately a million other places in Australia where you can stand and watch the sun glinting on the water and reflect that it's a step up from Allerton Bywater. Provided you have the price of a beer or a cup of coffee, you can sit in some comfort and think the same comforting thought. I have a couple of favourite spots. One is a little shack on Sydney Harbour, where you can drink Cooper's Sparkling Ale and eat oysters, looking out at – from left to right – Circular Quay, The Rocks, the Harbour Bridge and the Opera House, with all the bustle of Sydney's water-borne traffic in the foreground. The other is The Gap, a spot on the narrowing spit of land that eventually becomes South Head, one of the crags guarding the entrance to the harbour. From The Gap, you have the harbour and the city skyline in the distance, with the little boats bobbing on the quiet waters of Watson's Bay directly in front of you. Behind you, the Tasman Sea – or the Pacific, if you want to take it in its broader context – is thrashing itself into a frenzy at the foot of sheer cliffs. It is startling to discover that this is a favourite suicide spot. I have no statistics to prove it, but I am convinced that the majority of the people who choose this as the place to end their lives must have been told that they are going back to live in Allerton Bywater. If my theory is correct, I don't blame them at all; it would be the logical spot from which to end it all, before they could be dragged back to the real world.

So Australia – and particularly the League-loving bits of it – is a country to die for. But, without that lethal combination of monumental skill and mongrel meanness that Reilly had at his command, or Phil Lowe's tackle-smashing running, or Andy Currier's dazzlingly white legs, how is your average whingeing Pom

14

to share in the cornucopia? Only one way in my case – lacking the skill, the meanness, the running and the white legs – and that was by writing about the game.

The pioneer in this line of work was Eddie Waring who, long before he went senile and couldn't distinguish between Castleford v Hull Kingston Rovers and *It's a Knock Out*, paid his own passage on HMS *Indomitable* to travel with Great Britain on their 1946 tour of Australasia. Little in the way of deathless prose came out of Waring's return trip on the aircraft carrier; but, hell, it got him there. Uncle Eddie at least had the luxury of travelling with the team and, as far as I know, was not expected to stoke the boilers in the way that folklore insists the players did. Forty-two years later, there seemed no very good reason to me why I should not follow the 1988 Lions tour under my own steam, doing whatever work I could grab and making my own arrangements along the way. I had, after all, done a fair bit of travelling in Australia on previous visits; I knew roughly where things were. I had a cheap flight with Indonesia's finest, Garuda, a few hundred quid, and some orders from papers which had no intention of sending out their own man. It should be enough for a few beers and cups of coffee, the occasional train and hotel bill. And Australia is an easy country, isn't it? Even Australians survive there.

By the time I arrived in Sydney Shaun Edwards was on his way home, having wrecked his knee after just seven minutes of the only match in Papua New Guinea. My only other memory of the first jet-lagged, convivial days back in Australia, however, is of lending David Stephenson my shoes for the official team picture at the Sydney Football Stadium. This was the first tour on which the picture was not one of those classic Melba Studios team line-ups at the Sydney Cricket Ground, but tradition had not been abandoned to the extent of allowing players to appear in blazer, flannels and flip-flops. But for my intervention with a suitable pair of size 10½s, Stephenson would have appeared barefoot, in the manner of my erstwhile neighbours in Bondi. Not even Eddie Waring could boast of averting such a hammer-blow to British sartorial prestige; although, when I study some photographs of the 1946 tourists, that does rather look like his trilby that Gus Risman is wearing. Be that as it may, if you peruse the 1988 tour photo you will see the Wigan centre in a rather smart pair of grey, lace-up moccasins. I wonder if I ever got them back.

The Lions won comfortably enough in Newcastle, which itself is just a comfortable train ride from Sydney, including a breathtaking stretch over the Hawkesbury River. The next match, in Tamworth, was altogether less straightforward, whichever way you look at it. The only way to get to Tamworth, where Great Britain were to play New South Wales's Northern Division, involved arriving at three in the morning, a time at which a town renowned as the country music capital of Australia is fit only for broken-hearted cowboys. The only thing to do was to tramp the streets, grateful for the return of one's shoes, kipping intermittently in shop doorways, until what appeared to be the only hotel in town opened its doors at dawn.

A short digression on Australian terminology is required here. As befits a country which is, whatever anyone might say, upside down, they have the whole distinction between pubs and hotels completely inverted. A pub is called a hotel, and a hotel is known as a pub. Thus a fibreboard shanty in Torrowangee with a beer-pump or a street-corner ale-house in Allerton Bywater is a hotel. Conversely, the Savoy, or for that matter the Manly Pacific, is a pub. The first joint to open its doors in Tamworth that morning was definitely a hotel (which is to say, of course, that it was really a pub).

And who should be inside that pub/hotel, each tucking grimly into the standard Australian country breakfast of fillet steak, a couple of lamb chops, ten rashers of bacon, half a kangaroo's tail and a dozen eggs, but the members of the Northern Division team. A gloomier, more doom-laden group of men you would not meet outside the lyrics of Tamworth's country 'n' western industry. They looked and sounded like men condemned to execution that afternoon, working their way through their last meal because it was expected of them. Sitting down to my own platter of early-morning sustenance – which added up to rather more than the equivalent of an English pensioner's weekly shopping trolley – I heard that the wrong side had been picked, the training had been ratshit, the pub was more like a hotel (or was it the other way round?), and the food was frugal. All in all, it would be a bloody miracle if the match didn't produce a cricket score.

Those of you with either a long memory or a strongly developed sense of the inevitable will know what happens next. Our brave boys get thrashed 36–12 by a side of hicks from the sticks which, even now, includes just one name which anyone outside northern NSW will ever have heard of. That, incidentally, was Ewan McGrady, an aboriginal scrum-half who went to Sydney and, three years later, won the Rothmans Medal as the best player in the Winfield Cup. He was so shy that he declined even to show up for the ceremony and, when he was finally tracked down and frogmarched to the Hilton (a pub), he out-Stephensoned Stephenson by having to borrow the full evening dress, including frilly-fronted shirt, that was *de rigueur* for these events. On the official pictures of the presentation, he looks as though he has been sleeping out in a shop doorway in Tamworth.

There was to be no quick and easy access to the Great Britain changing-room after that ignominious defeat. It did not really matter; anybody hanging around in the general vicinity of the sheds that day could hear quite clearly what Reilly thought of his team's efforts. A bloke taking his dog for a walk in Werris Creek, 25 miles away, caught most of it as well, and a few distant relatives back in Allerton Bywater got the gist. As I left at three the following morning, again exploiting Tamworth's convenient links with the outside world, Northern Division were still celebrating. 'Told yer so!' said one of the characters who had looked over breakfast as though he was on his way to his own funeral. That's one of the great things about Lions tours: they can distribute unexpected dollops of happiness to unlikely people in improbable places.

Reilly had little cause to be much happier about the next defeat, 30–0 at his old club, Manly – something he had not foreseen as he had sat on that verandah 18 years before. The tour was rapidly turning into a joke, with the papers and commentators advising the Poms to go home and stop pretending to be a Rugby League team. Australians do this as soon as a tour side loses a couple of matches. Some, like the 1951 Frenchmen, shove those sentiments back down their throats; most do not.

It was not a bad time to be a few miles away from an increasingly fractious British camp, pleasant as it would have been to put the feet up in the Manly Pacific, with the surf purring and scraping up and down the beach just across the street. My own lodgings were slightly more basic – the spare bed in the baby's room at some friends' house across town in Drummoyne. My room-mate was 18 months old at the time and rather restless so, after a long day trying to find some encouraging news to send home, I found myself getting up every couple of hours to retrieve his dummy and shove it back in. Does Ian Wooldridge do that? Does he hell!

This is not a bad juncture, in fact, to pay tribute to the numerous Australians on whose spare beds, settees and floors I seem to have spent much of my adult life. There is one house in Sydney where I have slept in every room, including the kitchen. There is a bloke in

Cowra to whom I was able to give some help at a hotel reception desk on the French leg of the 1982 Kangaroo tour – his French being even worse than mine – and with whose family I have been staying ever since. Just this year, I was chatting to an Australian prop forward currently playing for a British club and, after I had known him for all of ten minutes, he was telling me: 'You can stop at our place in Brisbane on the next tour.' Such guarded, suspicious people.

Perhaps the most memorable temporary home, though, would be the one in Brisbane to which I decamped after Great Britain's defeat – a not dishonourable one, as it happened – in the first Test in Sydney. It was an arrangement set up by *Rugby League Week*'s man in that city, Tony Durkin. There were a few players from the local club, Fortitude Valley, he said, who had a spare room that they were quite happy for me to use. Spare room was a slight exaggeration. What they had was a walk-in wardrobe leading off a room already occupied by another itinerant Pom, Nick Grimoldby, now the chairman of the Rugby League Professional Players' Association but then guesting with Valleys and still signing his first name with a final 'k'. Having lived for several weeks in his wardrobe, I occasionally see him now, when he is out and about performing mighty deeds on behalf of the players' union, and think: 'I recognise that jacket.'

Sartorial matters aside – and Ewan McGrady would have thought all his birthdays had come at once if he had seen all that gear – it was an educational experience living with half the first-grade team from a club which had produced Wally Lewis, among others. For one thing, it answered a question which had perplexed me for some time: does anyone in Australia watch *Neighbours*? I thought for years that the answer to this was a resounding 'no', but this was the result of leading a culturally sheltered life in those various doorways and country hotels, not to mention floors, sofas and rooms, rather than wardrobes. It was here that I discovered that people did, but only if they were hairy-arsed footballers just back from their day-jobs as garbos – what we would call, rather more prosaically, bin-men – and not quite ready to go off to training. A big, solid bloke like Shane Kelly (who would later play for St George, London Crusaders and a renascent Newtown) would come in covered in dust and ash, get himself a big mug of tea and sit spellbound for 25 minutes while events in Ramsay Street unfolded. At the first chord of the closing theme tune, they would grab their training gear and dash down to Neumann Oval for the session. It was the ideal buffer between the bins and the equally sweaty business of training on a

18

balmy Brisbane evening. I've still seen no one else watch it in Australia, apart from my own children when I took them there. Don't give me any of that 'when in Rome' rubbish, I told them, only bin-men and footballers watch it here. I refrained from comment while the Valleys fellows were watching, though, and took care to keep the fridge topped up with beer for after training. That isn't as straightforward as it sounds because, apart from certain irrational brand preferences, some players would only drink stubbies and some only long-necks. With the honourable exceptions of Cooper's actually less-than-Sparkling Ale and the bar-top casks of Castlemaine XXXX at the Breakfast Creek Hotel (which is, of course, a pub), Australian beer is so devoid of distinguishing characteristics that the shape of the bottle is a more crucial issue.

A combined Brisbane side, including a couple of Valleys blokes but none of my immediate neighbours, formed the Lions' first Queensland opposition, before the tour went further afield in the state which an old colleague of mine, with ambitions to retire there, called 'the world's only fascist democracy'. By that he meant that it would suit him just fine, although possibly a little less so after the demise of its dominant political presence, Joh Bjelke-Petersen. Queenslanders are different. They regard other Australians as stuck-up, lah-di-dah and pretentious – apart from North Queenslanders, who feel much the same way about South Queenslanders. In far North Queensland, of course, they . . . oh, sod it, you get the idea. Rockhampton is in Central Queensland, so you can imagine the complexities that involves.

Rockhampton was also full; every pub, every hotel, every room, probably every wardrobe. Not because of the Lions tour, I must confess, as that was already being comprehensively rubbished, but because of the region's major agricultural shindig, which was in full swing. Thirsty men from the far west of Queensland, who reckon that life on the seaboard is irredeemably effete, had taken the place over. There became something almost biblical about the trek from pub to hotel, to be told each time that there was no room at the inn. The Last Chance Saloon was the Queensland Hotel, the sort of place where broken-hearted stockmen would stagger after they had been kicked out of everywhere else. An enormous woman behind the bar woke up the landlord, who was snoring in the corner of his jam-packed premises. There were no rooms, he confirmed. Except . . . no, you wouldn't want that. I assured him that I would; after ten hours on the bus from Brisbane and almost as long slogging around Rockhampton, I could have happily followed his lead by kipping down in the corner.

'She's pretty small. And she's a bit basic.' I'll take it. It sounds like paradise. I've been living in a wardrobe. And so it was that I was given a bunch of keys like the ones gaolers carry in cowboy films and directed on to the roof. The last room in Rockhampton was, in fact, the local lock-up, used to accommodate the hopelessly drunk. I had seen what passed for normality in the home town of Rod Laver and Rod Reddy, so I wondered just how blitzed one would have to be to qualify. But even a bare brick cell with an iron bedstead, a lightbulb and no window looked like the presidential suite at the Sheraton Wentworth to me. Give the place its due: it had been thoroughly hosed-out and disinfected since the Kelly Gang had last been incarcerated there. As the stockmen roared and bellowed below, I counted not sheep but my blessings. The official party got a good night's sleep in rather more salubrious surroundings, and Central Queensland were beaten 64–8.

There were other moments of improvisation to cherish in Queensland. At Toowoomba, home town of most of the bin-hoisting, soap-watching Valleys contingent, their recommendation was enough to secure use of the only phone, although I had to be locked in the secretary's office with the gate takings in order to use it. Nobody searched my pockets on the way out. At Gympie the only available line was in the bowling club next to the football ground, where a combination of footy fans and bowlers were kicking up a racket that would have put the stockmen in the Queensland Hotel to shame. The copy-takers on the *Hull Daily Mail* and the *Wigan Evening Post* earned their money that night.

Great Britain lost ignominiously in the second Test at Lang Park – when Lang Park was still called Lang Park – but that didn't stop the whole town of Orange turning out for the Lions' next match. Orange, in western New South Wales, is a place of extremes. Baking hot in the summer, it is high enough to get snow in the winter, something which always rates a couple of minutes on the television news in Sydney. Towns further west such as Parkes, Forbes and Dubbo have been as hot as hell when I've been there for country finals and tour matches, but I recall Mel Woodward, a man who has stood on the terraces at Thrum Hall in January, telling me that he has never been as cold in his life as he was at Parkes when France played there. Then again, he is virtually an Australian now and has undoubtedly gone soft. Orange closed down for the day so that everyone could turn out to see the tourists parading through the streets. The Whatmores from Cowra – whose son once played for Leigh – made a 200-mile round trip and, naturally, took me home for a couple of days' rest and recuperation. Great Britain were pretty ordinary, we agreed, but they at least avoided defeat by a bunch of hicks from the sticks this time around. But these hick towns are where so many of Australia's greatest footballers have come from; you underestimate the inheritors of that tradition at your peril.

The final match before the third Test was in Canberra and was played in conditions which the relevant *Rothmans* describes as 'theoretically suited to the British'. Even if you hadn't been there, that can only mean one thing. Pouring rain and knee-deep mud, which should – in theory – have slowed down players like Phil Blake and Mal Meninga sufficiently for the tourists to get a handle on them. So much for theory. The President's XIII gave them a good stuffing, I was dropped off by the coach on which I'd cadged a lift on the Parramatta Road with the rain still coming down in torrents, and my little room-mate spat the dummy all night.

The standing of the 1988 Lions tour could not now have been any lower. Half the party was injured; the other half was woefully out of form. My most vivid memory of the build-up to the third Test is of Kevin Ward hobbling across the foyer of the Manly Pacific – yes, we're back there – dragging one obviously useless leg behind him. Surely he wouldn't be playing?

'Have to. No bugger else,' was his ringing declaration of readiness for the task ahead. Hugh Waddell had, he confided, had a dream in which he played in a Test and Great Britain beat Australia. 'Ten Bellies' had seemed so surplus to requirements for most of the tour (recalling Des Foy, who was completely forgotten by the management four years earlier) that one prophecy seemed just about as unlikely as the other. Even when he was picked – on the Wardian basis that there was no bugger else – the obvious reflection was that one correct prediction out of two wasn't bad. Not Gypsy Petrulengo standard, perhaps, but not bad.

The withering scorn of Australia for the efforts of this particular set of Poms had now gone into overdrive. Newspapers advised their readers not to bother turning up at the Sydney Football Stadium for what would undoubtedly be the most embarrassing mismatch of all time. Was it really worth carrying on with Ashes Tests?

There were British fans in Australia who felt much the same way. They are the real heroes of this tour, spending their life savings to watch such lame performances from a side which they had really believed was going to be competitive this time. They were competitive, of course, but only with Western Division and Toowoomba. Resilient as they were, many had reached the stage by now when they no longer cared much. I know of several who made the policy decision that it was not worth subjecting themselves to further humiliation by even going to the third Test.

But we know the punchline, don't we? An unforgettable British victory – the first over Australia for a decade – wiped the slate clean of all the disgrace of the previous few weeks. The pleasure was all the more acute for being so utterly unexpected. Working for a dozen newspapers that day, I had deadlines so tight that I needed to collect quotes and conduct interviews while the victorious players were still on their laps of honour. They do not teach you on your journalism course how to take a legible shorthand note while running round the SFS with Henderson Gill, but they should. It was a long session on the phone that night, conveying the good news to Wigan, Hull and anywhere else that I thought ought to be told. David Stephenson had acquired some shoes of his own for the gala dinner, at which the Aussies threw a very gratifying sulk, and my cell-mate learnt that night – not before time – how to locate and retrieve his own dummy.

That was the rough – and I would do it again tomorrow if it was the only way of getting along in Australia. But, as Zsa-Zsa Gabor would vouch, smooth is, well, smoother. Life has been cushy in the extreme ever since. *The Independent* stumped up for the 1992 tour, enabling me to do my 'Man from Allerton Bywater' routine at the Manly Pacific, throwing open the balcony doors so that I could be vaguely aware of the surf on the sand all night. That was the tour on which Great Britain beat Australia 33–10 in Melbourne – the only time that any of us has been able to sit back and enjoy the sensation of a victory that was all neatly parcelled and labelled before half-time. The overspill press box that night also accommodated a ragbag of assorted celebrities, and I found myself sitting next to an actor whom I recognised from my cultural indoctrination in Brisbane as Jim from *Neighbours*. As Britain took total control in the first half, he remarked pleasantly, 'You just wouldn't believe this script.' I know I should have resisted but, considering what he did for a living, I had to tell him that was a bit rich coming from him. '*Touché,*' said Jim from *Neighbours*. The champagne flowed that night, much of it from the direction of Garry Schofield, who seemed to take it as a personal affront that anyone should have an empty glass. A couple of hours earlier, as he had stood on the sidelines at Prince's Park, doing countless interviews on a damp, chilly Melbourne night, the Great Britain captain had needed to be rescued for his own good. 'He'll have to come in now. He's getting cold,' said Lee Crooks, leading him off to the sheds.

But if that tour was comfortable – nay, luxurious – by comparison with working your way around Australia independently, true sybaritic indulgence had to wait until a remarkable weekend in 1995 when Rugby League in Australia made its biggest leap into the future. It is a myth much believed in Britain that the game in Oz has always been expansionist and outward-looking. Nothing could be further from the truth. It has had its moments, of course, notably the periodic attempts to crack the American question, but in Sydney in the early 1980s, the prevailing wisdom was that all the Rugby League that mattered stopped dead at Cronulla in the south, Manly in the north and Penrith in the far west. Beyond that, there might be dragons and cherubs blowing clouds across the map, but no Rugby League worth a stuff. The Poms couldn't play, the Kiwis couldn't play, the French certainly couldn't play, and the only real significance of the competitions in Brisbane, Newcastle, Wollongong and country areas across New South Wales and Queensland was as nurseries for Sydney. The decision to let Canberra and Illawarra into the Winfield Cup was widely perceived as watering down its excellence – Canberra would never be competitive, I was assured more than once – and as for a team in Brisbane . . . well, dream on, pal. So, for the Winfield Cup to be poised in 1995 to admit no less than four new clubs – in Perth, Townsville and Auckland, plus a second outfit in Brisbane – it was pretty cataclysmic stuff. Australians aren't as irony-deficient as Americans, by any stretch of the imagination, but it was still remarkable that the Brisbane Broncos and the Canberra Raiders should be at the forefront of those warning that the new sides would never cut the cake, would dilute the competition and so on, without being regarded as out-and-out hypocrites. At best, they must have had short memories for a time when everyone said the same things about them.

The Australian Rugby League was, by this stage, partial to the grand gesture. Some of them, like an outrageously over-the-top season's launch featuring music specially composed by an eccentric

Greek, misfire horribly. Friends of mine in Sydney still talk in tones of hushed horror about their interminable evening with Yanni and the city's glitterati. For the first weekend of games involving the new clubs, however, they had something planned that would be hard to beat – a private jet which, a tight schedule and a following wind permitting, would fly an invited party around all four inaugural matches, from Auckland on the Friday night to the Western Reds in Perth on the Sunday afternoon. There would be no time for things like sleep, unless you did it at the matches, but Yanni would not be playing. It was, in that most hackneyed of phrases which serves for a flight to the moon as well as for a fortnight's holiday in the sun, the trip of a lifetime. It would have been a dereliction of duty to make them do it without a Pom on board. Imagine all that unwanted champagne and all that surplus smoked salmon. Yes, from first assembling at Kingsford-Smith Airport in Sydney, the ARL do it in style. The term 'junket' was one that was bandied about, but only by those who didn't make the cut for the trip. But then 'work hard and play hard' has always been their motto. There was one famous meeting of the New South Wales Rugby League, which still ran the show in those days, where two committee members worked so hard that they finished up scrapping outside in Phillip Street. That great frilly shirt extravaganza, the Rothmans Medal ceremony, has been enlivened on more than one occasion by senior figures, who had worked hard all night on shedding their inhibitions, slugging it out on the dance-floor. It is all much more decorous these days; champagne doesn't seem to make you fighting drunk, it just makes you slump there feeling very pleased with life.

If it is a long way for me from the midnight bus to Tamworth and the drying-out cell on the roof of the Queensland Hotel, then it is also something of a contrast for the old players on board. Johnny Raper and Graeme Langlands, however, might claim to have been the pioneers of all this. League was strictly a blue-collar game when they started in the 1950s, but they would have a strong argument for being the first champagne footballers. They were partial to the good things of life when they were playing and have been partial to them ever since. Talk about horses for courses. Another old player who has done okay for himself is Rex Mossop – later an institution as a broadcaster. He is vaguely aware of where I come from and tells me the story of the second shower in Leigh. The first, it seems, was installed for Trevor Allan – guess which contributor to this book was named after him, by the way – when he arrived from Australia to grace the local club. 'Moose' Mossop called in another plumber to install the second, but he had never heard of such a thing and could not understand for the life of him why anyone should want a tap dribbling out water three-quarters of the way up the bathroom wall. What was wrong with the old zinc bath? 'Moose' assumed that things had changed a good bit in Leigh since then, but I was able to set him straight on that one.

With philosophical discourse of this calibre, the miles soon fly past, especially with the help of in-flight champagne refuelling, an area of transport technology in which Australia leads the world. Hospitality is another strong suit. If I had a glass of champagne for every time Ken Arthurson, the head honcho whose show this is, tells me 'Mate, I'd just like to say how very delighted we are that you could come with us', I would have had, well, a lot of champagne. And he appears to mean it. The suspicion that I'm going to be rumbled at some stage of the trip and left to make my own way to Auckland by outrigger canoe, or back from Perth on foot, gradually recedes.

We make Auckland by more conventional means, in plenty of time for . . . a champagne reception. That night at the Ericsson Stadium is dealt with elsewhere in these pages, but there was little time to dwell on it at the time before getting back on the plane for the flight to Brisbane. Our own box at what I will forever call Lang Park for the South Queensland Crushers against Canberra, a motorcycle escort to the airport to get us off to Townsville on time; this is the way to go to the footy. Mind you, it helps when Queensland's minister for sport is on board; small matters like cordoning off key road junctions to give us a clear run to the plane seem to present no problems at all.

Anyone who doubted the viability of a club in North Queensland should have been at Stockland Stadium that night. It has rained, the place is steaming gently in the sub-tropical heat, and the whole town seems to have jammed its way in. Okay, the Cowboys lose to Canterbury and also lose most of their other matches that first season, but there was a time too when the Raiders couldn't have raided a sweet-shop. It is in Townsville as well that I realise that, in terms of the stamina required for serious junketing, I'm strictly English second division standard. While Raper, Langlands and the heavy-duty mob head for the casino at 1 a.m., it's a toss-up whether I get to bed and then fall asleep or the other way around.

The 6 a.m. flight to Perth – more champagne with your bacon and eggs, anyone? – takes us across the great girth of Australia, red and parched shading into khaki and parched as we go west. Perth looks like a pristine, life-sized mock-up of a city, waiting for its population to arrive from central casting and mess it up. Where is everyone? Well, enough of them are in a baking-hot WACA ground to take the total attendance for the four matches beyond the magic 100,000 mark. The Western Reds round off the weekend by becoming the first of the four new sides to win their opening fixture, and Arko looks exhausted but vindicated. There is no time to bask in any glow of satisfaction, however, as the plane has to take off within half an hour of the final hooter in order to reach Sydney before the airport shuts down for the night. The alternative is a diversion to Melbourne which, without Great Britain thrashing Australia and the chance to put Jim firmly in his place, is a dreadful prospect. We make it to Sydney, which is just as well for the various film crews waiting there, galvanised by the news that a breakaway Super League is once more on the cards.

It seems inconceivable after the success of that opening weekend of the Winfield Cup that, within weeks, three of the four new clubs will turn around and bite the hand that has opened the door for them – but that, of course, is what happened. Arko doesn't believe it will happen either. 'I'm certain that, after this weekend, everyone will be able to see that we are on the right track,' he says. 'By the way, I'd just like to say how pleased we were that you could come along with us.' But Arko is an old man and, for the first time, is beginning to look it. If Super League does declare war, it is hard to imagine him being able to stand up to them. How wrong can you be? In many ways, the whole trip has been the sort of thing which made the ARL vulnerable to criticism as a jobs-for-the-boys, Good Time Charlie type of organisation, cosy, self-contained and self-protective. The lavish nature of the jaunt around Australasia created plenty of adverse comment, but that part of it which came from the Super League camp would have been more convincing if their main movers and shakers had been any more fond of roughing it. Doing the thing in as much comfort and conviviality as possible is simply the Australian way. And nobody – least of all other Australians – can condemn Australians for being Australian. Did I need a hotel in Sydney for the next few nights? If so, there was one waiting. I had to turn it down; not because I feared for my objectivity becoming compromised in the months of upheaval which lay ahead, but because I had a prior booking on Danny Lane's floor. You have to return to the real world at some stage . . .

Two days later, I'm in Newcastle with Malcolm Reilly, who is just a few weeks into his appointment as coach of Newcastle Knights. He has that same look on his face that he must have had as he sat on the front porch of the Manly Pacific in 1970; that expression which says 'How the hell did I cop for all this?'. He is excited about the set-up at the club, the depth of talent available to him, the way that he can have the whole playing staff in for training twice a day, every day, if he wants to. Within a few more weeks, he will have seen virtually all the club's administrative staff decamp to the ill-fated Hunter Mariners, but he will stay where he is, a decision made easier by one of the biggest 'loyalty bonus' payments in the whole, cash-strewn saga of Super League versus the ARL. I'm sure he would have been pretty excited by that as well.

At this stage, though, the excitement is generated simply by being back in a place which so often seems too good to be true. And this is Newcastle, mind you, a coal, iron and steel town which Australians tend to talk about as though it was a southern hemisphere clone of Middlesbrough. It is, of course, except that it has miles of beaches that way, the lake that way, and the Hunter Valley, with its stud farms and wineries, that way. We have a drive around, stopping on various shores and headlands to take in the scene. This is where he comes for a run in the morning. Down there, in the salt-water pool in that cove, is where he brings his players to soak and swim their bumps and bruises away on a Monday. Here, in what ranks as one of Australia's least superficially glamorous cities, you could live the rest of your life in a T-shirt and a pair of shorts, with or without several hundred thousand dollars from the ARL tucked in the back pocket. It seems further away from Allerton Bywater by the minute.

Content as he is with his own situation, the former Great Britain coach is curious about how I've grabbed my own tiny slice of the house-special deep-pan pizza that is Australia. How have I managed it? Who's paid?

Well, I have, I argue with myself. Paid my way out here four times in a decade. Paid my dues by doing it the rough way, before I really knew that there was a smooth way. Persuaded a newspaper that it was worth sending me out again on this particular treat.

But, in the end, it's a fair cop. Okay Australia, you've got me. I'm a lucky bastard as well, I suppose.

# Pastis with Pipette

## Harry Edgar

Throughout the first two decades of my adult life, the years in which I've published *Open Rugby*, one thing, one place, constantly haunted me. It was that eerie feeling of having been somewhere before in a different time, a different age. Or maybe a kind of frustration that you really belonged somewhere else, but life hadn't quite dealt the cards you wanted.

It was Carcassonne – a place so visibly steeped in history that it seemed forever looking back, forever melancholy; a constant reminder of the past and of another way of life. It was also a reminder of lost vitality for a game which has brought so much joy for the young men of the Midi. Carcassonne, a southern French town in the *départment* of Aude, has always been the ultimate symbol of the glorious youth of French Rugby League.

It was at the centre of the game's golden age in France in the years immediately after World War II. That golden age peaked, although it didn't die, in 1951 when the first French touring team went to Australia and took the game by storm. In an era when British and Australian touring teams still travelled around the world by boat, the 1951 Frenchmen were the Rugby League pioneers of air travel. They flew by military plane to Saigon, then south to Australia, and proceeded to blitz the Aussies in both Sydney Cricket Ground Tests to take the series with a swashbuckling brand of football that left their opponents face-down in the turf and the spectators in open-mouthed awe.

Australia still hasn't forgotten the 1951 French team, and neither has France, because everything about French Rugby League since has been measured against what happened in '51. That was the year when Puig-Aubert became the best-loved sportsman in the whole of France, and the best-loved Frenchman in the whole history of Australia and Rugby League.

In the 20 years I've been following the game in France I have sipped *Cinquante-et-uns* in most of the *Treiziste* towns whose communities have given our game sustenance, from Toulouse, the great city on the banks of the Garonne, to tiny villages like Pia. Other historic towns I have visited include Villeneuve-sur-Lot, Avignon, Albi and Perpignan, who were among the pioneers of the 'new' rugby back in the 1930s and who also provided much of the strength which brought about the golden age and created the passion to keep the flame burning in some of the darker days which have followed. But I always came back to that one place, and three things remained reassuringly constant about Carcassonne: the River Aude always flowed past the Stade Domec (albeit sometimes with a struggle in the driest days of a burning summer); La Cité, the medieval fortress which dominates the skyline, always looked down imposingly over the town and its people; and Puig-Aubert, Carcassonne's most famous citizen, was always there. Only two of these three would last for ever.

The walled city of Carcassonne has a history stretching back to its earliest traces of man in the sixth century BC. Two important roads dating from the earliest times intersect at Carcassonne, one running east to west and linking the Mediterranean with the Atlantic, and the other running north to south, from the Massif Central to Spain. In 122 BC the Romans conquered both Provence and Languedoc, and proceeded to fortify the settlement they called Carcasso. They occupied the region until the middle of the fifth century AD.

Between 1082 and 1209 the city of Carcassonne wielded tremendous influence, and these prosperous times saw the swift rise of the Cathar religion, better known perhaps as the Albigensian heresy, which was bitterly opposed to the contemporary decadence of Catholicism. When Pope Innocent III mounted his crusade in 1209, Carcassonne found itself in the direct line of fire and, on 15 August of that year, after a siege which lasted for two weeks, the city fell and the Albigensian heresy was over. Carcassonne was assigned to the military commander of the crusade, Simon de Montfort.

In 1355 the city of Carcassonne was destroyed by fire by Edward, the Black Prince, but it was rebuilt almost immediately. However, the charring of their town's memory left its mark on the modern Rugby League players of Carcassonne. I can recall a couple of times in the 1980s, when French international teams were on duty in England, seeing small groups of players who had enjoyed one drink too many after their game relieving themselves at the foot of the statue in Leeds's City Square. I only found out that this was not an unavoidable accident but a quite deliberate ploy when another player, a Catalan, sneered (in French with an accent you could grind rocks on): 'Those Carcassonnais . . . they're nutters. They teach them at school they have to piss on the Black Prince!'

La Cité has watched over the colourful story of Rugby League in Carcassonne since the game began in the '30s, as it sits on the hill overlooking the Stade Domec. At times you almost feel as if the ghosts of days gone by are stirring, and it was never more sinister than in December 1978 when France, against everybody's expectations, beat Bobby Fulton's Kangaroos. The afternoon went strangely and suddenly dark, and the driving rain and sleet was blown harder into the faces of the players by a bitter wind, as the Australians' nightmare was realised.

My introduction to the Domec had come a year earlier, in March 1977, when I travelled from Spain to Carcassonne to see France play against England. The scene, and the weather, could hardly have been more different. It was the first time I had watched Rugby League in person outside England, and the culture shock was enormous as, riding on the English team bus, we drove through the famous narrow entrance gate (now infamous for a host of Wallace Arnold bus drivers!) to the Stade Domec, to be greeted by a jam-packed capacity crowd of 12,000 who were roaring their approval at a juniors' curtain-raiser. This was over an hour before kick-off time in the international, and the feeling of Christians being ferried into the Colosseum to be fed to the lions was never more apparent.

I remember being shocked by the sheer brutality, mixed with breathtaking adventure, of many of the French team in 1977. The referee was a young man from Carcassonne, Monsieur Masse, of whom David Oxley said he'd never seen an official look so afraid before a game. This was in the pre-Bonnery era of French League, when organisation, discipline and links with the English-speaking outside world were unheard of, and people on the British side of the Channel hadn't a clue about the French game, or even the names of any of their players.

If I tell you that the French pack included Henri Daniel, Jean-Pierre Sauret and a pre-conversion J.J. Cologni, you start to get my drift! It was no holds barred up front, but when the French backs got the ball, they produced sheer poetry, usually orchestrated by their captain Jose Callé. It was the match in which a certain teenager called Jean-Marc Bourret gained his reputation, and the one where that old cliché about the French loving to play with the sun on their backs was never more true. Nothing more was ever heard of Monsieur Masse, but France had won a stunning victory to take the European Championship, and I'll swear the ghosts in La Cité were smiling that day!

Twenty-four hours earlier, I had had my introduction to another Carcassonne institution for Rugby League visitors from overseas – the Hotel Terminus. The old Terminus was exactly the same last time I was there, in 1995, as it was on that first occasion 18 years previously. Its enormously high mirrored ceiling still presided over a lobby area that was dominated by a marble staircase which would not have looked out of place in one of those southern mansions in *Gone with the Wind*.

The Terminus has been witness to a large chunk of Rugby League history. All visiting international teams have stayed there and many of the game's most important meetings have taken place there, but none would be more memorable than the International Board get-together in 1978, while the Kangaroos were staying there. It was the meeting at which Kevin Humphreys signed the document pledging the Australians' support for Mike Mayer's American Rugby League project, but when Mayer tried to follow it up and get the funding he was promised, the details of the agreement suddenly became a little murky. Humphreys later denied that he had ever signed the agreement with the American League, but both David Oxley and Bill Fallowfield, who were at the same meeting, told me that he did.

Fallowfield loved the cut and thrust of those verbal battles with the Australians as he presided over the International Board. The general perception was that the Aussies could get their own way on anything they wanted, but the French loved Bill because he would always stand his ground for Europe. Raymond Forges, like Fallowfield a wartime fighter pilot and one of Carcassonne's best-known Rugby League officials, summed it up succinctly when he said: 'Fallowfield wouldn't take any crap from Humphreys, and Humphreys knew it!'

Monsieur Forges would always call a spade a spade. He'd become very much an Anglophile during the war when he flew with the Free French, and had been given help and shelter by English families. As a young Carcassonne official in the years after the war, his command of the English language provided a natural progression to international affairs, and Raymond managed many French Test and tour teams, including the 1968 World Cup side which reached the final in Sydney. His perfect English included a knowledge of just about every swear word you'll never see in the *Oxford Dictionary* – but it went down well with the players in the dressing-room.

Raymond took me under his wing a few times whilst in Carcassonne. He was quite a playboy, despite his advancing years, and I'll never forget the time he gave me a lift back to Carcassonne from Perpignan where we'd been watching the 1982 Kangaroos. Raymond had a Porsche, and a journey which normally takes about an hour and a half took just 50 minutes, and that included a stop for petrol! It was a real white-knuckle ride through a particularly dark winter's night, and was made even more nerve-racking because Raymond was one of those drivers who insisted on looking at you when he spoke rather than keeping his eyes on the road.

Safely back in Carcassonne but still trembling, I expected the elderly Monsieur Forges to drop me at the Hotel Terminus before he retired to his mansion, grandly titled 'Pont du Forges', at Trèbes (one of several small villages a few miles out by narrow country road from Carcassonne, all of which had a little local League team). Not a bit of it. Despite the late hour he insisted on drinking a few more whiskies in his favourite watering-hole, the Café Continental, and then transferring to a nightclub on the outskirts of town.

That nightclub, Le Privé, was very much the hub of after-hours social life among the Rugby League players of Carcassonne because its owner was one Pierre Pavanetto, who was then president of the Sporting Association of Carcassonne, colloquially referred to either as ASC or by its nickname 'Les Canaris' (the latter deriving from the yellow jerseys worn by its members). Pavanetto also owned the Café Continental which, as the clubhouse of ASC, was a Rugby League institution. Upstairs at the 'Conti' were the club offices and meeting rooms which housed a treasure-trove of old photographs which brought to life the great history of France's most respected League club. Pride of place went to team groups of the Puig-Aubert-inspired team which won countless cups and championships in the early post-war years, and a huge blow-up of a picture of 'Pipette' in midair after kicking the ball for France at Sydney Cricket Ground in 1951. Years later, when ASC moved their headquarters to a new bar, La Davilla, the photographs went with them.

Downstairs behind the bar in the 'Conti' only one football picture hung. It was a Carcassonne team group from the late 1950s, and standing proudly on the back row as a dashing young second-rower was one Pierre Pavanetto, even then with the perfectly manicured moustache which was to become his trademark. He was an immensely proud club president, always eager to look after his players when they won, but brooding and impatient when they lost. It's a fair bet that, during Pavanetto's time at the helm, the number one expense on the ASC balance sheet was champagne!

I arranged for a couple of players to travel from England to join Pavanetto's Carcassonne in 1981. I flew down with the first, a young Australian called Gary Crawford, and on arrival we were treated to dinner at the 'Conti' where I apparently made some kind of history by eating no less than three platefuls of Madame Pavanetto's home-made cassoulet. It was only later that I learned what an honour it was seen as in Carcassonne to be invited to dine at Monsieur Pavanetto's personal table. Five years later they were still cracking jokes about the Englishman who ate three plates of the famous local dish which consisted largely of haricot beans. They obviously knew what the after-effects were going to be long before I did!

It wouldn't have been so bad, but Gary and I had to spend the next night at another dinner hosted by Pierre Rayssac, then secretary of the French Rugby League federation, and also a Carcassonne man through and through. Guest of honour was Ron Willey, the coach from Australia, who was on the first of his several visits to France in which he tried to impart some of his coaching knowledge.

It was obvious from the first time I met him that Pavanetto was held in some kind of awe by all the local people connected with League. Whilst he was very quietly spoken and incredibly charming, you had that immediate gut feeling that this was not a man to be crossed. A month later, I found out why. One morning in December 1981, the police called at the Café Continental and arrested Pavanetto at gunpoint. He went to jail for the best part of a year for his part in a whisky-smuggling racket, where bottles were being brought in from Spain via Andorra without payment of the necessary duty. Several leading politicians in Carcassonne were also implicated in the scam, but it seemed that 'Pava' took the rap for them all. I never did find out what his pay-off was, but you can be sure there would have been one!

A couple of days after he was arrested, I drove with some Carcassonne officials across country to Marseille, where the Test between Great Britain and France was being staged at the Vélodrome. Madame Pavanetto came with us, and sobbed all the way there, all the way back, all the way through lunch and all the way through dinner. Even the fact that France produced one of their best performances of modern times to beat the British 19–2 (in a match in which Greg Hartley was the referee) could not cheer her up.

Also down in the dumps when he arrived in Carcassonne to find the club president was in jail was their second import player, one Glenn Knight. He was as Yorkshire as a plate of parkin, and I didn't think he would last five minutes in France, but he was eager to give it a shot. He was even more eager to hang me from the nearest tree when he discovered that the man who was supposed to be paying his wages and travel expenses was being detained elsewhere. But, like dozens of other guest players from overseas, Glenn was made very welcome by Felix and Madame Bergèse at their café in the centre of Carcassonne, and although he moaned incessantly about wanting to go home, he stayed for a full season, led ASC to a cup final, and became the Canaries' favourite Englishman.

Although Glenn gave a good impersonation of someone who was hating every minute of it, secretly he was loving the celebrity status he enjoyed, the fact that he could enjoy free meals and free drinks in almost every café in town, and the fact that for the first time in his life he was a full-time footballer, with no worries about getting up for work in the morning. All he had to do each day was mosey down to Felix's café, munch on as many ham sandwiches as he could eat, and do a spot of training whenever he felt like it.

Thirteen years later in 1994, I stood behind the fence at the Stade Domec and watched Glenn Knight run through training with the French Test team the day before they played Great Britain. He was France's assistant coach, and later went on tour with them and worked with them throughout the 1995 World Cup. I'm hoping that by now he has come to realise that going to Carcassonne wasn't such a bad move, and that he's forgiven me enough to let them start dismantling the scaffold.

In the very centre of the town of Carcassonne lies the Place Carnot, a market square which bustles every Saturday morning as the traders set up their stalls and sell their goods. The lower town developed its commercial strength through the wine trade and the linen industry, but now tourism, attracted by La Cité, is just as important. At the centre of Place Carnot is a modest little café called Chez Felix which has, since the early post-war years, been not only a geographical centre spot, but also the spiritual centre of Carcassonne.

Felix Bergèse was known as the 'Basque Sorcerer' when he joined AS Carcassonne in the late 1930s. A great stand-off and tactician, he came from Bayonne in the west to join the growing power of *rugby à XIII*. Tragically, the best years of his playing career were cut short because of the war, when Rugby League was banned by the Vichy Government and Felix spent four years in a German prisoner-of-war camp. During the war the Germans set up their operations headquarters in the Hotel Terminus, and just a couple of hundred yards away, under a bridge by the Canal du Midi, stands a plaque which pays tribute to a group of Carcassonnais who were shot dead by the Nazis in that very spot. Several of the names are from some of Carcassonne's best-known Rugby League families.

When liberation came, the *Treizistes* did not look back. Felix Bergèse became player-coach, later just coach, of a mighty ASC team built by a young, go-ahead president named Paul Barrière. While still in his 20s, Barrière became president of the French federation during their golden age around the 1951 tour, and was the founding figure of Rugby League's World Cup competition. It was Barrière who, in 1945, recruited Carcassonne's, and France's, most famous footballer, Puig-Aubert.

Just 18 years old, and already nicknamed 'Pipette' (which was Catalan slang for cigarette, meaning literally 'little chimney'), young Puig-Aubert became the ultimate legend. It is said that, when the ASC directors Messieurs Barrière, Noubel, Ramon and Bousquet (who became his father-in-law a few years later) went to sign him, they beat off a massive offer from the Narbonne Rugby Union club (true amateurs even in those days!) by producing a suitcase filled with 120,000 francs in crisp banknotes (approximately £1,200) at a time when the average monthly salary in southern France was 3,000 francs.

Puig-Aubert went on to play 46 times for France and in no less than 16 finals, eight of which were championship finals and eight of which were finals of the Lord Derby Cup. He was twice a 'double' winner with Carcassonne, in 1945 and 1952.

It was impossible to visit Carcassonne and not see 'Pipette'. On one occasion I went unannounced to his house in the Rue Jean-Mermoz, accompanied by Joe Chamberlain and Bob Brown, as we returned from our original trip to Venice. We were just strangers passing through, but 'Pipette' was delighted to see us, and made a big fuss of Joe in particular whom he had seen win a cup semi-final for Albi at the Carcassonne ground a few years earlier. He liked Joe because he, too, was an old full-back. On his dining-room wall hung a beautiful old Melba Studios panoramic-view photograph of the packed Sydney Cricket Ground in 1951. 'I played zis match against Clive Churcheeel,' he grinned in not-bad English between tokes on his Gitane. 'I know,' I said, 'I know . . .'

Carcassonne had become not just a place in France where I went to watch Rugby League, but a place with which I now had a huge emotional tie. As 'Pipette', Felix and all the old men who once were the mighty warriors of ASC experienced the melancholy of reflecting on their lost youth, I realised the same was happening to me. In Carcassonne I'd fallen in love, fallen out of love, proposed marriage, had great fun and happy adventures, and more recently felt my heart breaking and been helpless to stop it.

Most of the fun factor of Carcassonne centred around a bunch of people who made their names not with the mighty ASC, but with the town's other Rugby League club, St Jacques. They haven't existed for well over a decade now, but people in Carcassonne still talk about them, always doing so with a big smile on their faces.

St Jacques peaked in 1978 when, to everybody's surprise (especially their own), they won promotion to the first division. That meant that they had to play a couple of local derbies against the Canaries and, as you would expect, plenty of blood and feathers flew – and that was in Felix's bar before they even got out on to the field together!

Mick Murphy played that season for St Jacques. Mick used to write to me during his time in Carcassonne, trying to ease the boredom of painting walls for a day-job, while sending his wife Rosie out to find any kind of shop that sold chocolate digestive biscuits. Mick told me he used to have great conversations with Puig-Aubert, who was the team manager, as they always sat up at the front of the bus together when travelling to away games. No doubt at the back of the bus would be the two rascals whom you'll still find in Felix's bar almost 20 years later, Christian Burgos and

36

Jean-Pierre Olivier. Mick gave them both nicknames that stuck: Burgos became 'Ginger', for obvious reasons, and Olivier became 'Charmant' because he was renowned for being charming, at least while in female company.

Burgos, whom I'd first met when he played for France in an Under-19 international at Whitehaven back in 1971, was also an extremely able and funny journalist. He regularly wrote satirical articles for *Treize* magazine, and it was he who coined the nickname for the doyen of French journalists, André Passamar of *L'Equipe*, who became forevermore known as 'Le Pap' (The Pope). Burgos was also the inspiration for France's first Rugby League fanzine, the Carcassonne supporters' club magazine *Dropi*. The name was perfect. Christian later dropped out of Rugby League to join a travelling theatre company. If he'd been born eight or so centuries earlier, you just know he would have been a Cathar, standing up there on the battlements of La Cité, fighting off the crusaders.

I didn't see him for five or six years, then I bumped into him at the Stade Domec after a Test match in 1993. He told me that he'd just run in the New York marathon, and was off to Barcelona soon, with former ASC internationals José Moya and Manuel Caravaca, to run another. We talked about the changes in Carcassonne and the continuing decline of League in France.

One big change was that Pierre Pavanetto was gone. Blew his head off with his own gun. Well, we knew 'Pava' was never destined to die at home in his sleep, but nobody expected him to go out with quite such a bang! It happened after he was the victim of an attempted robbery in the early hours one morning as he came out of his nightclub. Pierre would always have the night's takings with him in a bag, and the would-be robbers got to know this. Shaken by this attempted mugging, Pavanetto took to carrying a gun as a security measure. The story goes that he was getting out of his car one night, and did not have the safety catch engaged on the gun. The trigger, unbeknown to him, was caught behind his handbrake, and when he pulled it up to park his car . . . bang! Rumours abounded that it had been suicide, but Christian Burgos, who worked as a theatre nurse at the local hospital, had seen the autopsy notes and confirmed the coroner's findings that it really was a terrible accident.

Not long after, the Café Continental was no more, sold and turned into a McDonald's – the ultimate nightmare for southern Frenchmen who cherished their own culture. Even Carcassonne was falling victim to the sanitised uniformity of the western world.

It's hard to believe that I won't see 'Pipette' again, shuffling into Felix's bar or holding court at the back of the grandstand at the Domec after a game. The inevitable happened on Friday, 3 June 1994. On that day a small group of elderly men emerged into the Midi sunlight from the house on the Rue Jean-Mermoz. All were former players from the glory days of ASC, among them Messieurs Poch, Guilhem and Ribes. With great sadness and gentility the old men filed away through the gardens, the air sweet with the scent of roses and marguerites, after paying their respects to Madame Andrée Puig and her family.

These men, who were giants in the golden age of French Rugby League, shed another tear for their own lost youth, but this time they were also shedding tears for their 'Pipette', their great friend and colleague who was gone. Puig-Aubert had been pronounced dead at 7.30 on that Friday morning. At the age of 69, a cardiac arrest saw him pass away after a long struggle against cancer. For a man who was rarely seen without a cigarette in his hand for over 50 years, it came as no surprise that he should eventually succumb to cancer.

The last time I had seen 'Pipette' was in November 1993 when the Kiwis were based in Carcassonne during their tour. The changing attitudes and demands of modern-day football teams meant that the Hotel Terminus was no longer deemed to be of the required standard. British teams had long since preferred to stay in the air-conditioned luxury of Toulouse and travel by bus into Carcassonne just for the game, yet the journalists who travelled with them still requested to stay at the Terminus, with its high ceilings, rickety plumbing, iron bedsteads and suicidal stair-carpet. The wooden-shuttered windows looked out on to the Canal du Midi and the railway tracks, and it was easy to transport your mind back to the war years as you peered through the curtains, imagining you were a resistance fighter planted in the enemy camp. The Kiwis in 1993 stayed at a brand-new luxury hotel in the shadow of La Cité, and promptly saw two of their players disappear through the railings and fall from a first-floor balcony on the first day they were there!

Puig-Aubert came down to that hotel to meet the New Zealanders and to exchange pleasantries one lunchtime; it had to be during the day because his illness meant that he got too tired to go out in the evenings. It was a melancholy moment seeing Puig-Aubert, looking very frail, shaking hands with the tourists. Kiwi manager Richard Bolton was honoured and overwhelmed that this great legend of

Rugby League should have made a special effort to come down and greet them. Most of the New Zealand players were unaware who this elderly little Frenchman was. They would have understood better if 'Pipette' had known enough English to tell them, 'Hey, when I was your age I beat the crap out of the Australians in Sydney . . . twice!' The Kiwis would have appreciated that!

It was as if 'Pipette' had made that special effort to meet the 1993 Kiwis because he knew they would be the last visitors from Down Under he would get to see. Later that afternoon Richard Bolton and I strolled through a near-deserted Cité. It seemed the right place, the only place, to take our thoughts and pay our respects.

The funeral of Puig-Aubert saw the Cathédral Saint Michel in Carcassonne overflowing with old friends and colleagues. Among them was Paul Barrière, still alive, and still active every year in organising the Arts Festival of Carcassonne, although he has lived for many years in the Basque country of the far west. Puig-Aubert called Barrière his 'spiritual father'. Also there was Felix Bergèse, now into his 80s, the man who had guided and coached 'Pipette' from the teenage prodigy to the legend in his own lifetime.

As the sun grew hotter on the Rue Jean-Mermoz on that Friday in June, Carcassonne woke up and life went on. The River Aude still winds its way past the Stade Domec on its way to the sea, and the medieval Cité still looks down over Carcassonne. Sure, life goes on in Carcassonne – but it isn't the same.

# En Famille

## Margaret Ratcliffe

It must have been fate's decree. Why else would I particularly note and react to an advertisement in a Batley programme to travel with the Great Britain team to France? I'd never thought of it before – and I haven't been the same since. Following that first trip in 1989 we haven't missed a year. We've grown in confidence and developed our techniques – varied our game plan.

Sadly, the French can't really say the same. Their play was poor then, and it's still poor. So why do I support them so avidly? Why follow so closely the careers of any French players who come over here, willing them to do well? What attracts me is that they are so different, so Latin. It seems natural that Aussies and Kiwis should play our game, but faintly bizarre that these dusky, 'proper' foreigners should take on Great Britain. And they do love the game, and they stick to it through thin and thin. My idea of hell would be to see a France v Australia game live. I've always avoided that one.

Bearing in mind especially that they are virtually amateurs, the French never get a fair go from anyone. Not from referees of whatever hue; not from opposition players who, stirred up by parochial press reporting, are obsessed with historical anecdotes of alleged dirty tactics; and, most important of all, not from their own 'establishment'.

I can truthfully say that, but for Rugby League, I would never, ever, have visited any of the following beautiful and memorable spots. The thrill of travelling with the players – rarely talking to them, but just being 'around' them – has been special too, and continues to be in every passing year. It's a bonus to be both with and of the official party.

FEBRUARY 1989 – CARPENTRAS AND AVIGNON
Everyone's heard of Avignon, but how many get to go there in February? How do you know what to take to wear? It's okay for the players (seniors and Under-21s in this case, though just the latter on our plane); all their gear is provided for them.

Flying from Heathrow to Montpellier, the baked-bean brigade sniffed suspiciously at the Air Littoral lunch. But we loved playing with the varied little packages and fancy terrines, and certainly weren't saying no to the cute complimentary bottles of wine and champagne. (Neither were the Under-21s, who saved theirs for later.)

We were so green. No idea what to expect – not a clue. On arrival, we were terrified. We drove the hire car to Avignon and began to search for our pre-booked hotel, which proved to be on a station platform. This was our first experience of the Ibis chain. This is not an ad, but we've been addicted to Ibis hotels ever since. You know where you are with them. They are identically comfortable and, at 30-odd quid a night for a room for three, they're good value.

We awoke to a soft, gentle blue sky and cold sunshine. The Under-21 game was at Carpentras and, with a good map, we made it there for lunch. Omelette and *frites*, and a chat with some Leeds fans who had driven up from Monte Carlo. Then, at the ground, we spoke to a couple of Wigan fans living in exile in Bordeaux.

Continentals promenade in the evening as a matter of course. In winter they simply adapt by wearing their furs. Spoilt for choice of restaurants, we still remember the meals that weekend, not forgetting our Sunday lunch of *saucissons en baguettes* at the stadium. We never did see the Pope's Palace in daylight, but did just manage a late-evening photo close to the Pont d'Avignon.

Oh! The matches? Right. The Under-21s lost, and Tim Street was sent off. In the big boys' game, it was France 8, Great Britain 30. Four heroes of mine – Hugues Ratier, David Fraisse, Gilles Dumas and Jacques Moliner – all played, and Ratier's try, possibly the best ever scored by a winger, was never shown to best advantage by the single Yorkshire TV camera. There were great names in the GB side too – Lydon, Andy Gregory, Kevin Ward, Crooks and Hanley – and Denis Betts was a *Grande-Bretagne Espoir*.

MARCH 1990 – PERPIGNAN

We flew with the big boys this time, again to Montpellier. It was a little later in the year, so we drove down to Perpignan in daylight on the *autoroute, la Languedocienne*, marvelling that it really was the Mediterranean sea just visible on the left.

Perpignan has the best Ibis we know. Excellent – a room with a view of the Pyrénées, peaks snow-dusted. In the early morning we drove in sunshine to Narbonne and watched little old guys in black berets and slippers playing *boules*. Then a quick dash to Carcassonne for lunch in La Cité – outside, in March, with snow on the peaks! We strolled to the *gare* to buy the local *Midi-Libre* and hunted avidly for previews of the match, but instead found ourselves wading through a morass of coverage on the *Quinzistes*.

We just had time on Sunday morning to dash down the coast to Collioure and Port-Vendres close to the Spanish border, which had been recommended to us earlier by two fans. I am for ever in their debt. When I win the Lottery my apartment, with balcony, will be there in that corner of Corbières.

Back at Perpignan there was a good crowd, but the New Zealand ref did his best for Great Britain who duly won 8–4. Still, they should have heeded the warning signs. Three weeks later France reversed this result – with interest – at Headingley, winning 25–18 against a team including Gerald Cordle and David Bishop. Serves them right, really. For France, all last year's heroes were still there, along with Cyrille Pons, Danny Divet and Patrick Entat. Now here's a quiz question: which was the greater Leeds misjudgement – rejecting Jason Robinson as a lad, or not giving Patrick a fair go? It's a close call.

Although we paid for the smallest hire car possible, somehow we'd been allocated a Datsun Bluebird, with electric windows. After the match we drove on to the deserted beach at Port-Baccarés as dusk drew in, and dipped our hands in the Med.

Our *pièce de résistance* meal didn't quite work this time, because we were sitting a little too near the draughty door and we were insufficiently experienced to know that our seafood selection on a bed of ice was cold and didn't come with chips. In fact, it didn't come with anything. We know now.

JANUARY 1991 – LIMOUX AND PERPIGNAN

Early, this one, and a new point of departure: an official chartered flight from Manchester to Perpignan, with fancy GB Rugby League luggage labels and complimentary GB Rugby League scarf.

Husband Joe swapped his only this year for an Albi counterpart, which is a fabulous design but the colours don't go with anything. He then wore it at Wembley and said 'bonjour' to a surprised Wigan fan – who replied accordingly.

The Monarch Airlines Flight 1040 departed at 9.50 a.m. Well, it should have done. Was it the Gulf War? Whatever it was, the airport was like a fortress, with machine-gun-toting security men everywhere. We were held up for hours because our luggage didn't match our passengers. Up and down the gangway, on and off the aircraft several times to identify each individual piece. Rumours abounded.

'We're waiting for Lee Jackson.'

'No, we're not, I'm here.'

And so on, with the inevitable: 'I'm sure we must be waiting for Paul Newlove.' The journalists checked with each other: are we going to report this or not?

The delay played havoc with our tight touring itinerary, depending as it always does on daylight hours. We did at least make it to Castelnaudary in the Canal du Midi basin, so now, when we sample authentic *cassoulet*, we can say we've been to its home town.

The Under-21 match was on Saturday afternoon, so we scraped the early-morning frost off the car and headed for Mirepoix, with its half-timbered, galleried walkways, and Foix because that's where Jacques Moliner comes from, and you never know . . .

Limoux was just clearing up after a carnival. I've never been anywhere when a carnival or procession has actually been on – it's always being prepared or dismantled. The stadium for the Under-21s was a little out of town, and 'town' closes in France on a Saturday at lunchtime (or at least it does in January – believe me). So we had a *fromage baguette* on a stool at a scruffy petrol station with a cup of unspeakable coffee. A real foreign thing to do.

I can't remember the game, I'm afraid. All I do remember is that one of our Under-21s was chastised for wearing his baseball cap during the national anthems, and that David Despin was a bit wild for them.

Big-match Sunday was glorious – a factor three day on the terraces. Still, I didn't enjoy it: France 10, Great Britain 45. I sulked all the way down to Collioure, where we had a cup of hot chocolate in the Hôtel des Templiers, where Impressionist artists left pictures when they couldn't pay their bills. Beat that for a tourist experience.

## FEBRUARY 1992 – PERPIGNAN

To be truthful, vibrant is not the word for Perpignan in February. So this time we opted for a bespoke-tailored package, to travel with the lads but stay for two nights in Sète – a fishing village at the Mediterranean end of the Canal du Midi, on the Cap d'Agde. Highly recommended by a millionaire yacht owner of my acquaintance . . .

To quote from the tourist office brochure: 'Between the blue shades of the sky and sea, Sète embroides [*sic*] its lace with the streets and canals, coiling up round the Mont Saint-Clair.' I don't know what that means, but we met a Bramley fan as we strolled into a bar for our first *pastis* of the evening. Damn: Sète was supposed to be *my* secret. Everything we ate was *à la Sètoise* – which, in fact, meant stuffed with sausage-meat in a tomato sauce.

We had landed at Montpellier Airport twice but never actually been there, so we remedied that and had a 'Spot the Soccer Stadium' day tracking down Montpellier's ground and the Stades des Costières at Nîmes. A few *frites* from a stall in the *place*, and then a quick whizz round a Roman amphitheatre, which was pretty cool. Our personal guide told us all about the vomitories for the plebs, so we felt at home.

The front cover of the match programme was excellent, although it flattered to deceive; the contents were as disappointing as ever. The match? France 12, Great Britain 30, with the French forwards particularly uninspiring. Jason Robinson and Andy Farrell played in the Academy international curtain-raiser, which GB won 28–7. I'll bet I sulked and blamed the referee. But it was another glorious day, as you would expect in February, and I vividly recall the English fans frantically waving to the pilot of a huge jet who seemed intent on landing at the ground, telling him the airport was a little – but not *too* much – further away. There were lots of Huddersfield and Bramley shirts in evidence, so I wore my Batley scarf.

Restaurants in Perpignan are firmly *fermés* on Sundays in February so, for the first time ever, we ate in the hotel. Son Christian ordered beautifully in soon-to-be-a-Grade-A-at-GCSE French, and the meal was brilliant, unforgettable. The *crème brûlée* . . .

MARCH 1993 – CARCASSONNE
This was a whole new ball game – a really big adventure. Joe took the car across the Channel from Portsmouth to Caen and drove down to Toulouse, while Christian, with school, and I, with a miserly holiday allowance, again flew with the players from Manchester. Joe and the car met us at Toulouse Airport,

which was perfect. Having been there for 24 hours, he had a courier's confidence and expertly guided us round this wonderful city. (Christian says his Lottery-win apartment is to be in Toulouse.)

Our Hôtel Arcade (part of the Ibis Group) was also perfect – dead in the city centre. The players stayed at the much more grand Holiday Inn Crowne Plaza – but they still went across the road to McDonald's after breakfast.

There was no game on the Saturday, thank goodness; we have found that the rugby on these trips tends sometimes to get in the way. So we decided to drive north a little. First stop Castres, with its Goya museum and horsemeat stalls in the market. Then on to fabulous Albi and the Toulouse Lautrec museum, although Christian, in contemplative mood, went to the cathedral instead. There was just time then before the light went for a quick glance at Cordes, a time-warped citadel atop a hill in the middle of nowhere.

Our waiter in Toulouse that evening – who, by the look of him, was definitely one of the Southernwood family – noticed our Leeds shirts and asked what we were doing. He'd never heard of *rugby à treize* but was keen to know why Howard Wilkinson had sold Cantona. I thought that was a good question myself.

Bright blue skies overhung the Stade Albert Domec in Carcassonne on the Sunday, and the smell from the barbecues was tantalising. You pay your francs at the gate – 120 for *tribune d'honneur* or 50 for *entrée générale* – but you don't know where you'll end up inside. One or two displaced Wiganers risked their lives begging Alsatian-accompanied, gun-toting cops to let them join their mates round the other side of the ground.

France 6, Great Britain 48. GB included Connolly of St Helens, Molloy of Leeds and Currier of Widnes but, for France, there was no Entat. I was miserable. The *Midi-Libre* and *L'Indépendent* headlines were 'Et toujours le même dénouement' and 'Comme d'habitude'. There was a good crowd, though.

MARCH 1994 – CARCASSONNE
Joe travelled Portsmouth to Caen again – followed, I'm told, by a *brmm! brmm!* down the Mulsanne straight at Le Mans, which just happens to be part of the route south. For Christian and me, there was a wonderful innovation: the trans-Pennine express train direct to Manchester Airport. Fancy luggage labels again as part of the official party.

I thought I'd cracked it this time. I spotted a guy who wasn't a player, wasn't an official, and wasn't a journalist. Perhaps, like me, he'd actually paid for the trip – with his own money! I asked him, and ended up disappointed. He was a Wiganer, and the trip was a prize in a newspaper competition.

The car met us at the airport again, and it was off to Montauban – but not before we'd shed a layer of clothing. Soft sunlight, pavement café: it felt just like home. We called at the Leclerc supermarket in Gaillac to restock the wine rack, and then returned to Toulouse for an evening meal in the most inaptly named Place Wilson.

There was no game again on the Saturday: brilliant. So a special trip, to Lourdes via Saint-Gaudens. Gilles Dumas comes from Saint-Gaudens, and you never know . . . On from there to Lourdes. I have lots to thank Rugby League for, but I never in my wildest dreams thought it would lead me to Lourdes – never thought I'd have an Access chitty from an Esso petrol station in Lourdes.

I blame the fish pie at the Grand Café de l'Opéra. Or I did until I remembered recently that Maurice Lindsay came across to our table and said: 'What's the grub like here – is it all right?' That must have been it: Maurice poisoned my fish pie. Joe and Christian had something else, and they were both okay. I was very poorly.

When you've only got two days you can't afford to waste a moment, let alone a full day. But I was really badly. I lay down with a pillow in the back of the car as we drove to Carcassonne, along the banks of the Canal du Midi. I lay down while Joe and Christian sampled the barbecue outside the *stade*; I lay down while a coach from Barcelona disgorged its fans, one of whom was wearing two sombreros draped in Cas scarves. I crawled gingerly to my place on the bench in the *tribune d'honneur*.

Patrick Entat was back for France, but Dumas had retired. Poor Gilles: destined to play his whole career behind a beaten pack. Patrick Torreilles emerged as a possible new hero, though. France 4, Great Britain 12. I was too poorly to care.

I didn't go out that night. They did. They left me.

MARCH 1995 – ALBI AND CARCASSONNE
There was no France v Great Britain fixture this year: Wales instead, in the revived European Championship. 'I'm not going to watch Wales play anybody,' I said.

'Might be a better game,' mused Harry Edgar.

Right, then. I was persuaded. Another tailored package, another chartered plane from Manchester to Toulouse, with three teams this time. Both Pennines and Pyrénées were snow-dusted, although de-icing the wings before take-off doesn't worry me – much.

I know what a school exchange is now. Christian was asked by a teacher to bring back a bottle of duty-free Johnny Walker; the exchange would then take place in the playground . . .

This time we were determined to visit the vineyards and count the vines in Gaillac, rather than relying on the Leclerc *supermarché*. Most unusually – in fact, for the first time ever – we had to take refuge in the nearest café as it lashed it down. The coffee was wicked – and the beer and the hot chocolate and the wine . . .

It was up to Najac on Saturday, *en route* to Albi. Perched on a hill, redolent of Cathar and Albigensian legend, it was deserted, delightful. Raining and raw in Albi, where *France Espoirs* beat *Grande-Bretagne* 17–16. The vines lay under water. There was no fish pie this year.

A huge crowd gathered in Carcassonne on Sunday, despite it chucking it down again. I kept very quiet when the guy next to me in the stand produced a nasty little knife for his *saucisson en baguette* and told me his opinion of the English referee in a universal language. We were tightly packed together with not a centimetre to spare, but space was miraculously found a few rows behind when Guy Delauney and Gilles Dumas appeared. I took my specs off just in case Gilles remembered our interview in the Leeds Hilton some five years earlier. He didn't, of course. Moliner and Dumas, 'Jacques and Gilles'. Both gone now, and my French worse than ever.

When you're as big as Paul Moriarty, how do you get through life without banging your head all the time? He had been nearly bent double on the plane. I knew then France had no chance. Still, it was a good display by the French and, without two-thirds of the Wigan-Welsh front row, they might have run them closer than the 22–10 scoreline.

That evening the weather never let up. There was no strolling around the Place Wilson. The rain lashed into the exquisitely appointed Restaurant Batifol, where we dined on *pot-au-feu* and *canard à l'orange*. I was frustrated, too, on Monday morning because the shops didn't open until 10 a.m. or, in some cases, not at all *le lundi*. Perhaps I should have stayed with Joe and Christian and strolled by the river, probably for the last time.

After one match in Carcassonne, I heard an English fan say: 'It's a long way to come for a game like that.' One of us is missing the point.

You will observe that, in the course of this narrative, I have barely mentioned money, save to say that the hotels were good value. In truth, we've never counted the precise cost. We daren't: we know it wouldn't stack up logically. You could probably have two weeks on a beach in Benidorm for what we spend each year in just over two days in France. But then they don't play Rugby League in Benidorm. Yet.

When the first Super League fixtures for 1996 were announced, the only one I diarised there and then was Paris v Leeds. *Vive la France! C'est un monde ovale!*

# Roussillon Roulette on the Vomit Express

## Dave Hadfield

If there is one lesson I have learned from various travels, it is this: if a particular trip seems farcically cheap, there is usually something drastically wrong with it. That cut-price cruise might look tempting, but expect to be issued with your own oar.

Now France means many things to many people. The romance of Paris, the rolling vineyards, the vivid colours of the Mediterranean, 400 cheeses. For me, however, it will for ever be linked inextricably with scenes of squalor on a biblical scale, on a bargain coach trip from Wigan.

Oh yes, it was cheap. Cheap enough to get me and the photographer, John Leatherbarrow, to a Test match in Carcassonne that we would otherwise have missed. But cheap enough also to recommend itself as a sort of extended stag night to a group of fellow-travellers who still, from time to time, haunt my waking dreams in the early hours of the morning – that long, black stag night of the soul.

The prospect was attractive enough initially. A long time to be on a bus, of course; but, armed with a good book, a Walkman and plenty of wibbly-wobbly music, and a discreet bottle of Armagnac, that held few terrors. Doze till Dover, imbibe some bracing sea air on the ferry, and then watch France quietly slip past the window as we speed down the *autoroute*. What could be more agreeable?

The first inkling that something was about to go very wrong came before our companions even arrived at the coach, the lower deck of which was already full with the sort of family groups who go in for cheap and cheerful Rugby League weekends in France, leaving the top deck free for me and Leatherbarrow. Dropped lucky here, we're thinking; plenty of room to spread out. And then it starts to come down the street – the muffled roar of collectively arseholed humanity, like a mob on its way to the guillotine but a lot less decorous. Out of their skulls before even climbing aboard and staggering under the weight of further supplies for the journey, these are the men who are going to be sitting alongside you, in front of you, behind you and, when the radar breaks down completely, on top of you, all the way from Wigan to the South of France. Pass the brandy. Turn up the music. Good evening, gentlemen, how very nice to see you.

This scenario was actually even worse than it sounds, because I soon realised that I knew several members of the 20-strong task force that was lurching and belching its way down the aisle. Fortunately, it was well into the second day of the idyll before it dawned on any of them that we had, in fact, previously met upon the field of play.

'Know yer, dunt'er? Yer team's crap.'

But insults about the relative strengths of sides in the fifth division of the North-West Counties League were not one of the major inconveniences that lay ahead. Until Dover, I have to hold up my hands and admit, they were merely a bog-standard conglomeration of piss-artists, alternately sleeping, spewing and fighting among themselves. But, in the traditional manner of the young Englishman abroad, they really hit form once tyre-rubber touched the foreign highway.

That was not all that touched the foreign highway, because one of their ideas of fun was to dismantle the chrome fittings and fling them out through the skylight. At every stop on the *autoroute*, they would descend on the shop like a swarm of locusts and simply remove whatever they fancied, especially bottles of booze and hard-core porn. And their enthusiasm for fighting among themselves reached its height when one of their number was thrown downstairs – breaking his ankle in the process, it later transpired, although it took him a couple of days to realise it. My own vivid memory is of the chap seated immediately in front of me who, shortly after clearing the outskirts of Calais, was not only on the Continent but also incontinent. Even Leatherbarrow, who had been sitting through this Strangeways riot on wheels with stoical imperturbability, was seen to wrinkle his nose slightly at this development.

There was little, though, that you could do. The passengers downstairs, plus the two drivers, were keeping their heads down, trying to ignore the odd carcass bouncing down the stairs or the occasional handrail flying past the window. That left two of us to say: 'Come on, now. Is this any way to carry on?' Better on balance, I think, to turn up the tape player, put a clothes peg over the nose, and pretend to be asleep. Toulouse 300 km. *Mon Dieu!*

Call me unsociable if you like, but I had one overriding ambition by the time we reached journey's end. That was to stay as far away as possible from anyone who even looked as though they might have travelled there by coach. I succeeded until shortly before kick-off time on Sunday – and then I saw them, weaving down the middle of the road, banging on car roofs, leering and leching at the horrified occupants. It was definitely our pals – and yet there was something different about them. Every man-jack of them had a big, round splodge of jam over his nose and much of the rest of his face. You know the way these ideas take hold over breakfast and, well, one in, all in. God help the party-pooper who decided he didn't fancy wandering around all day with wasps circling a head oozing with strawberry mush. So they were all of one mind, all wearing their jam like, to paraphrase Stephen Crane's novel of the American Civil War, a red badge of imbecility. One who vaguely recognised me staggered over, produced a little pot of preserve from his pocket, handed it to me, pointed at the pot, pointed at my nose, and grinned in sheer delight at his own magnanimity. It was a touching moment.

The journey home was more of the same, except that mooning became very fashionable. Even the incontinent man on the Continent had a go. But, as we counted down the kilometres and then the miles back to Wigan, a feeling of euphoria began to creep over me, secure as I was in the knowledge that I was never, ever going to travel like this again. Annual visits to France have had their ups and downs since then, notably the night when the Foreign Legion reduced a bar in Avignon to sawdust; another trip to the same city when the Great Britain captain – I leave you to surmise which one – declined to pay an 800-franc bar bill and told the waiters that I had the money; and the night when the Under-21s walked up the main street along the roofs of parked cars. There was also the night I overdosed on garlic to an extent where I couldn't sleep for three days – they should warn you about that in the guidebooks. By comparison with life on the Vomit Express, however, every moment since has been pure bliss.

As the bus was decanted in Wigan, my man with the jam took me by the shoulder, pointed to his nose (by now encrusted in dried conserve), pointed to mine (its normal jam-free self) and laughed like a maniac.

'Yer team's still crap, but yer can come wi' us next year,' he said, like a man bestowing a rare honour.

But there was to be no next year. Like Alex Murphy and his drop goals, the coach trip from hell succeeded in changing the ground rules. When the advert appeared for the equivalent journey 12 months later, it was quite explicit about one thing. In big, bold type it read: 'Families and couples only. No groups of men.'

It might have added, but didn't: 'No scenes from Dante's *Inferno*. No jam on noses.'

# Kraut-Bashing with Judith Chalmers

## Dave Hadfield

The players of Bolton Rugby League Club knew that there was something radically wrong when they woke on the morning of the match without hangovers. It was not as though they did not deserve to have banging heads and inside-out stomachs. The night before had witnessed a fiendish Teutonic plot to debilitate all of them for the following day. And they had gone along with it enthusiastically, downing copious quantities of Altbier, Kölschbier, Dunkelbier, Rauchbier, Bock, Doppelbock, Weizen, Hefeweizen, and every other *Bier* that Germany had to offer. And yet now, when day dawned, they felt as though they had spent the evening with the World Service and a good paperback. To a man, they fancied a hearty breakfast of black bread, cheese and *Wurst*, followed by a little light training and a match against the prime of German manhood which now held few terrors. Not for the first time in the history of the twentieth century, the home team's plan for European domination had gone badly astray. 'Ze English Schweinhunds, mein Kapitan, zey are sober!'

We were in Bocholt, a pristine little town between the Ruhr and the Dutch border, as guests – indeed, if measured by the litre, honoured guests – of the only Rugby League club in Germany, and the idea that we could be reduced to quivering wrecks in advance of the match was back on the drawing-board. Our hosts had been the victims of their own government's punctiliousness, in the shape of a piece of life-saving legislation called the *Reinheitsgebot*. Under this law, German brewers cannot throw any old crap they like into their beer, only malt, hops and water. To highly trained sportsmen accustomed, because they were of an age to know no better, to the cocktail of chemicals and additives that is British canned beer and the national scandal that is British-brewed 'lager', anything produced in Germany was mother's milk: pure, soothing and health-giving. We greeted the dawn feeling like a million Deutschmarks – which was roughly what it had cost to put us in that condition.

Having said that, it was understandable that Bocholt should try to give us a good and preferably disabling time on the night before they played us. Their previous visitors from England had been a side from Hull, who had treated the whole expedition with absolute seriousness and had approached their match as though it had been a National Cup-tie. The result was a hundred-point winning margin, and several Germans shipped off to hospital. Good fun for the lads from Hull, of course, but hardly likely to advance the cause of Rugby League in Germany very much.

Bolton were – the past tense is required here, I'm afraid – a side of a very different stamp. From its inception, the club had itchy feet. Indeed, our first – and some would say best – season consisted entirely of travelling all over England, playing equally raw teams in unlikely places. I still remember vividly the way the paint peeled in the phone box the time I called home on the way back from Cheltenham, with the glad tidings that I should be back in the bosom of the family by midnight. 'Cheltenham?' came the blistering roar down the wires. 'You told me Chadderton.' I had, it must be admitted, mumbled a bit. That was the day we had to take our own referee with us, picked up in Wigan but unfortunately damaged a little when his hand was slammed in the minibus door at Keele services. We got precious little from him that afternoon.

Cynics used to claim that we put all those miles on the clock because it was so difficult, in our own immediate area, to find someone we could beat. The truth is that we were ablaze with missionary fervour. There have been better teams – between six and eight of them in our division every season, on average – but never one which loved a trip more.

It makes me laugh when I hear the proposals for reducing the game to 11-a-side – or it does until I realise that they might not be joking. What they don't seem to understand is that clubs like Bolton, playing around the corner in places like, well, Chadderton, pioneered this idea long ago. In fact, if Super League was to refine its mathematics still further by insisting on 11-a-side, two of whom must be complete strangers dragged out of the pub on the way, then it would be tapping into the true spirit of the game in the north-west. But matches scheduled for the other end of the country, or outside the country, were a different matter altogether. Suddenly, we had more players than we knew what to do with. Players not seen since the last major outing would reappear as if by magic, as reliable an indicator of what was in the offing as the first swallow of summer or the first screening of *Wish You Were Here* or *The Holiday Show*. There was one part-timer who would vanish – injured, unavailable, married, hung up boots? – for months at a time. But come the mere mention of a jaunt beyond the M62 corridor, and there he would be at training, his distinctive crinkled perm matted with sweat as he strove to show how indispensable he was to the enterprise. And we would say to each other: 'Hello. We must be going somewhere.' I think of him as the Judith Chalmers of Rugby League.

One way and another, we were the ideal club for the German job: good value socially, and unlikely to cause embarrassment by stomping all over the opposition. Nonetheless, we still had to have a little 'England expects' pep talk from BARLA's main man, Maurice Oldroyd. The only thing he had never fathomed about us was why we refused to have the word 'Amateur' in our title. That was the only argument I ever won with him: you don't boast about not being good enough to get paid. And we were not good enough to be paid by anyone, although we did once acquire the services of a prop who had played for Trafford Borough and, on the other hand, lose a player to Chorley's 'A' team – never to be heard of again.

As tourists, though, we were world class. With three times the number of players we could normally scrape together for a match at Leigh, plus assorted camp-followers, we filled a coach where three cars were usually more than adequate. Any space remaining was packed with cartons of cash-and-carry beer, and we were on our way.

Now I already had a soft spot for Germany. Discounting a brief transit through Belgium, it was the first foreign country I had ever been to as an impressionable 16-year-old spending six weeks with his pen-friend. She had turned out to be an exceptionally fun-loving *Fräulein* whose family owned a vineyard, so that first venture abroad was an eye-opener in several respects. Not the least of those revelations was that you rarely find what you expect when you meet people on their home turf. I had been brought up to have certain preconceptions regarding the Germans, but on the Mosel – a wine-growing tributary of the Rhine – there was nothing dour or industrious about them. Life on the Mosel seemed to me to consist of drinking a lot of beer while waiting for the grapes to ripen sufficiently for you to make the wine. It didn't alter the opinion of my grandma, who thought I shouldn't have gone at all, not after they had bombed her street. Subsequent visits to Munich helped to confirm my view, though, that Germany was pretty much a knockabout, fun sort of place.

My last taste of Germany before Bolton's adventure, however, had been a rather different matter, with a strange Rugby League twist at the end of it. I was sent to cover NATO manoeuvres on the north German plain, which proved to be one of the most uncomfortable weeks of my life. There was an opportunity to make a brief escape from the barracks in Paderborn, which happens to be Bolton's twin town, but it was frowned on because we were supposed to be pretending that the Russians were out there, no doubt with snow on their boots. Just for a couple of hours, though, I decided I wasn't playing. Instead, I discovered that Paderborn had a *Boltonstrasse*, complete with a *Bolton Bar und Grill* – and very welcoming it was, too. But the rest of the week consisted of crapping in woods and sleeping in trenches, leaving me not only with a suspicion that, if it came to saving Western civilisation, we might be better off with Bolton Rugby League Club as our first bulwark; but also somewhat bedraggled.

The officers' quarters at Sennelager represented sybaritic luxury by comparison and, when a batman came with the message that the Earl of Derby would like me to join him for dinner, I knew it was not going to be baked beans out of a mess-tin. The Earl and I had one thing in common because, apart from his being commander-in-chief of the regiment, he was also, far more importantly, the president of the Rugby Football League. It was surely the first time in that setting that military tactics took a poor second place in the conversation to the question of what on earth should be done about the scrums. His Lordship favoured the referee feeding them, but he was getting on a bit by then.

Nothing against Lord Derby, whose death in 1995 deprived Rugby League of a good friend; but my own aristocracy, could I create one, would consist of those people in various unpromising parts of the world who have broken their backs and often their bank balances in trying to carve out a niche for the game. Arise, Count

Mario of Majone. Arise, Sir Michael Mayer. And arise also, Stefan Nienhaus. Stefan was typical of many League pioneers in that he had fastened on to the game by pure chance – some Australian matches on an obscure German cable channel – and had immersed himself in messianic zeal. Against all probability, he had put together a team comprising a number of sports enthusiasts who used the same gym, plus a few local students who would give anything a go. There was no Rugby League background there at all, and precious little exposure to Union either – always a good thing, in my experience – but plenty of willingness to learn.

And they knew how to promote a match. There was hardly a shop window, and certainly not a licensed establishment – we know, because we checked – without a poster announcing the Bocholt Eagles' clash with the champion side from England. What had Maurice Oldroyd been telling them about us? The match venue could also have been a mite off-putting to men of less moral fibre. It was a proper stadium, with a stand and a running track. It was flat, covered with grass, and correctly marked out. To a club accustomed to playing on what had been, and still smelled like, a pig farm, it looked like Wembley.

The combination of all this and a night on the *Bier* should have been enough to render us wobbly-legged on match-day. But, as I think I mentioned, the effect of large amounts of German refreshment on the human body is simply to cleanse the system. There were men among the 13 players and nine or ten substitutes who felt better than they had for years. So, in front of what could without exaggeration be termed a crowd, we set about our task with gusto. One difference from our normal experience was immediately apparent: uninhibited by any macho code of silence, when you hurt them, they yelled. In fact, they sounded like cartoon-strip squareheads struck by Captain Hurricane's cricket bat. They went 'Aaaaaargh' and 'Yeeooowk'. After playing in a league where you could drive a stake through your opponent's heart and stir only a muffled grunt or a contemptuous 'Is that the best tha can do, grandad?', this was hugely gratifying. It took us all our restraint not to enter into the spirit of the thing by shouting: 'Take that, *Sauerkraut*-eater!'

Apart from this inability to maintain a stiff upper lip, their other problem was with the rules, especially around the scrums. It was fortunate, therefore, that we had a distinguished and bilingual referee in the shape of Fred Lindop. Now Fred, throughout his memorable career with the whistle, has always been an active supporter of the game's development. This and the fact that he claimed to be fluent in German made him the ideal man to officiate on such an occasion, although it transpired that he was in fact a graduate of the Captain Hurricane school of European languages. 'I'm going to have to have a word with them,' he said, as the Bocholt scrum-half stood transfixed with the ball in his hands, looking into the tunnel between the two packs and wondering where to insert it. 'Eh oop! Fritz! Putten ze ball in ze scrum!' It perhaps loses something in translation, but Fritz got the general idea.

By this stage, Bolton had built up a comfortable lead, and Fred had a message for us that required no interpretation: 'About time you gave them one or two.' We were, after all, meant to be on a diplomatic mission, not an ego trip designed to demoralise our hosts. And so it was that members of the Bolton side seized the opportunity to display histrionic skills which had hitherto lain dormant, throwing out extravagant balls which begged to be intercepted. The temptation was there to ham it up, and it was not resisted. I say, old chap, rather a careless pass. I know, skipper, I feel an absolute mug. If Bocholt cottoned on to what was going on they gave no sign of it, and the result was a nice, face-saving 50–30 or thereabouts – a scoreline which was far more unusual then than it is now.

Naturally enough, Bocholt provided enough goulash and beer to satiate a small army, after which some members of both sides felt so terrific that they just had to take part in a series of races around the running track. Even when we were poured back on to our coach at midnight, we were in the very best of health and spirits, swearing undying friendship – or something rather stronger in the case of one or two of the lads who had, like me 20-odd years earlier, been doing their bit for Anglo-German understanding – and promising to return for a second match in the series. It never happened. Within a few months, Bocholt had run out of opponents willing to make the trip from England and had succumbed to the blandishments of the nearest little pocket of Rugby Union activity, which held out the promise of regular fixtures. *Gott im Himmel!* They should have got in touch with us. We would have gone back every weekend. Several of us would have been prepared to live there permanently.

But that was all in the future. We travelled home full of the euphoria of having done our share for the cause of international expansion, and feeling well capable of playing another match in

Holland in the early hours of the morning if required. ('I think I know why that lot thought they could take over the world,' said Judith Chalmers.) Some of us felt so good, even after getting stuck into the remains of the beer we had brought with us, that when we got back to Bolton we went to watch Wigan play Hull.

This was a mistake, at least for me, because I did something I generally try to avoid doing when I dozed off in the press box during the second half.

And when I woke up, I had a hangover.

# HOLLAND

# Very Flat

## Trevor Gibbons

As a travel destination Holland has two principal qualities: it is very flat, and it is very near. The Netherlands are hardly the glittering jewel in the crown of Rugby League adventuring if exotic experiences are what you want, lacking as they do the inspiration of Australia, the colour of Papua New Guinea, and the adrenalin rush of a vibrant South African township. Thrills are at a premium there.

Travel not only broadens the mind, it awakens the appetite. But Holland leaves the bon viveur wondering what he can do in the face of a nationality whose major culinary achievement is to cover chips liberally in mayonnaise. Voyagers stepping off the boat on to Dutch soil after the overnight sailing from Hull might be excused for thinking they had journeyed, but not arrived. Meanwhile, the Dutch speak the English language better than many a native, which reduces the opportunities for bellowing loudly in our own tongue in an effort to feel superior. The detachment is increased when you realise that the entire output of the BBC is available on Dutch TV screens: how can this be abroad when the soothing tones of Auntie are so readily available?

All, however, is not as it seems. The Dutch are different; they just do not show it on the surface. They are so laid-back, they have more phlegm than the Belgians. Steady would be the word. But, as a race, they should be treated with caution because, by and large, they have not come under the civilising influence of 'The Greatest Game of All' – although once upon a time they did play Rugby League, in a forest clearing in the magical land of Papendrecht.

How did they come to see the light? As oft before in Anglo-Dutch relations, it was links between Hull and Holland which got this particular (rugby) ball rolling. For centuries there has been warfare and commerce between the two sets of seafarers across the North Sea. The effects of that interchange have been profound in Hull, whose people are soul-mates with the Dutch, in that theirs is a city clinging to the water at the edge of a flat coastal plain. Before the Humber Bridge was built, generations of Hullensians crossing the river alighted from the ferry at a place named, after the landscape, New Holland. There was extensive market-gardening in the area (the Rozenbroek family being leading local exponents), and the local vet was named Doutre. Still not convinced of the myriad links? Well, the bobbers on Hull's Fish Dock used to wear clogs. QED.

Among the exports which went the other way from Hull, however, Rugby League was conspicuous by its absence. In that instance at least, this is not the story of two maritime nations. We can instead narrow it down to one dogged Dutchman – Hans Modderman.

Hans arrived from his native country to work in Hull in 1974 and stayed for two years. He discovered Rugby League by playing for local team Ace Amateurs, and returned to Holland wanting to take his new passion back with him. That is how I personally learnt of Modderman. He was the crazy Dutchman who had *Open Rugby* and match programmes sent over the water to him by my father.

It was not until 1988, however, that the game in all its glory trundled into Holland. Hull University was the pioneer team who played the first Rugby League match on Dutch soil, and I was right in the middle of it – literally – being loosely described as the referee. At the end of that Saturday in March, Hull University had beaten Drechtstreek 46–32 at Papendrecht. 'Niets Dan Loft' screamed a massive headline in the local paper, and League was away.

Papendrecht stands on one side of the broad River Merwede, Dordrecht on the other. The town of Dordrecht is reputed to be the oldest in Holland, and a trip there will show classic architecture to convince you of that claim. Its narrow, many-storeyed buildings gaze across the river at the hamlet of Papendrecht, which is a quiet settlement not unlike a thousand other locales of similar size in Holland. Neat, red-brick streets are marshalled by 'sleeping policemen' and complemented by an extensive network of cycle-ways. Stout black bicycles are pedalled across numerous courses of water by way of low, sturdy wooden bridges. All is tidy, practical and well maintained. Yet behind this façade of normality, for a while in the late 1980s, revolution was fermenting. For a few heady, seditious months, Papendrecht was the epicentre of Dutch Rugby League.

At the end of a deceptively unassuming track outside the town lay the headquarters of Drechtstreek Rugby Club, the nerve-centre of the operation. A modest wooden structure, it looked like a cross between a barrack block and a Boy Scout meeting-place – although that second evocation was blown as soon as one realised that there was a fully stocked bar running the width of the room. Outside, the rugby pitch was surrounded by woodland; here, in a sleepy Dutch glade, was the European beachhead for League.

After the initial foray by the students, nirvana was reached one weekend in 1989. For that short time, Rome stood aside; no doubt about it, all roads led to Papendrecht. Holland was the proud host of the '1th [sic] International Rugby League Tournament'. That is how the extravaganza was rather quaintly billed on the souvenir T-shirts, while alongside that proud legend were emblazoned the national flags of Holland, France and Great Britain, so establishing the scope of this tournament. From Paris came Lisses and Montgeron, two teams who competed in France's National Division Three. Playing in Holland represented a relatively short away journey for them, faced as they usually were with the epic trek to fulfil fixtures in the south-western heartland of their own country. England provided four teams, half of the total dramatis personae. The capital was represented by Hornsey Lambs, while the short drive up the M1 brought along with them Hemel Hempstead; the northern-based entrants were Irlam Town and Atherton. Local interest focused on the two home-grown participants: Drechtstreek flew the Dutch version of the red, white and blue (though they played in Leeds's amber and yellow), but the real colour was provided by the Pink Panthers of Papendrecht.

The Panthers really did play in baby-pink shirts, the first – and quite possibly the last – team I have seen to do so. They also did much to sum up the spirit of the whole venture, when their novice Dutch players were joined by a party of Germans eager to try their hand at League. These last had been roped into the escapade through the work of Tas Baitieri, who was then Rugby League's European development officer. Tas (an Australian with Italian roots living in France) brought his own assortment of cultural baggage with him and threw his expertise on the playing field, as a former prop forward with Penrith and Canterbury-Bankstown, behind the motley crew. The tournament had also attracted the usual pilgrimage of pioneer League people, among whom was Calvin Wilkes. Born in the Caribbean, in addition to numerous amateur sides Wilkes had played for Leeds, Bramley, Doncaster, Keighley and even Southend Invicta. So nobody was in the least bit surprised when he arrived to lend a hand to the Panthers' cause. Baitieri and Wilkes: verily, the twin peaks of streetwise Rugby League know-how.

Twin peaks maybe, but even director David Lynch could not have manufactured the general suspension of disbelief which was in the air over the weekend. On the field the prize was contested in the only way League can be – for real. Off-field there prevailed a kind of alternative reality which began with the pre-tournament social event, which was held for all the teams and supporters at a local bar. Nothing unusual in that, you might think, except that it happened to be next door to the municipal swimming-pool. And, this being Holland, the subtle quirk was a connecting door between the two venues which was set in a plate-glass wall. People were encouraged to make dual use of the facilities, and it therefore seemed entirely reasonable to find a prop forward, clad only in swimming trunks, dispatching a litre of Oranjeboom as he dripped gently at the bar. How's that for a dress code? There were, of course, some rules to maintain standards: no beer in the pool, for one . . .

Game-day dawned at the scout hut, with several people claiming swimming-induced hangovers. Perhaps it was the alcohol which had seen off a few million brain cells the night before but, for once, the admirable Dutch mastery of English slipped slightly. 'How are you tomorrow?' boomed an affable Dutchman to a bemused Englishman. If only we could all answer that question, life would be much simpler.

Out in the clearing, order was restored to this topsy-turvy universe as Drechtstreek and the Pink Panthers played off to decide seventh and eighth places in the rankings. The final saw victory for Hemel Hempstead, the record books solemnly declaring a 34–2 win over Atherton. Don't tell the players, but nobody had really been counting . . . The toasts afterwards were all to the success of Dutch Rugby League. A minute pinprick had been made on the surface of Holland's obsession with soccer.

For a while after that, things looked promising. A Dutch Students' team was raised which came to this country to do battle in the Student Rugby League World Cup in York later that year. They certainly looked the part, dazzling the crowds with their orange shirts and the quality of their play, and they became a leitmotif for the whole tournament. It was the pinnacle of achievement for Dutch Rugby League. So what happened?

Like many voluntary League gospel-spreaders, Hans Modderman found that the twin demands of launching a foreign game and doing a full-time job were irreconcilable. Help aplenty there had been from England but, in the end, it was no substitute for a Dutch-based development campaign. Looking back, those halcyon days for an embryonic organisation were but a small window of opportunity. Before Drechtstreek, that window had been bolted firmly shut by Union bigotry; now, in the 1990s, Rugby Union – such as it is in Holland – can openly advertise and pay for its wares, and so the window is shuttered. As for Hans, having suffered the tribulations of organising the famous tournament, he then underwent the trials of a dislocated shoulder during it. Now he has retired from all things rugby, but he still dreams.

The last hurrah for League we now know came across the river in Dordrecht, when a London Crusaders (as was) team played the Koalas (a team of Australians resident in France). It was shown on local TV, and this time Modderman took the safer option of commentating for the station. Somehow he had fitted that duty into the '1th Tournament' too.

Talking of TV, if you want to remember the weekend the tournament took place, think only of Joe Lydon. It was the day when, in the semi-final of the Challenge Cup at Maine Road, Manchester, Joe helped Wigan on their way against Warrington with a mammoth 60-yard drop goal, the likes of which had not been seen for many a year. That shot and the rest of the match were broadcast via the BBC over the North Sea to an unmoved country. Unmoved except in Papendrecht, where the recording was eagerly devoured. Holland: so near, yet so far.

Although they do play another 'English' game in Dordrecht in the form of cricket, the clearing in the woods no longer echoes to the cries of 'gerremonside' from our own peculiar sport. The experiment is over; Europe's most benign and well-adjusted populace is safe from a frenzied debate on the death of 'real' hookers – but it was a close shave. Throughout it all, though, one thing has remained the same: Holland is very flat.

IRELAND

# Forty Shades of Blue

## Dave Hadfield

It was my latest fix of Irish music – the latest of many – and your man with the bouzouki said it perfectly. At least, I thought it was a bouzouki. It turns out to have been a mandocello, but that's another story. Whatever the precise nature of his stringed instrument, he struck a chord. He was apologising for his rather bedraggled and bleary-eyed condition: he had, he explained, just arrived from Dublin. It had been a late night, playing and drinking there, followed by an early morning. 'And sure, you know the way of it well enough yourselves.'

Sympathetic nods and chuckles all round. We knew the way of it well enough – though it's strange that what is a short hop between two neighbouring countries should be so immediately recognisable as a disorientating, even pleasantly debilitating experience. Men go to the moon and back and arrive in a better state.

It has more to do with circumstances than with distance. You are almost invariably saying goodbye to someone or meeting someone at the other end, sometimes both. The greeting and the leave-taking always involve a few glasses of something, late at night or early in the morning. Sure, you know the way of it – and that had certainly been the way of it the first time I had gone across the sea to Ireland.

It was on a ferry from Liverpool, on which any resolution to rest or repose was rescinded by the presence of the All-Ireland Ladies' Tug of War team, returning in triumph from some festival of hemp-hauling in Europe. All the way from the Mersey to Dublin, they demonstrated their prowess by taking on all-comers, their rope threaded through bars, cafeterias, the duty-free shop and the purser's office as they took up the slack and dragged relays of sweating, guffawing passengers from one end of the boat to the other.

A few hours later, on Custom House Quay on the banks of the Liffey, a few of us vanquished found ourselves pulled into a pub that was packed to the gunnels at 7.30 in the morning. 'Now would you just have come off the boat from Liverpool?' asked the barman. 'But you'd be more from the Manchester end of things, if I'm not mistaken. Do you, by any chance, get yourself down to Old Trafford at all?'

He was part of a massive Dublin exodus who get themselves on to the ferry and down to Old Trafford and, to a lesser extent, Anfield and Goodison, every other week. By contrast, your man Brian Corrigan was part of what they might call in Ireland the minority tradition. A minority of one, in fact, in that he used to get on the ferry of a weekend and make for Wigan, Widnes, St Helens or Warrington to watch Rugby League. In the accidental way of these things, it was Saturday-afternoon TV and a workmate from Hull that got Corrigan on board. 'He told me about this other kind of rugby, where the ball was in play a lot more and, after that, it was masochism that had me hooked.' We all know the way of that.

Years down the road, and despite a uniquely Irish situation in which three other rival codes of football were already clamouring for attention, Corrigan had succeeded in reviving Rugby League in Dublin. I say reviving because the 1950s and 1960s saw numerous exhibition games involving English teams. The late, lamented Roy Evans used to tell me about one such he had played in for Wigan. The celebrated Irish athlete Ron Delaney was attempting a world mile record on the track around the rugby pitch at the same time as the match, but the fight that broke out stopped not only the game but the race as well. For Rugby League in Ireland, Corrigan started the race up again, first with the Irish Students side in 1989, and then with the formation of a club, the Dublin Blues.

Now the very mention of a club in a far-flung corner of the Rugby League universe, a club looking for visiting sides to travel out there to play them, will have alerted you to the imminent appearance in this narrative of the Travelling Wilburys of the code, Bolton. This, I promise you, will be the last such account I write, because it was the last such journey we made; the club is now, all too literally, going nowhere. Back in 1993, though, we could still raise a team in the North-West Counties, and could still fill trains and boats and planes if there was a chance of getting out of those counties.

Thus it was that the night ferry from Holyhead to Dún Laoghaire was full of sporting types who, if not quite as muscular as the All-Ireland Ladies' Tug of War team, were giving the Guinness an equal degree of welly. I have to say, in all modesty, that the organisation for our trip was impeccable: a restful night on the ferry, rocked gently by the friendly waters of the Irish Sea, followed by an early-morning arrival in Dublin, where crisp linen sheets would be folded back in readiness at our hotel, just nice for several hours' deep and dreamless sleep in preparation for the match in the afternoon. The club, I reflected, was indeed fortunate to have a course and distance man such as myself making the arrangements. Someone who had heard Paddy Keenan play the uillean pipes in the upstairs room of a pub just off O'Connell Street, and Barney McKenna the banjo in the only room of one on the west coast; who had immersed himself in Brendan Behan, J.P. Donleavy, Flann O'Brien, and even some of the easier bits of James Joyce, and could point out which corner of which bar each had used for his serious drinking. As one imbued with the culture of the place, all the way across I was able to give inspiring little tutorials on what was to be expected.

'I'll say one thing about Dublin,' said one of my pupils as our coach pulled into the city in the early-morning light. 'It's got the best-dressed drunks I've seen in my bloody life.'

And, sure enough, there were few bus shelters or shop doorways that morn which were not piled two or three deep with young men in full evening dress and young women in ballgowns, blissfully and picturesquely sozzled and spent. It was the aftermath of the Trinity College May Ball we were witnessing and, just to mop up any stragglers still left standing, the cafés on Grafton Street, Nassau Street and thereabout were serving champagne breakfasts. Not many dinner jackets or full-length dresses in our party, but it seemed a good idea all the same.

As for that deep and dreamless sleep, there was a good deal of it going on in those doorways and bus shelters, and more to follow on the floor of the public bar at our hotel. There was, you see, a small problem with our rooms. There were people in them – people who, though perhaps not quite in a May Ball state of suspended animation, nonetheless had a good few hours' sleep left in them yet. But we were welcome to make ourselves comfortable in the bar until the rooms were ready. Comfortable, in this context, meant flat out, snoring, and oblivious to the opening of that bar a couple of hours later. In the imperturbable way of the Dublin drinking man, the first customers of the day merely strode over the comatose bodies. The nearest thing to an expression of surprise might have been a mild remark to the effect that it had clearly been a heavy night in here last night.

Time between those linen sheets varied between a couple of hours for the lucky ones to around ten minutes in some sadder cases, before Corrigan and his men rousted us out. Now it is almost compulsory in these matters that there should be late changes of plan and venue, and here was no exception. The original scheme had been for us to play on the prestigious sports grounds of University College, where the Rugby Union types had finished with the pitches come Easter. After that, the Dublin Blues were welcome to do their thing there, which was all very friendly and democratic and Irish of them – until they changed their minds. Reseeding, you know – which ranks pretty high in the list of cockamamie excuses traditionally used to prevent a person getting a pitch to play on or, indeed, a pot to piss in. Anyway, a pox on the college. I hope people go home sober from their next ball.

So we had the usual business (see Venice, for instance) of having to go miles out of town to find a plot of earth, a humble sod to call our own. Almost into County Wicklow, in fact, to a Christian Brothers college with a Gaelic football pitch doing nothing much that afternoon. There's actually a bit of a historical irony there because, apart from your Rugby Union men, your Gaelic games fellows would be the only ones in the world who have tried to impose a ban on the playing of another sport. In the case of the Gaelic Athletic Association, the prohibition extended to just about everything other than Gaelic football and hurling. You could not only get banned for dabbling in soccer or (tee-hee) Rugby Union, but it was widely presumed that you might go to hell as well. There's a good display about all this in the bar of the Irish Heritage Centre in Manchester – where they also have some pretty good music from time to time. So, you can see, there has been no stone left unturned in the name of research.

When we lobbed up on the doorstep of the Brothers, however, the problem with using Gaelic facilities was not so much ideological as spatial. We had played on a Gaelic football pitch before – in Bolton, in fact, when the council had forgotten to put up the posts or mow the meadow on our own acres. We had no happy memories of it, as it had been enormous – bearing out Brian Corrigan's contention that Gaelic footballers are excellent potential League fodder, simply because they have to be so fit, as well as slightly mad. Now, too, this great swathe of Irish pasture was not a welcome sight. It was not quite big enough to encompass all 40 shades of green; but there were, by my count, 37 of them, plus what looked like a herd of Kerrygold cows grazing contentedly in one corner. It looked as big as a golf course at a time when we, frayed around the edges as we were, would have preferred something more the size of a tennis court.

In spite of all that, we won. And we won in the best possible way, with a try in the very last minute. By that stage, though, I had already decided that, despite having bought a new pair of green boots for the occasion, I had played my last match. My last part-match, to be precise; I gave the sporting public of Ireland a 25-minute exhibition of why this decision was overdue, before handing over to somebody even bigger, slower, lazier, and 20-odd years younger. The rest of the afternoon I spent motivating my replacement with the threat that, unless he got his finger out and kept it out, he was going to suffer the humiliation of being replaced himself by an old fart twice his age. It worked, although I think I was perhaps guilty of 'over-motivation': he played himself to such a standstill that we never saw him again.

It almost amounts to racial stereotyping to say that our hosts lived up to expectations in the après-match department. Not for them the tatty little pub around the ring road; they had an arrangement with a converted hunting lodge whereby everyone got a four-course meal and all the stout they could drink. Most impressive of all, though, was the fact that the Blues had their own 'Rugby League Nuts' – those little painted figurines which enjoyed something of a collectors' vogue a few years ago, until people realised that they broke into a myriad pieces if they got knocked over. An authentic touch, that, in the case of some teams I could mention, but not a great selling point. That the Dublin Blues had commissioned their own batch – one of them now stands in two separate and precariously balanced pieces on my son's bedroom shelf – struck me at the time as proof that the game in Ireland was going big-time. I saw no 'Hurling Nuts', at any rate.

The average North-West Counties match is not followed by the two sides going on a pub crawl together. Somehow, that prospect in Higginshaw or Hindley seems less than irresistible. Dublin, however, is a rather different matter and, I need hardly tell you, all our fellows were eager to visit the various literary shrines and historic sites about which I had waxed lyrical. But in

O'Donoughue's, where a middleman climbs a step-ladder on to the bar to hand out the pints above the heads of the crowd, I got stranded, trapped in an angle between the Guinness pumps and the fiddlers, with no hope of escape.

It was only after a couple of hours without the benefit of any observations on the sociable habits of Flann O'Brien or the early days of the Bothy Band that my absence from the main body of the crawl was noticed. Not to worry about him, says your stand-off, who knows of my whereabouts; he's in Hadfield Heaven.

The following morning, as we're passing the same O'Donoughue's, whiling away those few awkward hours between breakfast and Sunday opening time, there's a stage-whispered 'Pssst!' from down the adjacent alley. 'Youse after coming in, lads?' Now here's special treatment for you, and a sure sign of a favourable impression created the night before: to be the only dry-throated band of men with time on their hands to be invited into this famous watering-hole at this scandalously early hour of a Sunday morning. Down the alley, through the door, and into a bar that is still as packed as it was the previous evening. Same fiddlers, same pint-passer up on the bar, same crowd, same *craic*.

In a calmer moment that afternoon, down the road in Toner's, a couple of us get chatting with an old fellow up from the country who used to be the Irish scout for Everton. 'Rugby League is it now, lads? Well, good on youse, there's a proper game.' Locked in with us during the holy hour, he says that Toner's hasn't changed much, not since he was last in, anyway. That was in 1951.

Rugby League in Ireland has been a small but significant success story, for which Bolton claim no credit at all. Matches against the USA in Washington, runners-up in the 1995 Emerging Nations World Cup, a Charity Shield at the Royal Dublin Showgrounds: it adds up to remarkable progress since the Blues were beginning their pioneering work three years ago. Sure, we knew it all along. Players from Hitro O'Kesene to Martin O'Ffiah are discovering their Irish roots. A Dublin team will be fast-tracked into Super League at some stage, not a doubt about it. My lad's Dublin Blues Rugby League 'Nut' (slightly distressed) will be worth a fortune. People will ask us what it was like to be there at the birth of it all, and we will say . . . well, there was this bloody huge field and a bar with a man stood on it. And sure, you know the way of it well enough yourselves.

ITALY

# Venice Visited

## Harry Edgar

'*Prego . . . prego . . .* ah, Mario? *. . . prego . . .*' Bob Brown's heavily Australian-accented words revealed a surprisingly impressive knowledge of the Italian language and could be heard, along with his subsequent sigh of relief, loud and clear outside the phone booth.

Bob was having to shout to make himself understood above the noise of a chaotic throng of bedenimed and rucksacked American girls, who were easily recognisable by their perfect dentistry and wide hips, and the ever-present accompanying gaggle of Italian boys who were eager to welcome them to their city of Venezia. But when, eventually, he heard the reply '*Prego . . . si,* this is Mario . . .' down the phone, a look of enormous salvation came over Bob's face, and he turned with a grin to give me and Joe the thumbs-up, everything's-gonna-be-okay sign.

Yes, we were in the right place. This was Venice, and we were here on a mission to discover just whatever did happen to Italian Rugby League. It was July 1981. Joe was Joe Chamberlain, whom I'd first met when he played full-back for Rochdale Hornets, and who later made some kind of history when he player-coached and inspired the Racing Club of Albi to win the French Cup in 1974. Joe was a pioneer, keen to do something for the game he loved, and a real Europhile – although this didn't always come easy for a boy from Warrington. Joe told me he had lived in France for a whole year and ate nothing but bread and chicken, and would rather dive into a river full of alligators than take a sip of red wine.

Despite all this, and the fact that he was on his way to becoming

71

a first-grade touch judge (I tried to talk him out of it!), Joe and I got on famously. We smiled at each other, and at the American girls, as Bob Brown, our leader on this expedition, bundled his perspiring frame out of the phone booth and instructed us to follow him to the jetty, where we joined another throng to queue for the boat which was to take us to meet our man Mario Majone.

All the trendy tourist guides say that the way to arrive in Venice for the first time is either to fly into Marco Polo Airport, or to step off the Orient Express straight into a water taxi. In our case, however, we had to take the ferry, having first driven across a long, narrow causeway, and so our initial impression of the approach to the famous water city was of a giant parking-lot.

But, once on board the ferry, that's when it really hit me. Venice: I'd heard a lot about it and, for 20 years, I'd stared at the Canaletto prints of the place hanging in my mother's house. But now it was actually here, coming to life in front of me. Joe and I had that glazed look of wonderment on our faces, like kids in a dreamland, as we rode majestically into the Grand Canal.

As we glided towards St Mark's Square, everything looked familiar, just as it was depicted centuries ago in the paintings. Only the sounds were different, I guessed. Back then there would have been dogs barking (check out any Canaletto, and you'll see he always managed to slip in a few Venetian mutts in his quest for realism) and the swish of sail-boats. Now those had been replaced by the purring of outboard motors, the endless flicking of phrase-book pages, and the clicking of several thousand Nikons.

The scramble to disembark began as soon as the boat conductor shouted: '*Prego . . . Place San Marrrrrrco.*' Mario stood there on the pier, just as any League fan might welcome a guest on the platform at Wigan Wallgate, beaming from ear to ear. For him a 15-year wait was over: at last he had made contact again with Rugby League. 'The cavalry has arrived,' I remarked to Joe. 'More like the three bloody musketeers,' growled Bob as he clasped Mario's outstretched hand.

Mario Majone had played for Venice in the last Rugby League games to have featured Italian teams. It was the 1965–66 season, and Venice had been joined by Padua and Casale in contesting regular matches against French clubs. He had also played in England in the early 1960s for Blackpool Amateurs, and spoke with pride about the strength of the team in which he was a dashing young second-rower. Mario had been in Lancashire as an English language student, earning his living (surprise, surprise) in the catering industry. Now he was running a successful screen-printing business from an office plum in the middle of Venice. 'The new headquarters of the Italian Rugby League,' he joked, while looking deadly serious.

Mario's dream was to relaunch the League game in Italy. There were others, he said, who retained a similar love for Rugby League, more than 20 years after Keith Barnes's Kangaroo touring team had played two internationals against Italy. We looked over the programmes for those matches played in Padua and Treviso, and Mario pointed out some familiar names in the home team. One was Ferdi Sarterato who, as Ferdi Corsi, had gone on to play for Rochdale Hornets. Another was Antonio Danielli, better known to English ears as Tony Rossi, who had toured this country with the Padua (Padova) Rugby League team in the late 1950s, scored a try against Wigan at Central Park and done cartwheels in celebration. He was then invited back to play for Wigan and eventually made a good first-teamer at Blackpool Borough.

'I don't know whatever happened to Tony,' sighed a momentarily melancholy Mario. 'Perhaps he's still in England.' After this trip I returned home and wrote a story in *Open Rugby* magazine headed 'Antonio Danielli, where are you?'. Would you believe it, a few days later, Reg Parker rang up to tell me this League legend was now the catering manager at Luton Airport! I kid you not.

Another name I recognised was that of Angelo Gerardi. He played in both those Tests against Australia in 1960 – 'a tough scrum-half and clever tactician' was how Mario Majone described him – and later became a leading member of the old Italian committee for *Rugby Tredici*. Now a very prominent businessman, his passion for the game still burned strong, and he was a key figure for Mario's hopes of getting something up and running again in Venice.

Both men still smarted at the bitter memories of how Rugby League had been allowed to die in Italy back in the 1960s. At that time there were over 40 clubs playing in three divisions, after the Rugby Football League had invested money in and provided coaching assistance for the Italian venture. The grants eventually ceased from Britain in the expectation that League, having proved itself over several years of competition, would be embraced and supported by the Italian Government's equivalent of the Sports Council. But, when the time for official recognition grew near, the old Achilles heel of Rugby League development reared its ugly head yet again – the Rugby Union stepped in. Pressure was brought to bear on the Italian Sports Council by influential Union sympathisers; when the League was denied acceptance by the authorities, it meant their players could no longer receive insurance cover.

It came as a body-blow for the game. Mario reflected, 'We could never understand why nobody from the British Rugby League ever came to Italy to find out what had gone wrong. They had supported us with money, and then the game just fizzled out almost overnight. Nobody from England ever contacted us to find out why. It was amazing. If somebody had come from England at that time, the Italian League could have been rescued. At least half of the 40 clubs had people who were willing to carry on, if only we could have had some encouragement. We needed to know that our struggle on behalf of the game was being supported. But nobody ever came.'

Joe and I reckoned that it was time for Mario to get upbeat; that the past was over, and something new needed to happen. So we headed back to Bob Brown's trusty (that said trusty, not rusty) Fiat – when in Rome, etc. – and crossed back over the causeway into real Italy in search of some of the old League players who, Mario claimed, were still around.

Mario did not drive. Nobody in Venice drove in these pre-Mondeo days. He navigated, however, hardly able to contain his excitement as we motored to Treviso, Padua and Casale to meet, in pure-chance, spur-of-the-moment calls, a whole batch of characters who had been involved in Rugby League back in the 1960s. They were now middle-aged men whom Mario had not seen for almost 20 years, but all exploded with emotion at this sudden and unexpected opportunity to talk again about the game they had been forced to give up in their youth.

All were currently engaged as officials of Rugby Union clubs. In one clubhouse we were shown a photograph of a 'Veterans' XV', and Mario identified no fewer than 11 men who had played Rugby League back in the old days.

The enthusiasm we encountered for League on that brief tour inspired Mario Majone and Angelo Gerardi to press ahead with plans for an exhibition game in Italy. In December 1981 they travelled to Marseille to meet officials at the France v Great Britain Test match at the Vélodrome, and got the go-ahead for a game between the two nations that would take place the following July, in Venice.

And so it came to pass that Bob Brown and I found ourselves in the same Fiat, 12 months down the track, this time without Joe, and heading back to north-east Italy. We took the same route, staying overnight in Munich to drink beer and eat lots of pork fat and suet-dumpling cannonballs – like you do in Munich – and arrived in the water city, this time not on a romantic journey in search of long-lost links, but instead to roll up our sleeves and get a game organised.

Mario had agreed to pay the travel and hotel costs for one night for two parties of 20 people each from the British and French Leagues. The British thought, wisely, that they should have their players arrive in Venice at least one day before the game, and were happy to cover the extra expense themselves. They were particularly eager for match practice as they prepared for the 1982 Test series against Australia. History suggests, however, that even building a dam across Venice's Grand Canal would not have stopped the Aussie tidal wave which was about to be unleashed.

Anyone who just happened to walk into Venice's Sant' Elena Stadium shortly before 8.45 p.m. on Saturday, 31 July 1982, would have been reasonably impressed. The majority of those who did so were young Italians who enjoyed the easy-going atmosphere and the music. I had taken the job of being in charge of the loudspeaker system at the stadium because, well, there was nobody else around to do it. Meanwhile, Bob was the gateman, collecting tickets, employed under much the same principle. Nobody except us knew the dramas we had gone through in the weeks, days, hours, even minutes leading up to the kick-off.

The problem in a nutshell was that Mario Majone had been doing everything alone and, already, the strain was beginning to show. We spent three days getting nowhere fast, shuttling back and forth between newspaper offices and television stations trying to whip up publicity for a match which was being billed as the European Championship decider. Being thrown out of an Italian media building is pretty much like being thrown out of any building anywhere else in the world – except that I don't think the various uniform-clad commissionaires appreciated my parting shot of 'What makes a Venetian blind?'. But this was work which should have been done weeks before; Mario just hadn't had the manpower to do it.

Then, on the Thursday, the day when the British team were due to fly in, some breaks started to come our way. Part of an article I had written and which had been translated by Mario appeared in the morning paper *Il Gazzettino*, which Mario saw as a major coup. In truth, it wasn't difficult to realise why it was such hard work getting the press interested in the match. Invariably we were shunted, in all innocence, on to the 'rugby correspondent', and 'rugby' meant, of course, Rugby Union. Under a strict edict from the Italian Rugby Federation, the 13-a-side code was taboo. But it was in a happier state of mind that we drove out to Marco Polo Airport to meet the Great Britain squad. They arrived on time, tired and hungry after a four-hour stopover in Milano. Half the act was here; having got them settled into their hotel, it remained only to pray that the French would also turn up, as they were not due to fly in until noon on Saturday – the day of the match.

Earlier, we had been to the City of Venice Sports Council to arrange a training ground for the British. Mario was constantly critical of the Council. He reckoned that obstacles had been deliberately placed in his way, despite the fact he was bringing a major international sporting occasion to the city. Certainly, the amount of support and backing he had received for his venture fell way behind that given to other sports events in Venice. Similarly, as he became increasingly aware that he was going to lose quite a slab of money on the match, Mario was also very bitter about the government system which demanded that he hand over 20 per cent of the takings in tax, especially since officially recognised sports – such as 'rugby' – were only obliged to give 4 per cent.

The players were based in a hotel at Punto Sabbioni, way out on the peninsula, about a 45-minute boat ride from the centre of Venice. If you have never been to Venice, it is impossible to appreciate just how difficult it is to get around there, and this was bound to have a severe effect on the size of the crowd at the match. In addition, the stadium itself was in a virtually inaccessible location, although finding any patch of dry land with grass on it is quite an achievement for Venice. Meanwhile, the real interest in Italian rugby lies on the mainland, in places such as Treviso, Padua and Co. With hindsight, it would perhaps have been better to have staged the game in one of those towns . . .

On the Friday morning, the British players took the hotel minibus to the Sports Council's training ground, some 15 kilometres along the lagoon. The bus wasn't big enough to fit everybody in, so the three substitutes, Les Dyl, Andy Gregory and Ray Tabern, waited, along with manager Colin Hutton, for a return trip. By this time, some gentlemen of the British press had arrived, so I could at least

start convincing myself that the game really was going to happen –
although nobody dared tell the media chaps that the French team
were not due to pitch up for at least another 24 hours. There was
Arthur Brooks of *The Daily Mirror* and Paul Harrison of *The Sun*;
Peter Ward and Jack McNamara, who had shared a car journey
down to Venice – Wardy cursing and complaining of backache
because Jack had omitted to tell him that he didn't drive, leaving
Peter to man the wheel all the way from Manchester; Dave
Hadfield, then an energetic young freelancer; and John Roberts, a
feature writer from *The Daily Mail*, who had flown in with
photographer John Sherbourne, ready to do a special story on this
'unique' sporting happening. Sherbourne was later to pay a smart-
ass gondolier almost 50 quid for the ten-minute hire of three boats,
so that he could get his exclusive picture of the British players on the
waterways of Venice.

The players trained well, but were delayed on the way back to the
hotel by the fact that they had to travel by public transport . . . and
the bus didn't turn up. At that, Mario promptly diverted his anger
from the Sports Council to the City Transport Department.

Saturday was the day of the match, and also the day when the
French were due to arrive. There was never a hint of worry. In
typical style, they breezed into Venice in a small charter plane,
touching down on schedule, with all the players looking cool in
their accepted uniforms of faded denims and *Treize* magazine T-
shirts. With them was the legendary Puig-Aubert, eager to see
Venice for the first time in his life. The French stayed in the same
hotel as the British, and later travelled on the same boat to and from
the match. Rarely has there been such fraternisation between
players from the two rival countries.

Having checked in, the French ate a big meal, and declined the
chance to go training. Instead, they went for a siesta. Both sets of
players took tea around 5 p.m. and were ready to catch the boat to
the stadium at 7 p.m. Thunder clouds had gathered during the
afternoon, and the downpour came a couple of hours before the
8.45 p.m. kick-off time. For the British, this was like a sign from the
heavens. The rain dispelled the humid atmosphere, and the evening
was clear and actually quite cool.

We arrived at the stadium to find there were no goalposts up. But
there was no need to panic; it was simply that the Italian
groundsmen didn't believe in exerting too much energy too soon,
and weren't going to make the effort to get the posts up until they

felt the time was right. It was only when the two teams arrived, ready to play, and eyed up the stadium incredulously, that the groundsmen decided that the time was right. It then took half a dozen of us to manoeuvre the uprights (which had been borrowed from the Venice Rugby Union Club on the say-so of Angelo Gerardi) into position, with the real heroes of this history-making exercise turning out to be the Great Britain coach Johnny Whiteley, and a young French lad who proved to be a dab-hand at shinning up the posts to drop the crossbars into their slots.

So the stage was set, the gates were opened, and the people began to filter into the stadium. Among them was a handful of British League fans who had made Venice their holiday destination for the summer, while one of the earliest arrivals was Ferdi Sarterato, whose first question was: 'How are the Hornets doing these days?' The tape for the national anthems arrived literally five minutes before the teams were due to walk out.

The match was played and proved a big success, with a crowd of around fifteen hundred – largely young – people, who warmed to the tenseness of the encounter as France ground out an 8–7 victory, and who came alive most when the dark stars, Des Drummond and Ivan Grésèque, got the ball and used their flashing pace. Bob Brown, who performed heroics as the gateman, and who took responsibility for calming down Mario when he got hassled by a 'spy' from the taxation department, reported that only four people actually left the stadium before the end.

The old-time League players from Italy said they couldn't believe the pace of the game. 'It was,' they said, 'much faster than when we used to play in the 1960s.' They were all heartened by the turn-out and the positive reaction to the game – all, that is, except Mario Majone who, by now, was deeply depressed in the sure knowledge that he was being stung by the taxman and was going to lose a lot of money. It seemed that, while the other Italians had predicted that only a few hundred spectators would turn up, Mario had set his sights too high. Still, the fact that fifteen hundred people had enjoyed the match gave the locals the incentive to get down to formulating a programme to bring League back to Italy and develop the game once more. Regular contact with the British and French Leagues was essential, we all agreed, if anything more was going to happen.

And, sadly, that's where the Italian dream started to falter. On the one hand Mario was, by his own admission, a players' man. He

78

loved being involved with football teams, and he had a vision for the promotion and presentation of Rugby League which was American-influenced because, at that time, American football was starting to make a big impression among young Italians. Unfortunately for him, that vision was something which British Rugby League didn't share until Super League came along in 1996.

On the other hand Mario was left in 1982 with a big debt. That wasn't the end of his attempts to get the game played in the Venice region; but, for the smart businessmen like Angelo Gerardi, the signs were clear that nothing had really changed since the 1960s when it came down to the established Rugby League nations following through with their enthusiasm and commitment to help the Italians.

For the next ten years I kept in some kind of contact with Mario. I sent him an *Open Rugby* every month, and every year he would write to say thanks and to send his good wishes. Then, one day, his magazine came back in the envelope, unopened, with the Italian words for 'gone away' scrawled across it. We never found out where he had gone. Bob Brown called his number after hearing the news, and it was no longer in use. For his part, Bob went on to make his Hemel Hempstead club the shining light of League development in England.

I'm tempted to write here 'Mario Majone, where are you?'. And you never know: somebody might, just might, call me up to say he's the new catering manager at Luton Airport!

# Venice Revisited

## Dave Hadfield

Do not go to Venice. Not if you are in any way susceptible to becoming obsessed with a place because, if you are, you will be swallowed whole by it. The very best that can happen then is that you will become a colossal bore on the subject.

There is, after all, nowhere else in the world where you can walk out of the railway station and find yourself in the middle of an oil painting; a masterpiece to which you add your own little scratched graffiti in the form of the experiences which you have there and the recollections you carry away. It happened to Byron and Shelley – and I noticed it happening to Johnny Whiteley as well. And me? The description 'sitting target' does not come close to hinting at my defencelessness. I walked down the steps from the station to the Grand Canal and I was a lost cause, sunk as comprehensively as Venice itself will be in a few hundred years, hooked like a trout.

I shouldn't reproach myself too much. After all, Byron never helped Johnny Whiteley to put up a set of rugby posts at Sant' Elena on his first visit. Shelley didn't have to run frantically around the city in a power cut, looking with mounting desperation for the main post office in order to phone back his match report. (If he had, he would have found that one stretch of canal, one hump-backed bridge, is very much like all the rest in the dark.) Neither of them took a vaporetto out to the Lido and sat at four o'clock in the morning by a hotel swimming pool with a still hale and hearty Puig-Aubert. It was little wonder I found myself dangerously intoxicated with the strutting, melancholy old fantasy.

This infatuation manifested itself in a couple of forms. I became fiercely partisan about Venice, quite capable of going for the throat of anyone who ran it down in any way. At the drop of a hat, I would shoe-horn references to Venice and all things Venetian into my copy – no small feat when you are covering the magistrates' court for *The Bolton Evening News*. On the basis that the purpose of writing in the first place is to write what you want to and not what your employer might require, my finest hour yet has to be a book review of an impenetrably dense history of Venice which I somehow persuaded the paper to print. It was about 20 paragraphs long and only got around to mentioning the book itself in the last of those paragraphs. The rest of it was a rant on behalf of Venice and, in particular, a defence against the charge, often levelled by day-trippers from the beach resorts, that it stinks to high heaven. 'Smell?' it read. 'How can it possibly smell, flushed out as it is twice a day by the fragrant waters of the Adriatic?' These were the ravings of a man besotted.

The other aspect of the obsession was the search for an excuse to go back there. Some in my family firmly believe that I only got married in order to be able to return there on honeymoon. That, of course, is completely untrue – although we did go to Venice for our honeymoon. Before that, though, another window of opportunity had flung itself open. The Venice International Sevens was an event entirely typical of Rugby League's expansionist efforts at the time, in that it was not international, it was not really a sevens tournament, and it did not take place in Venice. It did, however, fulfil a vital function by giving me a perfect excuse to go to Venice – which was far more important.

As international sporting events go, a turn-out of one team from Yorkshire and one from Hertfordshire might well be considered a little below par. The original plan – as original plans always are – was far more impressive, including teams from Britain, France and even Italy. But then the organiser, Signor Italian Rugby League, Mario Majone, started to run into a few logistical problems, like having nowhere for the teams to stay and nowhere for them to play. That was enough to deter most of the sides which had been intending to go, but not Oulton and Hemel Hempstead, who decided they were just damn well going to turn up anyway. It was an attitude with which I was in complete sympathy, because I certainly wasn't going to be deterred by a minor detail like there being no matches to write about.

To his credit, when Mario found that two teams were there despite the event being cancelled, he tried to salvage something from the sludge at the bottom of the canal which had once carried his dreams (oh no, I'm going into *Bolton Evening News* Venice-mode again). It was this attempt that brought us both into contact with the labyrinthine workings of Venetian bureaucracy, as we tried to get our hands on a pitch upon which Hemel and Oulton could battle for world domination.

Venice is not, by Italian standards, particularly sports-minded. Their idea of a big event is a boat race down the canal, and the city is said to be the one place in the country where an Italian World Cup victory can be greeted by something close to indifference. But, then again, when you have been the wealthiest and most confident power in the known world, why should you concern yourself overmuch with the pastimes of a barbarous hinterland to which, by some accident of history, you now belong?

There isn't any dry open space generous enough to stage anything bigger than a bowls match, Sant' Elena – the scene of the previous year's match between Great Britain and France – being the honourable exception. Something of a sporting backwater, then, but absolutely Olympic class when it comes to putting obstacles in the way of anyone who does want to organise anything. It was only when I accompanied Signor Majone to meet the officials of the city council who were nominally in charge of sports fields that I realised what a miracle it had been that the match a year earlier had ever taken place.

Those officials – I shall call them Signor Borgia and Signor Machiavelli – gave us the runaround for the best part of a day, bouncing us between the pair of them and then fobbing us off to various functionaries in other buildings. All those buildings appeared to be disused palaces of varying degrees of opulence and disrepair, so it was a good crash course in Venetian architecture, but very little use to two people hoping to stage a Rugby League match between Oulton and Hemel Hempstead. The state of play, when we finally managed to disentangle and divine it, was this: after consultation with – guess who – the local Rugby Union authorities, the city of Venice could not provide as much as a window-box for this titanic sporting contest, because Rugby League was not a recognised sport. In bureaucratic terms, it did not exist, so it would therefore be absurd to provide a patch of ground for it to be played. There was a logic to this that perhaps only the Jesuits could have truly appreciated.

There was, however, a Plan B. Outside the control of the Borgias and Machiavellis, and beyond the city limits, there was a pitch which we could use – provided we all liked peas.

There is a need here for a brief gastronomic digression. Among the many categories of visitors who can be wrong-footed by Venice are those who expect it to be a treasure-house of familiar Italian cuisine. But this isn't Italy; it's Venice. You can get better pizza in Pudsey and better pasta in Papua New Guinea. But if it's a lump of liver and a nice big plate of rice and peas that you fancy, then you've come to the right place. Venice and its surrounding area, the Veneto, is not pasta country, but they grow rice and peas like nobody's business. Hence it is only fitting that the pea harvest should be celebrated every year, deep in the heart of pea country, with some enthusiasm. All right, it isn't the Venice Film Festival or the Regatta Storico, but neither of those institutions showed much interest in grafting a Rugby League match on to their respective programmes of events. A shame, but there you go.

And so it was that the assembled cast of the Venice International Sevens piled into a coach and headed inland to the pea festival. To go across the lagoon and on to the mainland is to understand immediately how Venice manages to stay the way it is. All the trappings of the twentieth century, essential but unsightly, are on the other side of the long causeway; all the oil refineries, factories, sewage farms, and all the millions of rasping mopeds which infest the rest of the country.

After just a few days in Venice, it is a shock to the system to be back amid traffic. Even if it was not completely banned within Venice, there would be limited advantages in owning a vehicle in the city which caused Robert Benchley to cable famously to his office: 'Streets full of water. Please advise.' For a car-hater, Venice is close to heaven, although it is not a heaven which suits everyone. There is the man in that advert, for instance, sadly taking his leave of a palace on the Grand Canal, watched as he sails away by men, women – especially women, one of whom appears to be reluctantly marrying someone else – and children, all of them gazing after him with heart-stopping love and longing. And all so he can get in his bloody metal box, put his foot down and drive off, probably to a pea festival. Every time I see that advert, I think: 'You prat.' Anyway, the streets of Mestre, across the lagoon from the glories of Venice, are full of escapees from the streets full of water, roaring around and making up for lost time.

The venue for the sevens turned out to be a dusty school football field on the fringes of the funfair and open-air dance-floor which constituted the pea festival. It was not, in all honesty, destined to host a classic of the code, although the referee, Joe Chamberlain, did his best to make some sort of spectacle out of it for the benefit of a few raggedy village urchins and the occasional man on a moped who paused from their pea-eating for a while to watch what was going on.

One of those moped-riders, in fact, shares with me the distinction of having played on both sides that day, as liberal and creative use was made of the substitution rules. We should both have got two medals, if everyone had their just deserts; one winner's and one runners-up, although I'm blowed if I can remember after almost 15 years which team got which. Oh yes, there were medals. Even for a competition which had been cancelled and expelled from the city because it didn't exist, there were great shiny gongs. After all, it was Italy.

There were also peas. Plenty of them. As many as you could eat. And then some more. There was pea pâté, pea soup, huge steaming plates of rice and peas, followed by something that tasted suspiciously like pea ice-cream. It had been a good pea harvest, that much was abundantly clear.

But if it was a good year for peas, it was a poor one for Venetian Rugby League. The whole idea of Rugby League in Italy, in fact, had come to the end of its brief vogue, during which officials from the League were only too happy to head off to Venice for essential fact-finding, and it was now, like those massive vats of peas, firmly on the back-burner. Mario Majone, having gone through the usual pioneer's cycle of evangelical enthusiasm, dogged persistence and eventual despair, finally gave up on the project. And Oulton and Hemel Hempstead, sweating on that dusty football pitch, while the loudspeaker from a nearby tent yelled 'Rice and peas for everyone!', amounted to the Venice International Sevens to end all Venice International Sevens.

Not that such an outcome removed all reason to return to Venice, though. A year later, on that aforementioned honeymoon, I experienced what appeared at the time to be my second Venetian power cut while sitting outdoors at a restaurant in the Campo Santa Margherita, dining on something with no peas in it. All the lights suddenly went out, apart from a number of candles strategically placed in the upper-floor windows around the square. But the electricity had not given out; the scene was being prepared for a torchlit procession, an annual ceremony to transfer the relics of some saint or martyr from one church to another. In an eerie silence, the faithful carried the casket through the darkened square. It was the sort of moment at which the newly married might lean across the table and enquire tenderly what was in the other's mind. What was in mine was that I was very relieved that I didn't have to find that post office again.

# MOROCCO

# Like Webster's Dictionary

## Neil Tunnicliffe

The estimable Ralph Rimmer, erstwhile Rugby League development officer for Doncaster, now ploughing a similarly straight furrow in Sheffield, was unequivocal. 'It was the worst week of my life. A complete nightmare.' Belatedly, as an afterthought, he went on to add: 'Thanks for the opportunity, it was a great experience. But I'd never do it again for them.'

Ralph's colleague, Rick Rolt, delivered a more diplomatic verdict, as befitted a freshly appointed Rugby Football League staff coach still brailling his way around the corridors of power. The underlying sentiment, though, was the same. 'We had a lot of trouble getting them on the coach,' he mused helplessly. 'As soon as we'd got four or five on, the rest just disappeared. I've never seen anything like it.' One's heart went out to him. It must have been like trying to jam eels into a holster, three by three, with your bare hands.

Terry Flanagan, on his first nerve-racked engagement as a BBC TV commentator, famously and forgivably described the New Zealand Test team as 'a fine side, packed with internationals'. The members of the Moroccan ensemble which participated in the Halifax Emerging Nations World Cup in 1995, to whom Ralph and Rick were appointed liaison officers for the duration of the tournament, were neither of these things. Beaten in both their matches, by the equally *ingénue* Moldova and the rather less innocent Irish, they returned home at the earliest convenient stage with their 100 per cent international record chastely intact: played ten, lost ten. In truth, they were men fashioned in the image of their maker: wildly enthusiastic, extravagantly indisciplined,

86

inappropriately flamboyant, maddeningly mercurial and, in the end, surprisingly good.

The full story of Rick and Ralph's excellent adventure in Sheffield that week with their temporary charges has never been related – although I suspect it remains available for the right price, payable in the right currency, in the right environment. Personally, I must admit that I don't wish to hear it, torn as I am between red-faced guilt and near-maniacal *Schadenfreude*. You see, reader, I knew what it would be like for them, the spleen-inflating frustration that they would suffer in trying to nail this particular blancmange to the wall, in dealing with this infuriatingly perverse and contrary phenomenon. And still I let them go through with it, nay, urged them to do so. Did I forewarn them of the hydra-headed labour in store for them? Did I nuts.

The Moroccan Rugby League baby was conceived through the fertile mind and deeds of Hussain M'Barki early in 1993, went through a short and unusually active gestation period, and was subsequently brought to parturition under induction by the midwife Maurice Lindsay later that year. M'Barki is a man whom it is difficult not to like and admire, a warm and courageous human being whose achievements on and off a hundred square miles' worth of fields of differing provenances and orientations weave a yarn which forms a unique weft in the multicoloured and variegated tapestry that is the 100-year history of our game. There can be few if any sports which can top Rugby League for the sheer larger-than-life, man-of-the-world, seen-it-all, designed-the-T-shirt singularity and vivacity of its characters – Alex Murphy, Peter Fox *and* Maurice Bamford, all in the same generation, for God's sake; the pig-wrestling Cleal brothers, the Terry Clawsons, the Tim Wilbys, the Smokin' Joe Kilroys, and my own personal favourite, the one-armed Kerry Gibson who crossed the world to play for Runcorn. Even in this unlimited company, for reasons all of his own, M'Barki's short, wiry frame stands, like Alan Ladd on an orange box, shoulder to shoulder with the best of them.

Before the days when French Rugby Union systematically cherry-picked the best of the talent from its former colonies to grace its clubs and national XV, the young M'Barki was a *cause célèbre*. An almighty stand-up row erupted over France's invitation to the touchline-scorching winger to join them on tour, when the Moroccan Rugby Union understandably resisted this attempted piracy of their one genuine asset. Impatient at the prospect of a spell in dry dock, or indeed of missing the boat altogether, M'Barki promptly jumped ship when offered the opportunity of joining the SS *Fulham* on her maiden voyage in 1981. He subsequently became not just the only Moroccan professional Rugby League player in Britain, but also the most longeval and prolific – the best-rehearsed of his record 74 tries in 162 appearances for the appropriately nomadic London club being one of the hen's-teeth handful registered against the 'Invincible' 1982 Kangaroos. Brief tours of duty at Wilderspool, the Watersheddings and the Boulevard ended with migration back closer to the equator in the capital where, while performing sterling work on an ill-starred development project in Rotherhithe, he first began to think about taking this thing home. The rest, as they say, is history.

And yet, and yet . . . When the phone rings in the office on a weekday morning, and to answer it is to hear a serpentine hiss, a series of clicks, and then a hoarse, slurred voice say 'Gummornen Neil, iss 'Ussain', the spirits fall as if dropped by Paul Cullen. It's a segued sequence of sounds that invariably sends you diving for the Nurofen in the desk drawer.

The reason why M'Barki should have this effect may well lie rooted deep in the soil of his native heath, the evolution of which, informatively if untypically, was chronicled in an educational introduction to his original development plan, as submitted to the RFL in 1993. Since, and I quote, '*homo sapiens* first roamed across the then fertile plains and steep rocky mountains of Northern Africa and the adjunct [*sic*] sea shore', Morocco has been invaded, bullied, bought and sold, and generally batted about like a shuttlecock by all the major powers in the Mediterranean – Phoenicians, Carthaginians, Romans, Vandals, Muslims and Moors, Arabs and Turks and, most recently, the French. Throughout all those centuries the indigenous tribal inhabitants, most usefully parcelled under the title Berbers, have had continually to reinvent themselves in response to circumstance and the identity of this particular year's imperialists, to whom their vulnerability has had much to do with their country's susceptibility to the apocalyptic horsemen, Famine and Drought.

The end product of this seasoning and weathering process (and I generalise for simplicity's sake, while remaining conscious of the stereotype for the Englishman's one-dimensional view of Johnny Foreigner) is threefold: a people who are fiercely nationalistic, the straw to which they have tightly clung throughout the hurricane of history; a people to whom bartering, argument and negotiation in quest of a favourable compromise are as idiomatic as profanities to an Australian; but a people who will never answer a question with the answer to that question, but with what they think you want the answer to be.

M'Barki is a Berber. Had he not been, on the first of the aforementioned counts, then his stubborn vision of Morocco winning a speaking part on the world Rugby League stage would never have slipped through the fingers of the sceptics who wanted to know: 'Why there?' Had he not been, on the second count, then his association would not have been able to navigate the bureaucratic and administrative labyrinth in the state capital Rabat, where spiteful and suspicious Rugby Union lurked in ambush round every corner. And had he not been, on the third count, it might be a damn sight easier for his colleagues back at base to get a straight answer to a straight question and so find out what the hell he's up to. It can be worse than trying to plait fog.

Ask Hussain how many teams are on the go in Morocco at any given time, and he will reply, variously, five, six, eight or ten – depending on what he thinks you're driving at. Ask him what colour black is, and it's sometimes black, sometimes white, often grey and, when the mood is especially expansive, occasionally even pink. It's a national trait which falls a considerable distance short of actually lying (it would be a gross, stabbing insult to Moroccan integrity, and that of M'Barki in particular, to imply otherwise). But, with regard to the economics of the truth, it's the equivalent of a PhD from the Adam Smith Institute. And, as a conversational gambit, it has an effect on its recipient roughly equal to doing five *Times* crosswords at the same time as playing Boris Spassky at chess, with Motorhead blaring out full blast in the background. You just ask Rick and Ralph.

Given this chasm between information supply and demand, the only viable, forensic way to audit the state of Moroccan Rugby League is to go there and see for yourself. It's a dirty job, but somebody's got to do it . . .

I've been out twice now and, on both occasions, had experiences which it would be difficult, not to say invidious, to forget. The first time was in June 1994, at the end of M'Barki's first 12 months in office, in company with RFL development executive Tom O'Donovan. The Bob Hope and Bing Crosby of British Rugby League: 'Like Webster's Dictionary, we're Morocco bound.'

M'Barki (comparisons of whom to Dorothy Lamour would be, at best, laboured) met us at the airport together with three companions: two old coaches of his whom he had conscripted as lieutenants, one of whom seemed to have been personal mentor to, or once trained, or taught at the same school as, or lived in the same town as, or at least knew the name of, Said Aouita; and the neophyte captain of the Moroccan national team, a dreadlocked youth built like a Greek statue who was a junior javelin champion, starred in TV adverts for something or other, to whom the London Broncos wished to offer trials, all expenses paid . . .

Heads ringing with the tinnitus brought on by attempting to follow M'Barki's introductions, we boarded the minibus for the drive south-west down the coast from Casablanca to Safi, where a new initiative was primed and ready to explode. The protocol on Moroccan roads – doubly so if you have a right-hand drive vehicle in this drive-on-the-right country, as had M'Barki – is to wait to overtake until something large and momentous is approaching in the other direction; then, blowing your horn as hard as you can, you veer out in front of the oncoming vehicle and hammer your gears until they scream for mercy. At the moment when there appears to be only two possible eventualities – multi-car pile-up, or emergency bale-out into roadside ditches – then, and only then, change up and sidle through the eye of the needle on to the open road ahead.

Once we were inured to this periodic, ritualistic game of chicken, it was a pleasant trip punctuated by regular watermelon breaks as supplied by pushers who loitered opportunistically along the highway at one-mile intervals. (A life lesson: always dress down for a watermelon break and, as in the *Hitch-hiker's Guide to the Galaxy*, always carry a towel.) Morocco's Atlantic coastal plain is a largely rocky, inhospitable margin which, every so often, takes mini-bloom as a salad crop homes in on some alluvial delta or cultivable soil-well and gorges itself on these rare rations of nutrients. Otherwise, in common with many of its neighbours around the Mediterranean to the north-east, it's goats, goats and more goats – and the occasional camel, as a sop to the fact that this really is North Africa.

We sat in a café in Safi that evening as the local youngbloods buzzed around on mopeds like wasps attracted to our picnic. In time they landed, as many as 40, and M'Barki opened the hamper to unpack the bread and meat of his plan to establish Rugby League here. Again, we assumed that's what he said: to our ears the

Moroccan patois, with its preponderance of 'els' and 'als' and harsh glottal diphthongs, made each speaker sound as if he were about to break into song, but was prevented from doing so by the unfortunate intervention of catarrh. Whatever it was, the gleam it ignited in the eyes of this impressive legion of new recruits seemed testament to the inspirational evangelism of our man. (We just hoped he hadn't promised to pay them all with RFL money.)

In those early days, M'Barki's return to Moroccan rugby was considered not so much prodigal as prostitutional, and there were offered to him in greeting neither fatted calves nor the use of any fields on which they might have gambolled. With the Rugby Union authorities withholding their facilities in this high-, not to say petty-minded way, the majority of Rugby League training took place on public beaches. So it was that, the following morning, we wended our way from our hotel down to the harbour, past the docks, along the back side of a Quatermass-style industrial refinery, and on to the sands beyond.

There the previous evening's 40 multiplied to become around 80 throughout the course of an overcast morning which could have been Southport as easily as Safi. True, some of these were scallies who had come to the beach in ignorance of the intentions of Rugby League's Columbuses to plant their standard here on the shore and claim this territory for their game; rather than being instantly converted when the light fell upon them, they spent much of the morning trying to nick off with the marker cones which bounded the area of M'Barki's new domain. But the rest appeared genuinely and premeditatedly eager to get their hands on the forbidden fruit, to the extent that weight of numbers overwhelmed the organisation of the session and it degenerated into something of a shambles. The overriding image of the event is of M'Barki, alternately benign and ratty, pleading and shunting this vast, amorphous rabble through a hotch-potch of play-the-ball drills, handling games and touch rugby, trying desperately to ensure that each one had mastered the correct technique. Like Cecil B. de Mille trying to ensure that none of the extras in *Ben Hur* was wearing a wristwatch, it was a hopeless cause.

Afterwards we adjourned to a flimsy wooden shack in the arid, dusty shadow of the refinery, as the sun assumed its zenith, burned away the cloud and microwaved the atmosphere outside until it gasped for breath. M'Barki had promised to provide lunch here for the congregational multitude and, given that there were now so

91

many of them, it seemed that a loaves-and-fishes miracle would be required. Lucky, really: that's exactly what M'Barki had arranged. Pinned down by the deadly accurate blanket fire of the sun, we could do nothing for the next two hours but relax in the shade as a continuous food chain of sumptuously plump and exotic locally caught fish pumped from the harbour via a rudimentary iron barbecue on to our tables – a treat for both gourmet and gourmand. You could perhaps see the idea catching on in Hull or, more likely, Cumbria, at Workington after training, down on the beach near Sellafield. Except that you probably wouldn't need to cook the fish – they'd already be glowing. And they'd all have three eyes and two tails.

Thus sated, as the sun ran low on ammunition and its barrage subsided, we ambled through the snoozing no man's land of siesta-time docks and harbour up into the old town. There, in a cliffside corner carved by the coast road shimmying and side-stepping its way down to sea level, we found an ancient stone-built souk crawling its way back up the hill along a single street. Crumbling, cave-like shopfronts, once thresholds were crossed and eyes accustomed to the gloom, transformed themselves into treasuries wherein thousands of pots and plates of garish yet meticulous hand-painted designs were cradled by, or precariously slung from, teetering wooden shelves. Behind this primitive parade rose a row of blackened kilns in the shape of rondavels, or the beehive tombs in which the Mycenaean Greeks interred their heroes – ostensibly the factories which stoked this astonishing trade. M'Barki blithely remarked that this was the source of supply for much of the commercial ceramic demand of the likes of Habitat, at which it would have been easy to play the cynic: surely, somewhere in Safi, there was a high-tech, twentieth-century, mass-production enterprise churning out these pots like billy-oh, while leaving this baited line trailing for gullible tourists to bite on and swallow. But such was the magic of the place that it was more difficult not to be reeled in – even for mouths hardened to M'Barki's hooks.

That evening, back in Casablanca, we visited an authentic Moroccan restaurant, where there was advertised to be an evening of belly-dancing. Salaciousness vanished like snow in the sunshine when the practitioner turned out to be a wizened, black-eyed old man of 60-plus in baggy white nightshirt and pantaloons. Instead, we could only marvel at his skill and suppleness as he swooped and gyrated while balancing on his crown a two-foot tin tray bearing lighted candles and half-pint glasses filled to the meniscus line with water. It would be untrue to say that he spilled not a drop; but what he did spill wouldn't have washed a doll's handkerchief. Needless to say, we ended a memorable evening haggling over the bill – not with the waiters but with M'Barki, who was paying, wasn't paying, had credit cards, had no credit cards . . .

The same restaurant figured on the itinerary when I returned to Morocco some 12 months later as part of an Anglo-French mission with RFL coaching executive John Kear and Jean-Paul Ferré and Tas Baitieri of the Fédération Française de Rugby à XIII. This time, however, against anticipation, the belly-dancer was a geographical feature in female form: rolling hills, plunging rift valleys, a whole basket-of-eggs topography draped sparingly in silk and veils. The previous evening, too, on late arrival at the hotel we had gone in search of a nightcap beer and stumbled unwittingly (on my life) into a full-scale 'exotic revue', the principal features of which were a token handful of sequins, five ostriches' worth of feathers, and copious mounds of quivering flesh. It was as though Morocco, having wooed my heart and mind with its culture the previous year, had summarily decided in the interim to scrap that subtlety and instead go straight for the groin. (Another life lesson: expenses incurred with regard to belly-dancers are not tax-deductible.)

Poor old John. From Castleford to Casablanca – one small step, one giant leap. While Jean-Paul, Tas and I set off on the diplomatic round with M'Barki, invoking the familial spirit that formerly linked motherland and colony in the dingy offices of a dozen disinterested political pen-pushers, John was abandoned in a dustbowl sun-trap of an athletics stadium to impart his knowledge to the national team in advance of their participation in the Halifax Emerging Nations World Cup. We next found him two days later, as the training camp was breaking up. He was standing on the end of a short reception line of coaches and officials, along which the Moroccan players were proceeding to express their gratitude and farewells – by way of lustily kissing each of their seniors in the traditional, accepted Muslim manner. Not that there was much acceptance emanating from John: the way his shoulders were tensed, his body cocked and his brows beetled suggested that, should any of these buggers try it with him, the sort of kiss they'd receive in return would be that more usually associated with Kirkby.

As the first player approached him, there developed before our eyes the almost tangible manifestation of a cultural interface. Player looked at John, weighing up his options like any good half-back; John looked at player, eyeing him up, wondering if he could take him *and* all his mates. There was a moment's hiatus during which, to coin a cliché, you could have cut the atmosphere with a cricket stump. Then, with a suddenness and firmness which brooked no challenge, John thrust out a hand. The player shook it like an English gentleman, and moved away. There was a monsoon of relief: an international incident averted.

John told us later that he first thought he might struggle when, through a somewhat ropey interpreter, he asked the players to divide into pairs for tackling practice. The first to do so were two huge, glowering prop forwards with ears like root vegetables, anvils for noses, and three days' stubble – who cemented their bond by holding hands like junior school kids in a crocodile. Imagine that down Wheldon Road: Dean Sampson glides cutely up to Crooksy on the practice ground and entwines his fingers with those of his friend while waiting for the off. It'd be off all right. It'd be like the Wild West.

I suspect that it is this unlikeness, this foreignness, which is responsible for our Little England frustration with M'Barki and Morocco. After all, when we visit Australia and New Zealand, we speak the same language, we enjoy the same jokes, we share the same disciplines – but we still take them to task for preferring their beer cold and being less used to losing. And, when we go as far afield as France, we're quite capable of demanding their total excommunication from our association for the simple reasons that they don't fry their food and they drink wine instead of bitter. So when we collide with Morocco – its ponderous procedures, its inactive afternoons, its kissing cousins, its concentric circumlocutions – we are defenceless against our antipathy. We mistrust because we misunderstand.

Rugby League in Morocco is going to work out. These are still early days, but it's going to be a success. You can tell that from the fact that the only sports in which the country has ever excelled are athletics and martial arts – of which Rugby League might well be considered to be a leavened blend (albeit heavy on the latter, in the case of certain Widnes and Warrington teams of the 1970s). You can also tell that from the eagerness with which the country's youth is flocking to M'Barki's banner. Let's face it, if you called an impromptu training session on Brighton beach you wouldn't get 80 players turning up – not even if Linda Evangelista and Helena

Christensen were patronising the nudist area next door. But they turned up in Safi (where, I just happened to notice, there were no women at all, dressed or undressed).

So I suppose we'll just have to be more patient, tolerant and understanding in our dealings with M'Barki and his brethren; ask questions that are a little less leading, a little more straightforward. When the maverick young demagogue Alcibiades came to power in fifth-century Athens and shocked his fellow-citizens with his unorthodox politics, his 'modern' behaviour and libertine habits, the comedian Aristophanes drawled his told-you-so thus: 'It's really better not to rear a lion cub within the city; but, if you must, then you'll have to get used to its little ways.' Another life lesson learned in regard of Morocco – although I'm sure that, when we next need volunteers to wield the whip and chair, Ralph Rimmer and Rick Rolt will be conspicuous by their absence.

# Once Weren't Warriors

## Dave Hadfield

Rugby League has never, I think, staged an opening night soaked in such drama and sense of occasion as the Auckland Warriors' first match at Ericsson Stadium. It was the whole three-ring circus, that evening in March 1995: a full-scale Anzac mock-battle on the pitch, acrobats dangling from the stand roof, then a lone choirboy warbling plaintively in the pregnant silence. And when the Warriors ran out through the tunnel of fire into an otherwise darkened stadium, even someone from the opposite side of the world with a deep-seated indifference to pre-match entertainment got a lump in his throat. Vince Miller, where were you? And I must one day ask Dean Bell, who led the Warriors out that night, how he thought it compared with Leeds's first Super League match almost exactly a year later.

It goes without saying that the ground was packed; they could have filled it three times over. By the time the *haka* and the Polynesian drummers had done their worst, the emotional temperature was such that you felt fiercely proud to be a New Zealander – even if you weren't. This was clearly the start of something very, very big. But it was also the end of something: the end of the game in New Zealand being cosy and low-key; the end of the heroic little guy squaring up to the hulking power of the All Blacks; the end of innocence. The only traditional feature to be carried over was that the home team lost.

For the Leaguie far from home, there has always been something special about New Zealand. For an obvious start, it is so very far from home, and yet so achingly familiar. How strange that our colonising forefathers had to work their way to the furthest point of the globe before creating in Christchurch the perfect reproduction of the English country town. Alongside all the references to the mother country, however, New Zealand can be exotic to the point of weirdness. Next to something which looks like a suburban hotel in Surrey there will be a pool of boiling mud or a spouting geyser.

Their footballers are a mass of contradictions as well, especially the really scary ones – Kurt Sorensen, Kevin Tamati, Mark Broadhurst. The more intimidating they are on the pitch, the nicer blokes they are off it. We British get on well with Kiwis. They have that antipodean openness about them, without the edge and arrogance which we sometimes detect in Australians. They don't threaten us; in Rugby League terms, they make no claims to world domination.

Apart from that difference in attitude, the other most effective way to distinguish New Zealanders from their cousins across the Tasman is through sex. Let me explain. If 'sex' are something you carry coal in, and the way you make babies is through an activity called 'six', then you are talking to a Kiwi. By their vowels shall ye know them, and all Kiwis suffer from irritable vowel syndrome. Unlike Australians – and, indeed, Lancastrians – who can become distinctly crotchety when you take the piss out of their accents, New Zealanders treat the whole business with wry bemusement. We once had a Kiwi scrum-half at Bolton who was in charge of calling out our numbered moves. 'Tin!' he would shout, as the acting half-back was in the process of shipping the ball to him.

'What did he say?'

'Did he say "tin"?'

By which time he would be disappearing under the hooves of the Heysham Atoms or Leigh Victoria. The bloke in that shibboleth story in the Bible was surely a New Zealander.

That same, trampled scrum-half once took me white-water rafting near his home in Rotorua. Now, in this setting, he is meant to be the knowledgeable local and I'm supposed to play the role of the naïve foreigner. But when the captain of the craft asked for a volunteer to grab hold of a rope stretched over the river, in order (ho, ho) to stop the raft, it was Vance – or Vince, or Vence, we were never entirely sure – who put his hand up. The inevitable and intended result was that he was left suspended above the raging waters, while the rest of us sailed on happily downstream. 'Ah yis,' said our guide, 'there's one on every reft.' You can't help feeling at home with people like that.

On one level, just how much at home you feel in Auckland might depend on exactly which part of Auckland you are in. The city centre, on a bad day, can be reminiscent of a wet Sunday in Birmingham, but Auckland is also the biggest Polynesian city in the world – a magnet for Samoans, Tongans, Fijians and Cook Islanders, as well as housing a sizeable Maori population. Go far south of downtown, and you soon know that you are in the Pacific and not the Home Counties. This end of town – the modern heartland of New Zealand Rugby League – is vividly depicted in the much-acclaimed film *Once Were Warriors*. It is not the New Zealand of the tourist brochures, which is something the film exploits in its opening shot of a typical chocolate-box panorama of lakes and mountains. As the camera pulls back, you find that the pretty view is merely a hoarding, set among the crowded and often squalid sprawl of life as it is actually lived in South Auckland.

This is where Rugby League players come from and, apart from trying to keep track of 101 Ways to Open a Beer Bottle, one of the delights of the film is spotting the references to the game. All the men, and some of the women, look like they've survived a match or two, and you can pick out any number of club shirts and stickers – although nobody I noticed had a Mangere East jersey like the one I bought in a car park from their sponsor, the famous Mad Butcher. Not that I ever got much wear out of it. 'You are not walking around Bolton in a shirt with "The Mad Butcher" all over it,' I was told when I got home, proud as punch with the new garment. I bet none of the guys in *Once Were Warriors* gets ordered around like that. And their womenfolk have useful skills, too, like opening a quart bottle of Lion Red with a fish slice – which, for me, was one of the highlights of the film.

Plenty of people in New Zealand fervently disliked *Once Were Warriors*, because of the unflattering portrait of the country, and particularly of Maori urban domestic life, that it conveyed. They were especially unhappy about it being shown abroad, believing that the violence and drunkenness would put potential visitors right off. They had a right to their sensitivity. It's odd that the relationship between New Zealand and Britain is such a one-way street, even in an area – such as Rugby League – where we have so much in common. New Zealanders flock by the planeload to play in England; players who travel in the opposite direction have been, at least before Denis Betts and Andy Platt, a phenomenal rarity. They come on full-blown tours to Britain and France; we traditionally tag a couple of weeks there apologetically on to the end of the important business in Australia. They know all about us; we know only that they have a lot of sheep. And the game itself doesn't build much of a bridge for visitors to cross into a fuller understanding. The handful of people who have followed Great Britain tours of New Zealand have seen little outside the cities of Auckland, Christchurch and Wellington – because that is where the matches have been.

The one exception to these limitations was the 1990 Lions tour – the one which didn't go to Australia, and which therefore had the scope to take in League backwaters such as Napier and New Plymouth. In this pre-Warriors era, a touring team coming to towns where the code had always had to struggle for its existence was a big deal. Nowadays, the fans in those places can all go up to Auckland every other weekend to soak up the razzmatazz of the Winfield-cum-Optus Cup. In the relatively recent time of 1990, however, the game in New Zealand was still an intensely parochial affair, with each area running its own little competition, largely in isolation from the rest of the country. Places which had long given up hope of staging a representative match got one on the 1990 tour; these were places such as Huntly, a down-at-heel, closed-down, coal-mining town, which struck me as the Featherstone of the southern hemisphere. Huntly's greatest claim to fame is that it was the home town of Tawera Nikau. People there were greatly interested in how Nikau, who had returned for the Test series, had been playing in Britain with Sheffield Eagles, although they had a disconcerting way of asking: 'How's the black fellow going?' Tin out of tin for plain-speaking.

If Huntly was a backwater, then Thames, in the same far-flung Waikato competition, was a minor tributary of that backwater. Up on the Coromandel Peninsula, which thrusts out into the sea to the east of Auckland, Thames is small-town New Zealand to a tee: a couple of streets, a couple of shops, a couple of pubs and, because there were a handful of enthusiasts to run it, a Rugby League team. Such was the insistence of the Thames contingent at the Huntly match that I should come and see how the game was really played out in the sticks, that I felt obliged to go and have a look. It was, for one thing, supposed to be a beautiful part of the world. That may well be the case, but all I saw was rolling mist and pouring rain.

Rain is a major factor in New Zealand. On an average winter's day in Auckland, it might shower and clear up half a dozen times.

When I took the family there a couple of years after that tour, it rained all the time – something else that the brochures don't tell you. In 1990, Thames also succeeded in cutting out the interludes between downpours to produce a day-long deluge. Not to worry, the Thames secretary assured me; this amount of rain might have caused a few problems in the past, but now they had installed drains in the pitch. The show would go on.

Then there was the team. Had I seen *Once Were Warriors* by this stage, I would have typecast the Thames players as a bunch of would-be extras rejected by the film because they looked too mean. They were a motorbike gang of Maori wild-men who were just having a game of footy on a Saturday afternoon as a spot of light relief from looting, rape and pillage. Mind you, the visiting side were not dissimilar; same dreadlocks, same tattoos, same ancient leathers. The pitch was ankle-deep in mud which would have done Carlaw Park justice, and that was before anyone had as much as trodden on it. This was going to be World War I in Technicolor.

In fact, it was nothing like that. Even in impossible conditions, everyone wanted to be a ball-handler or, failing that, a thrilling broken-field runner, and some of the most fearsome-looking characters were among the more notable fancy-dans. It did degenerate into something reminiscent of trench warfare towards the end, but that was only because, by that time, there was a trench. Those much-vaunted drains, dug in a line across the pitch, started to sink, creating a distinct depression out of which the players had to scramble, like squaddies going over the top and into no man's land. Afterwards, the local newspaper turned out to interview me about my impressions of the game. I told them that I thought it could catch on: Rugby League with a ditch in the middle of the pitch. And, sure enough, Sky Sports have based much of their promotional material for Super League on exactly that concept.

Even if the game failed to live up to expectations, you would expect, would you not, the after-match festivities to be a little on the wild and woolly side. Not a bit of it. New Zealand is still a touchingly formal country in many ways and, for an official function, even in Thames, the denims and leathers are magically replaced by club sweaters and ties. Captains still make speeches after grass-roots matches in New Zealand.

'Youse blokes played real good and, if youse blokes carry on playing like that, we'll see youse blokes in the play-offs.'

Of course, this being Kiwidom, there are crates after crates after crates of Lion Red to shift, but it is done with a certain homespun decorum. Australians like to boast of being the world's greatest piss-artists, but the average Kiwi could put them under the table with ease, brought up as they are on a standard round of a crate of quart bottles. It's a rare example of New Zealanders being able to put one over on big brother across the Tasman.

Another is the unstoppable march of the Universal Interrogative. You know the one I mean? The rising inflection at the end of any sentence? Whether it is a question or not? It could be taken to denote a collective insecurity. Instead of saying 'I went to the game in Thames', a Kiwi has to say 'I went to the game in Thames?' – which is to say 'I think I went to Thames, if that's all right with you, but feel free to correct me if you think I might be mistaken'. In fact, it occurs to me now that I might have misled you about our wet, battered scrum-half Vance. What he actually used to shout was: 'Tin?' Anyone fancy that move at all?

The irony is that something which might be taken as a symbol of national indecision should have become New Zealand's leading export, replacing lamb, butter and all the other stuff which we now get from our friends in the EC. It is a widespread misconception that this upward inflection is Australian in origin, because it has been propagated worldwide through the medium of TV soaps such as *Neighbours?* and *Home and Away?*. But the Universal Interrogative is a Kiwi invention and can be heard in its purest form in the one New Zealand soap, *Shortland Street?*. What is certain is that, via Australia, the Universal Interrogative is sweeping the English-speaking world. A great Kiwi triumph?

If there is one place in New Zealand wetter than Thames, it would have to be New Plymouth, out on the west coast of the North Island in Taranaki, whence came such luminaries as the Tamatis and Graeme West – although nobody in 1990 asked us: 'How's the tall fellow doing?' Great Britain played a Taranaki Invitation XIII of returning Taranakians in a setting which resembled a washed-out early-'70s rock festival, with most of the crowd bringing sheets of polythene in which to swathe themselves. 'Jeez, she's a bit wet?' they said, as if requiring confirmation.

Connoisseurs of these matters say that if you really want to see New Zealand at its rainiest, though, you have to go to the West Coast of the South Island, to the area around Greymouth known simply as 'The Coast'. If you come from that part of the world you are a Coaster, which does not mean that you are a member of a close-harmony American singing group of the 1950s – the original purveyors of 'Poison Ivy', if I'm not mistaken – but that you are, even by Kiwi standards, one hell of a rum bastard. Even in the bad old days when New Zealand closed down for three days at the weekend and the pubs shut at teatime, the West Coast was a law unto itself. Famously gregarious, droll and thirsty, Coasters operated their own rules and regulations under which the only sin that was frowned upon was to be a 'piker', or to dodge your round.

It was the sort of area to give you a thirst. A gold rush brought the original population in, and they stayed on to mine coal and log the forests. Needless to say, there is not much left of either activity these days. The Coast retains its enviable reputation for precipitation, however. As if to prepare me, my book on the region quoted a visitor earlier this century who was moved to verse by the climate:

It rained and rained and rained.
The average fall was well maintained,
And when the tracks were simply bogs
It started raining cats and dogs.
After a drought of half an hour,
We had a most refreshing shower.
And then the most curious thing of all,
A gentle rain began to fall.
Next day was also fairly dry,
Save for a deluge from the sky
Which wetted the party to the skin
And after that the rain set in.

The other sphere of excellence for which the West Coast is renowned is Rugby League. The areas around Greymouth (population 14,000, and the biggest town on the Coast) must have produced more Test players per head than anywhere in the world – more than Wigan, more than the Bermuda triangle of Wakefield, Featherstone and Castleford, more than Sydney. The town is full of former Kiwis. Cec Mountford and his two Kiwi brothers come from Blackball, a village up the road which makes Featherstone look like Manhattan. Tony Coll, probably the last in a great line of born-and-bred West Coast forwards, has a sports shop on Greymouth's main street. And, as I was to find out, if you trip over a drunk on the pavement, the odds are that he has several New Zealand caps stashed away somewhere.

The Coast is the one place in New Zealand where League has always been the dominant code among the *pakeha*, or European, population. Uniquely in New Zealand now, the Coast remains largely monoglot – it is hardly a place where Polynesians would choose to live – but it resolutely declines to become excited by white New Zealand's sporting obsession with the All Blacks. This is League country, and it is far more important to know whether Waro-Rakau – 'Wood and Coal' – have beaten Cobden-Kohinoor, or whether the West Coast representative side has achieved one of its periodic victories over the other provincial teams.

This is a part of the world celebrated by Geoffrey Moorhouse in his inspiring collection of essays on the game, *At the George*. Moorhouse worked on the local paper, *The Grey River Argus*, in the late 1950s, a time when the mines were still thriving, and the West Coast side regularly broke out of its fastness to embarrass city teams and was considered close to unbeatable at home, especially when Wingham Park was shin-deep in the unusually cloying Greymouth mud. Memories were still fresh of the 1947–48 touring squad to Britain and France in which, of a party of 25, no fewer than seven were Coasters – rum bastards to a man.

This was a part of the world which, in 1990, simply had to be seen. One fortunate thing about the West Coast is that, like the Vatican, it has ambassadors everywhere. Such is the lack of job prospects in the area now that many Coasters have little option but to leave, which means that, wherever you go in New Zealand, there are exiles who grow dewy-eyed at the recollection of the rain, the closed-down mines, the Mountford brothers and Charlie McBride. This is particularly the case in Christchurch, the big metropolis over the mountains as far as Coasters are concerned. I mentioned my desire to see the Coast to the estimable John Coffey, the Rugby League writer on *The Christchurch Press*, and when he had recovered from the requisite pangs of nostalgia and homesickness, he got things moving. West Coasters – even expatriate ones – view the prospect of visitors as a challenge. We'll show you what makes us so stubbornly proud to come from this God-forsaken place, they say. Phone calls are made, welcoming parties are laid on, former Kiwis are told that, if they are in a certain bar at a certain time, there'll be a Pom who'd love to have a beer and a yarn about old times with them. Best of all, contact is made with Peter Kerridge, the

103

local chemist, who regards it as a sacred duty to organise a 24-hour crash course in the Rugby League heritage of the West Coast.

But first you have to get there. There is really only one sensible way to do this, and that, if you are in Christchurch, is the TranzAlpine Express. To call the scenery on this 145-mile rail journey varied would be like saying that the average Coaster quite likes a beer; it would be a gross and insulting understatement. Once out of Christchurch, you cross the Canterbury Plains, through the sort of green and sheep-dotted countryside which they might put on a hoarding in South Auckland. Then, gradually at first, but soon more dramatically, you start to climb the Southern Alps, up through tunnels and corkscrew bends, over gorges and viaducts to the high point of the line at Arthur's Pass, where the train obligingly stops for a while to allow you to throw snowballs. This – the pass, rather than the railway – was the route through which the Maoris reached the Westland and, when Rugby League became the source of contention between Christchurch and the Coast, that through which teams travelled by horse and cart for away games.

You drop from the summit of the journey into something quite different – a tropical rainforest watered by up to 200 inches of precipitation per year. Down through Otira, Aickens, Jackson, Inchbonnie, Poerua, Roto Manu, Te Kinga, Ruru, Moana, Kotuku, Kaimata and Kokira to Stillwater, Dobson and Greymouth. The middle section of that list might sound like one of Halifax's more exotic backlines, but what it actually denotes is a string of tiny settlements, clinging to the railway line and trying not to be washed down into the Tasman by the endless rain.

The one constant in the changing scene between Christchurch and Greymouth is the remarkable comfort in which you view it. New Zealand Railways have a penchant for sheepskin seats – largely as an attempt, I suspect, to use up a resource of which the country has far too much. It is one of the better-known facts about New Zealand that there are 30 sheep for every man, woman and child, so recycling a few of their overcoats as bum-warmers on the trains does not make much impression on the glut.

The other great cultural icon beneath which the country threatens to disappear is the kiwi fruit. If New Zealand has more sheep than people, then it has more kiwi fruit than sheep droppings – larger versions of which they superficially resemble. To an extent, the ubiquitous kiwi is one of New Zealand's great success stories. A rare delicacy a generation ago, New Zealand has intensively cultivated the little hairy eggs to the point where it ships them to all corners of the globe by the supertanker-load. Along with the Universal Interrogative, it is New Zealand's most bountiful export. But, even though they pump them out of the place by the millions of tonnes, they still have more left at home than they can possibly use. Supermarkets give them away by the sackful, rather than mess around with a few cents change. They are sold by the gross at the roadside for laughably low prices. In fact, the ultimate New Zealand roadside sign would read: 'Git yer kiwis here?'

One of the lesser-known facts about New Zealand is that it is illegal not to eat kiwi fruit. Under the terms of the Kiwi Fruit (Consumption) Act of 1985, any meal of two or more courses must include kiwi fruit somewhere along the line. In practice, most restaurants play safe by incorporating them in every course – indeed, in every item on the menu. Thus a typical repast might consist of kiwi-fruit soup, lamb in kiwi-fruit sauce, followed by sweet revenge on a trans-Tasman import, kiwi-fruit pavlova. Other meals can be kiwified equally effectively. Breakfast? A couple of lightly boiled kiwi fruit in their shells, with toast soldiers. A late-night supper after chucking-out time? A few kiwi fruit, battered and deep-fried with chips. There is even a kiwi-fruit liquor, although I have yet to hear the order: 'Hey, bro' . . . a crate of Lion Red and half a dozen kiwi-fruit liquors' in any New Zealand watering-hole.

Even with this concerted, constitutional effort to dispose of them, New Zealand groans under the weight of the surplus. Why do you think that the country is known as the Shaky Isles? Volcanic activity? That's what they want you to believe. In fact, New Zealand trembles under the burden of its national fruit, and rocks and rolls in time with Mount Kiwi Fruit shifting on its haunches. There was once a rumour that they had found a way to fuel the trains with them – well, it was either that or burning sheepskins. It turned out not to have been the breakthrough that would avert kiwi-fruit apocalypse, but it does remind me that we have veered off up a branchline here and had better return to Greymouth.

The aforementioned Peter Kerridge is the leading authority on the history of the game on the West Coast so, after a few kiwi fruit to sustain us, we set out to find it. It was not a difficult thing to locate, what with McBride – described by no less a pundit than Eddie Waring as just about the best forward he had seen after the 1946 tour – living virtually next door, and Bob Aynsley, the hooker on that same tour, the groundsman at a gratifyingly wet and muddy

Wingham Park. Both of them played in the old Blackball team with the three Mountford brothers. 'Old players always say that the game was better in their day,' says Aynsley as the rain rattles down on the tin roof, 'but, really, the best representative side that the Coast could put out now wouldn't be able to live with that old Blackball team.'

McBride, in his mid-60s by this stage but still seen regularly out running the streets of Greymouth, had an economic explanation for the Coast's strength in his younger days. 'We had all the coal-mines and the sawmills, and the blokes who worked there then were tough, hard men.' Never mind then; you wouldn't argue with him now.

Wingham Park itself has a few good tales to tell. In 1951 the French side – Puig-Aubert and all, fresh from their triumph in Australia – played the West Coast there, as did British touring sides in those days. In 1954, Greymouth became the smallest town in the world – smaller even than any of the towns in Papua New Guinea which have done so since – to host a Rugby League Test when a New Zealand side, including three Coasters, met and beat Great Britain. Generations of Coasters grew up expecting their home-grown players to be able to beat anyone who came to Greymouth.

'We were probably complacent,' the local league's president, Ted Gutbelert, told me. 'Because we were so strong, we thought it would go on for ever. But money governs everything in this country now, and if you're any good you're enticed away. Because there isn't much work here now, we lose a lot of young people to Australia. There must be 30 or 40 of our former young players there now.' That might not sound like many, but it's a big slice out of the playing resources of a small area like the Coast. Even Coffey trod that route once, playing in the Wollongong competition and taking over the jersey of one Bob Fulton when he moved on to bigger things. Trust a Coaster to come back with a tale like that to tell.

The supply-line of West Coasters to the Kiwi squad has virtually come to a stop. Gordon Smith was the last of more than 50 internationals from the Coast to hold a regular place in the New Zealand side, although more recent caps Whetu Taewa and Quentin Pongia spent part of their schooldays on the Coast and so count as honorary Coasters. The reason for the breakdown is easy enough to isolate even on a 24-hour crash course. Runanga, the mining village which produced Kiwis of the stature of George Menzies and Jock Butterfield, now consists of little more than retirement bungalows.

We drove on to Blackball, where the tiny oval had thrilled to the feats of what must have been New Zealand's best club side in the late 1940s and early 1950s, but where there is now nothing stirring. In fact, Blackball has been forced to amalgamate with the similarly depressed logging settlement of Ngahere in order to get a team on the field at all.

The mayor of Greymouth, Dr Barry Dallas, assures me that the decline is reversible: that Japanese companies are interested in exploiting the coal reserves which remain, and that the Coast's economy will rise again. He has also argued that the Coast should declare itself independent of the rest of New Zealand – which has come as a surprise to some locals, who were under the impression that it already was. Dr Dallas, a Greymouth 'character' as well as its first citizen, makes out a very plausible case, but it needs to be remembered that this is the same man who appointed his dog as mayoress. Not that Coasters consider this to be particularly bizarre behaviour. 'It's a smart dog,' they say.

Whatever the future of the mines, Greymouth retains enviable stocks of ex-Kiwis. A random trawl around town reveals another half-dozen, including Coll in his sports shop and one bloke in an especially bad state in the pub. He was a hero, too, in his day. And, when we trip over someone dead drunk in a doorway, Peter is able to reel off his Test record as well.

The West Coast has fallen off the international Rugby League map now. Tours – including this one in 1990 – no longer call there, a situation which Moorhouse for one calls 'a scandal . . . when they go to hopeless places like Taranaki'. Just as well, perhaps, I reflect on the station platform where another Coaster, Jack 'Chang' Newton, set out on tour with his gear packed in a sack from the pit, that Great Britain didn't include the Coast in their itinerary. Judging by their results to date in Christchurch, Wellington and Auckland, the Coast would probably have beaten them.

Back over the Southern Alps in Christchurch, the Canterbury provincial side did make history by beating the Lions at the Addington Showgrounds for the first time in 70 years – with, I must point out, a couple of expatriate Coasters in the side. It was a famous day for League in Christchurch, but the abiding memory I have of the city is of the unique arrangement in operation at the Showgrounds for local club matches. The trouble with the venue is that they customarily play two games simultaneously there, but there is only room for two pitches if they are marked out end-to-end and share the same in-goal area. This struck me as a circumstance that was bound to lead to spectacular collisions as play converged from the two different directions. Not so, said Coffey. He had been watching matches there for 20-odd years and had never seen such a thing happen. I therefore hold myself personally responsible for the fact that, before the words were fully out, two full-backs were being carried off after meeting head-on in pursuit of a matching pair of kicks behind the line.

Mark Broadhurst had never seen it happen either. Then coaching in Christchurch and, if you recall, number three in the all-time scariest list for New Zealand forwards, Mark saw it as incumbent on him to take me back to meet the family and have a good feed of kiwi fruit and all the trimmings. We had only met a couple of times before. If you are ever down and out in New Zealand, look out for the most battered ex-prop in the vicinity, and he will invariably look after you.

If the rest of New Zealand is justly famed for its rain, Wellington majors in wind. Chicago has no right to the title of the Windy City; alongside the Kiwi capital, it is merely the Breezy City. Papers in Wellington regularly record instances of people injured by being blown over as they step out of doorways. Mind you, this is the seat of Parliament and the vortex of the long expense-account lunch, so there is a suspicion that some of the casualties could involve forces other than wind-assistance. Wellington turned on both the wind and the rain in 1990 as a truly dreadful Great Britain made further history by losing to the locals for the first time ever. A few Wellington players were blown over after their celebrations that night.

Rotorua's distinguishing feature is its smell. When set alongside Rotorua, Widnes might be Maori for 'fragrant village by the clear waters'. Rotorua stinks to high heaven; a sulphurous, rotten-eggs odour to which it must take years to grow fully accustomed. I will not embarrass him by identifying the British journalist who changed his hotel room there three times, insisting each time that something had recently died under the bed.

I'm sure that parts of New Zealand which I missed on this and subsequent trips also have their own distinctive flavour. There's the whole stretch to the north of Auckland, for instance: Northland is known for the warmth of its rain and has an expanse of sand known as Ninety-Mile Beach – which, this being New Zealand, is 70 miles long. I have got no closer to it than the mail boat on the Hauraki

Gulf which runs from downtown Auckland three times a week; but one day there will be a convenient gap between matches. Most alluring of all is Chatham Island, population 750, and 500 miles out into the Pacific from Christchurch. This is an offcut of a remote country which is so remote that, in my guidebook, it appears after the index. I have a map of it in front of me now as I write, and I can just imagine the vibrant nightlife in the string of settlements along the shore of Petre Bay: Te Ngaio, Waitangi, Te One, Big Bush, Te Kairakau. The greatest living Chatham Islander is Brendon Tuuta – the artist formerly known as the Baby-Faced Assassin. He can be fairly scary, too, so, if I happen to mention to him on my next visit to Castleford that I'm thinking of visiting his birthplace, I should be assured of the fatted kiwi fruit. But then, Chatham Island might be sufficiently isolated from the mainstream of New Zealand life that it does not even have kiwi fruit. There is only one way to find out.

This ramble around the Shaky Isles, the Land of the Long White Cloud – and I've had that one dump on me a few times – should end where it started, in Auckland. Back before the Warriors, Rugby League, even at the most rarefied level it reached in New Zealand, carried the amiable air of an enjoyable hobby. One of the nicest men ever involved in it was Bob Bailey, the Kiwi coach in 1990. Bob had a wonderful record as the steward of Auckland sides which regularly beat touring teams as well as everyone else in New Zealand, but he was one of a succession of Kiwi coaches after Graham Lowe who seemed somewhat overwhelmed by the national job. One of the most likeable aspects of his approach was his complete lack of the guile and secrecy which characterised the rival regimes of Fulton and Malcolm Reilly. I was once suspected by the Lions manager, Maurice Lindsay, of passing information to 'the other side' simply because I was partial to sharing a few beers with Kiwi journalists such as Coffey. Contrast that with Bailey's attitude when a few of us Poms went down to watch the New Zealand side in training. They were running through a few moves but, because he feared that we might not have seen these clearly enough, Bob got his lads to go through them again at walking pace.

Unfortunately for Bob, his team lost the first two Tests, at Palmerston North and Auckland, to a far less relaxed and happy-go-lucky Great Britain. They only lost them narrowly; but they lost them, and the word was out in New Zealand that genial Bob Bailey was not up to the job.

I saw Bob again at Auckland Airport as both teams prepared to fly down to Christchurch for the final Test in a series which was, for him, already gone. He was anything but downcast. 'Great series, hasn't it been? Terrific rugby! I've really enjoyed it. But, would you believe it, there's been people grumbling about it. Blowed if I know what they want.'

I had to point out, as gently as possible, that what they probably wanted was for him to win a few Test matches – an insight which could not have struck him more forcibly had it been a double-decker bus on the road to Damascus. 'Cripes! You could be right. But how d'you reckon I could do that?'

Well, Bob, you've got to pick a few players who don't drop as many balls and miss as many tackles. Eureka! And, sure enough, New Zealand, armed with that new tactical master-plan, did win the final Test.

It was a long way in a short time from that to the opening night at Ericsson. It is hard to imagine Warriors' coach John Monie failing to appreciate the paramount importance of winning, or seeking advice on how to do so from a know-nothing in an airport departure lounge. It is a much more serious business now. On the other hand, the most professional Rugby League coach I've ever come across absorbed enough Kiwiness into his bloodstream during his first season that he played an extra substitute in one match by mistake, and later appeared at training in a dunce's hat. They would have enjoyed that down on the Coast.

# The White-Haired Man's Burden

## Dave Hadfield

The immigration officer at Port Moresby Airport studied my visa suspiciously, especially the line, painstakingly printed by the embassy in London, which said that I was there to follow the 1990 Great Britain Rugby League tour. He eyed and sniffed the statement, studied my picture, compared it with the real thing, and adopted the posture of a man who was not going to allow me to enter Papua New Guinea without having several things explained to him. This was a blow. That visa had taken several months to obtain, but with it, I had blithely assumed, the door to the place should swing open without too much further trouble. No such luck. It seemed to get even more oppressively hot in the entry hall, the ceiling fans whirring a little slower as the prospect of hours of interrogation began to loom.

'There is one thing you must tell me,' he said. Yes, yes, I'll try. God knows I'll try. It won't be necessary to test out any ways you might have of making me talk.

'Why are Ellery Hanley and Martin Offiah not here?'

That was a tough one. How was I to explain diplomatically that it probably had something to do with the fact that Port Moresby was not Sydney; that injuries which might just have allowed a person to cross his fingers, hope for the best and fly to Australia could instantaneously rule that same person out of a tour which offered only New Zealand and PNG. Hanley and Offiah – by far the two most important British players as far as supporters in PNG were concerned – were just two of about a dozen players who had withdrawn after being originally selected, leaving the coast clear for the likes of Ian Smales, Shaun Irwin and Chris Bibb, none of whom were exactly household names in Pontefract, let alone Port Moresby. PNG had been promised the big heroes – the big, black heroes at that – and the nearest thing it was getting was Roy Powell. Our man with the rubber stamp wanted an explanation, and the most tactful one seemed to be the official line that the two eagerly awaited stars were injured.

By now a little knot had formed in the background, consisting of others who also wanted to know why they weren't here. We told the immigration officer why. He turned to them and said: 'Hanley, Offiah *bugarap*.' Disappointed, but curiosity satisfied, they sidled away, and down came the rubber stamp.

*Bugarap*. Or *bagarap*, as it is sometimes rendered. It just about sums up the outside world's view of Papua New Guinea: a wild, primitive place where nothing works properly, a profoundly uncomfortable place to which you only go if you have to. There is an element of truth in this. From a western standpoint, life in PNG is indeed primitive, which is why anthropologists love the country so dearly. In the 1930s, when Australians first penetrated the mountainous interior of their mysterious northern neighbour, they found peoples who believed that they were the only inhabitants of the world. These people did not even know that there were other people, superficially like themselves but speaking a different language, living in the next valley and sharing the same mutual ignorance. So when men arrived who were white – the colour of ghosts – and who travelled in giant roaring birds, they were, not surprisingly, gobsmacked. The book *First Contact* by Bob Connolly and Robin Anderson describes these first incursions. Anyone looking for a visual definition of astonishment could do no better than the grainy photographs in this book of Highlanders encountering such unimaginable strangeness for the first time.

The country as a whole still sometimes seems stunned at what has happened to it over the last few decades. Calling it a country at all is a masterpiece of European wishful thinking; taking 178,000 square miles of mountain, swamp and island – variously administered by Britain, Germany, Australia, or nobody in particular – drawing a neat line around them, and declaring them a nation. The inhabitants of this invention speak 700 different languages and have, in some cases, as much in common with each other as a computer programmer has with a Stone-Age farmer. It is no wonder that things get a bit *bugarap* from time to time.

One of the jibes thrown at Rugby League's failure to conquer the world is that it is the national game in only one small, insignificant country. Yet PNG is twice the size of Great Britain, with the important difference that it does not, for the most part, have roads. And it has a habit of losing bits, with Bougainville trying to secede, and part of New Britain being buried under volcanic ash. It should, by rights, be twice as big as it is; but the Indonesians, the region's new imperialists, grabbed half the island of New Guinea and called it Irian Jaya. A low-level independence struggle still goes on there, which only comes to our attention when they take a few Brits hostage, as they did in 1995. It was when reports from their camp described the rebel army as spending most of its time playing soccer that I began to feel really angry with Indonesia. If New Guinea was all one, they would have been Rugby League players. Contact the United Nations. Indonesia has stolen our footballers.

Irian Jaya is even more *bugarap* than PNG, but PNG is *bugarap* enough. For one thing, it is just too damn hot. Not the go-to-the-beach-and-have-a-few-beers heat of Australia, but lie-down-and-die heat. Stepping off an air-conditioned plane in Port Moresby is like walking into a wall of hot, wet cotton-wool. You think at first that you must be standing in the wake of the plane's engines, before you realise that this is the normal temperature here, day and night.

Then there are the rascals. PNG has a bad name for rascals – a quaint way of bracketing together the various gangs of young men who hang around, especially in Moresby, ready to bop the unwary over the head and relieve them of their valuables. They are the reason for the armed guards on the doors of hotels and why, should you venture out on foot when the sun has as much as started to set, an Australian expatriate will screech to a halt, ask if you are bloody mad, and order you to get in. You hear so much about random acts of violence in PNG that your logical first assumption is that the garish red stains on every pavement are congealed blood. In fact, they come from betel nut, chewed for its mild narcotic effect and spat out wherever. The biggest notice at the Lloyd Robson Oval, the headquarters of Rugby League in Port Moresby, insists: 'No rascal T-shirts. No betel nut chewing.' Every house which might conceivably have something worth stealing is surrounded by a perimeter fence. It is not a relaxing place to be.

There is no avoiding it. PNG can be a violent country. Its main road, the Highlands Highway, is occasionally closed because two villages have set aside an afternoon for a pitched battle to settle some local grievance. Newspapers carry advance warning of this, almost like listing sporting fixtures. 'Payback' – the redress of wrongs suffered by an individual or community – is a dominant ethical concept, while head-hunting is something which the old-timers can still recall. No wonder they took to Rugby League in such a big way. As the PNG manager at the Centenary World Cup put it so succinctly: 'We like Rugby League because it is brutal.'

To say merely that they like Rugby League does not come close, however, to defining PNG's relationship with the code. It would be akin to saying that Wigan likes pies. PNG is besotted with the game. It's a job for the anthropologists to explain why, along with pidgin English, it is the one unifying factor in such a diverse, loosely bound-together country. It must just chime with their view of life, the remnants of the warrior culture, the centrality of tribal pride. They love it for the same reasons they love it in Featherstone. Whatever the technicalities, this bond adds a completely different layer to the experience of travelling in PNG if you happen to be a Rugby League man. Everything might be *bugarap*, but you are, in one important sense, a *wantok*.

This is lesson two in Essential Rugby League Pidgin. A *wantok* – literally 'one talk' – originally meant a fellow-tribesman, or someone who speaks the same language which, in PNG, cuts it down a bit. On a broader context, however, it can also mean someone with whom you have something significant in common. And in PNG, nothing, with the possible exception of betel nut, is more significant than Rugby League. So that, I am proud to argue, makes Bal Numapo and Joe Gispe my *wantoks*. I have this recurring notion that if I was ever set upon by rascals in the back doubles of Moresby – which I never was – I would whip out my membership card for the Huyton and Doncaster Appreciation Society and brandish it like an amulet. The rascals, of course, would back off, mumbling contrite apologies for not recognising a *wantok*, and offering betel nut by way of payback.

I might be kidding myself, and I have no particular desire to test the theory; but, whether or not Port Moresby rascals would consider themselves my *wantoks*, Peter Ward certainly falls into that category. More than that, in 1990, he was that most valuable of companions for someone encountering a country and a way of life right outside his experience: someone who had already done the course and distance. Not only had he been to PNG before, he had also acted as a sort of unofficial liaison man and guide during the

French leg of their previous European tour in 1987, much of which seemed to have been spent by the players huddling together for warmth in a porno cinema. His *wantok* credentials were therefore impeccable. He even looks the part: white of hair and moustache, and ruddy of complexion, like a particularly apoplectic colonel or the district commissioner of some troublesome corner of the empire. It is Peter's contention that his distinguished appearance has helped him to command respect among the Kumuls, as the national team are known. A strange thing, that, I told him, since he commands so little in Yorkshire; but I could see what he meant. If he had flown into your valley in a biplane in 1933, you would have been impressed.

Peter is rightly famous for taking no crap from anyone, especially when he is on his travels, and some of his encounters with French railway ticket-inspectors are the stuff of legend. He also has ways of dealing with recalcitrant fellow-travellers. A few months ago an article in *The Independent*'s 'True Gripes' series dealt with the vexed topic of people who hog more than their share of seats on public transport. It concluded with these words:

> . . . the most difficult seat-hoggers to dislodge are those found on late-night transport. They spread themselves over two seats in order to sleep off the evening's excesses. Few people have the nerve to disturb a dormant passenger. I saw it done once, and in some style. A large man with a great shock of white hair and an outsized personality simply scooped up the pile of coats, scarves and sweaters on which the sleeper's head was resting, and flung them to one side. He pushed the sleeper upright and then dropped into the vacant seat, where he immediately fell into a deep and snoreful slumber. I suspect he was drunk but, oh, what a performance.

Peter denies that he was the white-haired man involved. In that case, he has a *Doppelgänger* travelling around the country doing a more than passable impersonation of him. At the very least, we are looking at the closest of *wantoks*, or a twin from whom he was separated at birth.

Peter has been unjustly compared to Victor Meldrew – and there are parallels, up to and including an incredibly patient wife with a gentle Scots accent. But, compared to Ward when something stands in the way of him getting where he wants to go or threatens his comfort while he does so, Meldrew is an ingratiating old softie. In short, this man is the ideal travelling companion.

Thanks to Peter's forceful negotiating style that summer in 1990, we were able to hammer out a favourable room rate at the Great Britain hotel – indeed, the only hotel, apart from a few betel-stained flop-houses – in Port Moresby. The tour management didn't like people making their own arrangements in this way and tried to get the hotel to raise its price to the normal level. The desk staff took one look at Peter as he began to twitch with indignation, and reduced it further.

It was an interesting sojourn there, not least because of my introduction to the Ward way of working. After a sociable evening, it was his practice to retire with a large tumbler of Scotch and eventually doze off, propped upright, ostensibly incapable of coherent thought or speech for at least eight hours. But when the phone rang ten minutes after he went into his coma, he would instantly regale listeners to the BBC's World Service with five minutes of perfectly enunciated, stone-cold-sober insight into the state of the British tour. The phone would go down, and he would be insensible again; I believe he must have been wired up to it in some way.

The other early impression garnered in Port Moresby was of how popular the Great Britain squad was rapidly becoming. Even without Hanley, Offiah and most of the others they might have heard of, the locals really seemed to be taking the players to their hearts. That was obvious from the startling quantity of Great Britain gear you began to see worn on the street – something which was happening at the same time as the team itself was starting to run drastically short of kit. There was a moral here: don't leave damp gear on the balcony to dry, otherwise a gust of wind or an agile rascal would ensure that it had a proud new owner by the morning. Great Britain training gear became almost as much of a status symbol as Winfield Cup jerseys, which were worn as Sunday best in Moresby up to and beyond the point of disintegration. You would see some particularly fine specimens on the beach where, between the rocks and the rubbish, there was always a game going on. Kids and adults alike, many of whom seemed to believe that I was Ian Lucas – well, we do all look much the same – would point to their shirts and shout: 'Balmain! Nambawan!' or 'Parramatta! Nambawan!' Or, if they had got lucky in the balcony raffle, 'Chris Bibb! Nambawan!'

It was in Lae, on the north coast of the PNG mainland, that the tour really got sticky. The bad news about escaping from the overpowering heat and lurking rascals of Moresby was that Lae was

116

generally considered to be even hotter and more rascally. There was certainly a memorable outbreak of rascaldom during the match against the Northern and Highland Zones, with the first whiff of tear-gas in evidence after thousands of people who could not get into the packed ground tried to storm the gates. It was here that the tour manager, Maurice Lindsay, had what many consider his finest hour when, like a little drummer boy rescuing the regimental standard, he retrieved the gate takings. Maurice later became somewhat embarrassed by Peter's purplish reporting of this incident – he was under heavy pressure to make the very most of it from *The Daily Express* – to the extent of briefly banning him from the team bus to and from matches. Given the crowd trouble which we had just witnessed, that was a rather worrying punishment. It might have been kinder to shoot him there and then.

Nobody, however, could ban us from the bus we were due to board next. If Peter was in charge of the macro-economics of the trip – the hotels and flights – I was in command of the micro-economics of local transport and cheap places to stay in the sticks. It was thus that we discovered the three initials that go hand in hand with PNG: PMV, or public motor vehicle. PMVs are minibuses or trucks which run between all the major towns and quite a few minor ones. My guidebook advised me to ignore the warnings of expatriates about PMVs. They were safe, it assured me, because the drivers could not afford to have accidents; the payback consequences of running over somebody's pig were just too horrendous.

The PMVs in Lae clustered in the centre of town, their drivers and/or conductors leaning out of the doors and announcing their destination. 'Kainantukainantukainantukainantu!' No good to us.

'Where yu going?'

'Goroka.'

'Gorokagorokagorokagoroka!'

The worst thing that can happen to you on a PMV, short of running down a particularly well-liked pig, is to be sat next to a missionary. PNG is full of them – Australians, New Zealanders and Americans of sundry denominations, all full of fervour and as annoying as hell. Many of them have guitars, and none of them can play or sing a note; a clear case of the devil having all the best tunes. Some of them tried to proselytise Ward on the road to Goroka, but he was able to tell them in unambiguous terms that he was already very much at ease with his maker.

The missionaries descended on the interior of PNG like ravenous dogs on a bone, once the gold prospectors had blazed the way. All those lovely heathens to convert, they thought, and they competed for them furiously. Virtually every community is now beset by God-botherers of every hue and persuasion, and it is due to their influence that perfectly serviceable items of clothing such as arse-grass and penis gourds have been discarded in favour of Winfield Cup jerseys. I like to imagine one of these tuneless twangers encountering a villager in a red and white shirt and demanding of him: 'Yu laikim Jesus?' To which he replies: 'Nogat, mi laikim St George.'

Better company by far are local folk, like the tiny old lady who got on midway through one of our PMV journeys in the Highlands. She was carrying a sack of coffee berries – the one cash crop in these parts – which was rather bigger than her, and which she was transporting to market. The only slight problem was that, until she sold the berries, she had no money with which to pay the fare. So we waited in the market-place while she joined the line of other old ladies with sacks to transact. After about half an hour, our driver began to chew his betel nut with increasing agitation – a sure sign that he was running out of patience. After a little longer, he grabbed our lady's sack, shoved his way to the front of the queue, slammed it on the scales, took the money, subtracted his fare, and gave her the rest. She seemed happy enough, and off we went.

Goroka, being officially off the beaten track, fell within my sphere of responsibility, and I felt that I had done well by booking us into the National Sports Institute on the outskirts of town. I had not known it at the time, but this was also where the PNG team was staying in preparation for the first Test against Great Britain. In fact, apart from the Kumuls, we appeared to be the only people staying at the institute. Not a problem, we thought, especially with Ward being a fully fledged *wantok,* adorned with the white locks of sagacious seniority. That was the theory: no doubt our welcome would have been warmer if it had not been strongly suspected that we were there as spies, sent by Malcolm Reilly to snoop on the Kumuls in training and report back to Port Moresby, where the rest of the tour party was still preparing for the Test at sea-level.

The trouble with this preposterous notion was that there was a grain of truth in it. We had promised Reilly's assistant, Phil Larder, that we would pace out the nearby pitch and report back on any quirks and eccentricities it might possess. Having done so, we were able to tell him that it was roughly rectangular and had very little grass on it. I was able to throw in the extra insight from having seen the Kumuls train that they used neither of Bolton's moves, but they did have several others which I didn't recognise. Conveying this valuable information back to base was fraught with danger, because the only phone at the institute was nailed to a tree in the open courtyard. The use of this was normally a fairly congenial arrangement, despite the flying insects, because one could stand outside of an evening and bellow one's stories down the line to the various newspapers which had displayed the good sense to hire us. After the first day, we had the man who ran the canteen well trained: at the merest sound of a reversed-charges call, he would be there with two bottles of South Pacific beer and would continue to bring supplies until the evening's business was concluded. The inside story from the Kumul camp had to be relayed more discreetly, however, while Ward created a distraction by singing loudly in the communal shower.

Our espionage did Great Britain no good whatsoever. Unaccustomed to the thin Highland air, they lost a Test to PNG for the first time, amid stone-throwing from more would-be spectators who had, in some cases, walked miles through the scrub only to discover that they could not get into the ground. After the stones came the tear-gas, although the PNG military succeeded only in gassing most of the crowd inside the stadium, rather than the rioters outside. The disruption did the tourists no good either, but at least they were honest enough afterwards to admit that they had been beaten by a better side on the day.

Although I had wanted Great Britain to win – we had been with, if not of, their party for most of the trip – I couldn't help being happy for the Kumuls; but then my patriotism gland has never functioned reliably. Now, back at the institute and like it or not, we were at the epicentre of PNG's celebration of only their second Test victory. It was clear after about ten minutes of this party that they hadn't got a prayer in the second Test in Port Moresby a week later. They were going to be in no sort of state for that; the players were bent on the piss-up of their lives. Even spies got to share a few South Pacifics that night. With an early-morning PMV to Lae to catch, we made our excuses and retired, but it was not easy to sleep a few yards away from where the Kumuls were still toasting the best day of their lives. Ward's old mate Joe Gispe had the extra status of owning a ghetto-blaster but, sadly, he only had one cassette single to play on it – which he did, repeatedly, at top volume until, at three in the morning, Peter had had enough.

'Leave this to me,' he said. 'They'll listen to me.' And off he strode down the staircase into the courtyard, like General Gordon of Khartoum (and we all know what happened to him). 'Joe Gispe! What the bloody hell do you think you're playing at?' Joe said words to the effect that what he would shortly be playing at would be roasting an old honky spy on a spit, because he and his team-mates were starting to feel peckish, and Ward returned, his hair a fractionally paler shade of white.

It seemed only right to take the old chap to recuperate in Rabaul, at the eastern end of the island which the Europeans named New Britain, but which is as close to a South Seas paradise as PNG gets – at least until the tear-gas starts. Home here was the New Guinea Club – all mahogany panelling, ceiling fans and gin-slings. All the essentials of civilised life, in fact, including a television set which could pick up the State of Origin from Australia, with the result that the entire Great Britain party crammed into the bar one night to give the New Guinea Club its best takings for many a long year.

The tourists won their match in Rabaul comfortably enough – or perhaps comfortably is the wrong word, as we were all gassed once more. By this stage, one or two were developing a tear-gas habit and started to suffer withdrawal symptoms if they didn't have a whiff for a day or two. A police chief was later arrested by his own men for triggering the problems by firing off a few canisters prematurely. Getting away from the ground was a bit of a worry as well, as it involved running a gauntlet of seriously over-excited fans who were intent on making contact with the players. If they couldn't quite catch John Devereux or Carl Gibson they were quite willing to swarm over the occasional freelance writer or broadcaster, and Ward had cause to employ his basilisk glare on a few of them to make good our escape.

PNG duly lost the second Test in Port Moresby – no tear-gas required, for a change – and Great Britain's most extensive tour of the world's most League-mad nation came to a close. The Kumuls' reward for having taken a Test off the Lions was that the next visit two years later consisted of only three matches. The 1996 tour of the antipodes, meanwhile, was originally scheduled to consist of just one match in PNG. It looks like pretty shoddy treatment, until you compare it with Australia's record. They have managed just one full-scale tour of the League hotbed which exists on their own doorstep. When you challenged the ARL about this sorry state of affairs, they would argue that they had sent PNG all the equipment, coaches, referees, smiling administrators, et cetera, et cetera, that they could possibly want. Everything, in fact, apart from what they really wanted, which was a chance to see in the flesh the players who are so revered there. That one Australian tour, in 1991, was played in front of packed, capacity crowds throughout. But it was a bit hairy at times, so it has been virtually crossed off the itinerary. And yet the ARL were astonished when PNG threw in their lot with Super League.

The shortened Great Britain tour in 1992 had its moments, notably the failure of the Island Zone side to turn up on time for its match in Rabaul. Our brave boys were left sweltering in the sun for half an hour – there were no changing-rooms at Queen Elizabeth Park – and the match was shortened to 35 minutes each way, ostensibly to enable the team to fly out before the airstrip packed up for the night, but actually to get back to the motel to cool off in the swimming-pool.

Rugby League in the Island Zone has had even more problems since then. Not only is Bougainville still staging its breakaway, but the last time we saw Rabaul on our TV screens, it had disappeared under several feet of volcanic ash. No more New Guinea Club, no more Queen Elizabeth Park – I have a picture of its one stand groaning and collapsing under the weight of the debris, and a single goalpost standing askew. Eruption and secession – you just don't have to contend with these things in the North-West Counties.

The Danny Leahy Oval in Goroka is still there and so, I trust, is Danny Leahy, the son of one of the Leahy brothers who opened up the Highlands in the 1930s. My second visit to Goroka, in 1992, was also something of a seminar in local history – sitting with the man after whom the ground was named and listening to his recollections of his early days on the island. 'You know,' he said,'as soon as they saw this game they fell in love with it.'

In one respect, the profile of our *wantoks* in Papua New Guinea has never been higher. The Kumuls performed with great credit in the Centenary World Cup and they have a scattering of players now plying their trade as far afield as Sydney and Humberside. I hope that the little contingent in Hull find our summers rather more to their liking than Philip Ralda found our winters. He played for Bradford Northern – of all clubs – in the early 1980s, and I have never in all my life seen a man look so permanently frozen. Wherever he is now – and nobody in PNG seemed to know – I trust he has thawed out. Kumul tourists in Britain have traditionally been provided with three tracksuits, which they have worn all at once – even when inside the porno cinema.

Across that great cultural and climatic divide, though, they remain our *wantoks*, even if, on an official level, we insist on treating them as an unfortunate liability. Maurice Lindsay even proposed at one stage that, if the Lions have to play in the damn place, it should be on the basis of flying in from Cairns for one Test and flying straight out again. If we really want to make them feel good, I have a better suggestion: why don't we just go over there and spit on their ancestors' bones? All this trouble that the outside world goes to in order to avoid visiting PNG is deeply depressing. Okay, so it was hot, uncomfortable and occasionally dangerous on our one full-scale tour there; but nobody died. Indeed, the only serious international incident to have taken place on that trip was a scrap in a sedate bar-cum-restaurant in Auckland.

Ward and I have been unofficial ambassadors for the place for the last few years. But it's not done much good. We must have reported the rock-throwing and the tear-gas too vividly, because PNG remains synonymous in the western mind – that small section of the western mind which knows of its existence at all – with sudden and violent death. But I'll go back. I still want to see what it's like in Madang and up the Sepik and the Fly Rivers. And have they got a little local league running in Bougainville yet?

My mentor and *wantok* Mr Ward has no choice but to go back there at fairly regular intervals, because it is the only way he can get the money they owe him as Radio Kalang's voice of European sport. He could, you might think, just ring up the accounts department and complain, something he does very effectively in most other situations. But the phone there has been *bugarap* for several years now, and it seems simpler just to turn up at the office every now and again, *en route* to Australia or New Zealand. It's a long way to go for a few *kina*, but there's a principle involved. Besides, he's made up with Joe Gispe now and needs to check up on his *wantoks*. Papua New Guinea – the white-haired man's burden.

SOUTH AFRICA

# Bakkie to the Future

## Dave Hadfield

My friend Trevor Gibbons, whose musings on the quintessential flatness of Holland form one of the high spots – if that is not a contradiction – of this collection, has vivid memories of his first visit to Soweto. There were three of us and only two seats up front in the *bakkie*, that ubiquitous South African open-backed truck. Dave Southern and I had those seats, taking advantage of the ancient tribal custom that only people called Dave should be allowed to sit inside, while Trevor was in the back with 30 rugby balls. Don't waste too much sympathy on him. On a warm day, with the rugby balls arranged into an *ad hoc chaise-longue*, it was by no means an uncomfortable way to travel. So comfy was it, in fact, that by the time we were in Soweto proper Trevor was sound asleep, dreaming no doubt of old Hull triumphs.

He was jolted half-awake when we stopped at a crossroads. The first thing he saw when he opened his eyes was a burly black man leaping over the tail-gate and on to the *bakkie*, the pair of garden shears with which he was armed glinting under the African sun.

'Good morning!' he said, thrusting out his hand. 'I am Gordon.'

It's not true what they tell you about Soweto, thinks Trevor, his past life flashing before his eyes. Their muggers and murderers are the most polite in the world. But Gordon, you will be relieved to hear, was neither of those things. He was a schoolmaster, a Rugby League enthusiast and a part-time gardener – hence the shears – and he and people like him cut through an awful lot of our preconceptions over the next few weeks.

There is, as we observed in our sage and diplomatic way on our return to Britain, a vast amount of crap talked about South Africa, some of it by people like us who go for three weeks, but much of it by South Africans. Nowhere is that more true than in the matter of the townships. White South Africans, in my experience, simply refuse to accept that you can go unarmed into Soweto and Alexandra and emerge not only in one piece, but having had a marvellous time. Small wonder, then, that the first time you go there you do so in some trepidation – not helped when a man with a couple of sharp blades leaps towards you. Dave Southern spends most of his working day in these places. He is still alive – although there might be some who wish that he wasn't.

It is Southern's firm belief that Rugby League can establish itself as a thriving code in South Africa, but only if it goes out and evangelises for new participants among the majority black population. There are two strands of opposition to this. The first comes from those, both inside and outside the country, whose conviction, although they might dress it up in all manner of euphemism, is that the blacks aren't much good for anything, and time or energy spent trying to get them interested is bound to be wasted. The second is less ideological, and concedes that the black townships represent the right route for the game – but then dismisses it as too hard.

Rugby League has a big 'too hard' basket. All sorts of schemes and plans get pushed into it because they require too much thought and effort. It is far easier to say: 'Oh, Wales/South Africa/Fiji/France . . . Rugby Union is so powerful there. It's so difficult to compete with that.' And then if, in the face of those self-evident truths, you can persuade a few Rugby Union players to put on different shirts and moonlight in League for a while, you can convince yourself that you've made a major breakthrough. It's nice to see it happen, of course, and we all cheered when the South African Rhinos started to show some signs of discovering what the hell was going on during the Centenary World Cup. But it isn't Rugby League development. What Southern does is Rugby League development.

Southern is from Widnes; a stubborn, cussed sort of individual – which is not exactly the same thing. Many of his friends, both back home and in Johannesburg, reckon that the chemicals got into his brain at an early age. That is the only explanation they can find for the way he has clamped his jaws around the dream of black kids in Alexandra and Soweto growing up playing Rugby League, and refuses to let it go. At a time when the game has become increasingly associated with sharp suits, personalised number-plates and swish corporate offices, Southern runs his side of things from the front seat of his *bakkie* and his kitchen table.

The very least you can do when you come across a man on this type of mission is to go and have a look at it and try to help out in some way. So that's what we're doing in that *bakkie*, with 30 rugby balls and Gordon and his garden shears, blinking in the sunlight on this dusty South African morning.

It isn't, of course, like setting off into Widnes or Bolton on a similar initiative. No, sir. On the one venture you tend to run into indifference or outright hostility; on the other, you can run into hundreds of black South African kids whose enthusiasm and eagerness to learn almost overwhelms you. This isn't the township mentality that whites tell you about – interminably – at the pub or the barbecue. This is the real world.

That is not to say that South Africa is a safe place. It isn't, but there is a perverse delight in the way that residents and visitors alike reassure you about just how hazardous it is. The BARLA side which toured there in 1995, for instance, was told that in no circumstances could it ever step outside its hotel – as if 30-odd strapping young blokes were going to be instantly vaporised by the sheer intensity of the danger all around them. But it makes a good story when you get home, so you don't want to spoil it too much. The one violent incident we did see took place outside a virtually all-white pub around the corner from Southern's house. A man had been shot in the car park from a passing BMW; there had, it was rumoured, been an argument about a parking space. Such a crowd formed that the bar, which had closed when the shots rang out, opened up again to serve the thirsty bystanders as they discussed an interesting event triggered not by racial tension, but by aggravated road-rage.

And then there was Martin Birmingham, propped up in bed in Groote Schuur Hospital in Cape Town – the one where Christian Barnard marginally extended a few lives by swapping the odd heart around. Martin, ex-Foreign Legionnaire and ex-Hull trawlerman, was not in the market for a new ticker, but he did have several bullets lodged inconveniently about his person, which were doing an effective job of stopping him doing any Rugby League coaching. It had all been a terrible misunderstanding. After a night on the beer, he discovered that he had taken a taxi home without having the money to pay for it. Lacking even the modest pace he had enjoyed as a prop forward, Martin was shot down by the driver before he could get very far. The touching thing was, he didn't want his mum to find out – although you might imagine that, after the sands of the desert and the heaving North Sea, she would have exhausted her reserves of worry. It was not, he said, the sort of thing that would happen after a night out in Dewsbury.

So South Africa certainly can damage your health, but the closest thing to violence we saw actually in Soweto was Gordon pruning the roses in the gardens of bungalows which would not have looked out of place in the less swanky areas of Thornton-Cleveleys. Bloody disappointing if you were hoping to have tales of heroism to recount on your return to the white world. But that's the funny thing about people, isn't it? If you roll up on their doorsteps looking big and daft but essentially friendly, they tend to accept you as being okay. Strange business. I'll never work it out.

It had taken Southern rather more than a wide grin and a willingness to get his trainers dirty to make himself welcome in Soweto. He had needed to win the trust of the local ANC power-brokers, of the kids and of their teachers. He had to convince them that he was not on any sort of campaign of self-aggrandisement, not trying to gain points in the white world by playing Mother Theresa with rugby balls in the townships, but that he was doing it because it was worth doing for itself. It took about ten minutes of the first session to see that he was absolutely right.

The setting is a patch of arid, undulating spare land in the middle of Soweto, dignified by the title of the Alkah Stadium. If this is a stadium, then the Prescot Panthers play at the Bernabeu; but that is not the point. It is the wealth of human resources which is impressive, dozens of boys and girls, from toddlers up to gangling teenagers, who want to have a go at this strange, new game which is not, repeat not, Rugby Union, but Rugby League – a new game for a new South Africa. It's a good line, that, and Dave does not mind how often he uses it. Well, they harped on a fair bit about freeing Nelson Mandela, didn't they? And sure enough, in the end, they did.

It's not just the numbers, though; it's the level of concentration which is remarkable. Try talking about how to catch a rugby ball to the average mixed bag of kids in Stevenage or Stirling, and see how long it takes for their attention to wander away to whatever else they would rather be doing. Not in Soweto. This mob hang on your every word in a way that can be quite unnerving. It makes you think that you had better have something worthwhile to say.

126

Dave and Trevor, it seems to me from what I can hear, do have something worthwhile to say. So do Gordon and the other schoolteachers, male and female, who, in the manner of the Victorian monitor system, learn from the coaches and then, a couple of minutes later, pass it on to the children. I listen to what I'm telling my group, and I'm not so sure. Didn't do Bolton much good, did it? My own preferred role is to sweep around on the fringes of the session, roping in the ones who are too late, too young or too timid to join in with the main business. Specialist toddler coach, that's about my level. Once they can walk and talk, I feel dangerously close to being out of my depth.

One little lad hides behind his mother's skirt every time I try to catch his eye. Eventually, between us, we persuade him out into the open and, to the delight of the slightly less shy members of the stragglers' class, we get him catching and throwing a ball. What's his name? He won't say, but his mum tells me he's called Dopey. At least, it sounded like Dopey. It could have been Dophi or Dopee or any other way of rendering those two syllables but, thanks to my coaching, he will always be Dopey. Typical, I tell them; Dave and Trevor get the next wave of South African athletes, and I get the seven dwarfs.

There are three other sessions which stick in my mind. One was in Alexandra, the other notorious township on the outskirts of Johannesburg, and one which still looks for the most part like the shanty-town as which it began life. Approaching it on the motorway, the first sign that it is there is a greenish fug smudged across the horizon, the result of tens of thousands of wood fires heating tens of thousands of cooking pots. But, in the middle of this medieval scene, there is a smart little sportsground – one which hosted a match on the England cricket tour a year later, but which is a pretty handy facility for Rugby League as well.

The age range for our session there ran from two to 20 ('All right, lads, I'll take the two year-olds') and, at the end of two hours of non-stop activity, everyone walked the several miles back to their own corner of the sprawling, smoky rabbit-warren. Everyone, that is, apart from 20 or so who squeezed on to the back of the *bakkie* in order to be dropped off somewhere a little nearer home. Dave gave one lad a lift after playing in a tournament and found that home was a tarpaulin stretched under a tree.

At Kagiso, on the Western Rand, the sportsground had once had a fence around it, but all that wood and corrugated iron had now been removed to serve the rather more basic needs of providing roofs for makeshift houses. We didn't have the place to ourselves either, because one area of the field was being used by a group of serious and well-organised schoolchildren practising their Zulu dancing. That, as Dave concedes, is a problem you only rarely run across in Widnes. Worse than the Zulu dancers, though, is the late appearance of the local Rugby Union development officer. Late appearance is about right, because Rugby Union in South Africa had never shown much interest in introducing the game to blacks until the prospect of the World Cup being staged there created the desire for some speedy window-dressing. It's pretty galling when their man swans up to take over the ready-made crowd which we have assembled, dishes out oranges and T-shirts, and has photos taken to show the fine work that the South African Rugby Union is doing in the townships. Still, mustn't be small-minded about this. At least the kids have got an orange apiece – considerably more than that in the case of the quicker, craftier ones – and a shirt that will be perfectly serviceable for the Rugby League training that will make them quicker and craftier still.

Back in Soweto, a second session could have been a disaster. Indeed, in most parts of the world it would have been. The kids are supposed to be brought along by the teachers, but there are no teachers – because they are on strike over having their pay docked. Now if there is one group of people in South Africa which does not deserve to have its wages cut, it is township schoolteachers. Not for them the bell at four o'clock, and see you tomorrow. Their responsibilities extend well beyond school hours and involve children who go to different schools altogether. When Dave needs to gather his budding Rugby League players together, he rings up the few teachers who have telephones and they go out and knock on the doors – if there are doors – of the kids in their vicinity to tell them where to be and at what time. With the teachers all tied up in a meeting in some distant part of Soweto, the system breaks down. So we stand in the middle of the Alkah, with our rugby balls and our traffic cones – what would we do without them? – like the proverbial spare pricks at a wedding. Township life has led us to anticipate, however, that nobody with sports equipment and a tolerably convivial demeanour is alone for long.

The Alkah stands at a strategic crossroads, on the way home from school for children heading in several different directions. All you have to do is intercept them, throw them a ball, and ask if they fancy

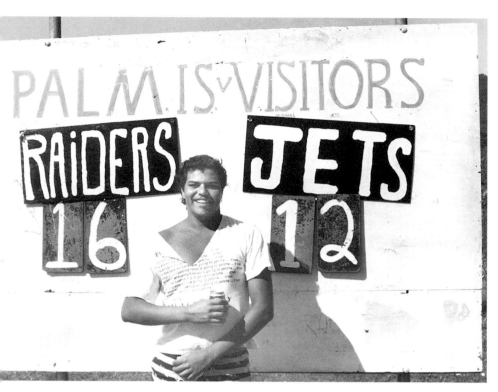

Australian Rugby League, rough and ready style. Palm Island, off the coast of Queensland

The bilingual referee Fred Lindop leads out the teams as Bolton play Bocholt

Carcassonne in 1945, with Felix Bergèse third from left and Puig Aubert third from right, front row

1948 - 1949.

Puig Aubert in 1948 . . .

. . . and at home in 1981, recalling great deeds at the Sydney
Cricket Ground 30 years earlier

The Dutch defy the mud

Oulton, winners of the first Venice International Sevens

British fans in Venice, 1981

LEFT: The world's greatest living Chatham Islander. Brendon Tuuta in his Featherstone days (photo © Andrew Varley)

RIGHT: Another of League's small triumphs. The Moldovan front row in the Emerging Nations World Cup

BELOW: Number three in New Zealand's all-time scariest list. Mark Broadhurst takes it up for Hull KR against Hull (photo © *Hull Daily Mail*)

Milwaukee gets its taste of Rugby League. Ellery Hanley locks horns with
Warrington (photo © Andrew Varley)

Wigan at Milwaukee, but putting players' names on their shirts will never catch on
(photo © Andrew Varley)

a go. Within minutes we have 80 of them, kids in blue uniforms from over there, kids in green uniforms from the other way, running little rugby-related relays, their satchels dumped unceremoniously on the cracked remnants of the basketball court. Before long, the word gets around that the Rugby League session which was cancelled has been magically reinstated, and the ones who were meant to be there arrive as well. Some come with their teachers, whose pay grievances are still unresolved but who are prepared to help out anyway. Try doing something like that in Widnes, Bolton or Hull, I thought to myself. You would finish up being mugged or reported to the Social Services.

There would have been a lot of kids late home from school that evening, we reflected later over a few bottles of Castle beer at Gordon's house. No great problem, he assured us. They would just tell their mums that the white fellow with the *bakkie* full of rugby balls had turned up unexpectedly, and everything would be explained.

There are other images, of activities even more unashamedly self-indulgent, which we carried home from South Africa: the compulsion to get up Table Mountain before someone snatched it away; an almost unbelievably glorious day touring the wineries of the Western Cape; the mother and father of all thunderstorms crashing around our sea-front, flea-pit hotel in Durban and sitting there, under a dripping canopy, talking about old times with an old mate from Blackpool Borough; the spectacle of black South Africa's soccer mania in full flow for the visit of Manchester United, and even – and this is how keen they are – Arsenal; being befriended by Kaiser Chiefs supporters, in their full tribal regalia; sitting under the stars *braaing boerwors* (barbecuing sausages to you). But, uniquely in my experience, it was the work which was the best part. As Dave was ferrying us to the airport – my turn in the back of the *bakkie* by now – we could reflect that if neither of us ever did anything of value again, which was entirely possible, we had at least done one thing which might just qualify. Just as well that I felt that way about the trip, really, because by going on it at a particularly fraught time in our family history I had inflicted damage on my marriage from which it has yet to recover. But never mind that: some ankle-biters in Soweto know how to pass a rugby ball and how to play it when they get tackled by other ankle-biters.

We hadn't done everything we would have liked to, of course. We had not, for instance, actually seen Rugby League being played –

apart from a suspiciously laid-on-specially-for-us effort at a place called Paradise Bend. It would be pitching it a little high to call that a match; in fact, what it truly represented was a total mismatch between the strapping lads from the private school down the road, who had boots and square meals, and the lads from Paradise Bend, who had neither. The functionaries from the South African Rugby League, as it was then constituted, got quite stroppy with the Paradise Bend crew for getting beaten so heavily, but it looked to me as though their main problem was that they hadn't been properly coached. Perhaps the SARL had been too busy with their political battle against Southern and his loose-cannon, renegade activities for mundane matters like that. At least one of their outfit had a line in racial theory which would have dovetailed neatly with the most blinkered of Afrikaners. 'You see,' he kept telling us, 'they can't concentrate. Their minds wander. Their heads go down.' Well, I've had crap coaches too, and I always found that my mind was more inclined to wander and my head to droop when they were at the helm.

By some quirk of fate, I sit on the plane next to a lifelong supporter of Bradford Northern, as they were then, who was flying home for one of his periodic refresher courses at Odsal. 'I love Rugby League, me,' he says. 'I'd love to see it take off in South Africa, but it never will. It's the blacks, you see – only bothered about football. You could take rugby balls and coaches into the townships, and they wouldn't be interested.'

It isn't even any good pointing out that we have done and they are, because any experience which doesn't fit with the theory is immediately ignored or inverted. 'That's right – not interested,' he agrees with himself. 'Nothing to be done about it.'

Rugby League in South Africa has had a bumpy flight since our visit. Southern and the SARL could not stand the sight of each other, and not even a high-powered delegation from Chapeltown Road, where the RFL was then still located, could change that. I doubt whether Mandela himself could have patched it up. The game was allowed to wither away in places such as Cape Town and Durban, where we had seen for ourselves that there was enthusiasm for it, if only it could have been effectively nurtured. Even restricted to its laager around Johannesburg, South African Rugby League was recognised by being given a berth in the Centenary World Cup – largely, we suspected at the time, to make up the numbers. That didn't look a bad assessment when the Rhinos – all white and Rugby

Unionish in just about everything they did – were thrashed out of sight by Fiji and Australia. None of these blokes was underfed, but they were playing out of their division just as surely as Paradise Bend had been. There was then something almost patronising about the way in which a 46–0 defeat by an off-key England was hailed as a moral victory. There were rows before and after the tournament about money which they claimed they should have received, and one player – a Grobbelaar, no less – tested positive for steroids, just like his fellow-countryman Jamie Bloem had done at Doncaster the previous year. All in all, it was a typically quiet and uneventful few weeks in the history of Rugby League in South Africa.

Through it all, Dave Southern carried on doing what he does, although the game he coaches in the townships which are his second home is now known as Mini-League, which the Rugby Union authorities reckon is Rugby League thinly disguised. Immediately after the World Cup, the Wigan and Great Britain forward Phil Clarke stopped off on his way to his new career playing in Sydney to lend a hand. He too came away convinced that he had spent the most enjoyable and worthwhile few weeks of his sporting life.

Mini-League South Africa is now grand enough to produce its own glossy annual report, full of pictures of grinning township kids, some of them now immaculate in the English club shirts contributed by supporters in this country. Not all the shirts get to their intended destination, however. One consignment somehow went astray between the Sports Council and Dave's kids and finished up with the South African Rugby Union – to be used, no doubt, in their belated and cosmetic development programme. Insult was added to injury when the video which SARU produced to show the world what a marvellous, non-racial job they were doing featured footage of kids playing Rugby League, the very game they would still cheerfully strangle in its infancy. Some mistake, surely.

Around the same time, a car which had been added to the *bakkie* in the Mini-League fleet was hijacked at gunpoint in Alexandra. The five hijackers were, according to MILSA's annual report, 'shamed into relinquishing the vehicle within an hour of it being stolen'. There is still no sign of the shirts.

# Barla Hai

## Trevor Hunt

'Don't forget you are pioneers!'

Oh, how those words from the BARLA chief executive Maurice Oldroyd drove us to distraction when whispered down a telephone 12,000 miles from the first ever Rugby League tour of the exotic South Pacific islands of Rarotonga, Western Samoa and Tonga.

At times – in fact, possibly every time – it would have given me the greatest satisfaction to have taken those five words of misguided encouragement and rammed each syllable, nay each consonant and vowel, slowly down Maurice's throat.

'Don't forget you are pioneers!' was Maurice's answer to everything.

'The accommodation is diabolical, Maurice!' we would say.

'Don't forget you are pioneers!' was his stock reply.

'We are overrun by cockroaches, Maurice!' we'd plead.

'Don't forget you are pioneers!' was sung down the line again.

Such incidentals as: 'Our lives have been threatened, Maurice! The hotelier is robbing us blind, Maurice! The plane's engine is under repair and, if we don't get off the island tonight, there isn't another flight to get us back to England for five weeks, Maurice!' were all greeted with the same pat little phrase delivered in that unique tone. Mother – or, in this case, Maurice – knows best.

But nothing could have been further from the truth in the summer of 1990 when the British Amateur Rugby League Association's open-age side ventured half-way around the world to take on the Pacific Islanders on their own islands. Maurice had visited Rarotonga, the largest of the Cook Islands, some two years previously as a fêted guest at the Pacific Cup, and his accommodation and perception of what would face the BARLA tourists were far removed from the reality eventually experienced by the 33-strong touring party.

But who was to have an inkling of what lay in store as the players, management and one referee, the very lean Mr Ian Ollerton of Wigan (who was to return even leaner), eagerly anticipated the trip into the unknown as they met at the Greyhound Motel on the East Lancashire Road – which, as far as BARLA is concerned, leads directly to the rest of the world. Perhaps even then we should have known that this was not a no-expense-spared trip of a lifetime, even though each of the tour party, with the assistance of their clubs, had paid around £1,200 for the privilege.

What a motley crew we must have looked as we assembled in pristine powder-blue blazers in front of the massed ranks of the media. The little and large team of big Paul Hankinson, the powerhouse prop with a slipping fan belt of a voice, and tiny scrum-half Peter Smith were in big photo-call demand. There were players destined to go to greater things, like Dave 'Mad Dog' Jones (Wakefield and Oldham), Henry 'Card' Sharp (Leeds, Halifax and Rochdale), Martin Oglanby (Workington Town), Chris Honey (Barrow and Chorley) and Graham Dale (Barrow). There was the captain Paul 'Messy' Messenger, his side-kick Stuart 'Pugs' Pugsley, Gary 'Lummy' Lumb the phantom barber, and Andy 'Cindy' Tindall, who were all eventually to make their mark across the Pacific.

The management was led by BARLA executive man Gordon Robb, a stalwart of the game and dedicated smoker who found the way to his bed of an evening by slicing through the smoke with a machete. He was a man who would never let them forget 'who you are and what you are!'. His team manager was Ivor Kelland, the former Barrow player who graced Wembley with the Shipbuilders back in 1967, and the coach was Ernest Wilby from Dewsbury, a man with an accent so thick that you couldn't spread it with a knife, and whose interview on Cook Islands television needed subtitles.

The trainer was former Barrow forward Tommy Thompson, who answered all jests at his expense – imagined or otherwise – with the single retort, 'I'll run ya! And then we'll see who's laughin'!' The physio was Julian Hatcher, who ran a tight and orderly surgery for an hour after breakfast and an hour after tea, and who spent the rest of the time trying to use up the entire photographic film stock of the

South Pacific. My job as 'media manager' was to get the stories back home. Maurice thought it meant through him, but I had other ideas. Nobody minded being called a 'pioneer' as they boarded the bus and said a fond farewell to weeping wives, grieving girlfriends and chattering children.

It was my misfortune, when we boarded our 747 at Heathrow the following day, to find that the seats had been allocated in alphabetical order. That placed me directly next to a man with a voice that would have put a siren to shame and saved many a shipwreck. Bryan 'Chissy' Hyslop was the elder statesman of the tour who developed a Peter Pan complex as soon as he began to fly. 'Where do you enrol for the mile-high club?' was his stock phrase in his rasping, Cumbrian accent. I have to admit that, as I desperately tried to snatch some kip, I was sorely tempted to let him use the outside loo on more than one occasion, although by the time we reached Auckland, I'm glad to say even Duracell Chissy was not firing on all cylinders. A mild spate of food poisoning had smitten him, Smithy and a couple of others including (inevitably, as it turned out) referee Ollerton. Who says there is no God!

Another slightly better-known squad had been on the same flight, as the Scotland Rugby Union squad were on their way to New Zealand to face the All Blacks. They weren't a bad lot on the whole, Gavin Hastings, Finlay Calder and the rest exchanging stories throughout the opening few hours of the flight, and they seemed genuinely interested in the BARLA boys' playing plans. The big Scots forwards were accommodated in first class, and the whole party eventually settled down on their prescribed sleeping tablets. Our travelling arrangements were somewhat less extravagant, however, and even though Air New Zealand aircraft are deservedly known as the 'Ritz in the Sky', it was still a mighty crush to get four BARLA men into four central seats in comfort.

As the plane landed in Auckland, the entire British party had changed from their tracksuit travelling gear to don their entire official tour party gear of blazers and slacks. Clean-shaven and resplendent, they negotiated customs, with manager Gordon Robb leading the party out into Auckland Airport's reception area, where he was immediately pounced upon by a camera crew and waltzed into a corner of the airport with a gaggle of media men in hot pursuit. What a reception, I thought – and this was only Auckland!

'How fit is Gavin Hastings?' they asked.

'Looks pretty fit to me,' said Gordon, somewhat puzzled.

'Will he be playing in your first game?' they went on.

'Not unless he's decided to join us,' said Gordon. 'We are the British Amateur Rugby League team touring the South Pacific islands.'

Cumbrian-Scottish, Scottish-Cumbrian, they all sound the same to a New Zealander desperate for a scoop, but slowly the penny dropped as Gavin loped around the corner in a team tracksuit and Gordon was dropped faster than a ball with dog muck on it.

The next leg of the journey involved a six-hour flight to Rarotonga, the largest of the Cook Islands, and had one saving grace for the weary travellers: *Steel Magnolias*. The highly acclaimed weepie film was just the type of in-flight entertainment to ensure that, at last, the entire party drifted into a weary slumber – even Chissy! However, the buzz of activity throughout the plane which precedes a descent gradually woke us, and the customary change into blazer and slacks was quickly effected as the lads vainly attempted to protect their modesty from unbelieving passengers. Were they really seeing 32 grown men desperately trying to don formal gear on a banking plane as cabin crew frantically tried to belt them into their seats?

The first thing that hits you as you step out of your air-conditioned aeroplane into the 5 a.m. pitch darkness of a South Pacific morning at Avarua Airport is the humidity. By the time I'd reached the bottom of the landing steps, rivulets of perspiration were streaming down the inside of the pure-wool, standard-issue flannels which had been designed to keep a heavy frost at bay, but which were now rapidly becoming a sodden thermal blanket flapping in a gentle Pacific breeze. But like the Hussars at Balaclava and countless bold boundary beaters of old we stood our ground, resplendent but wilting, in BARLA blue.

Rarotonga's airport and custom control is comparable with the check-out in a rather small corner shop, while the foyer where we were to be welcomed was equivalent to a good-sized garden shed and was like a sauna. It was there that I met John Kenning (known as JK), the president of the Cook Islands Rugby League, and Jack Madden, a former deep-sea fisherman who was the South Pacific Rugby League development officer and our liaison officer for the rest of the tour.

I met up with JK again at Wembley after the opening World Cup game between England and Australia in October 1995. He is a huge man with a disarming grin, the laid-back style of the islands, and a dry but acid wit. He had obviously enjoyed himself on some of the World Cup hospitality as he bellowed across the crowded banqueting suite, 'Hey Trevor, mate, do you know where London is?' It was his first trip to Europe, and London – never mind England – appeared bigger than a continent. Wide-eyed if not exactly legless, JK went with the flow to an East End pub where his bottle-green blazer cut quite a dash. In a place renowned for its gangland connections, it wasn't long before the besuited minder of some high ranker enquired, 'Who's the geezer in the green?'

'He's the president of the Cook Islands Rugby League,' I replied, as the band hit top note. No doubt the minder didn't quite catch it all, because soon there was a drink on its way for the President of the Cook Islands – and it was free beer all night! JK graciously accepted his elevated status, but was to be found sitting on the steps looking at the stars as the bubbling cauldron of human activity within the pub proved too much for a man reared on the sweet-scented air of Rarotonga.

Jack Madden's laconic humour was evident on our arrival in Rarotonga as he ceremoniously placed customary *lais* – garlands of exquisitely coloured flowers – around the necks of the British party.

'I thought these flowers were supposed to be presented by scantily clad island beauties,' I queried.

'I can put on a skirt and give you a kiss if you like,' retorted Jack, in a long New Zealand drawl, as he stepped forward, paunch first, in his 'player-of-the-day' T-shirt, baggy blue shorts and flip-flops – dress that was to prove *de rigueur* on the island. The sight of so many jaded travellers oozing sweat from under blue blazers attracted quite a crowd even at that time in the morning, as we bundled kit and players into a fleet of minibuses that trundled off into the blackness with wheels splayed and doors bulging. You could see nothing, but the driver did manage to cry out, 'Cook's Corner – best food on the island!' and what a tip that would prove to be!

The convoy pulled up at the hostel around 6.30 a.m. – just as dawn was breaking – and, as the sun rose, the weary travellers' visions of an island paradise plummeted. 'Tenko – it's like bloody Tenko!' was one of the more favourable descriptions of our intended abode as the players stepped across the opening verandah into the communal hall of the colonial-style building. The first-floor bedrooms were just wide enough for two beds, and a suitcase between them. There were no cupboards, wardrobes or hanging space. 'Have you any coathangers?' enquired Gordon of the obliging islander, who returned within minutes with a hammer and a huge bag of three-inch nails declaring, 'Coathangers, okay?'

The lads were deadly disenchanted, caught between the desperation for sleep and the unenticing situation. 'Give it a go,' bellowed Chissy as he stepped into the first-floor shower for a reviver, only for the rotten chipboard floor to give way under his weight and leave him hanging on and hollering as his feet dangled through the ceiling below.

'After we have a sleep things won't look as bad,' offered Gordon comfortingly. But that was before he realised that sleep was hardly going to be on his agenda, as the beds for the management were mattresses on the landing, presumably so that they could keep an eye on what the rest were up to. It was time for a summit meeting.

JK was bemused by our concern. 'It was okay for the lads from Samoa, and the other islanders – and they don't usually have mattresses,' he said. 'We can't afford anything else on our budget, and Maurice said it would be all right when he was here last June.'

'Bloody Maurice,' blasted Gordon, and within seconds he was hot on the pay phone to BARLA HQ, banging in coins like a pinball wizard. Then I heard those tell-tale words trill out of the earpiece: 'But Gordon, don't forget you are pioneers. You have a physio for Chissy, and the islanders might be offended if you move. We can't risk an international incident.'

The lads were told that we were in the middle of the ocean and, apart from one grossly over-priced five-star hotel, this type of accommodation was all there was on the island. They were heroes, every one of them, and they were prepared to do their bit for their country. Tenko was to prove home and hospital for the next eight days, but as a dining-room it drew a blank. Breakfast was cooked at around 7.30 a.m., regardless of the fact that the lads were generally out on the training field around that time, and really wanted their sustenance two hours later. By then the cockroaches had managed to find their way on to the menu, and it only took one rather crunchy mouthful of scrambled egg to send the entire party hotfoot to Cook's Corner (named after Captain Cook and not the fact that it did an excellent sausage, bacon and egg) where – surprise, surprise – the minibus driver was head cook and bottle-washer.

When there was time to study our surroundings, we realised that they were breathtaking. There just isn't anywhere in the world that is quite like the South Pacific and, for me, Rarotonga was the epitome of all that I would have expected that part of the world to be. Whether it is the surrounding lushness of the brilliantly coloured vegetation that proliferates in the hot and humid air, the turquoise sea glittering like the jewel in a belly-dancer's navel before lapping on to bleached white sands, or the warmth of the people it is difficult to say, but it was definitely good to be a pioneer at that stage.

The Saturday night was something special, as it appeared the whole island had turned out to party with the tourists, and our lads were happy to oblige. In fact, the islanders were happy to greet the money-laden Brits every night, with the world-famous Banana Court – a former banana warehouse – providing hot rock from local bands and cheap beer. It was a wild time and, with the uninviting Tenko the only alternative to a wander round the few bars which Avarua possesses, it was up to the lads to remember 'who you are and what you are!'.

At midnight it all stopped dead: right in mid-sentence as Wilson Pickett blasted out 'In the Midnight Hour', except he didn't get the last word out, as the needle was scratched across the record by an over-zealous policeman. It was now Sunday, you see, and everyone but everyone has to go to church at least a couple of times. Nevertheless the players and their party hosts had done enough to drink the entire island dry of its entire week's supply of Steinlager in just one night. From then on the players trained hard twice a day, Cook's Corner made a fortune, and I hadn't the heart to tell the lads that at least one of what turned out to be half a dozen reasonable beach hotels had offered to put them up for free if they could promise to drink at the same rate every night.

The first game was against the Cook Islands champions Tupapa, and a rousing 42–12 victory was hammered out against the background rhythm of island drums. But it was a win at a price, as the Brits picked up coral burns from the sandy soil, and bruises from the bludgeoning islanders.

Nevertheless, the scene was set for a memorable first international when the BARLA boys learned exactly what Pacific Test rugby was all about. No longer do the menfolk ram their war canoes into the splintering Pacific surf to pound their way across the ocean on the ultimate away game trip. Now their battles are fought often just as fiercely on the sportsgrounds of the few acres of terra firma amid the millions of square miles of glittering ocean. In that clash on 2 June the combination of a heavy deluge that made the humidity almost unbearable and the fleetness of foot of the powerfully built Cook Islanders ensured a 21–15 win for the home side, and celebrations long into the night for their committee, players and most of the 2,500 fans who had watched from the shelter of the stand or from under the coconut palms which generously fringed the pitch.

It had been a gripping game, and one that left me just as bruised as the players. I had been a summariser for the Cook Islands radio and television commentary team, which had broadcast the game alternately in English and Rarotongan. Every time that the Rarotongan man, Matt Feather, finished his spiel, the Cooks did something well or the Brits did something badly, he would dig me in the ribs with his elbow, then gesture apologetically as he heard me gasp. With a nest of hornets under the commentary desk, it was no picnic bringing news of this game to the waiting world.

JK could hardly disguise his delight and disbelief that the Cooks had beaten Great Britain and, as the players left to grab some shut-eye and pack their bags for a 7 a.m. flight off the island, Jack Madden chose his moment. 'Think those jokers were big?' he asked a dozen or so players within earshot, as he slugged back a rum and Coke. 'Well, wait till you get to Samoa,' he said, 'they are even bigger there. These jokers will look like kindergarten kids.'

And he wasn't wrong!

Western Samoa was a short hop away, just three hours or so, but it had suffered enormous damage at the hands of a cyclone a few weeks before. Electricity failures were frequent and long, and the whole island looked still to be in a state of emergency. Coconut trees were uprooted along the road from Apia Airport to our hotel, where the rooms offered innovations like showers and space to swing a cat. Luxury it wasn't, but neither was it Tenko. Ernest and Tommy were to be my room-mates, along with a handful of cockroaches – which were everywhere, including all the restaurants – assorted huge spiders and a six-inch gecko. Tommy wanted to throw him out, but I had learned a lesson on the Cook Islands when I had spent half the night chasing out a character half that lizard's size, only to be kept awake by the biting mosquitoes for the rest of it. The geckoes ensure the mossies leave you alone by the simple ploy of eating them, while themselves have no curiosity about how a human tastes.

It was apparent that the Samoans were under pressure from the Rugby Union from the first meeting with their officials. The RU were trying to prevent the game taking place at the Apia Stadium, and were using their influence to put a block on media attention and press coverage. Communications with the outside world were difficult at the best of times, and I once waited 17 hours in the hotel foyer for an international line to become available to send home my match previews. I did, however, have unlimited use of the hotel typewriter, as long as I didn't mind giving the hotel guests their keys and holding the fort while the manager was taking 40 winks.

The first game was played 48 hours after our arrival, and an Apia Select XIII stormed to a 28–16 victory in which Chissy was sent off by one of the most one-eyed officials I have ever seen. He was a Rugby Union referee, and at one stage even signalled a line-out until the error of his ways was explained. But the Samoans loved their first taste of live international Rugby League and howled with laughter at every big hit. Jack Madden had been right, these guys were built like tree trunks. Everyone in the English camp was bitterly disappointed by the result, but little did they know the storm that was now about to blow up.

The next day, Chissy attended his disciplinary meeting – and was fined a pig. The animals are seen as a great sign of wealth on the island and used as currency in all sorts of transactions. They wander the streets freely, going in and out of the Samoan homes with the same familiarity as a dog or cat back in England. Gordon and Chissy were distraught, as Chissy pondered the end to his tour because he was unable to pay his fine, and Gordon wondered what to do next. They needn't have worried; the Samoans themselves turned up with a small piglet for Chissy that afternoon, and the lads, bored by now, instantly adopted the boisterous baby boar as it chased footballs and caught sticks. Then the ball rolled round the back of the kitchen. A blood-curdling scream woke those who were asleep before, minutes later, little porky, skewered from top to bottom, was triumphantly carted to the barbecue.

The Samoan dancing was entertaining that night, but the show-stopper was a tall, lean brunette in a short, shimmering silver dress, with legs that went on and on. If Olive Oyl had walked into the bar, Popeye and Bluto's eyes could not have stuck out further on stalks than those of the BARLA boys. Bold as brass she planted herself in the middle of our company and asked for a drink. She could have been drowned three times over as the orders poured in. She looked too good to be true – and she was. Cindy was a *fafa-finia* – a 'fifty-fifty' – or a woman in a man's body, as the barman explained it to us as our jaws dropped. Was it fact or fiction? Nobody knew, and nobody admitted to finding out, despite Andy Parle drawing the short straw at the post-match disco whereby he was to go for a dance and generally feel for the lie of the land.

The Friday morning was to be one I will never forget. I was woken suddenly by the hotel manager with a copy of the *Western Samoan Observer* thrust under my nose. The headline referred to 'the scum from the slums of England'. The gist of the piece was an allegation that Henry Sharp had urinated on the pitch during the match against the Apia Select. It wasn't true; Henry would never have shown up himself or the team like that. But the video evidence was not available, and the Western Samoan officials were not able or willing to confirm one way or the other what had gone on. It was crisis time. We were informed that we may now not be safe on the streets, and that we should always take a taxi and never go anywhere in less than fours. We rang Maurice and, of course, were told that pioneers had to put up with things like this.

That night Tommy Thompson and I cautiously walked to a waterfront bar for a quiet ponder on the state of play. Tommy had no socks on, but was obligingly lent a pair from behind the bar to enable him to enter the establishment. Ties and long trousers were not essential, but socks were. At the bar, we had just about taken our first sip of an inviting beer when a generously proportioned lady with perhaps a little too much of the strong stuff inside her bared her thigh and said, 'Tonight I'm going to **** you!' The barman was drowned as we sprayed him from head to foot in cold lager while desperately trying to hang on to our stools. The bar erupted in laughter; apparently this was that particular lady's party trick to catch unsuspecting new arrivals. But, as the German ambassador's wife, she did have a great deal of information about what had been going on and who had accused Henry Sharp. It proved to be the coach of the national Rugby Union team, a great friend of the *Observer*'s editor, and suddenly something stank in Samoa.

The day of the game, everyone was nervous. Archie and Slats had been chased by a gang of youths down the high street of Apia early the previous night, and things were tense, but there was never a thought of calling off the game. The atmosphere at the ground was eerily silent, and after the minister of sport had poured oil on the troubled waters by asking for the Samoan people to forgive us for what we had done in the previous match, you felt you were sitting on a time-bomb that was ready to go off. I took my place in the area reserved for the press; a couple of the non-playing players insisted on accompanying me through the Samoan crowd, just in case someone took a swipe at me.

The game kicked off still in deadly silence, and all you could hear was the pounding of the tackles and the gasps as wind was knocked out of the players' bellies. Samoa blasted into a 12–0 lead, and there wasn't even a polite wave of applause. They had come to see what we would do and how we would behave. And if we did the unmentionable again, they would be ready to dish out retribution. But BARLA knocked down the big Samoans, and suddenly the ice began to melt as the raw courage shown in the face of some mighty hits seemed to prove at last we were not dishonourable men. When BARLA pulled back a 12–6 interval deficit to level, the crowd erupted into full voice.

The rest of the game was a magnificent testimony to the lads' character, as they clinched the finest BARLA win – a 20–16 success – that it has ever been my privilege to witness in 15 years with the national team. BARLA had won round the Samoans, but the earlier damage proved irreparable as the hastily cancelled civic reception was replaced with a low-key barbecue at the home of the British Ambassador.

Maurice was on the phone in the middle of the night (as he had been most of the week because he had never worked out the time difference). He just wanted to congratulate the boys for our pioneering spirit. I think that was when we got cut off.

Two days later we were on our way to Tonga, where the jokers were once again to prove even bigger. By some masterpiece of planning, the four-hour flight to Nuku'alofa (the City of Love) on Tongatapu, the largest of the Tongan islands, was to be followed that evening by the opening game against the Tongan champions, Ha'Ateiho Crusaders. BARLA's players were still bruised, battered and covered in horrendous, pus-weeping grass burns that were being drawn as if by a poultice by those flaming flannel trousers. But their blue blazers were outshone at the airport as the Honourable Vaha'i, Tongan nobleman, Member of Parliament and cousin of the omnipotent King Taufa'ahau Tupou IV led the welcoming party, resplendent in a bright red blazer festooned in representative badges. 'Bloody hell, it's Billy Butlin,' was the cry but, with a couple of extremely handy-looking associates either side of him, it was not too loud.

A man of influence, Vaha'i had been involved in Rugby Union until Jack Madden had convinced him that League was the game for Tonga. The story went that Union held the upper hand until one day they overstepped the mark and offended the Tongan sense of fair play when attempting to have a highly regarded player drummed out of his full-time job as a policeman because he was set to play for Tonga at Rugby League in the Pacific Cup. After that, League had the public sympathy, and the politicians knew where their bread was buttered.

That first evening, it was a princess who welcomed the BARLA guests. She was completely unruffled even though, seconds before, Vaha'i had tottered to the back of the podium and thrown up. Gordon and the lads couldn't believe what they had seen. Eighty minutes later it was the crowd who were rubbing their eyes in disbelief as their local champions won 12–8, running like a herd of charging buffalo against a team which defended doggedly and moved the ball well, but was battered into submission when attempting to take on the towering Tongans up the middle.

It was also a win which prompted the King to decree that the Test match against the Tongan national side should be moved back 24 hours in order that he could get back from diplomatic business in New Zealand to watch the game. It was news that was broken to the management early the next morning, and although the Brits argued long and hard that they were geared to a Friday-night game, it all boiled down to one unarguable fact. 'Nobody will go against the King's order, and he has said he wants to be there,' said Vaha'i. So by royal appointment BARLA were to play before the King on Saturday.

As the day of the Test approached, you could sense that the players were hungry for something more to do than coach schoolkids and train, and by now the novelty of touring was wearing thin as we neared the fourth week. Nevertheless, Ian Ollerton was way ahead in the whingeing stakes, having won the 'whinger-of-the-week' T-shirt on the Cook Islands, even though he was billeted with a New Zealand referee at the time instead of being in Tenko. He couldn't cope with the raw fish, hated the root vegetable taro that formed part of the islanders' staple diet, looked instantly nauseous when confronted with yet another underdone fatty piece of suckling pig, and refused to pay the rising prices for

143

Tongan beef steak. He was slowly starving to death, but his principles were not being eaten away. Wiganer Ian had to have a pie or he'd simply die.

But he was in luck. There was a former Rochdale man who had a restaurant down the road from our billet in the Friendly Islander, and although he was short of some ingredients for a traditional beef pie he could make shepherd's pie and he had some real English baked beans. It was the best we could do. There was a full turn-out for this 'island feast', as tomato soup was followed by a shepherd's pie with a potato crust so high that you couldn't see over it. Lashings of bread and butter were scoffed, and then chips arrived before the final *pièce de résistance* – apple crumble. A gang of shipwrecked sailors who had just crawled up the beach could not have eaten more, and Ian was almost ecstatic. But I think he clinched his 'whinger-of-the-tour' T-shirt by saying: 'It was good, but you would have thought he would have had some brown sauce. That would have just set it off!'

Bellies full and spirits revived, BARLA showed what solid English oak can do when suitably sustained, by thrashing the Tongans 58–12 with a breathtaking display of attacking rugby. I was summarising in English on an otherwise Tongan commentary, and my cue from their equivalent of Harry Carpenter was when the microphone was waved in my general direction. I hadn't a clue what the commentator was saying, but despite the drubbing he stuck the course. Which was more than he did four years later, when he disappeared to the sponsors' bar at the interval and never emerged for the second half.

As usual, I was getting the dispatches back home straight after the game, and this time it was on a variety of different typewriters that kept being found for me, but inevitably all needed repairing first. By now the bedroom I shared with Ivor Kelland looked like a junk shop, with hundreds of bits and pieces lying about. I rejoined the party just in time to see a huge blackened barbecued pig – as big as a hippo – carried by six hefty pall-bearers being planted right in the middle of the BARLA table – a gift from the Princess. I could see Gordon wondering how on earth he could get this in his suitcase, before one of the noblemen, aware of his quandary, suggested he donate it to the Tongan national team for their gallant effort.

Sunday was church as usual, followed by a short boat trip to Paradise Island, an offshore resort where tourists could buy beer and music could be played without offending the islands' religious scruples. It was wet and windy, but I was told the sea was relatively calm for those conditions. To me and the rest of the non-seafarers in our party, the small, overladen boat was just inches from being swamped by every second wave, and the smell of diesel made many lose their stomachs to a roaring swell. When we at last reached our destination I felt I had almost met my maker and I knew he wanted me to drink his health. I was not short of volunteers to assist me build up Dutch courage for the return trip on a sea that was now confirmed as 'getting a little choppy'.

There was one game left to play, three days later, against the might of the South Pacific, and Jack was picking up the rest of his squad from the airport the next day. He was bringing in the three-quarters from the Cook Islands to gel with the half-backs of Western Samoa, and a pack of the best of Samoa and Tonga. He was making them rough and mean, and when we did get down to counting the bodies for that final game, those dreadful coral wounds were now turning to sickening infections, despite all the administrations of Julian Hatcher, male nurse Ian Ollerton and any local doctors we could find. That last match was one too many for the Brits, and they never hit the dizzy heights of the Tongan romp, going down 28–17 in front of 5,100 spectators who again included His Majesty the King.

There was another pig for Gordon to give away graciously at the after-match reception, and a right royal knees-up to end the tour, with Ollerton losing count of the number of times he was thrown into the pool while living up to his whinger's title by proclaiming, 'Now I'll have to get changed again!' His suitcase was easy to spot as it dripped all the way home. That night the band left but the boys played on, and the next day Ivor was fuming because he couldn't sleep for that damned karaoke singer blasting out 'Wild Thing' for hours. I didn't dare tell him it was me and, besides, I felt sure I had someone else's head on. A window had been broken somewhere along the line, and a none-too-friendly landlady demanded recompense that could have paid for a glazier and joiner to travel from England to repair it. The lads chipped in and, when they departed, chose to show their appreciation in a traditional British two-fingered salute as she peered from behind closed curtains.

This, however, was not a wise move, as four hours later we were back there again – and this time the steaks were 12 dollars! Our plane had developed an engine fault one hour before take-off, and the local boys didn't know how to repair it. An engineer had been sent for, but nobody knew when he would arrive. 'Sometime soon, maybe tomorrow, maybe next week, is no bother. Pacific Airlines put you up on Tonga till then!' said the booking clerk.

No bother! We had to make a connecting flight in Fiji to Honolulu whence our plane would take us on to Los Angeles and then home. We were running out of cash fast, and a telephone call to the Air New Zealand tour operator in Nuku'alofa revealed that, after our scheduled plane departed, there wasn't one spare seat – never mind 33 – on a plane out of Los Angeles for the next five weeks. It was then we had to return rather sheepishly to the Friendly Islander, much like those rounded-up POWs in *The Great Escape*.

What could we do? First off was to get Vaha'i to use his influence to get something moving through the diplomatic circles. The second was to get Maurice Oldroyd back in England to work out some alternative passage home, even if it meant a paddle steamer and a worked passage stoking the boilers. At least the lads would stay fit. 'But it's three o'clock in the morning back home,' said Gordon. 'Maurice will be in bed.' What a sweet moment that was after all the adversity. He had rung me in the middle of the night for the past four weeks; now it was my turn.

'Get the bugger rung!'

Eventually we were summoned from our hotel, and shipped to the airport. Whatever had been done, it worked, and off we went on a wing and a prayer. We were chasing connecting flights now, and were some 12 hours behind schedule as the plane battled through an electrical storm, and all I could think about was James Stewart's classic film *The Flight of the Albatross*.

We should have had a day of sightseeing in Fiji, but as we landed at Suva we were already one hour late for our departure time on a flight out of Nadi. By the time we arrived in Nadi we were two hours late, but our flight to Honolulu had held on. Struggling against a headwind we added another half an hour to that delay before arriving in Honolulu, where an army of baggage handlers was waiting for our luggage and where a swarm of Air New Zealand officials acting like sheepdogs cajoled and hurried our limping band, heavily laden with wooden carvings and other souvenirs, through the transit terminals to the waiting plane.

The final leg of the journey was not without drama, as we hit heavy turbulence, a couple of passengers were knocked unconscious, and our happy-to-go-home heroes added 'Abide With Me' to a sing-song designed to lift everyone's spirits. By the time we

146

were back at the Greyhound, our loved ones were eagerly awaiting our arrival, and the lads, with festering wounds and aching limbs, couldn't wait either – for a drop of real English draught beer! A fleeting kiss, and a man-with-a-mission stride saw the long bar filled, Aussie commercial-style, with the BARLA blues as they raised their beers and downed them in one. Thirsty work, being a pioneer.

# Kazakh Attack

## Ian Lockwood

Try finding Alma-Ata on a map. It lies tucked away somewhere near the Chinese border with Kazakhstan, a million miles from anywhere. Benidorm it is not.

Yet here we were, two rugby teams from York and London, plus a clutch of directors, a physio, kitmen and a reporter, to teach the people of the capital of Kazakhstan all about the joys of Rugby League. It is, as we were to discover, an alien world. Where chicken for dinner means not Colonel Sanders's secret recipe, but a rooster's foot, complete with claw, floating in a bowl of water. Where every meal comprises cucumbers and caviare and not much else. The omens were not good. Chatting on the plane from Moscow, York's youngest squad member, a promising half-back from the Academy who had no need to pack any shaving tackle, revealed that in his 17 tender years his horizons had stretched beyond the Yorkshire border only so far as a few games in deepest Lancashire and, most exotically, an 'A'-team match at Workington.

Thrust into the world of Kazakhstan, it soon became apparent that this was as far from a tour of Australia as Huyton's old Alt Park was from Headingley. As the officials tried to sort out accommodation in a large skyscraper of a hotel, the players headed off to the place where all rugby players naturally congregate – the bar. Well, it was called a bar, but any resemblance to Billy Boston's hostelry ended with the fact that there was a wooden counter in a far corner. Cobwebs were everywhere, and behind the counter was row upon row of – nothing. No glasses, no pumps ready to serve foaming pints of Kazakhstan's answer to

148

Tetley's. Rule one in Alma-Ata: nothing is open, and nothing works.

Those quick on the uptake had the city summed up in five minutes. Let us use the words of that silver-tongued York scrum-half, Steve Dobson. It was, he proclaimed, 'a dump'. All slabs of concrete, crumbling roads, and not a drink to be had anywhere. There was, however, a chink of light at the end of the tunnel for some of us. Would the club officials and the gentleman of the press care to attend a civic reception to honour such distinguished visitors, drinks provided? What? And leave the players to mope around the dry hotel playing endless games of cards? Sorry, lads, no contest.

Together with Ian Clough, the club secretary whose ten-year-old beard had been forcibly shaved off by the players before the coach had even passed the racecourse in York, we greedily eyed the vodka. As each official from the Kazakhstan Ministry of Sport made a speech, a beakerful of the stuff appeared at one's elbow, and down in one go it went as a toast. To refuse was insulting.

Alas, the formalities went on, and on. Tongues were loosened, and it was the turn of the Brits to respond. Up sprang York chairman John Stabler to make some comment about sporting relations; Fred Lindop droned on and on about referees; the gentleman of the press burbled something about freedom of speech. Don't ask me how, but one minute I was standing up making the greatest peroration since Winston Churchill's 'we shall fight them on the beaches', and the next I was sitting on the steps of the hotel, watching Cloughie crawl out of a taxi and cement Anglo-Kazakhstan relations by regurgitating his meal at the feet of York captain Stewart 'Corgi' Horton. The thought 'thank God I'm just a little more sober than Cloughie' ran through my head as he was dragged up to some torture chamber for further punishment, involving the shaving of more hair from his body (the results of which exercise were fortunately hidden from view).

The next day it was down to the serious business of training in Kazakhstan's voluminous open-air stadium, a sort of Wembley without the roof, only even more decrepit if that is possible, and without the warm, £3-a-pint beer in a flimsy plastic container. The two sides divided, London to practise sneakily some new-fangled stratagem called sliding defence, York to go through some well-rehearsed routines which involve dropping the ball every second pass. The humidity was intense. And what could one do with an ageing hack other than give him a useful duty – such as fetching the cold water.

It sounded an easy job, and one which even a hungover journo could accomplish without too much difficulty. Yet here began an immense problem. This, remember, was still the Soviet Union, a land where nothing could be taken for granted. Each tap discovered ran dry, producing only powder, dust and, if one was really lucky, a yellow-coloured trickle of water. The problem was finally solved with a five-dollar bill and a visit to a stallholder who just happened to be outside the ground with enough bottles to supply an army. That's five dollars you owe me, lads.

Back then to our crumbling hotel, or prison, while the Rugby Football League official party – Fred Lindop, Mal Reilly and our beloved Maurice Lindsay – went off to somewhere more luxurious with, incredibly, a bar. Meanwhile, outside the players' *gulag*, word was spreading fast about these strangers with funny-shaped balls. Hordes of distinctly dodgy-looking youths were trying to sell old communist badges and militaria to an even dodgier-looking Greg Pearce. It was then that Ady Smith, a man whose yodelling and really quite brilliant singing were to prove the hit of the tour, pulled his masterstroke. As the arguments raged over whether a grimy Indian rupee, passed off by Mr Pearce as a perfectly acceptable new version of the US dollar, was a fair exchange for a Russian cap, Mr Smith pulled out his trump card – an old, dog-eared copy of *Playboy*. Kazakhstani eyes lit up and, in exchange for a single Playmate of the Month, Mr Smith came away with enough tin medals to decorate even the most pompous Russian grand marshal's chest.

So to the big day. A crowd of around 15,000 had entered the stadium to witness this strange foreign game played, first up, between the two British teams. They hadn't a clue what was going on. Nor, claimed York coach Gary Stephens, had referee Fred Lindop, who ensured that an honourable draw was secured. Then the missionary work was to begin – two halves of 20 minutes, first London v Kazakhstan, then York v Kazakhstan.

Both clubs had been firmly warned that this was an exhibition match to foster goodwill. No smacking, no high tackles, and ease off if the score looks like getting embarrassing. London behaved honourably as coach Ross Strudwick put into play his pride and joy, and some would say sole tactic, the sliding defence. In truth, this was not much use against a side who had had about 30 minutes on the training ground in the art of rugby. But the Londoners had spent so much time practising it, at the expense of everything else, that they were bewildered about what to do when they had the ball and so managed just one try in 20 minutes. A huge roar went up when the Kazakhstan side, who lacked nothing in commitment and strength, levelled the scores a minute from time.

It was time for Gary Stephens to deliver his pep talk. Remembering the spirit of the instructions he had received, he barked: 'Sling the ball out wide where they haven't got a clue, and let's stuff the so-and-sos.' Taciturn assistant Derek Foster added his sage words: 'And smack that big second-row around the ears – see if he wants to keep running.' In other words, good old-fashioned tactics.

York's wingers ran in some four tries apiece, the crowd was hushed, and the steam went out of the willing but, in rugby terms, incredibly naïve Kazakhstan forwards. Afterwards the crowd rushed on to the pitch to mob York's two Pryce brothers, Geoff and young Steve. These were allegedly the first negroes ever spotted by the public of Alma-Ata, and they were eager to touch the skin and hair of these beings who, they believed, were from outer space.

That night a reception was held in the presence of the President of Kazakhstan, a man with his finger on the button of more nuclear weapons than our own Prime Minister. Would his honoured guests like a visit to the Soviet space station, just 100 miles or so from Alma-Ata, the following day? A journalistic scoop of Watergate proportions suddenly took form in this reporter's mind. No western journalist had been anywhere near a place of such immense secrecy. So it was put to the vote: all those in favour of visiting the secret Soviet space station, hands up – total, one reporter. All those in favour of hanging about town and trying to find some beer – total, 30-odd rugby players.

The vodka flowed again (an ashen-faced Mr Clough being noticeably abstemious) and man-of-the-match Geoff Pryce was presented with his award and made his customary lengthy speech ('Erm, thanks, I don't know what to say, erm, that's it really').

All that was left was finally to show our hosts our appreciation of their hospitality by mounting a midnight raid on the stadium, climbing up the walls, and pinching the massive banner advertising the game. It eventually made its way back to York's dismal new stadium, where it can be found tucked in the secretary's drawer festering away alongside Maurice Lindsay's *Guide to a Golden*

*Future for Third Division Clubs* and the *Ray French English Grammar Masterclass*. Meanwhile, in Alma-Ata, puzzled Kazakhstanis are still trying to work out what happened the day 30-odd mad Englishmen played a funny game with an odd-shaped ball in their soccer stadium . . .

# May Night in Moscow

## Dave Hadfield

As communism entered its last throes, there were many things you could get away with in Moscow which would have been both frowned and stamped upon a year or two earlier. You could, as visitor or even Russian citizen, mock and deride the system, its achievements and especially its leaders to your heart's content. You could buy satirical versions of those traditional Russian dolls, with a lividly birthmarked Gorbachev opening up to reveal, in order, Brezhnev, Krushchev, Uncle Joe Stalin and, finally, a tiny, glowering Lenin, about the size of the top joint of your little finger. You could buy just about anything or anybody, in fact, provided you had the hard currency to pay the price. But you could not sing old Sam Cooke and Otis Redding songs in the restaurant of the Cosmos Hotel at midnight. As the fabric of the Soviet Union collapsed around them, they had to draw the line somewhere.

That was why police with riot-sticks were forcibly putting an end to the singing career of the Ryedale-York centre Steven Pryce – the lesser-known but more tuneful brother of Geoff – on the last night of British Rugby League's first incursion behind the Iron Curtain. Rugby League itself was permitted, even though one incredulous spectator in Leningrad had asked, 'Is this game legal in the Soviet Union?' It promised to bring in some longed-for hard currency, so it was obviously to be welcomed. But a mixed bag of Rugby League players and fellow-travellers enjoying themselves after the official banquet had been officially declared over – and not even paying hard-currency prices for the privilege? A stop had to be put to that very rapidly. Let them carry on like this and, Marx my words, they'll be ripping down the Berlin Wall next.

There were a number of things about this party of Fulham and Ryedale-York players which baffled the Russkies. What, for instance, were they to make of Fulham's black forward, Conrad Scott, who had had a handsome hammer and sickle shaved into his scalp? Was this some sort of bizarre yet sincere tribute to the host nation, or was he simply taking the piss? Black men such as Scott and the Pryce brothers were an unusual enough sight to draw small crowds on the streets of Moscow. The meagre resident population of African students generally kept well out of the way, for the very good reason that they were likely to be fraternally beaten up by the xenophobic Russians. But you couldn't really do that to a man with a hammer and sickle on his head.

Not only had Scott shelled out for his haircut, he and his team-mates and their opponents from York had made the whole project possible by agreeing to come and play for nothing – a figure that is the same in both hard and soft currency. It was an end-of-season trip with a few games thrown in, but it was also a journey into the unknown.

When the two clubs from what was then the second division embarked on this three-match tour in May 1991, Rugby League in the Soviet Union was little more than a year old. My own first contact with the Soviet players and officials had been at a venue which had surreal aspects of its own: Pontin's holiday camp in Blackpool, into which they were booked in spring 1990 for a week's intensive coaching under the RFL's Phil Larder before the holidaymakers arrived. It said everything about the country from which they had come that they regarded Pontin's as the height of decadent western luxury, and Blackpool's tackiest souvenir shops as Aladdin's caves stuffed to bursting point with unimaginable goodies. It was hard to conduct interviews with them, not because of the language barrier, but because they would feel obliged to try to buy your jeans. Through the culture shock, though, it was possible to discern one thing very clearly: they were mad keen to do well at a game that could be, literally as well as metaphorically, a passport.

The Soviet visa in my own passport was ten years out of date, a memento from a journey home from an Australian Rugby League season via Yokohama, Vladivostok and the Trans-Siberian Railway. The scenic route, you might say, except that in late November the scene for nine-tenths of that route was an unchanging one of ice, snow and endless steppes. It did yield, however, my favourite traveller's horror story of all time: The Man who got on the Wrong Train at Ulan-Ude. A group of around 20 of us was being shepherded through the Soviet Union by a very nervous guide and interpreter. Nervous with good cause, because the greatest sin in that line of work is to lose one of your party. And, in Ulan-Ude, she did just that. Mind you, it must be the most potentially disastrous railway junction in the world: three platforms, one for Vladivostok, one for Moscow, Warsaw and London, and a branch line to Ulaanbaatar and Beijing. Get on the wrong train here, and it isn't quite like hopping on the Circle Line instead of the District Line. I like to think that, somewhere in Mongolia, there is a very confused Australian still wondering when the next one to Earls Court is due. What I am sure about is that our minder, Natasha, will never have gained the Soviet tour guide's Holy Grail of a trip outside the country, to some paradise of conspicuous consumerism such as Poland or East Germany. As it was, she would have got little enough credit for getting the rest of us to Moscow in one piece; but she had committed her profession's equivalent of a knock-on on the first tackle on her own goal-line, and is probably now still serving her suspension in Siberia's newly privatised salt-mines.

The city to which she delivered the survivors was full of all the irritations and inconveniences about which visitors at the time were traditionally warned: bring your own bath plug – but better to bring your own bath and water as well. It was, however, a city still confident of its own place in the world, as the capital of a huge, if decaying, empire. To stand in Red Square at midnight and first to hear and then see the soldiers goose-stepping over the frozen cobbles to change the guard at Lenin's tomb was to be reminded forcefully of that status. No post-modern irony yet-a-while, if you please, and no unflattering caricatures of great communists for sale to tourists.

A decade later, the difference was not so much one in the physical environment as in prevailing attitudes. I don't doubt that the Muscovites of the 1980s used to chuckle, in the safety of their shared flats, at something so pompous and grandiose as the Exhibition of Economic Achievements, a 216-hectare monstrosity across Prospekt Mir (Peace Way, what else?) from the equally overblown Cosmos Hotel. They might privately have scoffed at the bathos of its pretensions and its contrast with the realities of their lives. But the party line, and the one that Muscovites would parrot for foreigners was, as my official guidebook from the time puts it, that it gave them 'a comprehensive picture of the present level and latest achievements of Soviet industry, agriculture, building, transport, science and culture'. In 1991, the Russians who attached themselves to the British party still advised us to go, but now only because it was so irresistibly kitsch and so hilarious to see the sort of crap in which their lords and masters had invested such pride. Next to it, too, there had developed by 1991 what amounted, in its own shabby way, to another Exhibition of Economic Achievements. This was a rambling open market, and the economic achievements being celebrated here were the acquisitions of old leather jackets, 1970s LPs and, inevitably, jeans from all points west, which were being sold on at a respectable capitalist profit. They loved Conrad Scott down there.

The players of Fulham and Ryedale-York had been through what they described as a mixed experience in their two games before arriving in Moscow. In Alma-Ata – not to be confused with Ulan-Ude, although you could get there on the Trans-Siberian if you changed at Novosibirsk – they had played in front of more people than most of them had ever seen. In Leningrad, that icy beauty then in the process of peeling off her greasy overalls and changing back into St Petersburg, there had been about as many as on a bad day at Crystal Palace, which was not very many at all.

In Moscow, all the preparations were on the grand scale. Press conferences, which were numerous, catered for the possibility that several hundred journalists might attend, each of whom would need a couple of plates of food in which beetroot always seemed to play a dominant role, and plenty of Georgian champagne to wash it down. By the time the four of us had done our best, there was still the equivalent of the output of one of the smaller republics to be disposed of – or, I rather feared, to be laid out again the next time we assembled. There was also a degree of overkill in the matter of interpreters. Interpreting was, and probably still is, a popular career path in those parts, holding out as it does the tantalising prospect of getting away from the damn place in the course of your work and coming back loaded down with jeans bought low to be sold high. (This facility, I need hardly add, is unavailable to interpreters who lose Australians in Ulan-Ude.) In Moscow, they were queuing up to interpret. I had four of them to myself at one stage, and such was their enthusiasm that one of them insisted on presiding over a conversation I had with Ross Strudwick. You could appreciate that he was only trying to be helpful; but Strudwick and I both spoke English, or something close to it.

The arrangements for the match itself were on a similarly generous basis. Dynamo Stadium is big enough to host a small war, but there seemed some doubt in the mind of the president of the Soviet Rugby League, Edouard Tatourian, whether it would suffice. He need not have worried. There were 3,200 people there that day, not all of whom had handed over the requisite roubles. There were some plates of beetroot that looked suspiciously familiar, and some Georgian champagne that was starting to lose its fizz – probably enough of both for a crowd which could have been regarded as derisory, had it not been rather better than any other (apart from in that famous hotbed of the game, Alma-Ata) that either side had attracted that season. You have to get these things into proportion.

The idea was that the two English sides should pool their strength as a Great Britain Select XIII for a match against the Soviet Union, which meant unlikely international honours for household names such as Dave Rotheram and David Kettlestring (two household names in himself, when you think about it), as well as London-based Australians such as Greg Pearce, Mark Lee and Russell Browning. The manner in which they dismantled a Soviet side fired up for great deeds was a salutary reminder of how good average players in an average competition like the English second division, *circa* 1990–91, really are. That was the cheerful way of looking at the British side's 42–10 victory, at any rate, while there was some truth in Phil Larder's explanation that the problem with the home team was not that they were Russians, but that they were all recently converted Rugby Union players. Larder, along with the RFL's then chief executive David Oxley, was firmly on the Russo-enthusiast wing of the British game. Indeed, he has the distinction of having a team in Moscow named after him – although there is no truth in the rumour that an eastern bloc car also owes its name to him.

Over the champagne and beetroot that night in the Cosmos, deals were being done – and not just the usual commerce involving the hard-currency whores in the hard-currency bar. Ryedale-York were signing a raftful of Russians; even more exotically, Leeds, having discovered him several thousand miles from home, were in the process of signing Greg Pearce. And Steve Pryce was sounding more and more like Sam Cooke. Reality wields a heavy riot-stick, however. The Russians never went to York, although one played a single game for what had by then become the London Crusaders.

157

Three of them, though, did sample the wealth and wonder of the West, signing on for that outfit perched on the pinnacle of professional sport: Trafford Borough. They must have gone home with interesting tales of just how green the grass was on the other side of the hill. It would not surprise me one day to see the names of Alexandre Diatlov, Valeriy Savikhine and Oleg Zotov among the candidates standing for election under the banner of the revived communist party. We have seen the way the West works, they could tell the electorate, and we were better off the way we were. Such are the insights when East and West are brought together by Rugby League.

# Apart from that, Mrs Lincoln . . .

## Neil Tunnicliffe

It was the first time that I had met the Rugby Football League's board of directors. I had been working at the old Chapeltown Road headquarters for just two months. I was a greenhorn junior under-secretary in the Ministry without Portfolio. I was dying for a chance, any chance. I had no idea.

Whisked away from my working drudgery, I was well met by these hale fellows and instantly entrusted with a vital mission: to go to Moldova in the company of development executive Tom O'Donovan, survey the state of the game there, and report back. There was an international tournament planned to take place between the nation states of what was the Soviet Union, thus providing a chance to meet all the major players in the Russian game at one fell swoop. Hereat, it seemed, order might appear out of the chaos created in Russian Rugby League by the recent crumbling of the communist carapace.

Like the suitors of Zuleika Dobson, I was at once captivated by this beautiful vision of a romantic, roving ambassadorial role. Blinded by the full glare of the spotlight, I merely laughed obligingly at the sardonic references to tin helmets. I didn't really understand.

Moldova. Or was it Moldava? Or Moldavia? Or Moravia? Nobody seemed to know for sure. It was not readily apparent whether we would be encountering Rugby League's newest nation, a fantasy kingdom from *Dynasty* ruled by an actor who otherwise doubled as Robin Hood, or a twentieth-century Italian novelist. It wasn't so much a fine line dividing fiction and reality as a tripwire.

Research for the expedition came in three equal parts. First, a file that was incomplete, inconsistent and, in part, in Cyrillic: not much help, all told. Second, a map of the world in the back of someone's desk diary: top left-hand corner of the Black Sea, or thereabouts, just around the back of beyond. Third, and perhaps most comprehensive, former RFL chairman Bob Ashby's reminiscences of a similar trip behind the Iron Curtain in the less than forensic history *When Push Comes To Shove*.

Chairman Bob's deliberate raconteurial style is geared towards proving two things beyond a shadow of a doubt: first, that being born and bred in Featherstone is no handicap to a man cultivating an easy, cosmopolitan *savoir-faire* no matter the circumstances; and second, that wherever you may wander, there is indeed no place like Fev. Thus, aplomb to the fore, Bob took mountains and deserts in his stride as he journeyed through Kazakhstan, ending his travels in a sheepskin house half-way up a hill, where there was laid on in honour of the distinguished guest exotic salads and caviare, mare's milk and vodka – and, of course, a whole sheep's head. Oh well, I thought, as I read that part: if I have to eat sheep's eyes, then at least they should see me through to breakfast . . .

The next few days were a flurry of activity – rearranging meetings planned for the days in question, couriering passports around to secure visas, arguing with travel agents over inflated air fares. Apparently, one can only fly direct to Tiraspol, whither we were bound, on a Tuesday; on any other day of the week, it's into Bucharest and then hop over the border. Since our schedule was supermodel-spare, to go in on Wednesday and back out again on Friday, Bucharest and the hop it was.

We also looked with interest into the inoculation requirements. Slowly and obliquely, it had emerged that at least part of the reason why Tom and I were asked to go was that a previous expedition to have been conducted by the board of directors themselves had had to be cancelled following an outbreak of diphtheria in Moldova. A wise precaution, we thought, repressing any unworthy thoughts of comparative expendability.

A final word of advice came in a somewhat oracular utterance from then RFL public affairs executive David Howes, who had accompanied chairman Bob on his epic trek. With a knowing wink and a familiar, crooked grin he divined: 'Make sure you buy plenty of cigarettes in duty-free.' But neither of us smoke, we protested. Never mind, he averred: just buy them . . .

It's tough on tour. The then Wigan trio of Martin Dermott, Billy McGinty and Andy Platt prepare to do battle with the Manly surf

Just five cornettos. Ray Tabern, Mike Smith, Brian Case, George Fairbairn and John Joyner in St Mark's Square, Venice

Italian pioneer Mario Majone

OPPOSITE
TOP: Morocco's guiding light Hussain M'Barki draws a line in the sand

BOTTOM: Morocco come to Dewsbury, with a few items from their National Portrait Gallery to remind them of home (photo © Sig Kasatkin)

RIGHT: Catching practice.
Alexandra township,
South Africa

BELOW: Dave Southern
and protégés in Soweto

Welcome to Rabaul. The Great Britain squad get ready to be garlanded

Taking a serious look at the warm-up game in Goroka, in the highlands
of Papua New Guinea

What the well-dressed tourist is wearing. Garland, headphones and shades for
Ellery Hanley in Papua New Guinea

Signing the visitors' book at the High Commission in Tonga

Arriving, slightly overdressed for the climate, in the Cook Islands

The opposition lines up at the Cook Islands' only stadium, in Avarua on Rarotonga

The USA in the Sydney Sevens

Then, at last, yet all too soon, the day of departure dawned – though not quite as I bleared my way into Wetherby to meet up with Tom. Black turned to purple turned to blue, red and orange, like a prop forward's eye sockets in the days following a match, as we sped down the A1, putting the world to rights and boiling and cracking in-jokes. It was only when we had traversed to join the M11 *en route* to Stansted that we realised we had neglected to ascertain exactly who would be meeting us in Bucharest, and exactly how we would recognise them. A brief yet solemn debate ensued regarding the most effective manner of identification – cloak and dagger, involving dark raincoats, red carnations, and a rolled-up copy of *Pravda*? full rugby kit, including shoulder-pads, strapping and headguard? – before we decided on the banal directness of asking them to carry a rugby ball.

On arrival at Stansted, we rang back to the office to ask them to relay this request to Tiraspol. Moments later, the office rang back: 'Sorry, they've already set off to collect you.' It took a while to compute the potential implications of this. Our connection was to be via Heathrow, wherefrom we were not due to land in Bucharest until 6 p.m. – some eight hours hence. Hmmm, we mused fractiously: either the hop over the border was one for the combined powers of Jonathan Edwards, Willie Banks and Bob Beamon; or our reception party had a devil of a lot of shopping to do on the way. Reluctant to countenance the former option, we plumped optimistically for the latter.

Less than daisy-fresh after 11 hours under way, we arrived in Bucharest. Granted, it was evening, and the shadows had already lengthened to gobble up most in their path. But there was an added gloom which owed little to nature. A frisson lay around like a carpet of frost crunching underfoot as we crossed the concourse. Revolution, repression, state terrorism: these were the handles and clasps of our portmanteau preconceptions of what it should be like, gleaned from news bulletins emitted by drama-conscious studios who understood that every sorry victim in an inexplicable foreign struggle was a priceless armament in a different, bloodless ratings war. If the ghosts of Ceaucescu's children hovered around us, it was because we had brought them with us. Still, it was awkward to know where the ordinary people stopped, and the torturers, murderers, widows and orphans began.

What the airport was full of was taxi-drivers, lean, hirsute, leather-jacketed wolves and mongrels of men who assailed us in packs one after another as soon as we had cleared immigration. Taxi to the hotel? To the town centre? The flaming torch we used to keep them at bay was our promise of transport, the mystery man with the rugby ball. But of him there was no sign.

Thirty minutes yawned and stretched into an hour. At its leisure, in its own sweet, unhurried time, that hour asexually reproduced to become two, while we paced and fidgeted like nervous fathers-to-be in a hospital corridor. The wolves looked on in amusement, as if this was some quaint western custom with which they were unacquainted: must be one of the luxuries of capitalism, surely, this refusal of the obvious help to rely instead on the invisible.

We took to approaching innocent bystanders who looked as if they might have held a rugby ball if there was one to hand: no joy. We went to the information bureau and, by the tried and trusted British method of shouting louder when misunderstood, got the message across to them that we wanted a tannoy announcement of our presence: no response to that, either. Finally, within spitting distance of desperation, we singled out a lone wolf on the edge of the pack and asked him, quietly for fear of embarrassment, how much to take us to Tiraspol. That we had to repeat the question seemed natural to us initially, given the language gap. It was only when he told us how far it was that we realised his hesitancy was probably caused by an internal debate over exactly where he thought he might retire on the proceeds. It was 600km from Bucharest to Tiraspol: roughly a 350-mile hop.

Our hearts sank like Leeds's title hopes after two bad mid-season defeats. Rocked by this rabbit-punch realisation of our repressed fears, and confronted by the grim yet tangible spectre of abandonment in the nightmare Bucharest of popular legend, we hastily regrouped. One more tannoy announcement, we agreed: then, and only then, will it be truly reasonable to panic.

Having whittled his vocabulary down to words of one syllable, Tom was vociferously using these to batter the poor, perplexed girl behind the information desk, when I noticed three new arrivals on the scene. One of these would have been noticeable under any circumstances, not merely by her stark contrast with the otherwise uniformly vulpine cast of this shadowy, Munschian theatre: for, with her long ebony hair, large green eyes, snub nose and full lips, she was strikingly attractive. I suspect that Tom could hardly believe his luck in more ways than one when his exaggerated, phonetic enunciation of the name 'O'Donovan' brought her swiftly to his side.

Students of the progression of Rugby League under the Moldovan banner (which, rather endearingly, carries the device of the national plant, a bunch of black grapes) will know that Natalya Konovalova is as vital to it as Geoff Fletcher is to Highfield, or as Tony Barrow has been of late to Swinton. As the only reliable Anglophone in the Moldovan set-up, she has established her apartment on the Boulevard Gagarina as its operational headquarters and become the charming, cheery conduit via whom Tests, tours, trips and tournaments have been organised. Communications with her can be a bit like shouting through an empty bean tin and down a length of string to your mate standing around two corners, while you never know whether your fax is travelling down the line to a similar machine or into the earphones of a monk with a quill pen and a scroll of papyrus. But experience has taught that, when the call goes out, Natalya answers and is as good as her word. It might not always be the most appropriate word for the situation, which can result in hilariously malapropian dialogue; but then it's rather more fluent than my Moldovan.

On this first, ice-breaking, siege-raising encounter she was accompanied by two men of variant stature. The first was a great hulking bear of a chap with Stalin's moustache and Chaplin's conversation, who turned out to be our driver, Erik. The strong, silent type, his willingness now to retrace ten-hour-long steps after a mere 15-minute break made us alternately awestruck at his stamina, and fearful lest narcolepsy should end our journey in a fond embrace with a Romanian tree-trunk. The second, a stocky, balding man with an open face, ready smile and ubiquitous leather jacket, was the general manager of the Moldovan Rugby League, Vladimir Dolgin, of whose name Natalya would commonly use the affectionate diminutive form 'Valody'. This apparent reference to an unseen fourth party confused us greatly at first, until we twigged that this was no different from calling Mike Stephenson 'Stevo' or Scott Quinnell 'Foo'.

Our three hosts were fulsome both in their apologies for their tardy arrival and in their welcome to their country – not that this was their country, though it seemed pettifogging to point that out. They led us from the airport transept across the car park to the four-wheel-drive off-road vehicle which was to be our *pied-à-terre* for the next God-knew-how-long. There we were treated to an ad hoc reception which was remarkable for its right royal trappings in this utterly incongruous environment. Cramped in the back seat,

163

illuminated only by courtesy lights and dashboard, we made ambassador's garden-party small talk and toasted our safe arrival with perfectly passable champagne in paper cups, and caviare-pimpled delicacies unfolded from coarse plaid handkerchiefs. Bizarrely out of context, it was a picnic scripted by Luis Buñuel.

With Erik thus stretched, refreshed and, like 'Ol' Man River', ready to roll on, we headed off into the Stygian gloom of the Romanian night. There were no streetlights by which to watch this other world go by, and Valody was evangelically keen to preach his sermon to this potentially influential audience while he held them captive. So, cheeks roasting gently from the champagne, and with little else to occupy us for the next third of a day, we settled back to listen to the machine-gun rattle of Valody's alien, backwards-sounding patter, turned to lyrical if halting English by the breathless, chiming voice of Natalya.

The story so far. In 1990, the Russian rugby authorities finally decided that amateur sport was incomprehensible within their totalitarian, Stakhanovite work ethic, where effort was rewarded with results and seemed wasted without them. Out, then, went the Tsarist decadence of Rugby Union and, in a revolution reminiscent of that 73 years earlier, in came the working-man's game, Rugby League. With the aforementioned enthusiastic support of Chairman Bob and Co., the Rugby League of Russia was constituted, otherwise known as the Fil League after its major sponsor. That organisation evolved, under the leadership of the machiavellian and ultimately discredited Edouard Tatourian, into the Euro-Asian Rugby League (EARL). This reorientation recognised the extent of a network which connected the 'headquarters' clubs in Moscow with far-flung co-operatives such as Tiraspol down here in Moldova, Kazan to the east on the upper reaches of the Volga, and the sheep's-head-consuming capital of Kazakhstan, Alma-Ata, hard up against the Chinese border.

Come 1993, Tatourian's misappropriation of the aid which the Rugby Football League had been supplying was rumbled. However, the blowing of the whistle on him was drowned out by the screaming sirens which heralded the end of the Soviet Union: the fissures which appeared in the still-damp plaster on the EARL's walls were nothing compared to the crevasses by which this leviathan of a nation was riven from border to border, top to toe.

What had hitherto been the straight path of consequential history then entered the catacombs of politics. Just as Gorbachev and Yeltsin had tussled with each other to impose their respective, idiosyncratic visions of post-diluvian capitalism on the blinking, dazzled masses, so Valody described the old-fashioned power struggle currently in train to fill Tatourian's muddied boots. On the one side stood our hosts, assembled in a fortress almost ironically christened 'Sodruzhestvo', or 'Harmony', a collective of those clubs who fancied themselves as professional – Eolis Tiraspol, Kazan Arrows, Moscow Magicians – and therefore the leading practitioners, and principal hopes, of the game in this part of the world. Against them was marshalled the National Rugby League, sundry survivors of the EARL who, Valody sneered, were not above exaggerating the number of clubs at their disposal. Although these characters had announced to the RFL that their league was 40-strong, stretching from Moscow across Georgia, the Ukraine, and into Kazakhstan, Valody dismissed these as paper teams, not substantial enough in quantity or infrastructure ever to take the field in anger. As a saga, it was saddeningly familiar: it seemed that British Rugby League was incapable of exporting its wares overseas without also loading on to the freighter the amateur-professional conflict which has dogged the last quarter-century of its existence.

We also heard tell in rhapsodic, reverential tones of a mission of Phil Larder and Fred Lindop to Moldova in 1991. It seems that the pair were received, not as visiting RFL officials come to conduct coaching and refereeing clinics, but as deities in human form, transported to earth to test the virtue and hospitality of mortals. We half-expected to find on our arrival in Tiraspol civic statues of the pair erected on street corners – Phil tracksuited, hunched and meditative, a Rodin-style bronze, and Fred straight-backed and immaculate in marble, gesturing a penalty for talking back. Imagine what they would think of that in the Humberside League: Lindop immortalised in sculpture. They'd be sending pigeons out by the crateload.

Periodically, and with increasing frequency the further we travelled, our seminar was interrupted by brief halts at turnpikes in the road. Here unsmiling, uniformed militia men would inspect our passports, speak curtly to Valody, and then wave us on – though never empty-handed. The cache of bottles which had enlivened our picnic began to diminish at a rate of knots as Valody ensured that it was never merely our passports which were offered to the guards. At once, the enigmatic wisdom of David Howes was revealed:

enlightened, we duly contributed our duty-free cigarettes to this war chest, to the effect that our passage through checkpoints while others stood and waited was remarkably fluid.

And how they stood and waited. The further we got from Bucharest, the more the run-ups to the checkpoints were lined with entire caravans of people. The scenes were reminiscent of *Fiddler on the Roof*, when the pogrom turns Topol and his fellow-Jews out of their homes and forces them to flee into exile; although now the vehicles of choice were largely battered beige or mustard Ladas and Deux-Chevaux, there were still handcarts and horse-drawn carts taking part in the procession, all of them topped by bulging hessian blankets moored precariously by untidy ropes.

When we asked the meaning of this apparent mass migration, Valody explained that people were so poor that they bundled all their possessions together, drove to the next town or state, and tried to sell their worldly goods at market. On the proceeds they would hope to start again, or at least survive a little longer. It was, in effect, the car-boot sale of last resort.

The drivers watched us pass with emotionless, expressionless faces, as though we were ciphers of some language, concept and culture which they could never hope to understand, nor were they intended to. Our presence, and our distinctly un-British queue-jumping, were simply accepted. So long as the guards were satisfied, it seemed, there was no need for their questions. It was the passivity of natural victims, seasoned by continual and institutionalised exploitation.

Around 2 a.m. we encountered the Lord Mayor's Show of these processions as we reached the Romania–Moldova border post. Where other checkpoints had been mere sentry boxes, this was the Charlie of them all, a whole complex that was part-motorway service station, part-military camp. This time Valody was compelled to leave the vehicle, loaded with comestibles as though he was delivering Christmas hampers to the housebound, and headed off into conference in an outbuilding. We sat patiently, awaiting his return, for a period that dragged into the disturbing.

Eventually he returned, hands naturally empty of everything except bad tidings. Although Tom and I had visas, these were only sufficient to guarantee us safe passage through Romania; they did not spirit us over the border and on into Moldova. For that transportation we would have to apply at the visa office in the border post – which, hardly surprising at 2 a.m., was closed.

Hindsight's 20:20 vision suggests that, on balance, waking the visa officer up at 2 a.m. and demanding that he open the office specifically for us may not have been the best tactical weapon to draw from the armoury. Civil servants possess the obstinacy of mules at the best of times when implored to trim the red tape to make life a little simpler for Joe Public. And 2 a.m., the smallest of hours, was not the best of times. We stood rather self-consciously outside his quarters in blazers and slacks that were every bit as tired and creased as we were, trying staunchly to resemble the diplomatic behemoths that Valody was making us out to be in justification of this outrageous violation of man's rightly earned rest – to no avail. Turning hard on his heel, the visa officer closed his bedroom door with a finality that spoke eloquently of a silent determination to open up 30 minutes late in the morning, just to get his own back.

Despair comes in many colours and, following the midnight blue of Bucharest Airport, we were really too bushed to push this one much beyond aquamarine. Tom and I set off on strolls in different directions, he to shake six hours' sitting out of his legs and me to shake a similar quantity out of my bladder. Entering the public area of the border post, I found that this was hardly Leicester Forest: no general shop, no video games, no Julie's Pantry. Instead, it was closer to one of Dante's circles of hell – an early one, given the generally moist atmosphere and the undead glaze on the faces of the occupants seated on bare wooden benches around the walls.

With the same dispassionate eyes as their confrères on the road, they watched me enter the lavatories. It is a byword among satirists and alternative comedians that the English, when travelling abroad, are obsessed with their middle-class scatalogical standards and personal hygiene. Here, however, it was difficult, nay impossible, to resist the reversion to type. Never have I encountered such a fetid, faecal cess-hole masquerading as a public convenience. Running water and toilet paper were the property of some plumbing Shangri-la a thousand miles and 20 years hence. Sinuses stinging and stomach turned roller-coaster, I abruptly resolved that, whatever intestinal discomfort or damage I might sustain in the attempt, I could wait.

Tom's perambulations proved rather more directly threatening to life, wind and limb. Absent-minded through the wit-robber fatigue, he was ambling along parallel to the main buildings when he heard a sharp, stentorian shout to his rear. Assuming this to be a routine, ear-bashing interchange between overweening NCO and put-upon

167

junior guardsman, he continued along his befuddled way. It was only the metallic, chain-rattle 'ching-ching' of a rifle being charged that pulled him up short. Somewhat sheepishly he was escorted back to the car park, hands raised, and withering before a parade-ground broadside of Slavonic abuse whose content was only too easy to guess at.

With characteristic British adaptability-cum-stiff upper lips, we did our best for the next six hours. Cat-napping with chattering teeth on the back seat of the four-wheel-drive, making desultory conversation with Natalya and Valody, exploring as far as we dare around the dismal compound and its purgatorial halls. Eventually daylight infiltrated the border post with the silent stealth of the SAS, and we repaired to the canteen, whose only other occupant was a solitary, youthful, sallow-skinned soldier nursing a tiny cup of pitch-like coffee. Some sort of soap opera was jabbering away on a TV in the corner of the bar, a flashing-eyed glamourpuss creating a scene with her swarthy, dreamboat lover. An old woman dragged herself away from the set's hypnotic hold to inspect us with now familiar absorbent, black-hole eyes, and serve us glasses of water, kerbs of stale bread, and a cold, fat-sealed turd of minced meat. To my addled mind and ravening craw, this last was the most revolting thing I had ever eaten. What I would have given then for a sheep's eye . . .

The visa office was due to open at 9 a.m., but there was an almost audible dragging of vindictive feet. When business did commence for the day, some 45 minutes in arrears, it was conducted with a pointed fastidiousness which, we were sure, was not a regular feature of Thursday's itinerary. Papers were shuffled, files consulted, small print examined, seals applied, documents checked, double-checked, triple-checked. Protestations, we were equally sure, were futile. And so, like every other civilian on the border post, we just waited with a patience which was not so much saintly, more plain dumb.

Finally, around 10.30 a.m., some 28 hours after leaving home, we entered our country of destination. Daylight added a perspective to our journey which we had lacked hitherto, but enlightening it was not. Moldova shares the geography of the Balkans and mainland, inland Greece to the south: naked, craggy half-mountains kept at arm's length by featureless, ochre plains in which occasional orchards of olive or orange make game stabs at greenery. The few other vehicles on the road were donkey-drawn, while the sparse humans dotting the landscape seemed to have all on to clothe themselves. Scarf-headed women in aprons and clogs, clawing worm-riddled fruit into rough-hewn wicker baskets; old-timers with cloth caps and clay pipes, vests and dungarees, vainly scratching at the unresponsive soil with hoe or adze; barefoot young goatherds in rags with skeletal mongrels fussily stewarding a handful of mangy nannies. How on earth did they survive? Even after what we had seen and heard in Romania, it seemed incredible that this state of medieval peasantry continued to exist in a country which, a short time earlier, had been part of a union which had colonised space.

We drove for two hours without seeing a single town, nor any settlement which could have been blithely mistaken for one. Our hosts were quiet, perhaps apprehensive as to our reactions to their tournament, perhaps inwardly cursing that their ambitions to impress had been so vasectomised at the border. Then there suddenly appeared on the horizon something like the Emerald City at the end of the Yellow Brick Road. You could clearly see its entire span, the limits where its suburbs at both extremes ended and the desert began, while in the middle it stretched upwards to a peak of gleaming marble towers and monuments. In the context of what had gone before, it was a remarkable sight.

This was Kishinev, the state capital, and driving through it almost gave the lie to the abject penury we had encountered that morning. Communism had been munificent here: well-watered, shrub-bound lawns grazed at the roadside, the sculpted, four-square chambers of state stood magisterially over stepped approaches of cyclopean granite paving, while imposing memorials preened themselves at every junction (though not, truth to tell, to Messrs Lindop and Larder). This was the irony of the system, the fatal flaw in the philosophy, writ large. If only the people themselves had benefited as much as the leaders of the people from the fruits of the people's democracy, the Berlin Wall would surely never have come down.

Good socialists both, Tom and I would none the less have cheerily swallowed our principles for a stopover in a city which was bound to have a decent hotel or two. Our hopes for a wash, brush-up and change of underwear were not out of short trousers before they were brutally smothered in their beds. There was to be the briefest of dalliances at the Romanian Embassy – one which did not even extend to our leaving the vehicle – and then off we went.

The purpose of the visit to the embassy was to write a new character into our drama, one who was never more than bit-part but who had enough lines to steal the odd scene – as might a peripheral misfit in a David Lynch production. Quiffed, goatee-bearded and clad in a linen suit, the terms of his presence were never readily apparent. As we drove out of Kishinev, we learned that his name was Popescu, he seemed to be from the Romanian Ministry of Sport, he was acquainted with the late, lamented Gilbert Dautant of the French *Fédération de Rugby à XIII*, and he harboured a harebrained scheme of unknown provenance, of a European Rugby League combining the known quantities of Great Britain and France, the unfulfilled prodigy Moldova, and the merely fanciful Spain and Romania. Given that Romanian sport generally was up for grabs following the dethroning of Ceaucescu, and that Rugby Union in particular was currently counting the cost of its brave, bloody and ultimately tragic role in the revolution, you could just make out the shape of his credibility through all the pinches of salt. But, really, it was straight out of Kafka: the man from the Ministry arrives, and events take a surreal turn.

Having passed out of Kishinev, the geography abandoned its all-or-nothing aspect and evolved a happy medium. Smaller towns came and went, some of which owned just the one horse, some of which more properly deserved the noun. The links in the chain which connected them one to another were more military checkpoints, different from their Romanian brethren only in the colour of the uniforms and the absence of queues, but identical in their avaricious plundering of our dwindling supplies in exchange for the craved-for wave-on.

Our next step was Benderi, on the outskirts of which we endured a particularly nit-picking negotiation before being allowed to continue. The place was a bastard cross between a derelict industrial estate and one of the grottier districts of Newcastle-upon-Tyne. Valody explained that the punctiliousness of the guards was due to the fact that we were passing from 'free' Moldova into an area which was in fact presently at war with the rest of the country. To illustrate this somewhat alarming point, he indicated a barn wall, pock-marked and blistered as if ravaged by some teenage hormonal condition, and off-handedly stated that these were bullet-holes from fighting which had taken place just the previous week. Perfectly safe now, though . . . I don't know what Tom was thinking, but the phrase which came fastest to my mind was both expression of surprise and literal evocation: bloody hell.

Benderi had played host that morning to the first round of matches in Sodruzhestvo's tournament, between Russia and

Kazakhstan, and now we were being taken to see the stadium. Tom and I were increasingly restive: having glimpsed the voluptuous vision of warm, soapy ablutions in a hotel room in Kishinev, it was difficult to exorcise it from our minds and so, the more eager our hosts were to gallop through their planned itinerary and make up for lost time, the more sulky and resentful we became.

Thus the enthusiasm with which we greeted the assembled coaches of the four competing nations at the stadium gates was muted in a way which would have done justice to the smokiest of late-night jazz trumpeters. The coaches themselves seemed neither to notice nor to care. Had they but known it, they represented the height of fashion – but only because of the nostalgic craze sweeping British football at the time which promoted old 1970s Adidas tracksuits, round-necked playing shirts and the memory of Frankie Worthington's coiffure as the apogee of hip. Smiling and gesturing magnanimously, we stepped through the excited throng into the stadium, puff-chestedly described by Valody as one of Moldova's better facilities. Given what we had seen in the countryside round about, it would have been churlish to sneer: but the single-stand, athletic-tracked, concrete bowl stirred little in the blood. It was as if our host had stood up and messianically declared: 'I have seen the future – and it's Barnet Copthall.'

Back in the car we thought, this time, it's got to be the hotel. Wrong again. At the head of a small convoy of juddering, chuntering 2CVs, we weaved our way down ever-dodgier country lanes until we reached a wooded site which Valody, as chuffed as he had been in Benderi, proudly introduced as the proposed centre of excellence for his national team. It still needed a bit of work, he conceded: but a lick of paint here and there, and it could transport Moldovan Rugby League into the twenty-first century.

Nineteenth, more like, we sniffed as we trampolined our way down pot-holed cart-tracks. There were two facilities to which the team would have access. First, an overgrown soccer field cum kiddies' playground, no better than the local council rec., complete with rickety swings and rusty chain-mail fence; and second, an abandoned, prefabricated accommodation block which might have stood empty since the Wehrmacht withdrew from this part of the world in the last war.

Damp, dank, dark and uninvitingly chilly, the block had one room which was ablaze with life, a surprise party springing forth atop a flight of unpromising stairs to perk up the birthday it seemed no one had remembered. Therein a makeshift barbecue had skewered meat chuckling with juicy warmth, hunks of cushioned bread clambered over each other in large wicker bowls, unexplained vegetables rolled and stewed in sturdy earthenware, and jars of vivid relish vamped it up to tempt the taste buds. Seated on low school benches around scarred, hefty oak tables, our ailing health was drunk and revivified with throaty red wine and smelling-salt brandy as speeches of welcome were finally made and formal pleasantries exchanged. It was the kiss of life for a mission that was all but dead on its feet: the aura of privileged respect which imbued these men and this woman who hung on our every faltering platitude brought us sharply yet spiritedly back to our purpose.

It did not, however, stop our chins crackling with stubble or our seams sagging. When our hosts tried to bustle us on again with post-prandial urgency, this time to the second match of the day, the foot went down with flat defiance. No, we said, like dogs who sit down on the pavement having decided that they will walk with their owners no further: we do nothing more without a shave, a shower, and a change of shirt. There followed a short round of plaintive cajoling, centred upon the desperate risk that we might end up not having seen any rugby at all, which we dead-batted with square jaws and left elbows high. In the end, the strength of our resolution was reluctantly accepted, and our wish was granted.

The hotel in Tiraspol – which was neither Kishinev nor Benderi, but somewhere in between – was the largest I have ever seen, a grander, more imposing, more baroque and more world-weary version of the Hotel Terminus in Carcassonne or the St Nicholas in Scarborough (depending, natch, on your cosmopolitanism), if such a thing can be imagined. Interminable stairways, route-march corridors, apparently thousands of doors before our respective ones – and then geysers of hot running water, an alabaster bath six cubits and a span, an acre bed on which to recline for a seductive moment before replacing the old cast-off slough with pristine laundered skin. Had we been gifted a longer sojourn there, I'm not convinced that our appreciation of it would have been as immense. Be that as it may, our concertinaed schedule had left us no room to explore this 1940s time warp and so, eyes brighter and tails bushier, we emerged inside the half-hour to be taken out to the ball-game.

The people to whom I have spun this yarn have, for the most part, begun by listening sympathetically and attentively, but then grown restless as the catalogue of hardship unfolds. Finally, half-way down the road to Kishinev, their feigned, fragile interest has snapped, and they have blurted out in spite of themselves: but what was the football like? Oh, yeah; apart from that, Mrs Lincoln, how was the show?

We arrived at Barnet Copthall II shortly before half-time, with the home team already enjoying a patent advantage in technique, physique, points and playing kit over Tatarstan. The visitors, wearing what looked like an old Manchester City strip airlifted in by the Red Cross, were neither up to it nor fancied it much, despite a sprightly, dancing display from a waif-like half-back who, from our vantage point, might have been either 14 or a 40-year-old with a tough paper-round. For their part, Moldova ran some neat patterns, held their shape well and, indeed, would have been picked out as a Rugby League team in any identity parade. But defences on both sides were woeful, the tackling frail as choux pastry, commitment mere clouds on the wind. Moldova cantered to the line as 40–11 victors, and our neighbours in the stand sagely opined that tomorrow's final against Russia (32–18 winners that morning) would be even-stevens. The same neighbours also gleefully recounted the watching crowd as 3,000-plus, when you could have knocked off a nought and several more and still been top-side. I wouldn't have bought a fitted carpet from any of them.

I didn't really know whether to be disappointed or impressed. No, neither side was yet ready to take on Great Britain and so broaden the base of European competition and, yes, there was much to be negative about, from the poor labourers in the fields through the obvious communication difficulties to the deficiencies in the sliding defences. But two of the eternal verities of the international development of Rugby League are that you can't force people to take up the game, and you can't always choose the places where they do want to play it. In many ways, it was little short of miraculous that Valody and his pals were running this tournament in the first place, let alone that they had plans for substantial internal development, let alone that they had their eyes trained on a viable professional future. What we had here was a start: it was incumbent on us to use our experience and expertise now to get them off the blocks and on their way down the track.

After the final whistle, the representatives of the competing nations huddled around us in the draughty grandstand (there can be no country in the world where grandstands are not draughty, including – not to say especially – Moldova) and asked us exactly that: where do we go from here? Their questioning emanated directly from the heart of the hungry fighter syndrome: help us, this is a one-shot deal, it's all we can do and it's our only way out. We listened again to the eager, hopeful tongues reiterating the story that Valody had told us in the car and, in return, preached reconciliation; it would be hard enough to hold the league together over the vast span of this sprawling continent, even without what few clubs there were squabbling and bickering over who got to sit in the comfy chair. We also encouraged them to press on with the youth development programme that would ensure the bloodline of the game long after we and they had passed on our way. Above all, we counselled patience, persistence: keep playing, keep putting teams on the park, keep plugging away. It seemed a trifle mealy-mouthed as we said it: one wanted to have more to be able to give. But this was neither the time nor the place. What we had seen and heard would, in time, give rise to the kind of promises our audience sought.

There was a further official engagement to fulfil and, for that, it was back in the car to another part of town. In Rugby League terms Moldova is, effectively, Tiraspol, and Tiraspol was then, effectively, the Eolis corporation, a shifting chimera which was at once major financial institution, oil company, retail outlet, chain of cinemas, and whatever else it could turn its hand to. Its patronage permitted the Moldovan players to be, nominally at least, professional. In the same way as the Japanese Rugby Football Union incorporates commercial companies whose representative teams are stocked with workers who are employed in positions within those companies, not necessarily because they are suitably qualified but because they can play rugby, so Eolis applied the principle to its particular circumstance.

Our meeting was with an Edouard Kosofskiy, the vice-president of Eolis's banking division, who was doubly keen to make our acquaintance in that he had trained in England on a Barclays Bank exchange scheme. His office could have been any sober, grey-suited bank manager's office anywhere in Europe – until he rose from his chair, turned to the large, rather sombre portrait painting which hung on the wall behind him, and opened it as a door to reveal a priest-hole lined with drinks and trophy cabinets and fine-quality antique furniture. Precisely why he needed this secret, opulent hide-away, or why we were furtively ushered into it and the door closed behind us, it seemed prudent not to enquire.

We were served with sickly herbal tea from a silver samovar and fiery, cauterising liqueur in tiny crystal thimbles as we talked serious money and investment and made the noises which beneficent sponsors like to hear. As our audience drew to a close, we ceremonially presented to Kosofskiy what goodies we had managed to salvage from the depredations of the checkpoint guards: RFL ties, pins, shields, the usual give-aways. In return we received a rather eclectic selection: a presentation set of match-boxes, each with a beautiful woman depicted on the front; two or three hang- 'em-ups in the colours of Eolis Tiraspol; ties woven in a texture not normally found outside an Edinburgh Woollen Mill; and a collection of plastic carrier bags. There was momentary hesitation: nice, we thought without conviction, to be given bags to carry our ties and matches in, until Valody's expression and subtle mime conveyed the truth that these were in fact an integral and valuable part of the gift. Seems that carrier bags are at something of a premium in Moldova – can't get them for love nor money. If I'd known that, I'd have had a big shop at Tesco's before we set off.

It had not taken us until the time we left Kosofskiy's office to calculate that, if we were to catch the 7.35 a.m. plane out of Bucharest the following morning, we would need to begin the return journey no later than 8.30 p.m. that evening. So much for sampling what local nightlife Tiraspol might have to offer. We adjourned to another, rather more functional hotel for dinner with the teams, where endless plates of cold meats, salads and caviare shuttled from the kitchen to jockey for position on a cluttered table, while a four-piece band played the sort of part-folk, part-country tunes which have given the Eurovision Song Contest its deserved reputation, at ear-ringing volume. Gorged and bloated on this sumptuous fare, Tom and I leaned back expansively in our chairs, only to discover that what had gone before was merely an hors-d'oeuvres: there were two more courses yet to be mastered. In Moldova, it seemed, the middle ground between famine and excess was almost entirely unoccupied.

We kissed Natalya goodbye in the street as she pressed into our hands rather too many bottles of wine and brandy which she had filched from the players' tables. She could not accompany us back to Bucharest, she said, as she had commitments in the morning. (The way that the otherwise non-contributory Popescu had set his cap at her over dinner, it seemed that she might have had a job on her hands that evening, too.) It was sad to bid her *au revoir*, not

175

only because our chances of understanding much thereafter remained with her on the corner as we pulled away. This was the sort of friendship forged under heavy shellfire which was responsible for reuniting long-parted ex-soldiers for the 50th anniversary of VE Day. It had only been 24 hours, but we felt like we'd been through a lot with her.

For an account of what happened on the way back to Bucharest, the reader should revise much of the first half of this chapter: more checkpoints, more queue-jumping, more bribes, more cat-napping. Skip over the episode at the border, though. Since we had a transit visa for Romania, we encountered no further problem there.

Only one incident remains snagged on the barbed wire of memory, which took place when we stopped at a roadhouse for what the Americans regrettably call a 'comfort break'. A youth in his late teens must have overheard an exchange between Tom and me and, recognising it as English, came over to engage me in conversation. Who were we, why were we here, where were we going, where had we been? Tired, irritable, and mentally on the plane, I was unforgivably short with him, though his English was well-nigh impeccable. None the less he continued, explaining that he was studying our language and intended in time to be able to leave his homeland to travel to and work in a country where his prospects might be rosier. Again, the hungry fighter: clinging to the drifting spars of hope that might carry him to shore. Again, I cut him dead, to the extent that he politely enquired as to the reason for my taciturnity: had he offended me in some way?

He hadn't really. It was simply that, by that stage, I had had a gutful of that part of the world. It seemed that Moldova – in common, I presume, with every other constituent state of the former Soviet Union – had its post-communism vacuum filled by two sorts of people. The first were Valody, Kosofskiy, this student here and their like, chancers who saw their new-found freedom as an opportunity, a choice, and were determined to make the best of it for their own betterment. Although the motivations of these named people had seemed pure, we had seen enough evidence during our trip of a dark side to the genre, a cadre of more shadowy figures to whom this was an opportunity to be not so much upwardly mobile as downright devious and dastardly.

The second were the people in the queues and in the fields, who were so used to doing as they were told under the communists that, when the orders stopped coming, they had not the wit to know what to do next. With doers in one camp, and done-tos in the other, the potential for large-scale exploitation and manipulation seemed alarming. At approximately 2 a.m., however, this was a political migraine which I didn't wish to incur, for which the poor student bore the brunt. I remain apologetic and self-reproachful; I didn't set a very good example on behalf of the free world.

It was the same sentiment which led Tom and me, on arrival back in England, straight up the M11 and A1 to the services at Retford, where there was known to be a McDonald's – westernised capitalism at its most familiar and reassuring. Back home in Collingham, I dropped my bags in the hallway, stripped off all my clothes there and then, marched into the bathroom and took a bath. Tom told me later that, when he got back to Dewsbury, he similarly deposited his luggage and went straight out for a haircut. Why we both chose these singular courses of action, I'm not entirely sure. My best offering is to share the rationale of the old joke: Why do dogs lick their balls? Because they can.

# USA

# What Made Milwaukee Infamous

## Harry Edgar

America had been a dream for Rugby League pioneers for as long as anyone could remember. I always blamed Harry Sunderland for sowing the seeds of the dream with his inspirational articles in Rugby League journals of the early 1950s. One boldly proclaimed 'New Fields in California' and featured a picture of a flying-boat on its front cover! Another was headlined 'Let's see an American Team at Wembley' and was accompanied by a cover photograph of Harry in Los Angeles, along with one-time Leeds and Salford player Cliff Evans, being interviewed by California journalist Ward B. Nash.

It was a classic photograph as Nash, complete with Panama hat, posed, notebook and pencil in hand, as if transfixed by Harry Sunderland's spiel on his hopes for a world tour by a team of American footballers. But hey, this was in Hollywood, and if you couldn't make dreams come true here, what hope was there for the rest of the world?

As early as 1921, Harry Sunderland was being described as 'a born hustler and advertiser of anything he has in hand', and it's true that the world of Rugby League has never had a better promoter. And it was in that year that the very first sign of League's 'American Dream' was given breath as the Kangaroo touring team travelled to England via the United States. On arrival in San Francisco the Australian players obliged movie cameramen with a demonstration of their war-cry, and on a visit to Stanford University Harry, who was then the secretary of the Queensland Rugby League and travelling with the Kangaroos as a visitor, discussed with local

178

sporting men the possibility of Rugby League being introduced to the West Coast of the USA.

In his memoirs of that 1921 tour another legendary Queenslander, Duncan Thompson, revealed that residents of Cheyenne, Wyoming, could claim to have been the first Americans to see some kind of Rugby League being played on their nation's soil – albeit the participants were dressed in blazers and bow-ties! It happened during the Kangaroos' five-day train trip across the USA when, late one night, the train stopped in Cheyenne. The players hopped off for ice-creams, all immaculately dressed for dinner, and on a stretch of grass near the station suddenly enacted a practice game. Thompson recalled that locals out for a stroll on that long-ago evening in Cheyenne were treated to the remarkable sight of these hefty Australians running and tackling, bumping into each other and laughing.

Seventy years later I planned to go to Cheyenne with Mike Mayer, to search for America's second most famous grassy knoll, and recount Duncan Thompson's story of Rugby League's first steps on American soil. I thought it would bring some light relief for Mike as he battled to overcome the financial ruin and millstones of debt which were placed like a noose around his considerable neck after his very own 'American Dream' had been shattered two years earlier in Milwaukee.

But we never did quite make it as far west as Wyoming. We'd crossed the Mississippi and were heading for South Dakota, although Mike didn't really appreciate the magnet that was drawing me to the sacred hills and he truly questioned my sanity at the thought of driving through the Badlands in the height of summer. Yet there we were, two overweight guys in Hawaiian shirts, sweating profusely as the temperature soared close to 100 degrees, driving due west and still talking about what went wrong in Milwaukee two years earlier. In fact, still talking about all the adventures we'd had in the 12 years before Milwaukee, since our paths first crossed when Mayer emerged on Rugby League's world stage in 1977.

It took him from 1977 to 1989 to get what he wanted – a major exhibition game featuring two top Rugby League teams played in an American stadium. When Wigan and Warrington finally ran out on to the turf of County Stadium, Milwaukee, on 10 June 1989, it should have been some kind of dream come true and the launch pad for Mayer's plan to attract major investors to the development of

Rugby League in the lucrative American sports market-place. Instead, however, it turned into a nightmare for him, both financial and emotional.

Just getting those two teams to the starting line had been a massive achievement. Mayer had, by virtue of his tremendous enthusiasm and meticulous attention to detail in his business plan, persuaded the English Rugby League and the International Board to back his United States Rugby League project in the late 1970s. He was helped enormously by far-sighted British officials such as Tom Mitchell, Brian Snape and Ossie Davies, who recognised the vast potential offered to the game if it could establish a professional presence in America.

Tragically, all Mayer's schedules were scuppered when Donald Trump's rebel USFL emerged in the early 1980s to challenge the NFL's monopoly and claim the vacant springtime months in the American sporting calendar which Mayer had specifically earmarked for Rugby League. He had no alternative but to sit it out and wait until the USFL fizzled out, as he confidently predicted it would. Although he was right, it meant three years of wasted time during which he went broke, had his house repossessed and was forced to move his wife and son, plus his office, into a tiny three-roomed apartment.

Since the 1970s Mayer had urged Rugby League officials to understand that television was the key to the promotion and expansion of the game anywhere, but especially in the United States. He also suggested they should set up merchandising operations and licensing agreements, build a hall of fame, and have an International Board with a full-time bureau who would actively pursue those world television and merchandising deals. What were, even then, accepted practices in American sports were way beyond the comprehension of British Rugby League. Only some 15 years later, with the arrival of Rupert Murdoch's Super League 'vision', did the game at last start talking about such things.

After the Australian Rugby League had staged a match between New South Wales and Queensland in Long Beach, California, in August 1987, Mike Mayer set up a meeting for British League officials with a leading American sports licensing company, which offered the British League the opportunity of securing potentially lucrative worldwide merchandising deals. Mayer was told the British would pay for his air fare to the UK because they wanted to talk in more detail about the licensing opportunities for the game. But, as it turned out, they changed their minds on both the plane ticket and the scheduled discussions. British League chairman Bob Ashby had become influenced by the Australians, whose League chief executive Ken Arthurson had long lost confidence in Mayer's ability to obtain the major investment required for his United States Rugby League project which he had been promising for so many years.

Bob, at least, was one man with the courage of his convictions. He called Mike up and told him straight: 'Don't bother coming over, you won't get past the door.' However, while the British Rugby League had joined the Australians in washing their hands of the United States Rugby League, Mike Mayer remained convinced that there were still opportunities for the game in the USA. He was determined to battle 'until the last tick of the clock' on behalf of the shareholders who had supported the launch of the USRL company, with by far the largest of them being the British Rugby League itself.

It was actually me who paid for Mayer's air ticket (carefully ensuring it was an open-ended return!) in December 1987. He came over to England, ostensibly to be a special guest at the celebration of *Open Rugby*'s 100th edition, but really to give him the opportunity to put his ideas back into the media spotlight and, more important, to get to talk with the more progressive League officials in Britain who might be persuaded it was worth giving America another shot. By far the most 'get-up-and-go' of those officials was Maurice Lindsay, then the chairman of Wigan and still on his way up in the RFL hierarchy. Maurice had had the courage, the confidence and the ambition to stage the Wigan–Manly game in October 1987 without support from the RFL, and it was only natural that he should recognise the potential offered by having Wigan become the first club to have a major stake in the American market. He was prepared to take a gamble, believing 'nothing ventured, nothing gained', and so Wigan agreed to help fund the promotion of an exhibition game in the USA, scheduled for June 1989 in Milwaukee. Soon after, Warrington agreed to become their partners in the venture, and the die was cast for these two fierce rivals of North-West (England) Rugby League to meet each other in the Mid-West in what was billed as 'The Great British American Challenge Match'.

And from that point onwards, the whole thing went downhill. Mike Mayer learned the hard way that dealing with people involved in Rugby League in the north of England wasn't quite the same as working with professional sports personnel in the United States.

Things that needed to be done didn't get done. In the 12-month build-up to the game, both Wigan and Warrington's faith in Mayer's ability to pull the project together dwindled drastically to the point that, had they not already invested some of the money, they would probably have pulled out of the whole deal. The Americans, and in particular the staff of the Milwaukee Tourist Board who were enthusiastic supporters of the project, could not understand why the British were so apparently reticent about trying to make the event a success. Meanwhile, the British just could not understand what was happening to their money! It was definitely a transatlantic case of two cultures divided by a common language.

So it was something of a surprise that the Wigan and Warrington teams actually flew into Chicago on schedule, five days before the 10 June showdown in Milwaukee, and even the act of getting there seemed to say something about the attitudes surrounding the whole event. The two clubs had added considerably to their journey time by flying via Amsterdam because they got a cheaper deal from KLM, and a bunch of British journalists, having handed their flight arrangements over to the Rugby Football League's official travel agents (who had also been entrusted with organising supporters' trips), found themselves on an engaging mystery tour which, in some cases, involved as many as four stopovers and flight changes in the act of getting from Manchester to Milwaukee!

They looked at me incredulously when I expressed surprise at their nightmare journeys which had, not surprisingly, already put them in a negative frame of mind. Travelling with my pals from *Open Rugby*, Trevor Gibbons and Andrew Varley, we had just jumped on a plane in England and flown direct to Chicago, and we couldn't understand why everybody else hadn't done the same. It all seemed too easy!

Arriving on the scorching tarmac of Chicago's O'Hare Airport, we were determined to enjoy a week of adventure. This should have been easy to do, because Chicago was such a vibrant city and the natives in Milwaukee were so welcoming to their British visitors, but in order to achieve it I had to distance myself from the events surrounding the game. I felt somewhat guilty that I was having a holiday while my friend Mike Mayer was being put under such intense pressure. Other friends from England had gone to help Mayer to pick up the pieces of the match organisation, which had almost fallen apart some weeks earlier when a company employed at considerable expense to recruit sponsorship and to promote the game in Milwaukee had come up totally empty, despite using up a major chunk of the money advanced by Wigan and Warrington. Mayer had to fire the company, but the money was gone and he was broke and desperate.

I'd known Mike broke several times before, but never desperate. He called me in England in May on the point of throwing himself out of the John Hancock Building (a skyscraper, the second tallest in the world at that time, which dominates the downtown Chicago skyline alongside the Sears Tower). Unless I could raise some money and get it to Milwaukee right away, there could be no further work done on promoting the Wigan–Warrington game, and the whole deal would be cancelled. Everybody would be left high and dry, including several hundred fans who had already booked flights to go to the USA. I was Mayer's last resort: he knew it, and I knew it.

I scratched together all the money I could from my business and my life-savings and managed to come up with the £15,000 required. Meanwhile Barry Wood, another long-time supporter of the USRL, mortgaged his house in Hull to raise another £15,000. We both knew we'd never see that money again, but as blind believers in Rugby League's 'American Dream' we could not allow it to disappear when it was so close to becoming reality.

Chicago is a great place to hear jazz, to eat the best Italian meatballs and pizza, and to look out over Lake Michigan and imagine just how cold it would be on a Sunday afternoon in December when the Bears were playing at Soldier Field. It also has a beach! Varley drove and Gibbons navigated, while I got the tourist ticket in the back seat, as we headed downtown from O'Hare. They call the Windy City the 'crossroads of America', as since the earliest days of the railway it has been the crossing point on the routes from east to west, and north to south. Union Station is still mobbed by a vibrant mass of people even today, when rail travel in America, other than commuter trains, is left largely to rich senior citizens and tourists from Europe. On the day we visited Union Station, it was awash with cherry-and-white Norweb-clad strangers with accents indecipherable to the English-speakers (as opposed to the Hispanics and Italians) of Chicago. Maybe they'd heard that the Union Station buffet was the best place to get a pie in Chicago!

The crossroads tag also applies to air travel and, as we drove on the freeway towards the city, planes looked to be within touching distance as they came from all directions to land at O'Hare. Distracted by the planes, we missed our exit and found ourselves heading into the notorious South Side. It was a tough baptism into Americana as we sped along the Dan Ryan Expressway. Aiming at Chicago's heart, that freeway cuts a devastating swathe from north to south, splitting the neighbourhoods of the city's South Side. Its 16 lanes have successfully dismembered the communities which lay in its path, in order that people who live somewhere else can get somewhere else again. There are also two tracks of rapid transit line running down the middle of this strip of freeway, appearing to have been added as an afterthought. What is tragically absurd is that even one track has the carrying capacity of ten lanes of road! 'Welcome to America, home of the automobile,' I sighed to myself. Meanwhile, my travelling companions were more concerned with the practicalities of getting us out of the oppressive mass of urban decay and rusting railtracks that were the South Side and, thanks to them, we made it safely downtown.

I loved Chicago. On subsequent visits we saw the real tourist sights (like Mike Ditka's bar and Max's Deli!) and, two years later, I even saw a soccer game at Soldier Field between the USA national team and AC Milan, played in front of over 45,000 people at the start of the build-up to the World Cup in 1994. But nothing could ever surpass our first night in Chicago, when the Wigan and Warrington teams rode on an open-topped double-decker London bus (honest, this is true!) to the Baja Beachclub. That name is etched on my brain. Later, at about 3 a.m., Mike Mayer (who was able to relax momentarily, safe in the knowledge that at least the two teams had turned up) took us for a ride in his home city. In a fair imitation of Gene Hackman as Popeye Doyle in *The French Connection*, he weaved his car in between the pillars that carried the overhead railway above Wabash Avenue. Popeye's run had been set in New York, but a similar scene in *The Blues Brothers* was actually filmed on this very avenue in Chicago where big Mike screeched in and out of the pillars, unloading a mass of aggression and pent-up tension. We were on too much of a high to feel any fear.

The next morning, everybody left Chicago and headed north to Wisconsin. It takes just an hour by freeway to get to Milwaukee, but we chose to take the scenic route along North Lake Shore Drive, home to anybody in Chicago who 'makes it' big enough to move into one of its impressive houses. I searched vainly for a sighting of the Max Wax sausage factory, the proceeds of which helped to give the proprietor's daughter Ruby such an affluent start in life. Now you can bet that all the doctors who star in *Emergency Room* live up there.

Once across the state line out of Illinois, we passed through small towns like Racine which belied Wisconsin's popular image as a dairy state. There were no signs of green pastures or Friesian cows, just empty shells of old steelworks and rusting railtracks. It reminded me of younger days in Workington or Wollongong, blue-collar Rugby League country, and it came as no surprise to learn that Racine supports a small semi-professional football club – a rarity in American sports. Such clubs seem to thrive only in this area of the Mid-West, sandwiched between two famous footballing legends – the Chicago Bears and the Green Bay Packers.

It was the semi-professional players from tough Mid-West towns with whom Mike Mayer had so much empathy. He was convinced that these were the people, largely priced out of watching NFL teams, who would take Rugby League to their hearts, striking an immediate bond between towns such as Racine and the industrial communities in northern England, such as Castleford, Featherstone and Widnes, which gave life to Rugby League.

Mayer's plan was that the exhibition game in Milwaukee would provide the first showcase for Rugby League to these people. Two things were essential to the plan: first, that the game be given good quality television coverage; and second, that there be absolutely no link between Rugby League and Rugby Union. The 15-a-side code, which 99.9 per cent of Americans perceived to be the one and only 'rugby', has an appalling image in the USA; one centred around drunkenness, college-boy behaviour and second-rate athletes.

As well as hiring a promotional company who proved to be all mouth and no action, Mike Mayer's costliest mistake was in paying big dollars – just about everything that was left in his budget, and then some – to an Atlanta cable TV company to produce full coverage of the game. Considering they knew so little about Rugby League they did a good job, and it was their coverage which portrayed a hugely positive image of the game when extensive highlights from Milwaukee were shown back in Britain on BBC's *Grandstand*. But it was hardly sighted in the USA, which had been the real object of the exercise.

While we were having fun in the multitude of bars in Milwaukee and cruising out of the city to exotic spots such as Germantown, Wisconsin, Mayer was being backed into a corner by Wigan and Warrington, who were unhappy over just about everything they could think of. Their worst fears – that they were not going to get any of their money back from this gamble – looked to be heading towards realisation, unless something incredible happened and 50,000 people suddenly bought tickets for the game in County Stadium. They didn't.

While Barry Wood was constructing a pair of rugby goal-posts with his bare hands, members of the Wigan team were deciding they didn't want to play on the pitch which had originally been marked and which included several patches of sand down one touchline from the baseball pitch which was currently in use at County Stadium. If you've ever seen football teams like the San Francisco Forty-Niners play at home, you'll have seen them happily run across large patches of sand while the baseball season is still *in situ*. Wigan, however, were not the Forty-Niners, and so a new pitch had to be marked out. It was, of course, unavoidably narrower than a standard Rugby League field, and this proved to be very restricting to the players when the match was played.

The ultimate nightmare for Mayer came on the eve of the game, as he hosted a reception for the business community of Milwaukee and their guests. It was then that threats were made that the teams would not take to the field unless certain legal guarantees were agreed to. Although it was after hours on Friday evening, Maurice Lindsay insisted that an attorney be found and summoned to the hotel. Mayer knew then that he was ruined, but he had to put a brave face on things to get through the reception and the game itself.

At that reception I looked on with a mixture of sadness and anger at the sight of some Wigan players refusing to give interviews to the local media. One even turned down the chance to talk with a highly respected radio presenter whose show was syndicated across the United States to over 60 black radio stations. Americans at the reception could hardly believe that people who had travelled several thousand miles to promote their sport in a new country seemed so apathetic.

Not all the Wigan players fell into this category. Some, like Martin Dermott and Ian Lucas, were as enthusiastic and helpful as ever, whilst Joe Lydon was brilliant. Joe flew into Chicago after the long haul from Sydney, where he was playing for Easts at the time, and was immediately whisked on to another plane by Peter Deakin and flown to New York, where an interview on a leading nationwide breakfast TV programme had been lined up. Joe got a four-minute slot, shown coast to coast, and achieved his ambition of eating doughnuts for breakfast on Wall Street.

The Warrington players seemed a much more relaxed bunch and, with Mike Gregory and Billy McGinty at the helm, seemed happy to enjoy the week-long party which was part and parcel of being a visiting football team from England. Les Boyd was a superb ambassador, giving countless interviews, mingling well at receptions and always speaking articulately about the game. What we didn't know then was that there was in fact anger simmering inside Les, who had put off his Warrington retirement to fly to America for this game. That anger manifested itself in the opening seconds of the game when he provoked a skirmish with Ellery Hanley. Rumour had it that they had already squared up to each other in Los Angeles International Airport in transit from Sydney, and the on-field altercation left Ellery's No. 13 ripped and hanging from his back. The game's biggest drawcard was sent to the sidelines for ten minutes by referee John Holdsworth, who didn't appear to realise the sense of anticlimax his 'show-'em-who's-boss' stance brought to the expectant crowd's appreciation of the event.

At just after 5 p.m. on that Saturday, 10 June, we were cruising through the wide streets of Milwaukee. With County Stadium two miles away, you get a strong waft of the Miller brewery – what *did* make Milwaukee famous? Then on to Highway 41 and the approach to County Stadium, home of the Brewers and, for three games a season, the Green Bay Packers. County Stadium is famous for its pre-game tail-gate parties, where people gather in the car parks, eat from barbecues and drink Miller. That night the conversations were different. They did not revolve around whether Molitor's hamstring would hold up (did it ever?) or whether Robin Yount would strike out in the first innings (did he ever?) and allow the Brewers' star batters to see out the game. And they didn't have fans wrapped up in minus-zero temperatures to keep out the icy blasts blowing in from Lake Michigan in winter, wondering if today would be the day the Packers didn't snatch defeat from the jaws of victory (don't they always?). North Sydney fans, even old-time Whitehaven fans, have an immediate affinity with the Packers.

An official attendance of 17,773 was given out by the County Stadium authorities as Wigan defeated Warrington 12–5 in a very tough and intense game which featured just one try, scored by Andy Goodway. Such a crowd wasn't enough to pay any of the bills, and the person who did the counting probably made a mistake by putting a one in front of the figure – 7,773 looked more realistic. But the majority of them were American people who went away from their first Rugby League game wanting more. They gave the teams a rapturous five-minute standing ovation at the end, despite another huge anticlimax provided by referee Holdsworth, who blew for full-time just as the crowd was getting ready to count down the last nail-biting 90 seconds on the stadium clock.

Sadly, those American people were destined not to get any more. Wigan and Warrington tried to gather up what little money they could from the game and went home, never to return. Not before there was a moment of true irony from Bob Ashby, however. The British RFL chairman, who had watched the game from the press box, turned to fellow-Britons and said, 'Well, we've bloody done it; we've got Rugby League played in America!' This was the same man who had earlier told Mayer not to bother coming to talk to the RFL because he wouldn't get through the door! And, despite all the encouraging words after the game by assorted individuals in the British Rugby League about the need for a follow-up, I was certain none of them had the slightest intention of actually doing anything about it. And they didn't.

Milwaukee had been targeted for the Rugby League challenge match between Wigan and Warrington because it is a blue-collar sportsville. All Mike Mayer's predictions proved correct in that public interest in Milwaukee was extensive and there was tremendous goodwill towards the project from the whole of the city, despite the numerous problems caused by lack of funding and insufficient manpower. People from Chicago had been so impressed by the game that they wanted to put on another Rugby League event, bigger and better promoted, in their city the following summer. For a while, Mayer's hopes for a 'Rock and Rugby League' festival in Chicago rose slightly, with the Beach Boys and Tina Turner (pre-Winfield Cup advert) in the frame. But with Wigan and Warrington licking their financial wounds, and the British Rugby League being presented with demands for payment of unpaid bills, there was no prospect of their ever giving Mike Mayer another chance.

Mayer himself, faced with massive debts accruing interest every year at a great rate of knots, entered a deep depression for a long time. Over the next couple of years I had to advance him several more thousands of pounds when he got desperate enough to ask. Mike never spelled out exactly which debts he was paying with my money, but I had a hunch the cash was to keep him out of gaol when he was being hounded by the State Taxation Department over money due from receipts at the game which never actually existed.

Several years later Mayer bumped into an old friend in Chicago who told him that he had been to the Milwaukee game and actually paid for two tickets for it. 'So you're the guy who bought all the tickets!' came Mayer's wry reply. The ability to laugh at himself and to bounce back from such massive blows has become second nature to Mike Mayer during his near 20-year love affair with Rugby League which had started when he saw the movie *This Sporting Life*.

When Andrew Varley and I returned to Milwaukee a year after the game, on a kind of rehabilitation mission for Mayer, we found that the city hadn't forgotten Rugby League. How could it when half of it was still chasing unpaid bills? Some of the players had made a big impression on the local girls, as had the fans who followed Wigan and Warrington. Mayer recounted that four marriages and two engagements had resulted from the English invasion in 1989 – 'I should have set up a marriage bureau, not a Rugby League,' he quipped.

In Madison, Wisconsin, we sat by Lake Mendota, where Otis Redding's plane crashed, and pondered on what could have been but what wasn't quite. We drove to Green Bay but, being in the summertime with no Packers, there was nothing to see. But it was from the Packers' front office that so much influence permeated Rugby League, from the footballing gospel preached by coach Vince Lombardi via Jack Gibson and Terry Fearnley. In just about any Under-11s game in England, you'll hear kids and their coaches talking about big hits, hard yards and playing catch-up football. Two different worlds bonded by a common language, and it all started here on Lombardi Avenue, Green Bay.

In the Packers' front office, visitors can hold the original Lombardi Trophy which was won in the first Superbowl, and the Packers' own hall of fame is a lesson in how to preserve sports history and heritage. 'It's not the same as the Whitbread Trophy Rugby League Hall of Fame,' remarked the always-observant Andrew Varley, showing the keen eye which has made him one of the world's top Rugby League photographers.

Since the ill-fated match in the United States, Mike Mayer has arranged for numerous Rugby League coaches and officials from Britain to visit the training camps of both the Chicago Bears and the Green Bay Packers in order to look and learn. One man who used his visits to maximum effect was Brian Smith, formerly at Hull and St George and most recently coach to the Bradford Bulls. But it was touching to see that the influences can work both ways across the Atlantic. When I went into the office of the Packers' public relations chief, Lee Remmell, the first thing I noticed was a copy of *Open Rugby* on top of a pile of magazines and newspapers on his desk. It was the issue which included a comparison feature between our own Ellery Hanley and America's Bo Jackson. Mr Remmell, delighted to learn his visitors were based in Yorkshire, was keen to pick up all the latest from his favourite TV series *All Creatures Great and Small*.

The disappointment for Mike Mayer was that the thousands of young American athletes who he knew would have loved to have played Rugby League were not now going to get that opportunity. In addition, the thousands of British players and fans would not get the chance to travel to the cities of the United States where they would have been given a great welcome and had a great time. Those who made it to Milwaukee in 1989 will vouch for that, just as Harry Sunderland knew it back in the 1920s.

Mayer could live with the personal financial ruin brought on him by the events of 1989 and the judgements made about him. What he found hardest to handle was the feeling that he had let down the people who had helped him in various ways, big and small, over the years, and his sadness that Rugby League was going to miss out on the riches he knew the USA could bring it.

What made Milwaukee famous may well have made a loser out of Mike, but as Varley and he sat in the front of the car making wisecracks, I settled back into the tourist seat again and dreamt of Crystal Lake. The 'American Dream' will never be over for Rugby League. In another time and another place it will resurface, and newcomers will talk about 1989 and going down the roads not taken then. From that day on, I was content to sit in the back seat and hum Don Henley's song of that summer, 'End of the Innocence.' And it made a great headline!